Contents

v

Introduction

This textbook provides an introduction to economics. It has been tailored explicitly to cover the content of the OCR specification for A2 economics, module by module, and follows on from the companion volume *OCR AS Economics*.

The text provides the foundation for studying OCR A2 economics, but you will no doubt wish to keep up to date by referring to additional topical sources of information about economic events. This can be done by reading the serious newspapers, visiting key sites on the internet, and reading such magazines as *Economic Review*.

The core content of the text is as follows:

OCR unit	Text
Common material for Units F583 and F584	**Part 1:** Firms and market structure Chapters 1–4
A2 Unit F583 The economics of work and leisure	**Part 2:** The economics of work and leisure Chapters 5–8
A2 Unit F584 Transport economics	**Part 3:** Transport economics Chapters 9–12
A2 Unit F585 The global economy	**Part 4:** The global economy Chapters 13–20

The structure of the optional units means that some topics appear in more than one place in the book.

The text also features the following:
- a statement of the intended learning outcomes for each chapter
- clear and concise but comprehensive explanation and analysis of economic terms and concepts
- examples to show these concepts applied to real-world situations
- definitions of key terms
- exercises to provide active engagement with economic analysis

A separate *Teacher Guide* is available that provides complete answers to all exercises, plus additional support material and exercises.

Assessment objectives

In common with other economics specifications, OCR economics entails four assessment objectives. Candidates will thus be expected to:

➤ demonstrate knowledge and understanding of the specified content
➤ apply knowledge and critical understanding to problems and issues arising from both familiar and unfamiliar situations
➤ analyse economic problems and issues
➤ evaluate economic arguments and evidence, making informed judgements

In the overall assessment of the A-level, the four assessment objectives count equally. However, a greater weighting is given to the first two objectives in AS, and to the final two objectives in A2.

All A2 units include an element of *synoptic* assessment. Synoptic assessment sets out to test '...candidates' understanding of the connections between different elements of the subject'. This will test the ability to:

➤ understand the ways in which many economic issues, problems and institutions are interrelated
➤ understand how economic concepts, theories and techniques may be relevant to a range of different contexts
➤ apply such concepts, theories and techniques in the analysis of economic issues and problems and in evaluating arguments and evidence

'The emphasis in synoptic assessment is on candidates' ability to think as economists and to use the economist's "tool kit" of concepts, theories and techniques effectively.'

(*See the OCR AS/A GCE Economics specification at* **www.ocr.org.uk**.)

In approaching the A2 part of the A-level programme, it is therefore important not to discard what has been learnt from the AS section. Where appropriate, this text will provide references to relevant chapters of *OCR AS Economics* to allow connections to be made. These references will appear in the form '*AS Economics, Chapter x*'. The *Teacher Guide* that accompanies this book contains some extension material that can extend your knowledge and understanding of economics. By studying these books, you should develop an awareness of the economist's approach to issues and problems, and the economist's way of thinking about the world.

Economics and the real world

The study of economics also requires a familiarity with recent economic events in the UK and elsewhere, and candidates will be expected to show familiarity with 'recent historical data' — broadly defined as the last 7–10 years. The following websites will help you to keep up to date with recent trends and events.

➤ Recent and historical data about the UK economy can be found at the website of the Office for National Statistics (ONS) at: **www.statistics.gov.uk**
➤ Also helpful is the site of HM Treasury at: **www.hm-treasury.gov.uk**

➤ The Bank of England site is well worth a visit, especially the *Inflation Report* and the Minutes of the Monetary Policy Committee: **www.bankofengland.co.uk**

➤ The Institute for Fiscal Studies offers an independent view of a range of economic topics: **www.ifs.org.uk**

For information about other countries, visit the following:

➤ **www.oecd.org/home**

➤ **europa.eu.int**

➤ **www.worldbank.org**

➤ **www.undp.org**

Another way of keeping up to date with economic topics and events is to read *Economic Review*, a magazine specifically written for A-level economics students, also published by Philip Allan.

How to study economics

There are two crucial aspects of studying economics. The first stage is to study the theory, which helps us to explain economic behaviour. However, in studying AS and A2 economics it is equally important to be able to *apply* the theories and concepts that you meet, and to see just how these relate to the real world.

If you are to become competent at this, it is vital that you get plenty of practice. In part, this means carrying out the exercises that you will find in this text and in the *Teacher Guide.* However, it also means thinking about how economics helps us to explain news items and data that appear in the newspapers and on the television. Make sure that you practise as much as you can.

In economics, it is also important to be able to produce examples of economic phenomena. In reading this text, you will find some examples that help to illustrate ideas and concepts. Do not rely solely on the examples provided here, but look around the world to find your own examples, and keep a note of these ready for use in essays and exams. This will help to convince the examiners that you have understood economics. It will also help you to understand the theories.

Enjoy economics

Most important of all, I hope you will enjoy your study of economics. I have always been fascinated by the subject, and hope that you will capture something of the excitement and challenge of learning about how markets and the economy operate. I also wish you every success with your AS/A-level studies.

Acknowledgements

I would like to express my deep gratitude to Mark Russell, whose thorough reading of the book's precursor and insightful and helpful comments were invaluable in improving the scope and focus of the book. I would also like to thank everyone at Philip Allan, especially Rachel Furse and Penny Fisher, for their efficiency in production of this book, and for their support and encouragement.

Many of the data series shown in figures in this book are drawn from the data obtained from the National Statistics website: **www.statistics.gov.uk** Crown copyright material is reproduced with the permission of the Controller of HMSO (PSI licence number C2007001851).

Other data were from various sources, including OECD, World Bank, United Nations Development Programme and other sources as specified.

While every effort has been made to trace the owners of copyright material, I would like to apologise to any copyright holders whose rights may have unwittingly been infringed.

Peter Smith

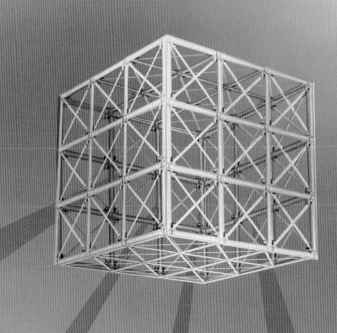

Firms and market
structure

Part 1

Chapter 1
Firms and how they operate

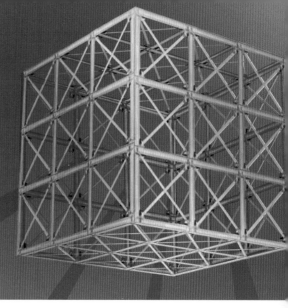

In studying the economics of work and leisure or of transport, firms play a central role. Firms employ workers, so are crucial in the economics of work; it is also firms that provide leisure services. Firms are also central to the study of transport economics: firms need to transport their products — and, of course, there are firms whose business it is to provide transport services. An important first step is therefore to investigate how firms operate, and how they take decisions designed to achieve their objectives. This requires some discussion of the costs and revenues faced by firms at different levels of output. The following chapters show how firms' decisions are influenced by the market environment in which they operate. Part 1 of the book serves as an introduction to both Part 2 (on the economics of work and leisure) and Part 3 (on transport economics).

Learning outcomes

After studying this chapter, you should:
➤ be aware of the reason for the birth of firms, and the desire for their growth
➤ be aware of the need for firms to grow if they wish to compete in global markets
➤ be familiar with short- and long-run cost curves and their characteristics
➤ understand the significance of economies of scale in the context of the growth of firms
➤ understand the profit maximisation motive and its implications for firms' behaviour
➤ be aware of the principal–agent issue, and its influence on the motivations of firms
➤ be familiar with alternative motivations for firms and how these affect decision making

What is a firm?

One way of answering this question is to say that **firms** exist in order to organise production: they bring together various factors of production, and organise the production process in order to produce output.

There are various forms that the organisation of a firm can take. The simplest is perhaps that of *sole proprietor*, in

term

firm: an organisation that brings together factors of production in order to produce output

which the owner of the firm also runs the firm. Examples would be an independent newsagent/corner shop, hairdresser or taxi driver, where the owner is liable for the debts of the enterprise, but also gets to keep any profits.

In some professions, firms are operated on a *partnership* basis. Examples here are doctors', dentists' and solicitors' practices. Profits are shared between the partners, as are debts, according to the contract drawn up between them. Some non-professional enterprises, such as some builders and hardware stores, also operate in this way.

Independent newsagents are often run by sole proprietors

Private *joint stock companies* are owned by shareholders, each of whom has contributed funds to the business by buying shares. However, each shareholder's responsibility for the debts of the company is limited to the amount he or she paid for the shares. Profits are distributed to shareholders as dividends. The shares in a private company of this kind are not traded on the stock exchange, and the firms tend to be controlled by the shareholders themselves. Many local businesses are operated on this basis: for example, double glazing installation firms and computer consultancies. If you look in your local *Yellow Pages*, you will see that some firms indicate that they are this sort of company by adding 'Ltd' after their name, referring to the fact that shareholders have *limited liability* for the firm's debts, as mentioned above. Many family firms operate in this way, with the families maintaining control through their ownership of shares.

Firms that are owned by shareholders, but are listed on the stock exchange are *public joint stock companies*. Again, the liability of the shareholders is limited to the amount they have paid for their shares. However, such companies are required to publish their annual accounts and also to publish an annual report to their shareholders. Day-to-day decision making is normally delegated to a board of directors (who are not major shareholders), appointed at the annual general meeting (AGM) of the shareholders. Examples of this sort of company abound — Tesco, HSBC, BP and so on. Again, your local *Yellow Pages* will reveal the names of some companies with 'plc' after the name, standing for *public limited company*.

Firm size

An important decision facing any firm is to choose its scale of operation. If you look around the economy, you will see that the size of firms varies enormously, from small one-person operations up to mega-sized multinational corporations. Such firms may need to continue to grow in order to compete with other large-scale competitors in global markets. There may be many reasons why firms wish to expand their operations. This chapter will begin to explain why this is so, and show how the decision about how much output to produce depends upon what it is that a firm is trying to achieve, and on the market environment in which it is operating.

In both leisure and transport sectors, there are examples of both large and small firms. For example, in the leisure sector, your local gymnasium may be a relatively small enterprise, but there are also some big players in the market, such as Chelsea FC or BSkyB. In transport, there may be small local taxi firms, but there are also large firms such as British Airways.

Exercise 1.1

Identify firms operating in your town or city that are active in either the leisure or transport sectors. Which of them would you classify as being relatively small-scale enterprises, and which operate on a more national basis?

Summary

➤ A firm is an organisation that exists to bring together factors of production in order to produce goods or services.

➤ Firms range, in the complexity of their organisation, from sole proprietors to public limited companies.

➤ Firms vary in size, from one-person concerns to large multinational corporations operating in global markets.

Costs facing firms

To understand why firms wish to grow, it is first important to examine the costs of production that they face. This section focuses on the relationship between costs and the level of output produced by a firm. Diagrams will be used to illustrate this relationship using a series of cost curves that apply in various circumstances.

For simplicity, it is assumed that the firm under consideration produces a single product. Of course, in reality this does not apply to all firms. There are many large conglomerate firms that produce a range of different products. However, this complicates the analysis unnecessarily, so the focus here is on a firm that produces a single product.

In order to undertake production, the firm uses productive resources known as factors of production. These include *human resources* (labour, entrepreneurship and management), *natural resources* (land, raw materials, energy) and *produced resources* (physical capital). These factors of production are organised by the firm in order to produce output. For example, in the leisure sector, your local gym uses capital in the form of exercise equipment, and labour in the form of the training staff and receptionist. In transport, a taxi firm uses capital in the form of the cars, and labour — the drivers and phone operators.

Notice that these factors have some differing characteristics that affect the analysis of firms' behaviour. In the short run, the firm faces limited flexibility. Varying the quantity of labour input the firm uses may be relatively straightforward — it can increase the use of overtime, or hire more workers, fairly quickly. However, varying the amount of capital the firm has at its disposal may take longer. For example, it takes time to commission a new piece of machinery, or to build a new sports centre — or a Channel Tunnel! Hence labour is regarded as a flexible factor and capital as a fixed factor. The definitions of the **short run** and **long run** are based on this assumption.

The production function

As the firm changes its volume of production, it needs to vary the inputs of its factors of production. Thus, the total amount of output produced in a given period depends upon the inputs of labour, capital and other inputs used in the production process. Of course, there are many different ways of combining these inputs, some combinations being more efficient than others. The **production function** summarises the technically most efficient combinations for any given output level. It specifies how the level of output produced by a firm depends upon the quantities of inputs of the factors of production that are utilised.

Key term

short run: the period over which a firm is free to vary its input of one factor of production (e.g. labour), but faces fixed inputs of the other factors of production

long run: the period over which the firm is able to vary the inputs of all its factors of production

production function: relationship that embodies information about technically efficient ways of combining labour and capital to produce output

law of diminishing returns: law stating that if a firm increases its inputs of one factor of production while holding inputs of the other factor fixed, eventually the firm will get diminishing marginal returns from the variable factor

The nature of technology in an industry will determine the way in which output varies with the quantity of inputs. However, one thing is certain. If the firm increases the amount of inputs of the variable factor (labour) while holding constant the input of the other factors, it will gradually derive less additional output per unit of labour for each further increase. This is known as the **law of diminishing returns**, and is one of the few 'laws' in economics. It is a *short-run* concept, as it relies on the assumption that capital and other factor inputs are fixed.

It can readily be seen why this should be the case. Suppose a firm has 10 computer operators working in a travel agency, using 10 computers. The 11th worker may add some extra output, as the workers may be able to 'hot-desk' and take their coffee breaks at different times. The 12th worker may also add some extra output, perhaps by keeping the printers stocked with paper. However, if the firm keeps adding staff without increasing the number of computers, each extra worker will be adding less

Computer operators add to production provided they have machines to use

additional output to the office. Indeed, the 20th worker may add nothing at all, being unable to get access to a computer.

Figure 1.1 illustrates the short-run relationship between labour input and total physical product (TPP_L), with capital held constant. The shape of the TPP_L relationship reflects the law of diminishing returns: as labour input increases, the amount of additional output produced gets smaller. An increase in the amount of capital available will raise the amount of output produced for any given labour input, so the TPP_L will shift upwards, as shown in Figure 1.2.

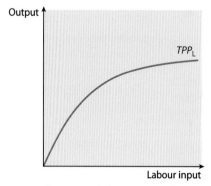

Figure 1.1 *A short-run production function*

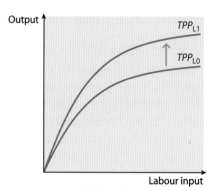

Figure 1.2 *The effect of an increase in capital*

The production function thus carries information about the physical relationship between the inputs of the factors of production and the physical quantity of output. With this information and knowledge of the prices that the firm must pay for its inputs of the factors of production, it is possible to map out the way in which costs will change with the level of output.

We can view the firm's decision process as a three-stage procedure. First, the firm needs to decide how much output it wants to produce. Second, it chooses an appropriate combination of factors of production given that intended scale of production. Third, it attempts to produce as much output as possible given those inputs. Another way of expressing this is that, having chosen the intended scale of output, the firm tries to minimise its costs of production.

Total, marginal and average costs

In talking about costs, economists distinguish between total, marginal and average costs. **Total cost** is the sum of all costs that are incurred in order to produce a given level of output. Total cost will always increase as the firm increases its level of production, as this will require more inputs of factors of production, materials and so on.

Average cost is simply the cost per unit of output — it is total cost divided by the level of output produced.

 Key term

total cost: the sum of all costs that are incurred in producing a given level of output

average cost: total cost divided by the quantity produced; sometimes known as unit cost

Equally important as these measures is the concept of **marginal cost**. Economists rely heavily on the idea that firms, consumers and other economic actors can make good decisions by thinking in terms of the margin. This is known as the **marginal principle**. For example, a firm may examine whether a small change in its behaviour makes matters better or worse. In this context, marginal cost is important. It is defined as the change in total cost associated with a small change in output. In other words, it is the additional cost incurred by the firm if it increases output by 1 unit.

Costs in the short run

Because the firm cannot vary some of its inputs in the short run, some costs may be regarded as fixed, and some as variable. In this short run, some **fixed costs** are **sunk costs**: that is, they are costs that the firm cannot avoid paying even if it chooses to produce no output at all. Total costs are the sum of fixed and **variable costs**:

total costs = total fixed costs + total variable costs

Total costs will increase as the firm increases the volume of production because more of the variable input is needed to increase output. The way in which the costs will vary depends on the nature of the production function, and on whether the prices of labour or other factor inputs alter as output increases.

A common assumption made by economists is that in the short run, at very low levels of output, total costs will rise more slowly than output, but that as diminishing returns set in, total costs will accelerate, as shown in Figure 1.3.

Short-run average and marginal curves are plotted in Figure 1.4, which shows how they relate to each other. First, notice that short-run average total costs (*SATC*) take on a U-shape. This is the form often assumed in economic analysis. *SATC* is the sum of average fixed and variable costs (*SAFC* and *SAVC*, respectively). Average fixed costs slope downwards throughout – this is because fixed costs do not vary with the level of output, so as output increases, *SAFC* must always get smaller, as the fixed costs are

Key term

marginal cost: the cost of producing an additional unit of output

marginal principle: the idea that firms (and other economic agents) may take decisions by considering the effect of small changes from the existing situation

fixed costs: costs that do not vary with the level of output

sunk costs: costs incurred by a firm that cannot be recovered if the firm ceases trading

variable costs: costs that do vary with the level of output

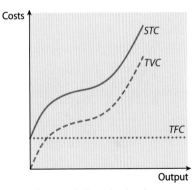

Figure 1.3 Costs in the short run

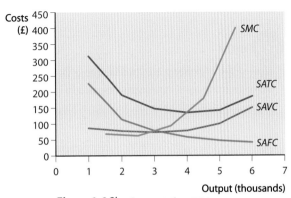

Figure 1.4 Short-run cost curves

spread over more and more units of output. However, *SAVC* also shows a U-shape, and it is this that gives the U-shape to *SATC*.

A very important aspect of Figure 1.4 is that the short-run marginal cost curve (*SMC*) cuts both *SAVC* and *SATC* at their minimum points. This is always the case. If you think about this for a moment, you will realise that it makes good sense. If you are adding on something that is greater than the average, the average must always increase. For a firm, when the marginal cost of producing an additional unit of a good is higher than the average cost of doing so, the average cost must rise. If the marginal cost is the same as the average cost, then average cost will not change. This is quite simply an arithmetic property of the average and the marginal, and always holds true. So when you draw the average and marginal cost curves for a firm, the marginal cost curve will always cut average cost at the minimum point of average cost. Another way of viewing marginal cost is as the *slope* or gradient of the total cost curve.

Remember that the short-run cost curves show the relationship between the volume of production and costs under the assumption that the quantity of capital and other inputs is fixed, so that in order to change output the firm has to vary the amount of labour. The *position* of the cost curves thus depends on the quantity of capital. In other words, there is a short-run average total cost curve for each given level of other inputs.

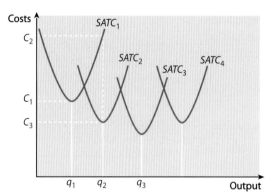

Figure 1.5 *Short-run cost curves with different levels of capital input*

Costs in the long run

In the long run, a firm is able to vary capital and labour (and other factor inputs). It is thus likely to choose the level of capital that is appropriate for the level of output that it expects to produce. Figure 1.5 shows a selection of short-run average total cost curves corresponding to different expected output levels, and thus different levels of capital. With the set of *SATC* curves in Figure 1.5, the long-run average cost curve also takes on a U-shape.

 term

economies of scale: occur for a firm when an increase in the scale of production leads to production at lower long-run average cost

Economies of scale

One of the reasons why firms find it beneficial to be large is the existence of **economies of scale**. These occur when a firm finds that it is more efficient in cost terms to produce on a larger scale.

It is not difficult to imagine industries in which economies of scale are likely to arise. For example, recall the notion of the division of labour, which you encountered during the

AS part of the course. When a firm expands, it reaches a certain scale of production at which it becomes worthwhile to take advantage of division of labour. Workers begin to specialise in certain stages of the production process, and their productivity increases. Because this is only possible for relatively large-scale production, this is an example of economies of scale. It is the size of the firm (in terms of its output level) that enables it to produce more efficiently — that is, at lower average cost.

Although the division of labour is one source of economies of scale, it is by no means the only source, and there are several explanations of cost benefits from producing on a large scale. Some of these are industry-specific, and thus some sectors of the economy exhibit more significant economies of scale than others — it is in these activities that the larger firms tend to be found. There are no hairdressing salons that come into the top ten largest firms, but there are plenty of oil companies.

Technology

One source of economies of scale is in the technology of production. There are many activities in which the technology is such that large-scale production is more efficient.

One source of technical economies of scale arises from the physical properties of the universe. There is a physical relationship between the volume and surface area of an object, whereby the storage capacity of an object increases proportionately more than its surface area. Consider the volume of a cube. If the cube is 2 metres each way, its surface area is $6 \times 2 \times 2 = 24$ square metres, while its volume is $2 \times 2 \times 2 = 8$ cubic metres. If the dimension of the cube is 3 metres, the surface area is 54 square metres (more than double the surface area of the smaller cube) but the volume is 27 cubic metres (more than three times the volume of the smaller cube). Thus the larger the cube, the lower the average cost of storage. A similar relationship applies to other shapes of storage containers, whether they be barrels or ships.

What this means in practice is that a large ship can transport proportionally more than a small ship, or that large barrels hold more wine relative to the surface area of the barrel than small barrels. Hence there may be benefits in operating on a large scale.

Furthermore, some capital equipment is designed for large-scale production, and would only be viable for a firm operating at a high volume of production. Combine harvesters cannot be used in small fields; a production line for car production would not be viable for small levels of output. In other words, there may be *indivisibilities* in the production process.

In addition to indivisibilities, there are many economic activities in which there are high *overhead* expenditures. Such components of a firm's costs do not vary directly with the scale of production. For example, having built a factory, the cost of that factory is the same regardless of the amount of output that is produced in it. Expenditure on research and development could be seen as such an overhead, which may be viable only when a firm reaches a certain size.

Notice that there are some economic activities in which these overhead costs are highly significant. For example, think about the Channel Tunnel. The construction (overhead) costs were enormous compared to the costs of running trains through the tunnel. Thus the overhead cost element is substantial — and the economies of scale will also be significant for such an industry.

There are other examples of this sort of cost structure, such as railway networks and electricity supply. The largest firm in such a market will always be able to produce at a lower average cost than smaller firms. This could prove such a competitive advantage that no other firms will be able to become established in that market, which may therefore constitute a **natural monopoly**. Intuitively, this makes sense. Imagine having several underground railway systems operating in a single city, all competing against each other!

The Channel Tunnel — the construction costs were enormous compared to the costs of running trains through the tunnel

Key *term*

natural monopoly: monopoly that arises in an industry in which there are such substantial economies of scale that only one firm is viable

diseconomies of scale: occur for a firm when an increase in the scale of production leads to higher long-run average costs

Management and marketing

A second source of economies of scale pertains to the management of firms. One of the key factors of production is managerial input. A certain number of managers are required to oversee the production process. As the firm expands, there is a range of volumes of output over which the management team does not need to grow as rapidly as the overall volume of the firm, as a large firm can be managed more efficiently. Notice that there are likely to be limits to this process. At some point, the organisation begins to get so large and complex that management finds it more difficult to manage. At this point **diseconomies of scale** are likely to cut in — in other words, average costs may begin to rise with an increase in output at some volume of production.

Similarly, the cost of marketing a product may not rise as rapidly as the volume of production, leading to further scale economies. One interpretation of this is that we might see marketing expenses as a component of fixed costs — or at least as having a substantial fixed cost element.

Finance and procurement

Large firms may have advantages in a number of other areas. For example, a large firm with a strong reputation may be able to raise finance for further expansion on more favourable terms than a small firm. This, of course, reinforces the market position of the largest firms in a sector and makes it more difficult for relative newcomers to become established.

Once a firm has grown to the point where it is operating on a relatively large scale, it will also be purchasing its inputs in relatively large volumes. In particular, this relates to raw materials, energy and transport services. When buying in bulk in this way, firms may be able to negotiate good deals with their suppliers, and thus again reduce average cost as output increases.

It may even be the case that some of the firm's suppliers will find it beneficial to locate in proximity to the firm's factory, which would reduce costs even more.

External economies of scale

The factors listed so far that may lead to economies of scale arise from the internal expansion of a firm. If the firm is in an industry that is itself expanding, there may also be external economies of scale.

Some of the most successful firms of recent years have been in activities that require high levels of technology and skills. The computer industry is one example of an economic activity that has expanded rapidly. As the sector expands, a pool of skilled labour is built up that all the firms can draw upon. The very success of the sector encourages people to acquire the skills needed to enter it, colleges may begin to find it viable to provide courses and so on. Each individual firm benefits in this way from the overall expansion of the sector. The greater availability of skilled workers reduces the amount that individual firms need to spend on training.

Computer engineering is by no means the only example of this. Formula 1 development teams, pharmaceutical companies and others similarly enjoy external economies of scale.

Economies of scope

There are various ways in which firms expand their scale of operations. Some do so within a relatively focused market, but others are multi-product firms that produce a range of different products, sometimes in quite different markets.

Key term

economies of scope: economies arising when average cost falls as a firm increases output across a range of different products

For example, look at Nestlé. You may immediately think of instant coffee, and indeed Nestlé produces 200 different brands of instant coffee worldwide. However, Nestlé also produces baby milk powder, mineral water, ice cream and pet food, and has diversified into hotels and restaurants — not to mention locally popular items such as lemon cheesecake-flavoured Kit Kats (a strong seller in Japan).

Such conglomerate companies can benefit from **economies of scope**, whereby there may be benefits of size across a range of different products. These economies may arise because there are activities that can be shared across the product range. For example, a company may not need a finance or accounting section for each different product, nor human resource or marketing departments. There is thus scope for economies to be made as the firm expands.

Exercise 1.2

Which of the following reflects a movement along a long-run average cost curve, and which would cause a shift of a long-run average cost curve?

a A firm becomes established in a market, learning the best ways of utilising its factors of production.

b A firm observes that average cost falls as it expands its scale of production.

c The larger a firm becomes, the more difficult it becomes to manage, causing average cost to rise.

d A firm operating in the financial sector installs new, faster computers, enabling its average cost to fall for any given level of service that it provides.

Returns to scale

In Figure 1.6, if the firm expands its output up to q^*, long-run average cost falls. Up to q^* of output is the range over which there are economies of scale. To the right of q^*, however, long-run average cost rises as output continues to be increased, and the firm experiences diseconomies of scale. The output q^* itself is at the intermediate state of **constant returns to scale**.

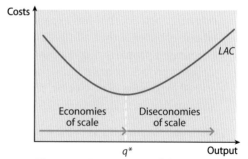

Figure 1.6 *Economies and diseconomies of scale*

It is important not to confuse the notion of returns to scale with the idea introduced earlier of diminishing marginal returns to a factor. The two concepts arise in different circumstances. The law of diminishing returns to a factor applies in the *short run*, when a firm increases its inputs of one factor of production while facing fixed amounts of other factors. It is thus solely

Key term

constant returns to scale: found when long-run average cost remains constant with an increase in output — in other words, when output and costs rise at the same rate

a short-run phenomenon. Diseconomies of scale (sometimes known as *decreasing returns to scale*) can occur in the *long run*, and the term refers to how output changes as a firm varies the quantities of *all* factors.

If the firm is operating at the lowest possible level of long-run average costs, it is in a position of *productive efficiency*. For example, in Figure 1.6 the point q^* may be regarded as the optimum level of output, in the sense that it minimises average cost per unit of output.

Summary

➤ A firm may face inflexibility in the short run, with some factors being fixed in quantity and only some being variable.

➤ The short run is defined in this context as the period over which a firm is free to vary some factors, but not others.

➤ The long run is defined as the period over which the firm is able to vary the input of all of its factors of production.

➤ The production function shows how output can be efficiently produced through the input of factors of production.

➤ The law of diminishing returns states that, if a firm increases the input of a variable factor while holding input of the fixed factor constant, eventually the firm will get diminishing marginal returns from the variable factor.

➤ Short-run costs can be separated into fixed, sunk and variable costs.

➤ There is a clear and immutable relationship between total, average and marginal costs.

➤ For a U-shaped average cost curve, marginal cost always cuts the minimum point of average cost.

Exercise 1.3

A firm faces long-run total cost conditions as shown in Table 1.1.

Output ('000 units per week)	Total cost (£'000)
0	0
1	32
2	48
3	82
4	140
5	228
6	352

Table 1.1 Output and long-run costs

a Calculate long-run average cost and long-run marginal cost for each level of output.
b Plot long-run average cost and long-run marginal cost curves on a graph. (Hint: don't forget to plot *LMC* at points that are halfway between the corresponding output levels.)
c Identify the output level at which long-run average cost is at a minimum.
d Identify the output level at which $LAC = LMC$.
e Within what range of output does this firm enjoy economies of scale?
f Within what range of output does the firm experience diseconomies of scale?
g If you could measure the nature of returns to scale, what would characterise the point where *LAC* is at a minimum?

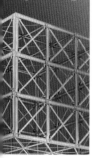

Revenue of firms

In the AS part of the course (see *AS Economics, Chapter 4*), you saw how the total revenue received by a firm varies along the demand curve, according to the price elasticity of demand. In the same way that there is a relationship between total, average and marginal cost, there is also a relationship between **total revenue**, **average revenue** and **marginal revenue**.

Figure 1.7 reminds you of the relationship between total revenue and the *PED*. The marginal revenue (*MR*) curve has also been added to the figure, and has a fixed relationship with the average revenue (*AR*) curve. This is for similar mathematical reasons as the relationship between marginal and average costs explained earlier in this chapter. *MR* shares the intercept point on the vertical axis (at point *A* on Figure 1.7), and has exactly twice the slope of *AR*. Whenever you have to draw this figure, remember that *MR* and *AR* have this relationship, meeting at *A*, and with the distance *BC* being the same as the distance *CD*. *MR* is zero (meets the horizontal axis) at the maximum point of the total revenue curve.

Motivations of firms

The opening section of this chapter stated that firms exist to organise production by bringing together the factors of production in order to produce output. This begs the question of what motivates them to produce particular *levels* of output, and at what price. This section considers alternative objectives that firms may set out to achieve.

 Key *term*

total revenue: the revenue received by a firm from its sales of a good or service; it is the quantity sold, multiplied by the price

average revenue: the average revenue received by the firm per unit of output; it is total revenue divided by the quantity sold

marginal revenue: the additional revenue received by the firm if it sells an additional unit of output

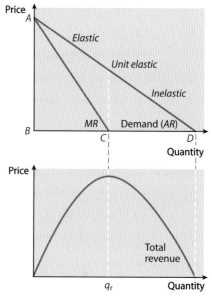

Figure 1.7 *Elasticity and total revenue*

Profit maximisation

Traditional economic analysis has tended to start from the premise that firms set out with the objective of maximising profits. In analysing this, economists define profits as the difference between the total revenue received by a firm and the total costs that it incurs in production:

profits = total revenue − total cost

Total revenue here is seen in terms of the quantity of the product that is sold multiplied by the price. Total cost includes the fixed and variable costs that have already been discussed. However, one important item of costs should be highlighted before going any further.

Consider the case of a sole proprietor — a small local business such as a gym or a taxi firm. It seems reasonable to assume that such a firm will set out to maximise its profits. However, from the entrepreneur's perspective there is an *opportunity cost* of being in business, which may be seen in terms of the earnings that the proprietor could make in an alternative occupation. This required rate of return is regarded as a fixed cost, and is included in the total cost of production.

The same procedure applies to cost curves for other sorts of firm. In other words, when economists refer to costs, they include the rate of return that a firm needs to make it stay in a particular market in the long run. Accountants dislike this, as 'opportunity cost' cannot be identified as an explicit item in the accounts. This part of costs is known as **normal profit**.

 Key *term*

normal profit: the return needed for a firm to stay in a market in the long run

abnormal, supernormal or economic profits: profits above normal profits

Profits made by a firm above that level are known as **supernormal profits**, **abnormal profits** or **economic profits**.

In the short run, a firm may choose to remain in a market even if it is not covering its opportunity costs, provided its revenues are covering its variable costs. Since the firm has already incurred fixed costs, if it can cover its variable costs in the short run, it will be better off remaining in business and paying off part of the fixed costs than exiting the market and losing all of its fixed costs. Thus, the level of average variable costs represents the shut-down price, below which the firm will exit from the market in the short run. In situations where firms in a market are making abnormal profits, it is likely that other firms will be attracted to enter the market. The absence or existence of abnormal profits will thus be important in influencing the way in which a market may evolve over time.

How does a firm choose its output level if it wishes to maximise profits? An application of the marginal principle shows how. Suppose a firm realises that its marginal revenue is higher than its marginal cost of production. What does this mean for profits? If it were to sell an additional unit of its output, it would gain more in revenue than it would incur additional cost, so its profits would increase. Similarly, if it found that its marginal revenue was less than marginal cost, it would be making a loss on the marginal unit of output, and profits would increase if the firm sold less. This leads to the conclusion that profits will be maximised at the level of output at which marginal revenue (*MR*) is equal to marginal cost (*MC*). Indeed, this *MR* = *MC* rule is a general rule that tells a firm how to maximise profits in any market situation.

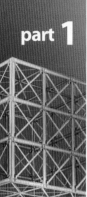

The principal–agent problem

The discussion so far seems reasonable when considering a relatively small owner-managed firm. In this context, profit maximisation makes good sense as the firm's motivation.

However, for many larger firms — especially public limited companies — the owners may not be involved in running the business. This gives rise to the **principal–agent (or agency) problem**. In a public limited company, the shareholders delegate the day-to-day decisions concerning the operation of the firm to managers who act on their behalf. In this case the shareholders are the *principals*, and the managers are the *agents* who run things for them. In other words, there is a divorce of ownership from control.

If the agents are in full sympathy with the objectives of the owners, there is no problem and the managers will take exactly the decisions that the owners would like. Problems arise when there is conflict between the aims of the owners and those of the managers.

Key term

principal–agent problem: arises from conflict between the objectives of the principals and their agents, who take decisions on their behalf

satisficing: behaviour under which the managers of firms aim to produce satisfactory results for the firm — for example, in terms of profits — rather than trying to maximise them

X-inefficiency: occurs when a firm is not operating at minimum cost, perhaps because of organisational slack

One simple explanation of why this problem arises is that the managers like a quiet life, and therefore do not push for the absolute profit-maximising position, but do just enough to keep the shareholders off their backs. Herbert Simon referred to this as '**satisficing**' behaviour, where managers aim to produce satisfactory profits rather than maximum profits.

Another possibility is that managers become negligent because they are not fully accountable. One manifestation of this may be *organisational slack*: costs will not be minimised, as the firm is not operating as efficiently as it could. This is an example of what is called **X-inefficiency**. For example, in Figure 1.8 *LAC* represents the long-run average cost curve showing the most efficient cost positions for the firm at any output level. With X-inefficiency, a

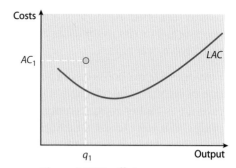

Figure 1.8 *X-inefficiency*

firm could end up producing output q_1 at average cost AC_1. Thus, in the presence of X-inefficiency the firm will be operating *above* its long-run average cost curve.

Some writers have argued that the managers may be pursuing other objectives. For example, some managers may enjoy being involved in the running of a *large* business, and may prefer to see the firm gaining market share — perhaps beyond the profit-maximising level. Others may like to see their status rewarded and so will want to divert part of the profits into managerial perks — large offices, company cars and so on. Or they may feel that having a large staff working for them increases their

Some managers may be pursuing other objectives than profit maximisation

prestige inside the company. These sorts of activity tend to reduce the profitability of firms.

Revenue maximisation

The industrial economist William Baumol argued that managers may set out with the objective of maximising revenue. One reason is that in some firms managerial salaries are related to turnover rather than profits. The effects of this can be seen by looking back at Figure 1.7. You can see that total revenue is maximised at the peak of the *TR* curve (where $MR = 0$) at q_r. A revenue-maximising firm will produce more output than a profit-maximising one, and will need to charge a lower price in order to sell the extra output. This should be apparent from the fact that profits are maximised where $MR = MC$, which must be at a positive level of MR — and thus to the left of q_r in Figure 1.7.

Baumol pointed out that the shareholders might not be too pleased about this. The way the firm behaves then depends upon the degree of accountability that the agents (managers) have to the principals (shareholders). For example, the shareholders may have sufficient power over their agents to be able to insist on some minimum level of profits. The result may then be a compromise solution.

Sales maximisation

In some cases, managers may focus more on the volume of sales than on the resulting revenues. This could lead to output being set even higher, to the point at which total revenue only just covers total cost. Remember that total cost includes normal profit — the opportunity cost of the resources tied up in the firm. The firm would have to close down if it did not cover this opportunity cost.

Again, the extent to which the managers will be able to pursue this objective without endangering their positions with the shareholders depends on how accountable the managers are to the shareholders. Remember that the managers are likely to have

much better information about the market conditions and the internal functioning of the firm than the shareholders, who view the firm only remotely. This may be to the managers' advantage.

Summary

➤ Traditional economic analysis assumes that firms set out to maximise profits, where profits are defined as the excess of total revenue over total cost.

➤ This analysis treats the opportunity cost of a firm's resources as a part of fixed costs. The opportunity cost is known as normal profit.

➤ Profits above this level are known as abnormal profits.

➤ A firm maximises profits by choosing a level of output such that marginal revenue is equal to marginal cost.

➤ For many larger firms, where day-to-day control is delegated to managers, a principal–agent problem may arise if there is conflict between the objectives of the owners (principals) and those of the managers (agents).

➤ This may lead to satisficing behaviour and to X-inefficiency.

➤ William Baumol suggested that managers may set out to maximise revenue rather than profits; others have suggested that sales or the growth of the firm may be the managers' objectives.

Chapter 2
Perfect competition and monopoly

The AS economics course introduced the notion of market failure — describing situations in which free markets may not produce the best outcome for society in terms of efficiency. One of the reasons given for this concerned what is termed 'imperfect competition'. It was argued that, if firms can achieve a position of market dominance, they may distort the pattern of resource allocation. As a prelude to the modules covering the economics of work and leisure and transport economics, it is now time to look at market structure more closely in order to evaluate the way that markets work, and the significance of this for resource allocation. The fact that firms try to maximise profits is not in itself bad for society. However, the structure of a market has a strong influence on how well the market performs. 'Structure' here is seen in relation to a number of dimensions, but in particular to the number of firms operating in a market and the way in which they interact. This chapter considers two extreme forms of market structure: perfect competition and monopoly.

Learning outcomes

After studying this chapter, you should:
- ➤ be familiar with the assumptions of the model of perfect competition
- ➤ understand how a firm chooses profit-maximising output under perfect competition
- ➤ appreciate how a perfectly competitive market reaches long-run equilibrium
- ➤ understand how the characteristics of long-run equilibrium affect the performance of the market in terms of productive and allocative efficiency
- ➤ be familiar with the assumptions of the model of monopoly
- ➤ understand how the monopoly firm chooses the level of output and sets its price
- ➤ understand why a monopoly can arise in a market
- ➤ understand how the characteristics of the monopoly equilibrium affect the performance of the market in terms of productive and allocative efficiency

Market structure

Firms cannot take decisions without some awareness of the market in which they are operating. In some markets, firms find themselves to be such a small player that they cannot influence the price at which they sell. In others, a firm may find itself to be the only firm, which clearly gives it much more discretion in devising a price and output strategy. There may also be many intermediate situations where the firm has some control over price, but needs to be aware of rival firms in the market.

Economists have devised a range of models that allow such different **market structures** to be analysed. Before looking carefully at the most important types of market structure, the key characteristics of alternative market structures will be introduced. The main models are summarised in Table 2.1. In many ways, we can regard these as a spectrum of markets with different characteristics.

Key term

market structure: the market environment within which firms operate

	Perfect competition	Monopolistic competition	Oligopoly	Monopoly
Number of firms	Many	Many	Dominated by few	One
Freedom of entry	Not restricted	Not restricted	Some barriers to entry	High barriers to entry
Firm's influence over price	None	Some	Some	Price maker, subject to the demand curve
Nature of product	Homogeneous	Differentiated	Varied	No close substitutes
Examples	Cauliflowers Carrots	Fast-food outlets Travel agents	Cars Mobile phones	PC operating systems Local water supply

Table 2.1 *A spectrum of market structures*

Perfect competition

At one extreme is perfect competition. This is a market in which each individual firm is a *price taker.* This means that there is no individual firm that is large enough to be able to influence the price, which is set by the market as a whole. This situation would arise where there are many firms operating in a market, producing a product that is much the same whichever firm produces it. You might think of a market for a particular sort of vegetable, for example. One cauliflower is very much like another, and it would not be possible for a particular cauliflower-grower to set a premium price for its product.

Such markets are also typified by freedom of entry and exit. In other words, it is relatively easy for new firms to enter the market, or for existing firms to leave it to produce something else. The market price in such a market will be driven down to that at which the typical firm in the market just makes enough profit to stay in business. If firms make more than this, other firms will be attracted in, and thus abnormal profits will be competed away. If some firms in the market do not make sufficient profit to want to remain in the market, they will exit, allowing price to drift up until again the typical firm just makes enough to stay in business.

Monopoly

At the other extreme of the spectrum of market structures is monopoly. This is a market where there is only one firm in operation. Such a firm has some influence over price, and can choose a combination of price and output in order to maximise its profits. The monopolist is not entirely free to set any price that it wants, as it must remain aware of the demand curve for its product. Nonetheless, it has the freedom to choose a point along its demand curve.

The nature of a monopolist's product is that it has no close substitutes — either actual or potential — so faces no competition. An example might be Microsoft, which for a long time held a global monopoly for operating systems for PC computers. At the time of the famous trial in 1998, Microsoft was said to supply operating systems for about 95% of the world's PCs.

Bill Gates held a global monopoly on PC operating systems through his company Microsoft

Another condition of a monopoly market is that there are barriers to the entry of new firms. This means that the firm is able to set its price such as to make profits that are above the minimum needed to keep the firm in business, without attracting new rivals into the market.

Monopolistic competition

Between the two extreme forms of market structure are many intermediate situations in which firms may have some influence over their selling price, but still have to take account of the fact that there are other firms in the market. One such market is known as monopolistic competition. This is a market in which there are many firms operating, each producing similar but not identical products, so that there is some scope for influencing price, perhaps because of brand loyalty. However, firms in such a market are likely to be relatively small. Such firms may find it profitable to make sure that their own product is differentiated from other goods, and may advertise in order to convince potential customers that this is the case. For example, small-scale local restaurants may offer different styles of cooking.

Oligopoly

Another intermediate form of market structure is oligopoly, which literally means 'few sellers'. This is a market in which there are just a few firms that supply the market. Each firm will take decisions in close awareness of how other firms in the market may react to their actions. In some cases, the firms may try to collude — to work together in order to behave as if they were a monopolist — thus making higher profits. In other cases, they may be intense rivals, which will tend to result in abnormal profits being competed away. The question of whether firms in an oligopoly collude or compete

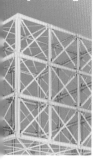

Small-scale local restaurants differentiate what they have to offer by serving particular kinds of food

has a substantial impact on how the overall market performs in terms of resource allocation, and whether consumers will be disadvantaged as a result of the actions of the firms in the market.

Barriers to entry

It has been argued that if firms in a market are able to make abnormal profits this will act as an inducement for new firms to try to gain entry into that market in order to share in those profits. A barrier to entry is a characteristic of a market that prevents new firms from joining the market. The existence of such barriers is thus of great importance in influencing the market structure that will evolve.

For example, if a firm holds a patent on a particular good, this means that no other firm is permitted by law to produce the product, and the patent-holding firm thus has a monopoly. The firm may then be able to set price such as to make abnormal profits without fear of rival firms competing away those profits. On the other hand, if there are no barriers to entry in a market, then if the existing firms set price to make abnormal profits, new firms will join the market, and the increase in market supply will push price down until no abnormal profits are being made.

Summary

➤ The decisions made by firms must be taken in the context of the market environment in which they operate.

➤ Under conditions of perfect competition, each firm must accept the market price as given, but can choose how much output to produce in order to maximise profits.

➤ In a monopoly market, where there is only one producer, the firm can choose output and price (subject to the demand curve).

➤ Monopolistic competition combines some features of perfect competition, and some characteristics of monopoly. Firms have some influence over price, and will produce a differentiated product in order to maintain this influence.

➤ Oligopoly exists where a market is occupied by just a few firms. In some cases, these few firms may work together to maximise their joint profits; in other cases, they may seek to outmanoeuvre each other.

Perfect competition

Assumptions

At one end of the spectrum of market structures is **perfect competition**. This model has a special place in economic analysis because, if all its assumptions were fulfilled, and if all markets operated according to its precepts (including the markets for leisure goods and services, and for transportation services), the best allocation of resources would be ensured for society as a whole. Although it may be argued that this ideal is not often achieved, perfect competition nonetheless provides a yardstick by which all other forms of market structure can be evaluated. The assumptions of this model are as follows:

Key term

perfect competition: a form of market structure that produces allocative and productive efficiency in long-run equilibrium

➤ Firms aim to maximise profits.
➤ There are many participants (both buyers and sellers).
➤ The product is homogeneous.
➤ There are no barriers to entry to or exit from the market.
➤ There is perfect knowledge of market conditions.

Profit maximisation

The first assumption is that firms act to maximise their profits. You might think that firms acting in their own self-interest are unlikely to do consumers any favours. However, it transpires that this does not interfere with the operation of the market. Indeed, it is the pursuit of self-interest by firms and consumers that ensures that the market works effectively.

Many participants

This is an important assumption of the model: that there are so many buyers and so many sellers that no individual trader is able to influence the market price. The market price is thus determined by the operation of the market.

On the sellers' side of the market, this assumption is tantamount to saying that there are limited economies of scale in the industry. If the minimum efficient scale (that is, the level of output at which a firm's long-run average costs reach their minimum) is small relative to market demand, then no firm is likely to become so large that it will gain influence in the market.

A homogeneous product

This assumption means that buyers of the good see all products in the market as being identical, and will not favour one firm's product over another. If there were brand loyalty, such that one firm was more popular than others, then that firm

would be able to charge a premium on its price. By ruling out this possibility the previous assumption is reinforced, and no individual seller is able to influence the selling price of the product.

No barriers to entry or exit

By this assumption, firms are able to join the market if they perceive it to be a profitable step, and they can exit from the market without hindrance. This assumption is important when it comes to considering the long-run equilibrium towards which the market will tend.

Perfect knowledge

It is assumed that all participants in the market have perfect information about trading conditions in the market. In particular, buyers always know the prices that firms are charging, and thus can buy the good at the cheapest possible price. Firms that try to charge a price above the market price will get no takers. At the same time, traders are aware of the product quality.

Perfect competition in the short run

The firm under perfect competition

With the above assumptions, it is possible to analyse how a firm will operate in the market. An important implication of these assumptions is that no individual trader can influence the price of the product. In particular, this means that the firm is a **price taker**, and has to accept whatever price is set in the market as a whole.

As a price taker, the firm faces a perfectly elastic demand curve for its product, as is shown in Figure 2.1. In this figure P_1 is the price set in the market, and the firm cannot sell at any other price. If it tries to set a price above P_1 it will sell nothing, as buyers are fully aware of the market price and will not buy at a higher price, especially as they know that there is no quality difference between the products produced by different firms in the market. What this also implies is that the firm can sell as much output as it likes at that going price — which means there is no incentive for any firm to set a price below P_1. Thus, all firms charge the same price, P_1.

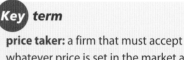

Key term

price taker: a firm that must accept whatever price is set in the market as a whole

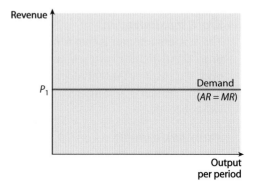

Figure 2.1 The firm's demand curve

The firm's short-run supply decision

If the firm can sell as much as it likes at the market price, how does it decide how much to produce?

Chapter 1 explained that to maximise profits a firm needs to set output at such a level that marginal revenue is equal to marginal cost. Figure 2.2 illustrates this rule by adding the short-run cost curves to the demand curve. (Remember that *SMC* cuts *SAVC* and *SATC* at their minimum points.)

As the demand curve is horizontal, the firm faces constant average and marginal revenue and will choose output at q_1, where $MR = SMC$.

If the market price were to change, the firm would react by changing output, but always choosing to supply output at the level at which $MR = SMC$. This suggests that the short-run marginal cost curve represents the firm's short-run supply curve: in other words, it shows the quantity of output that the firm would supply at any given price.

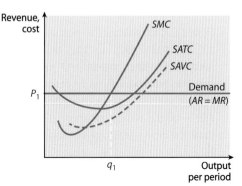

Figure 2.2 *The firm's short-run supply decision*

However, there is one important proviso to this statement. If the price falls below short-run average variable cost, the firm's best decision will be to exit from the market, as it will be better off just incurring its fixed costs. So the firm's **short-run supply curve** is the *SMC* curve above the point where it cuts *SAVC* (at its minimum point).

Industry equilibrium in the short run

One crucial question not yet examined is how the market price comes to be determined. To answer this, it is necessary to consider the industry as a whole. In this case there is a conventional downward-sloping demand curve. This is formed according to preferences of consumers in the market and is shown in Figure 2.3.

On the supply side, it has been shown that the individual firm's supply curve is its marginal cost curve above *SAVC*. If you add up the supply curves of each firm operating

> **Key term**
>
> **short-run supply curve:** for a firm operating under perfect competition, the curve given by its short-run marginal cost curve above the price at which $MC = SAVC$; for the industry, the short-run supply curve is the horizontal sum of the supply curves of the individual firms

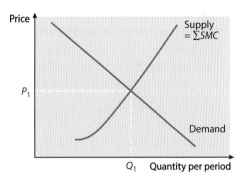

Figure 2.3 *A perfectly competitive industry in short-run equilibrium*

in the market, the result is the industry supply curve, shown in Figure 2.3 as Supply = ΣSMC (where 'Σ' means 'sum of'). The price will then adjust to P_1 at the intersection of demand and supply. The firms in the industry between them will supply Q_1 output, and the market will be in equilibrium.

The firm in short-run equilibrium revisited

As this seems to be a well-balanced situation, with price adjusting to equate market demand and supply, the only question is why it is described as just a *short-run equilibrium*. The clue to this is to be found back with the individual firm.

Figure 2.4 illustrates the position facing an individual firm in the market. As before, the firm maximises profits by accepting the price P_1 as set in the market and producing up to the point where $MR = SMC$, which is at q_1. However, now the firm's average revenue (which is equal to price) is greater than its average cost (which is given by AC_1 at this level of output). The firm is thus making supernormal profits at this price. (Remember that 'normal profits' are included in average cost.) The total amount of supernormal profits being made is shown as the shaded area on the graph. Notice that average revenue minus average costs equals profit per unit, so multiplying this by the quantity sold determines total profit.

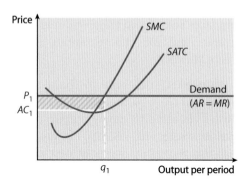

Figure 2.4 *The firm in short-run supply equilibrium*

This is where the assumption about freedom of entry becomes important. If firms in this market are making profits above opportunity cost, the market is generating more profits than other markets in the economy. This will prove attractive to other firms, which will seek to enter the market — and the assumption is that there are no barriers to prevent them from doing so.

This process of entry will continue for as long as firms are making supernormal profits. However, as more firms join the market, the *position* of the industry supply curve, which is the sum of the supply curves of an ever-larger number of individual firms, will be affected. As the industry supply curve shifts to the right, the market price will fall. At some point the price will have fallen to such an extent that firms are no longer making supernormal profits, and the market will then stabilise.

If the price were to fall even further, some firms would choose to exit from the market, and the process would go into reverse. Therefore price can be expected to stabilise such that the typical firm in the industry is just making normal profits.

Perfect competition in long-run equilibrium

Figure 2.5 shows the situation for a typical firm and for the industry as a whole once long-run equilibrium has been reached and firms no longer have any incentive to enter or exit the market. The market is in equilibrium, with demand equal to supply at the going price. The typical firm sets marginal revenue equal to marginal cost to maximise profits, and just makes normal profits.

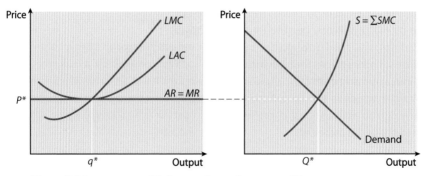

Figure 2.5 *Long-run equilibrium under perfect competition*

The long-run supply curve

Comparative static analysis can be used to explore this equilibrium a little more deeply. Suppose there is an increase in the demand for this product. Perhaps, for some reason, everyone becomes convinced that the product is really health promoting, so demand increases at any given price. This disturbs the market equilibrium, and the question then is whether (and how) equilibrium can be restored.

Figure 2.6 reproduces the long-run equilibrium that was shown in Figure 2.5. Thus, in the initial position market price is at P^*, the typical firm is in long-run equilibrium, producing q^*, and the industry is producing Q^*. Demand was initially at D_0, but with the increased popularity of the product it has shifted to D_1. In the short run this pushes the market price up to P_1 for the industry, because as market price increases, existing firms have the incentive to supply more output: that is, they move along their short-run supply curves. So in the short run a typical firm starts to produce q_1 output. The combined supply of the firms then increases to Q_1.

However, at the higher price the firms start making supernormal profits (shown by the shaded area in Figure 2.6), so in time more firms will be attracted into the market, pushing the short-run industry supply curve to the right. This process will continue until there is no further incentive for new firms to enter the market – which occurs when the price has returned to P^*, but with increased industry output at Q^{**}. In other

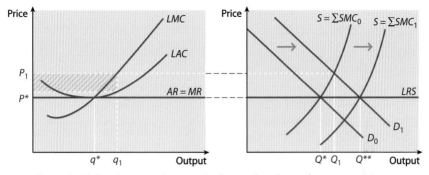

Figure 2.6 *Adjusting to an increase in demand under perfect competition*

words, the adjustment in the short run is borne by existing firms, but the long-run equilibrium is reached through the entry of new firms. This suggests that the **industry long-run supply curve** (*LRS*) is horizontal at price *P**, which is the minimum point of the long-run average cost curve for the typical firm in the industry.

Key term

industry long-run supply curve: under perfect competition, a curve that is horizontal at the price which is the minimum point of the long-run average cost curve for the typical firm in the industry

Efficiency under perfect competition

Having reviewed the characteristics of long-run equilibrium in a perfectly competitive market, you may wonder what is so good about such a market in terms of productive and allocative efficiency.

Productive efficiency

For an individual market, productive efficiency is reached when a firm operates at the minimum point of its long-run average cost curve. Under perfect competition, this is indeed a feature of the long-run equilibrium position. So, productive efficiency is achieved in the long run — but not in the short run, when a firm need not be operating at minimum average cost.

Allocative efficiency

For an individual market, allocative efficiency is achieved when price is set equal to marginal cost (see *AS Economics, Chapter 5*). Again, the process by which supernormal profits are competed away, through the entry of new firms into the market, ensures that price is equal to marginal cost within a perfectly competitive market in long-run equilibrium. So allocative efficiency is also achieved. Indeed, firms set price equal to marginal cost even in the short run, so allocative efficiency is a feature of perfect competition in both the short run and the long run.

Exercise 2.1

Figure 2.7 shows the short-run cost curves for a firm that is operating in a perfectly competitive market.

a At what price would the firm just make 'normal' profits?

b What area would represent total fixed cost at this price?

c What is the shutdown price for the firm?

d Within what range of prices would the firm choose to operate at a loss in the short run?

e Identify the firm's short-run supply curve.

f Within what range of prices would the firm be able to make short-run supernormal profits?

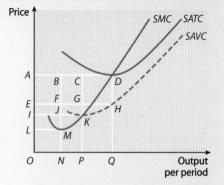

Figure 2.7 *A firm operating under short-run perfect competition*

g What conditions must hold for supernormal profits to be competed to zero in the long run?

Exercise 2.2

Starting from a diagram like Figure 2.5, track the response of a perfectly competitive market to a decrease in market demand for a good — in other words, explain how the market adjusts to a leftward shift of the demand curve.

Evaluation of perfect competition

A criticism sometimes levelled at the model of perfect competition is that it is merely a theoretical ideal, based on a sequence of assumptions that rarely holds in the real world. Perhaps you have some sympathy with that view.

It could be argued that the model does hold for some agricultural markets. One study in the USA estimated that the elasticity of demand for an individual farmer producing sweetcorn was −31,353, which is pretty close to being perfectly elastic.

However, to argue that the model is useless because it is unrealistic is to miss a very important point. By allowing a glimpse of what the ideal market would look like, at least in terms of resource allocation, the model provides a measure against which alternative market structures can be compared. Furthermore, economic analysis can be used to investigate the effects of relaxing the assumptions of the model, which can be another valuable exercise. For example, it is possible to examine how the market is affected if firms can differentiate their products, or if traders in the market are acting with incomplete information. This scenario was in fact explored in *AS Economics, Chapter 7*, describing the effects of asymmetric information on a market.

So, although there may be relatively few markets that display all the characteristics of perfect competition, that does not destroy the usefulness of the model in economic theory. It will continue to be a reference point when examining alternative models of market structure.

Summary

> The model of perfect competition describes an extreme form of market structure. It rests on a sequence of assumptions.

> Its key characteristics include the assumption that no individual trader can influence the market price of the good or service being traded, and that there is freedom of entry and exit.

> In such circumstances each firm faces a perfectly elastic demand curve for its product, and can sell as much as it likes at the going market price.

> A profit-maximising firm chooses to produce the level of output at which marginal revenue (*MR*) equals marginal cost (*MC*).

> The firm's short-run marginal cost curve, above its short-run average variable cost curve, represents its short-run supply curve.

> The industry's short-run supply curve is the horizontal summation of the supply curves of all firms in the market.

> Firms may make supernormal profits in the short run, but because there is freedom of entry these profits will be competed away in the long run by new firms joining the market.

> The long-run industry supply curve is horizontal, with price adjusting to the minimum level of the typical firm's long-run average cost curve.

> Under perfect competition in long-run equilibrium, both productive efficiency and allocative efficiency are achieved.

Monopoly

At the opposite end of the spectrum of market structures is **monopoly**, which strictly speaking is a market with a single seller of a good. However, there is a bit more to it than that, and economic analysis of monopoly rests on some important assumptions. In the real world, the Competition Commission, the official body in the UK with the responsibility of monitoring monopoly markets, is empowered to investigate a merger if it results in the combined firm having more than 25% of a market. In a situation where a single firm dominates a market, it may be able to act as if it were the only firm — a dominant monopoly. Some discussion of the theory of how monopoly markets operate is necessary in order to understand why such monitoring is required. First, consider a pure monopoly market, in which there is a single seller.

Key term

monopoly: a form of market structure in which there is only one seller of a good or service

Assumptions

The assumptions of the monopoly model are as follows:

> There is a single seller of a good.

> There are no substitutes for the good, either actual or potential.

> There are barriers to entry into the market.

It is also assumed that the firm aims to maximise profits. These assumptions all have their counterparts in the assumptions of perfect competition, and in one sense this model can be described as being at the opposite end of the market structure spectrum.

If there is a single seller of a good, and if there are no substitutes for the good, the monopoly firm is thereby insulated from competition. Furthermore, any barriers to entry into the market will ensure that the firm can sustain its market position into the future. The assumption that there are no potential substitutes for the good reinforces the situation. (Chapter 3 explores what happens if this assumption does not hold.)

A monopoly in equilibrium

The first point to note is that a monopoly firm faces the market demand curve directly. Thus, unlike perfect competition, the demand curve slopes downwards. For the monopolist, the demand curve may be regarded as showing average revenue (notice that for a firm charging the same price for all units sold, price is the same as average revenue). Unlike a firm under perfect competition, therefore, the monopolist has some influence over price, and can make decisions regarding price as well as output. This is not to say that the monopolist has complete freedom to set the price, as the firm is still constrained by market demand. However, the firm is a *price maker* and can choose a location along the demand curve.

Chapter 1 recalled the nature of the relationship between the own-price elasticity of demand (*PED*) along a straight-line demand curve and total revenue. The key graphs are reproduced here as Figure 2.8. The analysis pointed out that the price elasticity of demand is elastic above the mid-point of the demand curve and inelastic in the lower half, with total revenue increasing with a price fall when demand is elastic, and falling with a price fall when demand is inelastic.

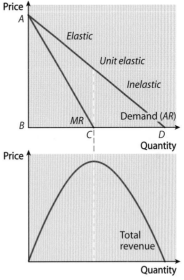

The marginal revenue curve (*MR*) has been added to the figure, and it has a fixed relationship with the average revenue curve (*AR*). Remember that *MR* shares the intercept point on the vertical axis (point *A* in Figure 2.8) and has exactly twice the slope of *AR*. Whenever you have to draw this figure, remember that *MR* and *AR* have this relationship — meeting at *A*, and with the distance BC being the same as the distance *CD*. *MR* is zero (meets the horizontal axis) at the maximum point of the total revenue curve.

Figure 2.8 *Elasticity and total revenue*

As with the firm under perfect competition, a monopolist aiming to maximise profits will choose to produce at the level of output at which marginal revenue equals marginal cost. This is at Q_m in Figure 2.9. Having selected output, the monopolist will then set the price at the highest level at which all output will be sold — in Figure 2.9 this is P_m.

This choice allows the monopolist to make supernormal profits, which can be identified as the shaded area in the figure. As before, this area is average revenue minus average cost, which gives profit per unit, multiplied by the quantity.

It is at this point that barriers to entry become important. Other firms may see that the monopoly firm is making healthy supernormal profits, but the existence of barriers to entry will prevent those profits from being competed away, as would happen in a perfectly competitive market.

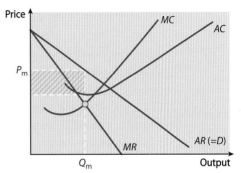

Figure 2.9 *Profit maximisation and monopoly*

It is important to notice that the monopolist cannot be guaranteed always to make such substantial profits as are shown in Figure 2.9. The size of the profits depends upon the relative position of the market demand curve and the cost curves. If the cost curves in the diagram were higher, the monopoly profits would be much smaller, as the distance between average revenue and average costs would be less. It is even possible that the cost curves will be so high as to force the firm to incur losses, in which case it would be expected to shut down.

Exercise 2.3

Table 2.2 shows the demand faced by a monopolist at various prices.

a Calculate total revenue and marginal revenue for each level of demand.

b Plot the demand curve (*AR*) and marginal revenue on a graph.

c Plot total revenue on a separate graph.

d Identify the level of demand at which total revenue is at a maximum.

e At what level of demand is marginal revenue equal to zero?

f At what level of demand is there unit price elasticity of demand?

g If the monopolist maximises profits, will the chosen level of output be higher or lower than the revenue-maximising level?

h What does this imply for the price elasticity of demand when the monopolist maximises profits?

Demand (000s per week)	Price (£)
0	80
1	70
2	60
3	50
4	40
5	30
6	20
7	10

Table 2.2 A monopolist's demand schedule

Exercise 2.4

Draw a diagram to analyse the profit-maximising level of output and price for a monopolist, and analyse the effect of an increase in demand.

How do monopolies arise?

Monopolies may arise in a market for a number of reasons. In a few instances, a monopoly is created by the authorities. For example, for 150 years the UK Post Office held a licence giving it a monopoly on delivering letters. From the beginning of 2006, the service was fully liberalised, although any company wanting to deliver packages weighing less than 350 grams and charging less than £1 can do so only by applying for a licence. The Post Office monopoly formerly covered a much wider range of services, but its coverage was gradually eroded over the years, and competition in delivering larger packages has been permitted for some time. Nonetheless, it remains an example of one way in which a monopoly can be created.

The patent system offers a rather different form of protection for a firm. The patent system was designed to provide an incentive for firms to innovate through the development of new techniques and products. By prohibiting other firms from copying the product for a period of time, a firm is given a temporary monopoly.

In some cases the technology of the industry may create a monopoly situation. In a market characterised by substantial economies of scale, there may not be room for more than one firm in the market. This could happen where there are substantial fixed costs of production but low marginal costs: for example, in establishing an underground railway in a city, a firm faces very high fixed costs in building the network of track and stations and buying the rolling stock. However, once in operation, the marginal cost of carrying an additional passenger is very low.

For 150 years, the Post Office held a licence giving it a monopoly on delivering letters

Figure 2.10 illustrates this point. The firm in this market enjoys economies of scale right up to the limit of market demand. The largest firm operating in the market can always produce at a lower cost than any potential entrant, so will always be able to price such firms out of the market. Here the economies of scale act as an effective barrier to the entry of new firms and the market is a **natural monopoly**. A profit-maximising monopoly would thus set $MR = MC$, produce at quantity Q_m and charge a price P_m.

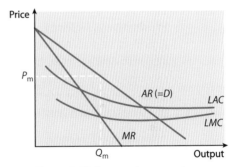

Figure 2.10 *A natural monopoly*

Such a market poses particular problems regarding allocative efficiency. Notice in the figure that marginal cost is below average cost over the entire range of output. If the firm were to charge a price equal to marginal cost it would inevitably make a loss, so such a pricing rule would not be viable.

There are markets in which firms have risen to become monopolies by their actions in the market. Such a market structure is sometimes known as a *competitive monopoly*. Firms may get into a monopoly position through effective marketing, through a process of merger and acquisition, or by establishing a new product as a widely accepted standard.

> **Key term**
>
> **natural monopoly:** monopoly that arises in an industry in which there are such substantial economies of scale that only one firm is viable

In the first Microsoft trial in 1998, it was claimed that Microsoft had gained 95% of the world market for operating systems for PC computers. The firm claimed that this was because it is simply very good at what it does. However, part of the reason why it was on trial was that other interested parties alleged that Microsoft was guilty of unfair market tactics and predatory behaviour.

Exercise 2.5

In 2000, AOL merged with Time Warner, bringing together an internet service provider with an extensive network and a firm in the entertainment business.

One product that such a merged company might produce is a digitised music perform-ance that could be distributed through the internet. Think about the sorts of costs entailed in producing and delivering such a product, and categorise them as fixed or variable costs. What does this imply for the economies of scale faced by the merged company?

Monopoly and efficiency

The characteristics of the monopoly market can be evaluated in relation to productive and allocative efficiency (see Figure 2.9).

Productive efficiency

A firm is said to be productively efficient if it produces at the minimum point of long-run average cost. It is clear from the figure that this is extremely unlikely for a monopoly. The firm will produce at the minimum point of long-run average cost only if it so happens that the marginal *revenue* curve passes through this exact point – and this would happen only by coincidence.

Allocative efficiency

For an individual firm, allocative efficiency is achieved when price is set equal to marginal cost. It is clear from Figure 2.9 that this will not be the case for a profit-maximising monopoly firm. The firm chooses output where *MR* equals *MC*; however, given that *MR* is below *AR* (i.e. price), price will always be set above marginal cost.

Summary

➤ A monopoly market is one in which there is a single seller of a good.

➤ The model of monopoly used in economic analysis also assumes that there are no substitutes for the goods or services produced by the monopolist, and that there are barriers to the entry of new firms.

➤ The monopoly firm faces the market demand curve, and is able to choose a point along that demand curve in order to maximise profits.

➤ Such a firm may be able to make supernormal profits, and sustain them in the long run be-cause of barriers to entry and the lack of substitutes.

➤ A monopoly may arise because of patent protection or from the nature of economies of scale in the industry (a 'natural monopoly').

➤ A profit-maximising monopolist does not achieve allocative efficiency, and is unlikely to achieve productive efficiency in the sense of producing at the minimum point of the long-run average cost curve.

Chapter 3
Monopolistic competition and oligopoly

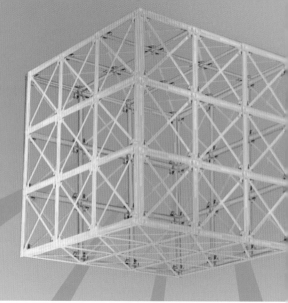

*The previous chapter introduced the models of perfect competition and monopoly, and de-
scribed them as being at the extreme ends of a spectrum of forms of market structure. In between those two extremes are other forms of market structure, which have some but not all
of the characteristics of either perfect competition or monopoly. It is in this sense that there
is a spectrum of structures. Attention in this chapter is focused on some of these intermediate
forms of market structure, including a discussion of the sorts of pricing strategy that firms may
adopt, and how they decide which to go for. This chapter also discusses ways in which firms
may try to prevent new firms from joining a market, in terms of both pricing and non-price
strategies. The theory of contestable markets completes the discussion.*

Learning outcomes

After studying this chapter, you should:
- ▶ be familiar with the range of market situations that exists between the extremes of
  perfect competition and monopoly
- ▶ understand the meaning of product differentiation and its role in the model of monopolistic competition
- ▶ understand the conditions under which price discrimination is possible and how this
  affects consumers and producers
- ▶ understand the notion of oligopoly and be familiar with approaches to modelling firm
  behaviour in an oligopoly market
- ▶ understand the benefits that firms may gain from forming a cartel — and the tensions
  that may result
- ▶ be aware of the possible pricing rules that can be adopted by firms
- ▶ understand the notion of cost-plus pricing, and how this may relate to profit maximisation
- ▶ be familiar with the idea of predatory pricing
- ▶ understand the notion of contestable markets and its implications for firms' behaviour
- ▶ be familiar with other entry deterrence strategies

Monopolistic competition

If you consider the characteristics of the markets that you frequent on a regular basis, you will find that few of them display all of the characteristics associated with perfect competition. However, there may be some that show a few of these features. In particular, you will find some markets in which there appears to be intense competition among many buyers, but in which the products for sale are not identical. For example, think about restaurants. In many cities, you will find a wide range of restaurants, cafés and pubs that compete with each other for business, but do so by offering slightly different products.

Indian restaurants operate in monopolistic conditions

The theory of **monopolistic competition** was devised by Edward Chamberlin, writing in the USA in the 1930s, and his name is often attached to the model, although Joan Robinson published her book on imperfect competition in the UK at the same time. The motivation for the analysis was to explain how markets worked when they were operating neither as monopolies nor under perfect competition.

 term

monopolistic competition: a market that shares some characteristics of monopoly and some of perfect competition

product differentiation: a strategy adopted by firms that marks their product as being different from their competitors'

The model describes a market in which there are many firms producing similar, but not identical, products: for example, package holidays, hairdressers and fast-food outlets. In the case of fast-food outlets, the high streets of many cities are characterised by large numbers of different types of takeaway — burgers, fish and chips, Indian, Chinese, fried chicken and so on.

Model characteristics

Three important characteristics of the model of monopolistic competition distinguish this sort of market from others.

Product differentiation

First, firms produce differentiated products, and face downward-sloping demand curves. In other words, each firm competes with the others by making its product slightly different. This allows the firms to build up brand loyalty among their regular customers, which gives them some influence over price. It is likely that firms will

engage in advertising in order to maintain such brand loyalty, and heavy advertising is a common characteristic of a market operating under monopolistic competition.

Because other firms are producing similar goods, there are substitutes for each firm's product, which means that demand is relatively price elastic (although this does not mean that it is never inelastic). However, it is certainly not perfectly price elastic, as was the case with perfect competition. These features — that the product is not homogeneous and demand is not perfectly price elastic — represent significant differences from the model of perfect competition.

Freedom of entry

Second, there are no barriers to entry into the market. Firms are able to join the market if they observe that existing firms are making supernormal profits. New entrants will be looking for some way to differentiate their product slightly from the others — perhaps the next fast-food restaurant will be Nepalese, or Peruvian.

This characteristic distinguishes the market from the monopoly model, as does the existence of fairly close substitutes.

Low concentration

Third, the concentration ratio in the industry tends to be relatively low, as there are many firms operating in the market. For this reason, a price change by one of the firms will have negligible effects on the demand for its rivals' products.

This characteristic means that the market is also different from an oligopoly market, where there are a few firms that interact strategically with each other.

Overview

Taking these three characteristics together, it can be seen that a market of monopolistic competition has some of the characteristics of perfect competition and some features of monopoly; hence its name.

Short-run equilibrium

Figure 3.1 represents short-run equilibrium under monopolistic competition. D_s is the demand curve and MR_s is the corresponding marginal revenue curve. AC and MC are the average and marginal cost curves for a representative firm in the industry. If the firm is aiming to maximise profits, it will choose the level of output such that $MR_s = MC$. This occurs at output Q_s, and the firm will then choose the price that clears the market at P_s.

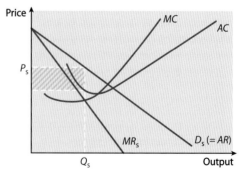

Figure 3.1 *Short-run equilibrium under monopolistic competition*

This closely resembles the standard monopoly diagram that was introduced in Chapter 2. As with monopoly, a firm under monopolistic competition faces a downward-sloping demand curve, as already noted. The difference is that now it is assumed that there is free entry into the market under monopolistic competition, so that Figure 3.1 represents equilibrium only in the short run. This is because the firm shown in the figure is making supernormal profits, shown by the shaded area (which is $AR - AC$ multiplied by output).

The importance of free entry

This is where the assumption of free entry into the market becomes important. In Figure 3.1 the supernormal profits being made by the representative firm will attract new firms into the market. The new firms will produce differentiated products, and this will affect the demand curve for the representative firm's product. In particular, the new firms will attract some customers away from this firm, so that its demand curve will tend to shift to the left. Its shape may also change as there are now more substitutes for the original product.

Long-run equilibrium

This process will continue as long as firms in the market continue to make profits that attract new firms into the activity. It may be accelerated if firms are persuaded to spend money on advertising in an attempt to defend their market shares. The advertising may help to keep the demand curve downward sloping, but it will also affect the position of the average cost curve, by pushing up average cost at all levels of output.

Figure 3.2 shows the final position for the market. The typical firm is now operating in such a way that it maximises profits (by setting output such that $MR = MC$); at the same time, the average cost curve (AC) at this level of output is at a tangent to the demand curve. This means that $AC = AR$, and the firm is just making normal profit (i.e. is just covering opportunity cost). There is thus no further incentive for more firms to join the market. In Figure 3.2 this occurs when output is at Q_1 and price is set at P_1.

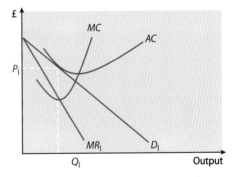

Figure 3.2 *Long-run equilibrium under monopolistic competition*

Efficiency

One way of evaluating the market outcome under this model is to examine the consequences for productive and allocative efficiency. It is clear from Figure 3.2 that neither of these conditions will be met. The representative firm does not reach the minimum point on the long-run average cost curve, and so does not attain productive efficiency; furthermore, the price charged is above marginal cost, so allocative efficiency is not achieved.

Evaluation

If the typical firm in the market is not fully exploiting the possible economies of scale that exist, it could be argued that product differentiation is damaging society's

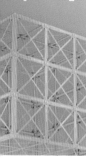

total welfare, in the sense that product differentiation allows firms to keep their demand curves downward sloping. In other words, too many different products are being produced. However, this argument could be countered by pointing out that consumers may enjoy having more freedom of choice. The very fact that they are prepared to pay a premium price for their chosen brand indicates that they have some preference for it. For example, some people may be prepared to pay £50 to watch Chelsea although they could watch 90 minutes of football at Wimbledon AFC for £10.

Another crucial difference between monopolistic competition and perfect competition is that under monopolistic competition firms would like to sell more of their product at the going price, whereas under perfect competition they can sell as much as they like at the going price. This is because price under monopolistic competition is set above marginal cost. The use of advertising to attract more customers and to maintain consumer perception of product differences may be considered a problem with this market. It could be argued that excessive use of advertising to maintain product differentiation is wasteful, as it leads to higher average cost curves than needed. On the other hand, the need to compete in this way may result in less X-inefficiency than under a complacent monopolist.

Exercise 3.1

Figure 3.3 shows a firm under monopolistic competition.

a Identify the profit-maximising level of output.

b At what price would the firm sell its product?

c What supernormal profits (if any) would be made by the firm?

d Is this a short-run or a long-run equilibrium? Explain your answer.

e Describe the subsequent adjustment that might take place in the market (if any).

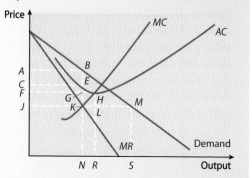

Figure 3.3 A firm under monopolistic competition

f At what level of output would productive efficiency be achieved? (Assume that *AC* represents long-run average cost for this part of the question.)

Summary

➤ The theory of monopolistic competition has its origins in the 1930s, when economists such as Edward Chamberlin and Joan Robinson were writing about markets that did not conform to the models of perfect competition and monopoly.

- The model describes a market where there are many firms producing similar, but not identical, products.

- By differentiating their product from those of other firms, it is possible for firms to maintain some influence over price.

- To do this, firms engage in advertising to build brand loyalty.

- There are no barriers to entry into the market, and concentration ratios are low.

- Firms may be able to make supernormal profits in the short run.

- In response, new entrants join the market, shifting the demand curves of existing firms and affecting their shape.

- The process continues until supernormal profits have been competed away, and the typical firm has its average cost curve at a tangent to its demand curve.

- Neither productive nor allocative efficiency is achieved in long-run equilibrium.

- Consumers may benefit from the increased range of choice on offer in the market.

Price discrimination

One thing that monopoly and monopolistic competition have in common is that by setting price above marginal cost, there is some allocative efficiency, with output lower than would be implied by the $P = MC$ outcome. This section examines a special case of monopoly, in which a monopolist will produce the level of output that is allocatively efficient.

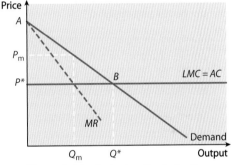

Figure 3.4 *Perfect price discrimination*

Consider Figure 3.4. Suppose this market is operated by a monopolist that faces constant marginal cost *LMC*. (This is to simplify the analysis.) Chapter 4 shows that under perfect competition the market outcome would be a price P^* and quantity Q^*. (See Figure 4.1 for an explanation of this.) What would induce the monopolist to produce at Q^*?

One of the assumptions made throughout the analysis so far is that all consumers in a market get to pay the same price for the product. This leads to the notion of consumer surplus, which was introduced in *AS Economics, Chapter 5*. In Figure 3.4, if the market were operating under perfect competition and all consumers were paying the same price, consumer surplus would be given by the area AP^*B. If the market were operated by a monopolist, also charging the same price to all buyers, then profits would be maximised where $MC = MR$: that is, at quantity Q_m and price P_m.

But suppose this assumption is now relaxed; suppose that the monopolist is able to charge a different price to each individual consumer. A monopolist is then able to charge each consumer a price that is equal to his or her willingness to pay for the

good. In other words, the demand curve effectively becomes the marginal revenue curve, as it represents the amount that the monopolist will receive for each unit of the good. It will then maximise profits at point *B* in Figure 3.4, where *MR* (i.e. *AR*) is equal to *LMC*. The difference between this situation and that under perfect competition is that the area *AP*B* is no longer consumer surplus, but producer surplus: that is, the monopolist's profits. The monopolist has hijacked the whole of the original consumer surplus as its profits.

From society's point of view, total welfare is the same as it is under perfect competition (but more than under monopoly without discrimination). However, now there has been a redistribution, from consumers to the monopoly — and presumably to the shareholders of the firm. This situation is known as **perfect price discrimination** or **first-degree price discrimination**.

> **term**
>
> **perfect/first-degree price discrimination:** situation arising in a market whereby a monopoly firm is able to charge each consumer a different price

Perfect price discrimination is fairly rare in the real world, although it might be said to exist in the world of art or fashion, where customers may commission a painting, sculpture or item of designer jewellery and the price is a matter of negotiation between the buyer and supplier.

However, there are situations in which partial price discrimination is possible. For example, students or old-age pensioners may get discounted bus fares, the young and/or old may get cheaper access to sporting events or theatres etc. In these instances, individual consumers are paying different prices for what is in fact the same product.

There are three conditions under which a firm may be able to price discriminate:
➤ The firm must have market power.
➤ The firm must have information about consumers and their willingness to pay — and there must be identifiable differences between consumers (or groups of consumers).
➤ The consumers must have limited ability to resell the product.

Market power

Clearly, price discrimination is not possible in a perfectly competitive market, where no seller has the power to charge other than the going market price. So price discrimination can take place only where firms have some ability to vary the price.

Information

From the firm's point of view, it needs to be able to identify different groups of consumers with different willingness to pay. What makes price discrimination profitable for firms is that different consumers display different sensitivities to price: that is, they have different price elasticities of demand.

Ability to resell

If consumers could resell the product easily, then price discrimination would not be possible, as consumers would engage in **arbitrage**. In other words, the group of consumers who qualified for the low price could buy up the product and then turn a profit by reselling to consumers in the other segment(s) of the market. This would mean that the firm would no longer be able to sell at the high price, and would no longer try to discriminate in pricing.

> **Key term**
>
> **arbitrage:** a process by which prices in two market segments will be equalised by a process of purchase and resale by market participants

In the case of student discounts and old-age concessions, the firm can identify particular groups of consumers; and such 'products' as bus journeys or dental treatment cannot be resold. But why should a firm undertake this practice?

The simple answer is that, by undertaking price discrimination, the firm is able to increase its profits by switching sales from a market with relatively low marginal revenue to a market where it is higher.

An extreme form of price discrimination was used by NAPP Pharmaceutical Holdings, as a result of which the firm was fined £3.2 million by the Office of Fair Trading. NAPP sold sustained-release morphine tablets and capsules in the UK. These are drugs administered to patients with incurable cancer. NAPP realised that the market was segmented. The drugs were sold partly to the National Health Service for use in hospitals, but were also prescribed by GPs. As these patients were terminally ill, they tended to spend a relatively short time in hospital before being sent home. NAPP realised that GPs tended to prescribe the same drugs as the patients had received in hospital. It therefore reduced its price to hospitals by 90%, thereby forcing all competitors out of the market and gaining a monopoly in that market segment. It was then able to increase the price of these drugs prescribed through GPs, and so maximise profits. The OFT investigated the firm, fined it and instructed it to stop its actions, thus saving the NHS £2 million per year.

Exercise 3.2

In which of the following products might price discrimination be possible? Explain your answers.

a hairdressing

b peak and off-peak rail travel

c apples

d air tickets

e newspapers

f plastic surgery

g beer

Summary

➤ In some markets a monopolist may be able to engage in price discrimination by selling its product at different prices to different consumers or groups of consumers.

➤ This enables the firm to increase its profits by absorbing some or all of the consumer surplus.

➤ Under first-degree price discrimination, the firm is able to charge a different price to each customer and absorb all consumer surplus.

➤ The firm can practise price discrimination only where it has market power, where consumers have differing elasticities of demand for the product, and where consumers have limited ability to resell the product.

Oligopoly

A number of markets seem to be dominated by relatively few firms — think of commercial banking in the UK, cinemas or the newspaper industry. A market with just a few sellers is known as an **oligopoly** market. An important characteristic of such markets is that when making economic decisions each firm must take account of its rivals' behaviour and reactions. The firms are therefore interdependent.

 Key *term*

oligopoly: a market with a few sellers, in which each firm must take account of the behaviour and likely behaviour of rival firms in the industry

An important characteristic of oligopoly is that each firm has to act strategically, both in reacting to rival firms' decisions and in trying to anticipate their future actions and reactions.

There are many different ways in which a firm may take such strategic decisions, and this means that there are many ways in which an oligopoly market can be

High-street banking is an oligopoly market

PUBLISHING PICTURES

modelled, depending on how the firms are behaving. This chapter reviews just a few such models.

Oligopolies may come about for many reasons, but perhaps the most convincing concerns economies of scale. An oligopoly is likely to develop in a market where there are some economies of scale — economies that are not substantial enough to require a natural monopoly, but which are large enough to make it difficult for too many firms to operate at minimum efficient scale.

Within an oligopoly market, firms may adopt rivalrous behaviour or they may choose to cooperate with each other. The two attitudes have implications for how markets operate. Cooperation will tend to take the market towards the monopoly end of the spectrum, whereas non-cooperation will take it towards the competitive end. In either scenario, it is likely that the market outcome will be somewhere between the two extremes.

The kinked demand curve model

One model of oligopoly revolves around how a firm perceives its demand curve. This is called the kinked demand curve model, and was developed by Paul Sweezy in the USA in the 1930s.

The model relates to an oligopoly in which firms try to anticipate the reactions of rivals to their actions. One problem that arises is that a firm cannot readily observe its demand curve with any degree of certainty, so it must form expectations about how consumers will react to a price change.

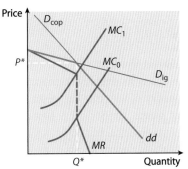

Figure 3.5 The kinked demand curve

Figure 3.5 shows how this works. Suppose the price is currently set at P^*; the firm is selling Q^* and is trying to decide whether to alter price. The problem is that it knows for sure about only one point on the demand curve: that is, when price is P^*, the firm sells Q^*.

However, the firm is aware that the degree of sensitivity to its price change will depend upon whether or not the other firms in the market will follow its lead. In other words, if its rivals ignore the firm's price change, there will be more sensitivity to this change than if they all follow suit.

Figure 3.5 shows the two extreme possibilities for the demand curve which the firm perceives that it faces. If other firms *ignore* its action, D_{ig} will be the relevant demand curve, which is relatively elastic. On the other hand, if the other firms *copy* the firm's moves, D_{cop} will be the relevant demand curve.

The question then is: under what conditions will the other firms copy the price change, and when will they not? The firm may imagine that if it raises price, there is little likelihood that its rivals will copy. After all, this is a non-threatening move that gives market share to the other firms. So for a price *increase*, D_{ig} is the relevant section.

On the other hand, a price reduction is likely to be seen by the rivals as a threatening move, and they are likely to copy in order to preserve their market positions. For a price *decrease*, then, D_{cop} is relevant.

Putting these together, the firm perceives that it faces a kinked demand curve (*dd*). Furthermore, if the marginal revenue curve is added to the picture, it is seen to have a discontinuity at the kink. It thus transpires that Q^* is the profit-maximising level of output under a wide range of cost conditions from MC_0 to MC_1; so, even in the face of a change in marginal costs, the firm will not alter its behaviour.

Thus, the model predicts that if the firm perceives its demand curve to be of this shape, it has a strong incentive to do nothing, even in the face of changes in costs. However, it all depends upon the firm's perceptions. If there is a general increase in costs that affects all producers, this may affect the firm's perception of rival reaction, and thus encourage it to raise price. If other firms are reading the market in the same way, they are likely to follow suit. Notice that this model does not explain how the price reaches P^* in the first place.

Game theory

A more recent development in the economic theory of the firm has been in the application of **game theory**. This began as a branch of mathematics, but it became apparent that it had wide applications in explaining the behaviour of firms in an oligopoly.

> **Key term**
>
> **game theory:** a method of modelling the strategic interaction between firms in an oligopoly

Game theory itself has a long history, with some writers tracing it back to correspondence between Pascal and Fermat in the mid-seventeenth century. Early applications in economics were by Antoine Augustin Cournot in 1838, Francis Edgeworth in 1881 and J. Bertrand in 1883, but the key publication was the book by John von Neumann and Oskar Morgenstern, *Theory of Games and Economic Behaviour*, in 1944. Other famous names in game theory include John Nash (played by Russell Crowe in the film *A Beautiful Mind*), John Harsanyi and Reinhard Selton, who shared the 1994 Nobel prize for their work in this area.

Almost certainly, the most famous game is the **prisoners' dilemma**, introduced in a lecture by Albert Tucker (who taught John Nash at Princeton) in 1950. This simple example of

Russell Crowe playing the part of mathematician and game theorist John Nash in A Beautiful Mind

game theory turns out to have a multitude of helpful applications in economics.

Two prisoners, Al Fresco and Des Jardins, are being interrogated about a major crime, and the police know that at least one of the prisoners is guilty. The two are kept in separate cells and cannot communicate with each other. The police have enough evidence to convict them of a minor offence, but not enough to convict them of the major one.

Key term

prisoners' dilemma: an example of game theory with a range of applications in oligopoly theory

Each prisoner is offered a deal. If he turns state's evidence and provides evidence to convict the other prisoner, he will get off – *unless* the other prisoner also confesses. If both refuse to deal, they will just be charged with the minor offence. Table 3.1 summarises the sentences that each will receive in the various circumstances.

		Des		Des	
		Confess		**Refuse**	
Al	**Confess**	10	10	0	15
	Refuse	15	0	5	5

Table 3.1
The prisoners' dilemma: possible outcomes (years in jail)

In each case, Al's sentence (in years) is shown in orange and Des's in blue. In terms of the entries in the table, if both Al and Des refuse to deal, they will be convicted of the minor offence, and each will go down for 5 years. However, if Al confesses and Des refuses to deal, Al will get off completely free, and Des will take the full rap of 15 years. If Des confesses and Al refuses, the reverse happens. However, if both confess, they will each get 10 years.

Think about this situation from Al's point of view, remembering that the prisoners cannot communicate, so Al does not know what Des will choose to do and vice versa. You can see from Table 3.1 that, whatever Des chooses to do, Al will be better off confessing. If Des confesses, Al is better off confessing also, going down for 10 years instead of 15; if Des refuses, Al is still better off confessing, going free instead of getting a 5-year term. John Nash referred to such a situation as a **dominant strategy**.

Key term

dominant strategy: a situation in game theory where a player's best strategy is independent of those chosen by others

The dilemma is, of course, symmetric, so for Des too the dominant strategy is to confess. The inevitable result is that, if both prisoners are selfish, they will both confess – and both will then get 10 years in jail. If they had both refused to deal, they would *both* have been better off; but this is too risky a strategy for either of them to adopt. A refusal to deal might have led to 15 years in jail.

What has this to do with economics? Think about the market for DIY products. Suppose there are two firms (Diamond Tools and Better Spades) operating in a duopoly market (i.e. a market with only two firms). Each firm has a choice of producing 'high' output or 'low' output. The profit made by one firm depends upon two things: its own output and the output of the other firm.

Table 3.2 shows the range of possible outcomes for a particular time period. Consider Diamond Tools: if it chooses 'low' when Better Spades also chooses 'low', it will make £2 million profit (and so will Better Spades); but if Diamond Tools chooses 'low' when Better Spades chooses 'high', Diamond Tools will make zero profits and Better Spades will make £3 million.

		Better Spades			
		High		Low	
Diamond	High	1	1	3	0
Tools	Low	0	3	2	2

Table 3.2 *Diamond Tools and Better Spades: possible outcomes (profits in £m)*

The situation that maximises joint profits is for both firms to produce low; but suppose you were taking decisions for Diamond Tools — what would you choose?

If Better Spades produces 'low', you will maximise profits by producing 'high', whereas if Better Spades produces 'high', you will still maximise profits by producing high! So Diamond Tools has a dominant strategy to produce high — it is the profit-maximising action whatever Better Spades does, even though it means that joint profits will be lower.

Given that the table is symmetric, Better Spades faces the same decision process, and also has a dominant strategy to choose high, so they always end up in the northwest corner of the table, even though southeast would be better for each of them. Furthermore, after they have made their choices and seen what the other has chosen, each firm feels justified by its actions, and thinks that it took the right decision, given the rival's move. This is known as a **Nash equilibrium**, which has the characteristic that neither firm needs to amend its behaviour in any future period. This model can be used to investigate a wide range of decisions that firms need to take strategically.

Key term

Nash equilibrium: situation occurring within a game when each player's chosen strategy maximises payoffs given the other player's choice, so no player has an incentive to alter behaviour

Exercise 3.3

Suppose there are two cinemas, X and Y, operating in a town; you are taking decisions for Firm X. You cannot communicate with the other firm; both firms are considering only the next period. Each firm is choosing whether to set price 'high' or 'low'. Your expectation is that the payoffs (in terms of profits) to the two firms are as shown in Table 3.3 (Firm X in brown, Firm Y in blue):

		Firm Y chooses:			
		High price		Low price	
Firm X	High price	0	10	1	15
chooses:	Low price	15	1	4	4

Table 3.3 *Cinemas X and Y: possible outcomes*

a   If Firm Y sets price high, what strategy maximises profits for Firm X?

b If Firm Y sets price low, what strategy maximises profits for Firm X?

c So what strategy will Firm X adopt?

d What is the market outcome?

e What outcome would maximise the firms' joint profit?

f How might this outcome be achieved?

g Would the outcome be different if the game were played over repeated periods?

Cooperative games and cartels

Look back at the prisoners' dilemma game in Table 3.2. It is clear that the requirement that the firms are unable to communicate with each other is a serious impediment from the firms' point of view. If both firms could agree to produce 'low', they would maximise their joint profits, but they will not risk this strategy if they cannot communicate.

If they could join together in a **cartel**, the two firms could come to an agreement to adopt the low–low strategy. However, if they were to agree to this, each firm would have a strong incentive to cheat because, if each now knew that the other firm was going to produce low, they would also know that they could produce high and dominate the market — at least, given the payoffs in the table.

 term

cartel: an agreement between firms on price and output with the intention of maximising their joint profits

This is a common feature of cartels. Collusion can bring high joint profits, but there is always the temptation for each of the member-firms to cheat and try to sneak some additional market share at the expense of the other firms in the cartel.

There is another downside to the formation of a cartel. In most countries around the world (with one or two exceptions, such as Hong Kong) they are illegal. For example, in the UK the operation of a cartel is illegal under the UK Competition Act, under which the Office of Fair Trading is empowered to fine firms up to 10% of their turnover for each year the cartel is found to have been in operation.

This means that overt collusion is rare. The most famous example is not between firms but between nations, in the form of the Organisation of Petroleum Exporting Countries (OPEC), which over a long period of time has operated a cartel to control the price of oil.

Some conditions may favour the formation of cartels — or at least, some form of collusion between firms. The most important of these is the ability of each of the firms involved to monitor the actions of the other firms, and so ensure that they are keeping to the agreement.

Collusion in practice

Although cartels are illegal, the potential gains from collusion may tempt firms to find ways of working together. In some cases, firms have joined together in rather loose strategic alliances, in which they may work together on part of their business, perhaps in undertaking joint research and development or technology swaps.

For example, in 2000 General Motors (GM) and Fiat took an equity stake in each other's companies, with GM wanting to expand in Europe and needing to find out more about the technology of making smaller cars. Such alliances have not always been a success, and in the GM–Fiat case GM and Fiat separated in 2005.

The airline market is another sector where strategic alliances have been important, with the Star Alliance, the One World Alliance and SkyTeam carving up the long-haul routes between them. Such alliances offer benefits to passengers, who can get access to a wider range of destinations and business-class lounges and frequent-flier rewards, and to the airlines, which can economise on airport facilities by pooling their resources. However, the net effect is to reduce competition, and the regulators have interfered with some suggested alliances, such as that between British Airways and American Airlines in 2001, which was investigated by regulators on both sides of the Atlantic. The conditions under which the alliance would have been permitted were such that British Airways withdrew the proposal. This proposed alliance resurfaced in August 2008, when the European Commission opened a new anti-trust investigation into a revenue-sharing deal announced between British Airways, American Airlines and Iberia.

Alternatively, firms may look for **tacit collusion**, in which the firms in a market observe each other's behaviour very closely and refrain from competing on price, even if they do not actually communicate with each other. Such collusion may emerge gradually over time in a market, as the firms become accustomed to market conditions and to each other's behaviour.

Key *term*

tacit collusion: situation occurring when firms refrain from competing on price, but without communication or formal agreement between them

One way in which this may happen is through some form of *price leadership.* If one firm is a dominant producer in a market, then it may take the lead in setting the price, with the other firms following its example. It has been suggested that the OPEC cartel operated according to this model in some periods, with Saudi Arabia acting as the dominant country.

The Star Alliance reduces competition

STAR ALLIANCE

An alternative is *barometric price leadership*, in which one firm tries out a price increase and then waits to see whether other firms follow. If they do, a new higher price has been reached without the need for overt discussions between the firms. On the other hand, if the other firms do not feel the time is right for the change, they will keep their prices steady and the first firm will drop back into line or else lose market share. The initiating firm need not be the same one in each round. It has been argued that the domestic air travel market in the USA has operated in this way on some internal routes. The practice is facilitated by the ease with which prices can be checked via computerised ticketing systems, so that each firm knows what the other firms are doing.

The frequency of anti-cartel cases brought by regulators in recent years suggests that firms continue to be tempted by the gains from collusion. The operation of a cartel is now a criminal act in the UK, as it has been in the USA for some time.

Exercise 3.4

For each of the following markets, identify the model that would most closely describe it (e.g. perfect competition, monopoly, monopolistic competition or oligopoly):

a   a large number of firms selling branded varieties of toothpaste

b   a sole supplier of postal services

c   a large number of farmers producing cauliflowers, sold at a common price

d   a situation in which a few large banks supply most of the market for retail banking services

e   a sole supplier of rail transport

Summary

➤ An oligopoly is a market with a few sellers, each of which takes strategic decisions based on likely rival actions and reactions.

➤ As there are many ways in which firms may interact, there is no single way of modelling an oligopoly market.

➤ One model is the kinked demand curve model, which argues that firms' perceptions of the demand curve for their products is based on their views about whether or not rival firms will react to their own actions.

➤ This suggests that price is likely to remain stable over a wide range of market conditions.

➤ Game theory is a more recent and more flexible way of modelling interactions between firms.

➤ The prisoners' dilemma can demonstrate the potential benefits of collusion, but also shows that in some market situations each firm may have a dominant strategy to move the market away from the joint profit-maximising position.

➤ If firms could join together in a cartel, they could indeed maximise their joint profits — but there would still be a temptation for firms to cheat, and try to steal market share. Such action would break up the cartel, and move the market away from the joint profit-maximising position.

> However, cartels are illegal in most societies.

> Firms may thus look for covert ways of colluding in a market: for example, through some form of price leadership.

Pricing strategies and contestable markets

Pricing rules

In the analysis of market structure, it was assumed that firms set out to maximise profits. However, Chapter 1 pointed out that sometimes they may set out to achieve other objectives. The price of a firm's product is a key strategic variable that must be manipulated in order to attain whatever objective the firm wishes to achieve.

Figure 3.6 illustrates the variety of pricing rules that are possible. The figure shows a firm operating under a form of market structure that is not perfect competition — because the firm faces a downward-sloping demand curve for its product shown by $AR (= D)$.

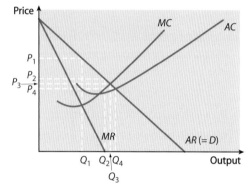

Figure 3.6 Possible pricing rules

Profit maximisation

If the firm chooses to maximise profits, it will choose output such that marginal revenue is equal to marginal cost, and will then set the price to clear the market. In terms of the figure, it will set output at Q_1 and price at P_1.

Revenue maximisation

As mentioned in Chapter 1, the economist William Baumol argued that, if there is a divorce of ownership from control in the organisation of a firm, whereby the shareholders have delegated day-to-day decision making to managers (a principal–agent situation), the managers may find themselves with some freedom to pursue other objectives, such as revenue maximisation. A revenue maximiser in Figure 3.6 would choose to produce at the output level at which marginal revenue is zero. This occurs at Q_2 in the figure, with the price set at P_2.

Sales maximisation

If instead managers set out to maximise the volume of sales subject to covering opportunity cost, they will choose to set output at a level such that price equals average cost, which will clear the market. In Figure 3.6 this happens at Q_4 (with price at P_4).

Allocative efficiency

It has been argued that allocative efficiency in an individual market occurs at the point where price is equal to marginal cost. In Figure 3.6 this is at Q_3 (with price P_3). However, from the firm's perspective there is no obvious reason why this should become an objective of the firm, as it confers no particular advantage.

Exercise 3.5

For each of the following situations, identify the pricing rule most appropriate to achieve the firm's objectives, and comment on the implications that this has for efficiency.

a A firm producing DVD recorders tries to achieve as high a market share as possible, measured in value terms.

b A local gymnasium tries to make as high a surplus over costs as can be achieved.

c A national newspaper sets out to maximise circulation (subject to covering its costs), knowing that this will affect advertising revenues.

d A garden centre producing Christmas trees finds that it cannot influence the price of its product.

Predatory pricing

Perhaps the most common context in which price wars have broken out is where an existing firm or firms have reacted to defend the market against the entry of new firms.

One example occurred in 1996, in the early years of easyJet, the low-cost air carrier, which was then trying to become established. When easyJet started flying the London–Amsterdam route, charging its now well-known low prices, the incumbent firm (KLM) reacted very aggressively, driving its price down to a level just below that of easyJet. The response from easyJet was to launch legal action against KLM, claiming it was using unfair market tactics.

So-called **predatory pricing** is illegal under English, Dutch and EU law. It should be noted that, in order to declare an action illegal, it is necessary to define that action very carefully — otherwise it will not be possible to prove the case in the courts. In the case of predatory pricing, the legal definition is based on economic analysis.

 term

predatory pricing: an anti-competitive strategy in which a firm sets price below average variable cost in an attempt to force a rival or rivals out of the market and achieve market dominance

Remember that if a firm fails to cover average variable costs, its strategy should be to close down immediately, as it would be better off doing so. The courts have backed this theory, and state that a pricing strategy should be interpreted as being predatory if the price is set below average variable costs, as the only motive for remaining in business while making such losses must be to drive competitors out of business and achieve market dominance. This is known as the *Areeda–Turner principle* (after the case in which it was first argued in the USA).

On the face of it, consumers have much to gain from such strategies through the resulting lower prices. However, a predator that is successful in driving out the opposition is likely to recoup its losses by putting prices back up to profit-maximising levels thereafter, so the benefit to consumers is short lived.

Having said that, the low-cost airlines survived the attempts of the established airlines to hold on to their market shares. Indeed, in the post-9/11 period, which was a tough one for the airlines for obvious reasons, the low-cost airlines flourished while the more conventional established airlines went through a very difficult period indeed.

In some cases, the very threat of predatory pricing may be sufficient to deter entry by new firms, if the threat is a credible one. In other words, the existing firms need to convince potential entrants that they, the existing firms, will find it in their best interests to fight a price war, otherwise the entrants will not believe the threat. The existing firms could do this by making it known that they have surplus capacity, so that they would be able to increase output very quickly in order to drive down the price.

Whether entry will be deterred by such means may depend in part on the characteristics of the potential entrant. After all, a new firm may reckon that, if the existing firm finds it worth sacrificing profits in the short run, the rewards of dominating the market must be worth fighting for. It may therefore decide to sacrifice short-term profit in order to enter the market — especially if it is diversifying from other markets and has resources at its disposal. The winner will then be the firm that can last the longest; but, clearly, this is potentially very damaging for all concerned.

Exercise 3.6

Discuss the extent to which consumers benefit from a price war.

Limit pricing

An associated but less extreme strategy is limit pricing. This assumes that the incumbent firm has some sort of cost advantage over potential entrants: for example, economies of scale.

Figure 3.7 shows a firm facing a downward-sloping demand curve, and thus having some influence over the price of its product. If the firm is maximising profits, it is setting output at Q_0 and price at P_0. As average revenue is comfortably above average cost at this price, the firm is making healthy supernormal profits.

Suppose that the natural barriers to entry in this industry are weak. The supernormal profits will be attractive to potential entrants. Given the cost conditions, the incumbent firm is enjoying the benefit of economies of scale, although producing below the minimum efficient scale.

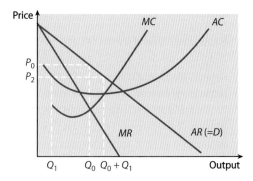

Figure 3.7 Limit pricing

If a new firm joins the market, producing on a relatively small scale, say at Q_1, the impact on the market can be analysed as follows. The immediate effect is on price, as now the amount $Q_0 + Q_1$ is being produced, pushing price down to P_2. The new firm

(producing Q_1) is just covering average cost, so is making normal profits and feeling justified in having joined the market. The original firm is still making supernormal profits, but at a lower level than before. The entry of the new firm has competed away part of the original firm's supernormal profits.

One way in which the firm could have guarded against entry is by charging a lower price than P_0 to begin with. For example, if it had set output at $Q_0 + Q_1$ and price at P_2, then a new entrant joining the market would have pushed the price down to a level below P_2, and without the benefit of economies of scale would have made losses and exited the market. In any case, if the existing firm has been in the market for some time it will have gone through a process of learning by doing, and therefore will have a lower average cost curve than the potential entrant. This makes it more likely that limit pricing can be used.

Thus, by setting a price below the profit-maximising level, the original firm is able to maintain its market position in the longer run. This could be a reason for avoiding making too high a level of supernormal profits in the short run, in order to make profits in the longer term.

Notice that such a strategy need not be carried out by a monopolist, but could also occur in an oligopoly, where existing firms may jointly seek to protect their market against potential entry.

Contestable markets

It has been argued that in some markets, in order to prevent the entry of new firms, the existing firm would have to charge such a low price that it would be unable to reap any supernormal profits at all.

This theory was developed by William Baumol and is known as the theory of **contestable markets**. It was in recognition of this theory that the monopoly model in Chapter 2 included the assumption that there must be no substitutes for the good, *either actual or potential*.

Key term

contestable market: a market in which the existing firm makes only normal profit, as it cannot set a price higher than average cost without attracting entry, owing to the absence of barriers to entry and sunk costs

For a market to be contestable, it must have no barriers to entry or exit and no sunk costs. *Sunk costs* refer to costs that a firm incurs in setting up a business and which cannot be recovered if the firm exits the market. Furthermore, new firms in the market must have no competitive disadvantage compared with the incumbent firm(s): in other words, they must have access to the same technology, and there must be no significant learning-by-doing effects. Entry and exit must be rapid.

Under these conditions, the incumbent firm cannot set a price that is higher than average cost because, as soon as it does, it will open up the possibility of *hit-and-run entry* by new firms, which can enter the market and compete away the supernormal profits.

Consider Figure 3.8, which shows a monopoly firm in a market. The argument is that, if the monopolist charges the profit-maximising price, then in a contestable market the firm will be vulnerable to hit-and-run entry – a firm could come into the market, take some of the supernormal profits, then exit again. The only way the monopolist can avoid this happening is to set price equal to average cost, so that there are no supernormal profits to act as an incentive for entry.

On the face of it, the conditions for contestability sound pretty stringent. In particular, the firm in Figure 3.8 enjoys some economies of scale, so you would think that some sunk costs had been incurred.

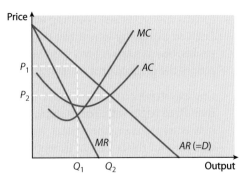

Figure 3.8 Contestability

However, suppose a firm has a monopoly on a domestic air route between two destinations. An airline with surplus capacity (i.e. a spare aircraft sitting in a hangar) could enter this route and exit again without incurring sunk costs in response to profits being made by the incumbent firm. This is an example of how contestability may limit the ability of the incumbent firm to use its market power.

Notice in this example that, although the firm only makes normal profits, neither productive nor allocative efficiency is achieved.

A moot point is whether the threat of entry will in fact persuade firms that they cannot set a price above average cost. Perhaps the firms can risk making some profit above normal profits and then respond to entry very aggressively if and when it happens. After all, it is difficult to think of an example in which there are absolutely no sunk costs. Almost any business is going to have to advertise in order to find customers, and such advertising expenditure cannot be recovered. Pricing is not the only strategy that firms adopt in order to deter entry by new firms. Barriers to entry are discussed in Chapter 4.

Summary

➤ There are many pricing rules that a firm may choose to adopt, depending on the objectives it wishes to achieve.

➤ Although price wars are expected to be damaging for the firms involved, they do break out from time to time.

➤ This may occur when firms wish to increase their market shares, or when existing firms wish to deter the entry of new firms into the market.

➤ Predatory pricing is an extreme strategy that forces all firms to endure losses. It is normally invoked in an attempt to eliminate a competitor, and is illegal in many countries.

➤ Limit pricing occurs when a firm or firms choose to set price below the profit-maximising level in order to prevent entry. The limit price is the highest price that an existing firm can set without allowing entry.

➤ In contestable markets, the incumbent firm or firms may be able to make only normal profit.

➤ Contestability requires that there are no barriers to entry or exit and no sunk costs — and that the incumbent firm(s) have no cost advantage over hit-and-run entrants.

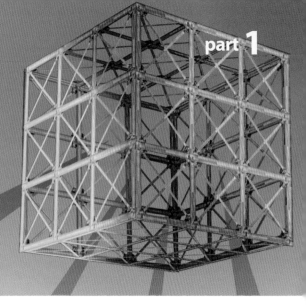

part **1**

Chapter 4
Markets and resource allocation

The previous two chapters have explored different forms of market structure that arise in the real-world economy. The significance of these forms of market structure is that they have different implications for the way in which resources come to be allocated within society. This chapter introduces some key issues that are relevant for both leisure and transport sectors.

Learning outcomes

After studying this chapter, you should:
➤ be aware of the relative merits of perfect competition and monopoly in terms of market performance
➤ understand the significance of concentration in a market and how to measure it
➤ be aware of the relationship between firm size and concentration
➤ understand what is meant by market dominance
➤ be familiar with factors that may give rise to natural and strategic barriers to entry
➤ be aware of some of the effects on a market if competition is limited

Perfect competition and monopoly compared

Chapter 2 set out the models of perfect competition and monopoly. Each has different implications for resource allocation. A monopoly by its behaviour distorts resource allocation, and by comparing a monopoly market with a perfectly competitive market, it is possible to identify the extent of the distortion. To do this, the situation can be simplified by setting aside the possibility of economies of scale. This is perhaps an artificial assumption to make, but it could be relaxed.

Suppose that there is an industry with no economies of scale, which can be operated either as a perfectly competitive market with many small firms, or as a monopoly firm running a large number of small plants.

Figure 4.1 shows the market demand curve ($D = AR$), and the long-run supply curve under perfect competition (*LRS*). If the market is operating under perfect competition, the long-run equilibrium will produce a price of P_{pc}, and the firms in the industry will together supply Q_{pc} output. Consumer surplus is given by the area $AP_{pc}E$, which represents the surplus that consumers gain from consuming this product. In other words, it is a measure of the welfare that society receives from consuming the good, as was explained in *AS Economics, Chapter 3*.

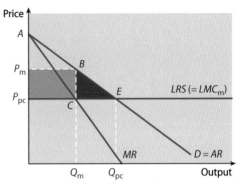

Figure 4.1 *Comparing perfect competition and monopoly*

Now suppose that the industry is taken over by a profit-maximising monopolist. The firm can close down some of the plants to vary its output over the long run, and the *LRS* can be regarded as the monopolist's long-run marginal cost curve. As the monopoly firm faces the market demand curve directly, it will also face the *MR* curve shown, so will maximise profits at quantity Q_m and charge a price P_m.

Thus, the effect of this change in market structure is that the profit-maximising monopolist produces less output than a perfectly competitive industry and charges a higher price.

It is also apparent that consumer surplus is now very different, as in the new situation it is limited to the area AP_mB. Looking more carefully at Figure 4.1, you can see that the loss of consumer surplus has occurred for two reasons. First, the monopoly firm is now making profits shown by the shaded area P_mBCP_{pc}. This is a redistribution of welfare from consumers to the firm, but, as the monopo-

> **Key term**
>
> **deadweight loss:** loss of consumer surplus that arises when a monopoly restricts output and raises price

list is also a member of society, this does not affect overall welfare. However, there is also a loss, which represents a loss to society resulting from the monopolisation of the industry. This is measured by the area of the triangle *BCE*. This is known as the **deadweight loss** that society incurs as a result of the restriction to competition. Notice that a small number of firms in collusion with each other may have similar effects to a monopoly.

This deadweight loss is a measure of the welfare loss imposed on society in a monopoly situation. However, there are two key aspects of efficiency, as was shown in *AS Economics, Chapter 5*. The loss in *allocative efficiency* shown in Figure 4.1 may be partly offset by improved *productive efficiency*: for example, because a monopoly is able to take advantage of economies of scale that would be sacrificed if it were to be split into many small firms, none of which would be able to reach the minimum average cost level of output.

The existence of the deadweight loss provides the rationale for intervention by the Competition Commission and the Office of Fair Trading, which have the responsibility for protecting consumer interests and attempting to promote competition.

Exercise 4.1

Figure 4.2 shows a market in which there are only two firms operating.

a The two firms competing in the market produce at constant marginal cost *OD*, which means that average cost is also constant and equal to marginal cost. Competing intensively, the price is driven down to a level at which no surplus above marginal cost is made. Identify the price charged, the quantity traded and consumer surplus.

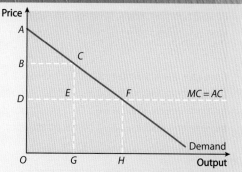

Figure 4.2 Anticompetitive behaviour

b Suppose the two firms decide to collude to raise price to a level *OB*. Identify the quantity traded and the consumer surplus.

c You should have found that consumer surplus is much smaller in the second situation than in the first. What has happened to the areas that were formerly part of consumer surplus?

Market concentration

The discussion above has shown that the models of perfect competition and monopoly produce very different outcomes for productive and allocative efficiency. Perfect competition produces a 'good' allocation of resources, but monopoly results in a deadweight loss. In the real-world economy it is not quite so simple. In particular, not every market is readily classified as following either of these extreme models. Indeed, you might think that the majority of markets do not correspond to either of the models, but instead display a mixture of characteristics.

An important question is whether markets such as oligopoly behave more like a competitive market or more like a monopoly. You have seen in Chapter 3 that there are many different ways in which markets with just a few firms operating can be modelled, because there are many ways in which the firms may interact.

It is helpful to have some way of gauging how close a particular market is to being a monopoly. One way of doing this is to examine the degree of concentration in the market. Later it will be seen that this is not all that is required to determine how efficiently a market will operate; but it is a start.

Concentration is normally measured by reference to the **concentration ratio**, which measures the market share of the largest firms in an industry. For example, the three-firm concentration ratio measures the market share of the largest three firms in the market; the five-firm concentration ratio calculates the share of the top five firms, and so on. Concentration can also be viewed in terms of employment, reflected in the proportion of workers in any industry that are employed in the largest firms.

Key term

n-firm concentration ratio: a measure of the market share of the largest *n* firms in an industry

Consider the following example. Table 4.1 gives average circulation figures for firms that publish national newspapers in the UK. In the final column these are converted into market shares. Where one firm produces more than one newspaper, their circulations have been combined (e.g. News International publishes both the *Sun* and *The Times*).

Firm	Average circulation	Market share (%)
News International Newspapers Ltd	3,470,711	36.3
Associated Newspapers Ltd	2,077,545	21.7
Trinity Mirror plc	1,318,168	13.8
Express Newspapers Ltd	1,292,330	13.5
Telegraph Group Ltd	799,021	8.4
Guardian Newspapers Ltd	292,909	3.1
Independent Newspapers (UK) Ltd	178,576	1.9
Financial Times Ltd	130,695	1.4

Table 4.1 *Concentration in the UK newspaper industry, July 2008*
Source: www.abc.org.uk

The three-firm concentration ratio is calculated as the sum of the market shares of the biggest three firms: that is, $36.3 + 21.7 + 13.8 = 71.8\%$.

Concentration ratios may be calculated on the basis of either shares in output or shares in employment. In the above example the calculation was on the basis of output (daily circulation). The two measures may give different results because the largest firms in an industry may be more capital-intensive in their production methods, which means that

Concentration ratios in the newspaper industry can be calculated on the basis of daily circulation

their share of employment in an industry will be smaller than their share of output. For the purposes of examining market structure, however, it is more helpful to base the analysis of market share on output.

This might seem an intuitively simple measure, but it is *too* simple to enable an evaluation of a market. For a start, it is important to define the market appropriately; for

instance, in the above example are the *Financial Times* and the *Sun* really part of the same market?

There may be other difficulties too. Table 4.2 gives some hypothetical market shares for two markets. The five-firm concentration ratio is calculated as the sum of the market shares of the largest five firms. For markets A and B, the result is the same. In both cases the market is perceived to be highly concentrated, at 75%. However, the nature of likely interactions between the firms in these two markets is very different because the large relative size of Firm 1 in Market A is likely to give it substantially more market power than any of the largest five firms in Market B. Nonetheless, the concentration ratio is useful for giving a first impression of how the market is likely to function.

Largest firms in rank order	Market A	Market B
Firm 1	68	15
Firm 2	3	15
Firm 3	2	15
Firm 4	1	15
Firm 5	1	15

***Table 4.2** Market shares (% of output)*

Figure 4.3 shows the five-firm concentration ratio for a number of industrial sectors in the UK. Concentration varies from 1.1% in tools and 15.6% in paper, printing and publishing to 96% in iron and steel and 99.2% in tobacco. In part, the difference between sectors might be expected to reflect the extent of economies of scale, and this makes sense for many of the industries shown.

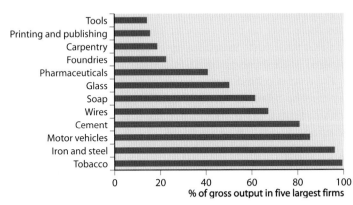

Figure 4.3
Concentration in UK industry, 1992

Source: Census of Production 1992.

Summary

➤ A comparison of perfect competition with monopoly reveals that a profit-maximising monopoly firm operating under the same cost conditions as a perfectly competitive industry will produce less output, charge a higher price and impose a deadweight loss on society.

➤ Real-world markets do not often conform to the models of perfect competition or monopoly, which are extreme forms of market structure.

➤ It is important to be able to evaluate the degree of concentration in a market.

➤ While not a perfect measure, the concentration ratio is one way of doing this, by calculating the market share of the largest firms.

Scale and market concentration

An important issue that arises as firms become larger concerns is the number of firms that a market can support. Suppose that economies of scale are available right up to the limit of market demand, as in Figure 4.4. If more than one firm were to try to supply this market, each producing at minimum average cost, there would be substantial excess supply, and the situation would not be viable.

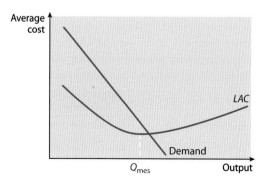

Figure 4.4 How many firms can a market support?

In this situation, the largest firm in the market will come to dominate, as it will be able to produce at lower average costs than any potential competitor. This will be reinforced if there are significant learning-by-doing effects, which will further entrench the largest firm as the market leader. Such a market is likely to become a *natural monopoly*.

Such substantial economies of scale are not available in all sectors. It will depend upon the nature of technology and all the other factors that can give rise to economies of scale. In some activities there may be little scope at all for economies of scale. For example, there are no great fixed costs in setting up a restaurant or a hairdressing salon — at least, compared with those involved in setting up a steel plant or an underground railway. The level of output at which minimum average cost is reached for such activities may thus be relatively small compared with market demand, so there may be room for many firms in the market. This helps to explain the proliferation of bars, take-away restaurants and hairdressing salons.

There may also be an intermediate position, where the economies of scale are not sufficient to bring about a monopoly situation, but only relatively few firms can operate efficiently. Such markets are known as *oligopolies*, which were investigated in Chapter 3.

How does this affect the way in which a market works? Is there any reason to believe that a monopoly or oligopoly will work against society's best interests? If market share is concentrated among a small number of firms, does this *inevitably* mean that consumers will suffer?

The answer to these questions depends upon the behaviour of firms within the market. There may be an incentive for a monopoly firm to use its market power to increase its profits. It can do this by restricting the amount of output that it releases on to the market, and by raising the price to consumers. In Chapter 2 it was shown that a monopoly has the incentive to act in this way, since by lowering output and raising price it can increase its overall profits. From the consumer's point of view, the result is a loss of consumer surplus.

If there is an incentive for a single firm to act in this way, there is a similar incentive for firms in an oligopoly to do the same, as they can increase their joint profits — with the same effects on consumers. However, the oligopoly case is more complicated, as there is always the possibility that individual firms will try to increase their own share of the market at the expense of others in the oligopoly.

Market dominance

A key issue is whether firms actually have the market power to exploit consumers in this way. Do firms have market dominance that can be exploited to bring higher profits? In other words, to what extent do firms have the freedom to set prices at their preferred levels, and to what extent do they have to take into account the actions of other firms or face other constraints?

Even monopoly firms have to accept the constraint of the demand curve. They are not free to set a price at any level they choose, otherwise consumers would simply not buy the product. The question is more one of whether firms are free to choose where to position themselves on their demand curve, rather than having to accept the market equilibrium price.

The fact that most countries have legislation in place to protect consumers from this sort of exploitation by firms recognises that firms might have market power and also have an incentive to use it. In the UK this monitoring is in the hands of the Office of Fair Trading and the Competition Commission. For these purposes, a firm is said to have a dominant position if its market share exceeds 40%. The existence of such bodies helps to act as a restraint on anti-competitive practices by firms.

There may also be natural constraints that limit the extent to which a firm is able to achieve a position of dominance in a market. An important consideration is whether a firm (or firms) in a market needs to be aware of the possibility of new firms joining the market. Remember that in Chapter 2 a competitive market was seen to tend towards a long-run equilibrium. In response to an increase in consumer demand, a key part of the adjustment involved the entry of new firms, which would be attracted into the market when the incumbent firms were seen to be making abnormal profits. This had the effect of competing away those profits until the incentive for entry was removed. Can firms in a market prevent this from happening?

Barriers to entry

Another way of thinking about this is to examine what might constitute a barrier to the entry of new firms into a market. If such barriers are present, the existing firm or firms may be able to continue to make higher profits.

Key term

barrier to entry: a characteristic of a market that prevents new firms from readily joining the market

Economies of scale

One source of entry barriers is the existence of economies of scale. If the largest firm has a significant cost advantage over later entrants, it can adopt a pricing strategy that makes it very difficult for new firms to become established.

This advantage of the existing firm is likely to be reinforced by a learning-by-doing effect, by which a firm becomes more proficient as it gathers experience of operating in a particular industry. This could produce an even stronger cost advantage that would need to be overcome by new entrants.

Ownership of raw materials

Suppose that the production of a commodity requires the input of a certain raw material, and that a firm in the market controls the supply of that raw material. You can readily see that this would be a substantial barrier to the entry of new firms. A key commodity in the fashion industry is diamonds. Until recently, DeBeers controlled the world's supply of uncut diamonds, and there was no way that new firms could enter the market because of the agreements that DeBeers had with mining companies and governments in those parts of the world where diamonds are mined. This monopoly lasted for many years and only began to break down in the early years of the twenty-first century.

The patent system

The patent system exists to provide protection for firms developing new products or processes. The rationale for this is that, unless firms know that they will have ownership over innovative ideas, they will have no incentive to be innovative. The patent system ensures that, at least for a time, firms can be assured of gaining some benefit from their innovations. For the duration of the patent, they will be protected from competition. This therefore constitutes a legal barrier to the entry of new firms.

Advertising and publicity

Advertising can be regarded as a component of fixed costs, because expenditure on it does not vary directly with the volume of output. If the firms in an industry typically spend heavily on advertising, it will be more difficult for new firms to become established, as they too will need to advertise widely in order to attract customers.

Similarly, firms may spend heavily on achieving a well-known brand image that will ensure customer loyalty. Hence they may invest a lot in the design and packaging of their merchandise. One example was the high-profile television campaign run by Sunny Delight when trying to gain entry into the soft drinks market in the early part of the twenty-first century.

Advertising to gain customer loyalty can be expensive

Notice that such costs are also sunk costs, and cannot be recovered if the new firm fails to gain a foothold. It has sometimes been suggested that the cost of excessive advertising should be included in calculations of the social cost of monopoly.

Research and development

A characteristic of some industries is the heavy expenditure undertaken on research and development (R&D). A prominent example is the pharmaceutical industry, which spends large amounts on researching new drugs — and new cosmetics.

This is another component of fixed costs, as it does not vary with the volume of production. Again, new firms wanting to break into the market know that they will need to invest heavily in R&D if they are going to keep up with the new and better drugs and cosmetics always coming on to the market.

Barriers to entry in the leisure industry

How likely is it that such barriers to entry will be present in the leisure industry?

In the UK, about half of leisure time for both males and females is taken up by watching television or DVDs or listening to the radio. Perhaps it could be argued that there are some economies of scale in the production and broadcasting of television programmes. There are some fixed costs involved in building studios and in purchasing cameras and broadcasting equipment. On the other hand, changing technology in recent years has reduced the costs of shooting film and broadcasting the results. This could help to explain the proliferation of television stations that has occurred, many of them catering to small niche markets. There are other contributing factors, but 50 years ago

it would not have been possible to support multiple television channels, even if the industry had not been so closely regulated.

In other segments of the leisure industry, there are some areas in which large firms have emerged. For example, consider professional football in the UK, now dominated by the Premiership and a few large clubs within it. Or consider the market position achieved by McDonald's and Burger King — these might be seen as large, but not dominant in the fast-food sector. Some of these markets will be discussed more fully later in the chapter.

Barriers to entry in the transport sector

How likely is it that such barriers to entry will be present in the transport sector?

In some segments of the sector, there are likely to be economies of scale. This particularly applies in the provision of infrastructure. A rail network, Channel Tunnel or airport entails substantial upfront investment, which could be seen as a fixed cost for the market segment. The marginal cost of transporting an additional passenger on a train or plane is relatively low. However, it is possible to separate out the provision of infrastructure from the provision of transport services, so although there may be barriers to entry in the infrastructure segment of the market, which may be viewed as a natural monopoly, the barriers to entry in the provision of services may be less severe — for example, think of a taxi firm set up to carry passengers to and from a major airport. You would find that every city in the south of England has such firms serving Heathrow and Gatwick.

The control of raw materials may not be a feature of many transport markets, but nonetheless there may be parallels to be drawn. For example, BAA plc has been responsible for running all three London airports — Heathrow, Gatwick and Stansted — since the privatisation of the British Airport Authority in 1987. BAA supplies takeoff and landing slots to airlines that wish to fly in and out of these airports. Given capacity constraints, BAA has effectively held a monopoly on this business, and it would be difficult for a new firm to build a new airport and set up in competition — in other words, there are barriers to entry in this segment of the market. One result of this market situation was an investigation by the Competition Commission, which published its findings in 2008.

Strategic and innocent barriers to entry

In the case of economies of scale, it could be argued that the advantage of the largest firm in the industry is a purely natural barrier to entry that arises from the market position of the firm.

In other cases, it may be that firms can consciously erect barriers to entry in order to make entry into the market more difficult for potential new firms. In other words, firms may make strategic moves to protect their market position behind entry barriers.

chapter  4

One example of this might be the advertising undertaken by firms. Some firms have become (and remain) well known by dint of heavy advertising expenditures. In some cases these expenditures have very little impact on market shares, and merely serve to maintain the status quo. However, for potential entrants they make life very difficult. Any new firm coming into the market has to try to match the advertising levels of existing firms in order to gain a viable market share. Effectively, existing firms have increased the fixed costs of being in the market, making entry more difficult to achieve. For example, when the soft drink Sunny Delight was launched, it had to undertake a large-scale television advertising campaign to try to break into a market dominated by Coca-Cola and PepsiCo.

An alternative method is for an existing firm to operate with spare capacity, making it clear to potential entrants that entry will trigger a price war. The surplus capacity adds credibility to this threat, as the existing firm is seen to be able to increase output – and thus force down price – very quickly.

Exercise 4.2

For each of the following, explain under what circumstances the action of the firm constitutes a barrier to entry and discuss whether there is a strategic element to it, or whether it might be regarded as a 'natural' or 'innocent' barrier.

a A firm takes advantage of economies of scale to reduce its average costs of production.

b A firm holds a patent on the sale of a product.

c A firm engages in widespread advertising of its product.

d A firm installs surplus capacity relative to normal production levels.

e A firm produces a range of very similar products under different brand names.

f A firm chooses not to set price at the profit-maximising level.

g A firm spends extensively on research and development in order to produce a better product

Market failure

How is the market affected if the extent of competition in it is limited? By restricting output and raising price, firms are able to increase their profits, effectively increasing the market price to a level above the marginal cost of production. This implies that there is a loss of allocative efficiency in this situation. From society's point of view, too little of the product is being produced.

To the extent that the monopolist is a member of society, the increase in producer surplus might be regarded as a redistribution from consumers to producers. However, more crucial is the fact that there is a loss of consumer surplus that is not recoverable.

Regulation of monopoly and mergers

The effectiveness of the market system in allocating resources requires prices to act as signals to producers about consumer demand. Firms will be attracted into activities where consumer demand is buoyant and profitability is high, and will tend to exit from activities in which demand is falling and profitability is low.

This process relies on the existence of healthy competition between firms, and on freedom of entry to and exit from markets. In the absence of these conditions, resources may not be best allocated according to the pattern of consumer demand. For example, if there are barriers to entering a market, the existing firms in the market may have the power to restrict output and raise the price, producing less of the product than is desirable for society. As explained above, such barriers to entry may arise from features such as economies of scale or the patent system. In some situations, existing firms may take strategic action to deter entry.

This is one area of the economy in which governments often choose to intervene to protect consumers. In the UK, the Office of Fair Trading (OFT) and the Competition Commission (CC) are responsible for this part of government policy. These bodies have the power to investigate markets that appear to be overly concentrated or in which competition appears weak. They can also take action to encourage competition in markets. This is known as **competition policy**. Notice that the OFT and CC have been active in a number of investigations involving the leisure sector.

One of the knotty problems that arises here is that if firms benefit from economies of scale, it may be more productively efficient to allow large firms to develop than to fragment the industry into lots of small firms in the name of encouraging competition. Thus, the authorities have to find a way of balancing the potential costs of losing allocative efficiency against the potential benefits of productive efficiency.

 Key term

competition policy: an area of economic policy designed to promote competition within markets to encourage efficiency and protect consumer interests

In seeking to evaluate the situation in a market, the competition authorities face a series of challenges. Apart from anything else, market conditions are always changing, so it becomes difficult to observe how firms are behaving. For example, the prices of foreign holidays could rise for many reasons other than the abuse of market power by tour operators or other firms in the market. Such price rises could be because of increases in the price of oil, affecting transport costs. They could equally be the effect of changes in the foreign exchange rate, or many other factors affecting the market. The authorities thus need to be careful in coming to a decision. They may need to investigate a variety of market conditions before judging a firm's behaviour. A key issue may be the extent to which the market is contestable. In other words, a judgement needs to be made as to the extent to which a firm faces potential competition, which may restrict the amount of market power that it can wield.

Merger and acquisition activity has led to the creation of some giant firms in recent years, and one responsibility of the competition authorities is to monitor such activity, which may be seen to have an effect on concentration in markets. Examples of recent cases can be viewed on the websites of the OFT and the CC. In one inquiry, the CC investigated takeover bids for the Safeway supermarket chain from Morrisons, Tesco, Sainsbury's and ASDA. The Morrisons bid was accepted, as it was least likely to lead to a less competitive market. In an earlier investigation, the CC blocked a proposed takeover of Manchester United Football Club by BSkyB on the grounds that this would not be beneficial for consumers.

Summary

> Cost conditions in a market may affect the number of firms that can operate profitably.

> Firms that attain market dominance may be able to harness market power at the expense of consumers, reducing output and raising price.

> This is especially the case where the existing firm or firms are protected by barriers to entry.

> When firms do use such market power, there is a deadweight loss to society that reflects allocative inefficiency.

> However, this may in part be balanced by a gain in productive efficiency.

> Competition policy is a set of measures designed to encourage competition in markets.

The economics of
work and leisure

Part 2

Chapter 5
The nature of work and leisure and trends in employment and earnings

This part of the book considers the economics of work and leisure. It examines the way that labour markets operate, which entails exploring the demand for and supply of labour. In addition, there is discussion of how economic analysis can be applied in order to understand the operation of the leisure industry, which has become an increasingly important sector in the economy. The study of the leisure industry will require some analysis of the markets that have been established to provide leisure opportunities, and the extent to which these operate to ensure an efficient allocation of resources. The present chapter introduces these topics, and provides some background to the labour market and the leisure industry in the UK.

Learning outcomes

After studying this chapter, you should:

➤ be aware of the structure of UK employment and earnings
➤ be able to compare the UK labour market situation with that of other countries in the EU and countries elsewhere
➤ be familiar with movements in labour productivity and hence unit labour costs in the UK and elsewhere
➤ understand the distinction between work and leisure and why this is important
➤ appreciate the significance of economic analysis in decisions related to the allocation of time
➤ be familiar with broad trends in the leisure industries

Work and leisure

At first glance, you may wonder why work and leisure should be linked together in this way. However, from an economic point of view, there are close connections between the two things. When an individual takes decisions about participation in the labour force, this also constitutes a decision about leisure. If I decide to occupy my time in writing an economics textbook (which most people would classify as

'work'), I forgo the opportunity of watching television or doing some gardening. So my leisure time can be regarded as the opportunity cost of writing this textbook. Similarly, if you decide to give up your Saturdays in order to work at a local super-market or department store, you forgo the chance of going to a football match, or going out with your friends.

In fact, the connections between work and leisure go beyond this simple notion of opportunity cost because another way of looking at this decision is that people work in order to be able to earn the income needed to enjoy their leisure time. The wage rate for an hour's work can be seen as the opportunity cost of an hour's leisure time, but wages are also needed to purchase the means with which to enjoy leisure time. These ideas will be explored in the following discussion, but first it is important to find out about these two important markets — the labour market and the market for leisure.

Employment and earnings in the UK

The way in which people earn a living is an important aspect of any economy. Indeed, it is a matter of concern to everyone at an individual level, especially those soon to join the labour force.

Looking at the overall situation for labour supply in the UK, in late 2011, about 63% of people aged 16 and above were **economically active**. This means that they were in employment, self-employed or unem-ployed. Unemployment may arise for a number of rea-sons. It may reflect the fact that some people may not be prepared to accept jobs at the going wage rate. To the extent that this is so, such people may be regarded as being part of *voluntary unemployment.* However, there may also be *involuntary unemployment* — that is, people who would like to work but who are unable to find employment. Chapter 8 examines whether such unemployment arises from market failure in the labour market.

 Key *term*

economically active: active in the labour force, including the employed, the self-employed and the unemployed

ILO unemployment rate: measure of the percentage of the workforce who are without jobs but are available for work, willing to work and looking for work

The official measure of unemployment used in the UK is known as the **ILO unemploy-ment rate**, as it is measured using the definition devised by the International Labour Organisation (ILO). This identifies the number of people available for work and seeking work, but who are without a job. The data are collected as part of the *Labour Force Survey.*

The overall percentage of the economically active does not vary much from year to year. Since 1992 it has only varied between 62.4% and 63.7%. There tends to be a slight increase when the labour market is relatively healthy, which may encourage some people to believe that it is worth their while to join the workforce. Of the 18.5 million people who were economically inactive in late 2011, 9.2 million were above the official retirement age.

Focusing on people aged between 16 and 64, 7.1 million (76%) of the economically inactive in this group did not want jobs. Of those who did want jobs, but had not been looking for work in the previous 4 weeks, a number were long-term sick, or were looking after family members, or were students. There were also small numbers of 'discouraged workers' — that is, people who had withdrawn from the workforce believing that they had no chance of getting a job.

Figure 5.1 shows how the population aged 16 and over have been divided between the various categories in each year since 1992. This shows a gradual rise in the number of employees and a slight fall in the numbers unemployed; this is easier to see in Figure 5.2, which shows the percentage unemployment rate over this same period. Notice that it rose again in 2009 as the recession set in.

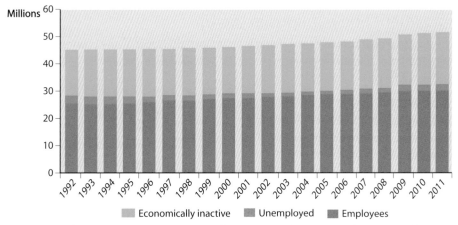

Figure 5.1 *Economic activity and inactivity in the UK (second quarter each year)*
Source: ONS.

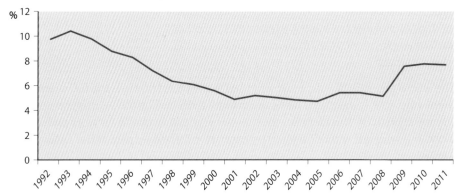

Figure 5.2 *Unemployment in the UK 1992–2011 (spring of each year)*
Source: ONS.

Over the past 25 years or so, the UK economy has gone through substantial structural change. You can see something of this in Figure 5.3, which shows the changing pattern of employment in the UK since 1978. One of the key features is the change

in the balance of employment between manufacturing activity and services. Back in 1978, 26.5% of workforce jobs were in manufacturing activity, and 61.5% were in services. By 2007, only 10.1% of jobs were in manufacturing, and 80.8% were in services. The finance and business services sector grew especially rapidly during this period, more than doubling their number of jobs between 1978 and 2007. Service activity is clearly important to the UK economy, particularly education, health and public administration, distribution, hotels and restaurants, and finance and business services. In contrast, manufacturing employment fell by more than a half in the period.

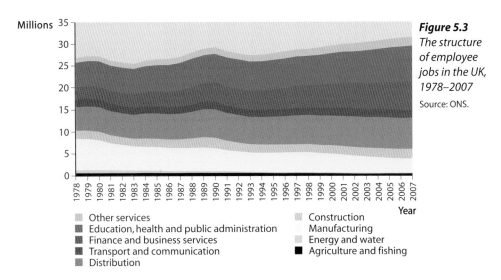

Figure 5.3
The structure of employee jobs in the UK, 1978–2007

Source: ONS.

You should not be too surprised at such changes in the pattern of activity over time. In part they may reflect changes in the pattern of consumer demand as incomes have increased. As real incomes rise, the demand for some goods increases more rapidly than for others. For luxury goods, which have an income elasticity of demand greater than 1, the proportion of income spent on them increases as income itself increases. It is worth noting that the demand for many leisure items is likely to be income elastic. So, for example, as real incomes rise, it would be expected that the demand for capital goods associated with leisure activity, such as digital cameras and iPods, would rise more than proportionately with income. At the same time, the demand for some other goods and services may slacken. If the market economy is working effectively in encouraging the production of those goods and services that people wish to buy, then the structure of economic activity should also change, with some sectors expanding and others contracting.

Patterns of international trade have also changed over time, especially in the context of closer European integration, which may have affected the pattern of specialisation between countries. For example, as China has become a source of competitively priced manufactured goods, economies like the UK have been able to focus on the sorts of service sector activity at which they excel.

Exercise 5.1

Figure 5.4 shows the contribution of the major sectors to GDP in a range of locations. Compare and contrast the changes that have taken place in these locations between 1986 and 2008/10.

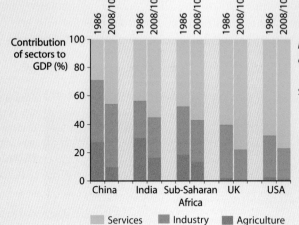

Figure 5.4 *The structure of economic activity, 1986 and 2008/10*

Source: World Bank.

Trends in earnings

Figure 5.5 shows the rate of change of earnings in the UK in the recent past, together with changes in the retail price index. Notice that it is important to look at both earnings and prices because changes in prices (inflation) affect the purchasing power of earnings. An extreme example is 1977, when the earnings index rose by 8.75%, but prices rose by even more (15.8%), so that the real purchasing power of earnings fell. This is seen clearly in Figure 5.6, which shows the annual rate of change of **real earnings**: that is, the rate of change of earnings adjusted for inflation. Notice how real earnings fell in the recession that set in after 2008.

Key term

real earnings: the level of earnings adjusted for the price level; the rate of change of real earnings is thus the rate of change of earnings adjusted for inflation (the rate of change of prices)

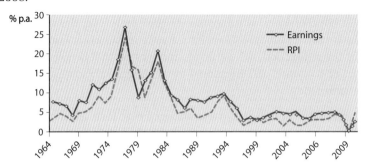

Figure 5.5 *Changes in earnings and prices, 1964–2010*

Source: ONS.

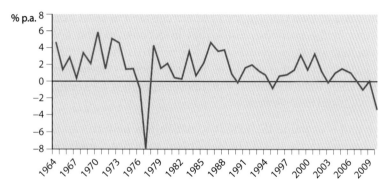

Figure 5.6 *Rate of change of real earnings, 1964–2010*
Note: rate of change of earnings index relative to retail price index.

In most years, earnings can be seen to rise more rapidly than prices. This may reflect increases in the productivity of labour. Whether a rise in real earnings also means an improvement in the standard of living will depend on a number of things. For a start, the fact that average earnings have increased does not mean that all workers share in the benefits, so the distribution of the increases across different groups of workers may be important. Furthermore, it may be argued that the standard of living does not only depend upon income (earnings), but may also reflect other aspects of the quality of life, such as the environment in which people live, or the quality of leisure time that they can enjoy.

It is also important to be aware that the earnings that people receive differ for a wide variety of reasons. For one thing, it is the case that earnings differ between the various kinds of economic activity that take place within the economy. Figure 5.7

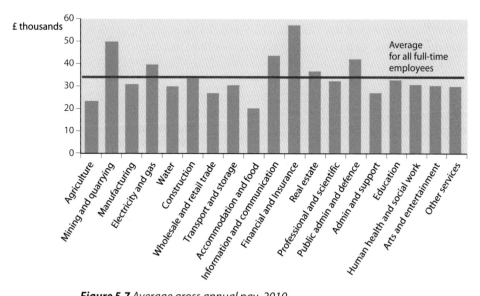

Figure 5.7 *Average gross annual pay, 2010*
Note: data are for full-time employee jobs.
Source: ONS.

shows something of this. You can see that average annual gross pay in 2010 varied across sectors in the economy. Employees in accommodation and food services and in agriculture received relatively low pay, whereas those in the financial sector enjoyed substantially higher levels of remuneration — indeed, average pay for employees in finance and insurance was almost three times the average for workers in accommodation and food services.

Chapters 7 and 8 examine the extent to which this pattern can be explained in terms of economic analysis. One obvious point to notice here is that some of the differences in earnings between economic sectors in the economy may reflect differences in occupational structure, which in turn may be associated with different skills requirements of different jobs. The differences in the wages earned by workers in different occupations can be seen in Figure 5.8, which shows average hourly earnings for various occupational groups. As might be expected, it is clear that managers, senior officials and professionals receive higher hourly earnings than less skilled occupations.

Figure 5.8 also serves as a reminder that there is a gender gap between earnings of male and female workers — and it would seem that the gap is more significant in some occupations than in others. The reasons for this are examined in Chapter 8. It is also the case that earnings (and employment) show differences between age and ethnic groups, and one of

> **Key term**
>
> **discrimination:** a situation in a labour market where some people receive lower wages that cannot be explained by economic factors

the important issues to be examined is the extent to which such differences reflect **discrimination** in the labour force, or the extent to which they may be explained by other economic factors at work in the market. It is noticeable that the gender gap has narrowed somewhat over the past decade — as you can see in Figure 5.9. However, it is still the case that men (on average) earn more than women.

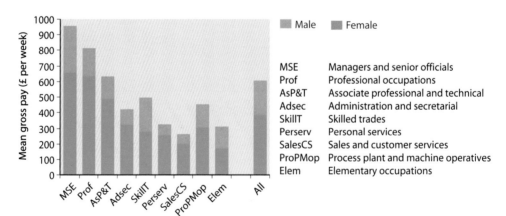

Figure 5.8 *Earnings in the UK by occupation, 2010*
Note: data are for full-time employee jobs.
Source: ONS.

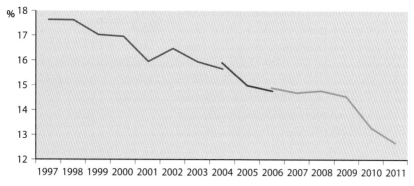

Figure 5.9 *The gender pay gap, 1997–2011*

Note: data refer to full-time employees whose pay for the survey period was unaffected by absence; data show the percentage pay gap between women's and men's median earnings.

Source: *Social Trends*.

There are also some differences that emerge between ethnic groups within society. As with the gender differences, variations between ethnic groups reflect a number of factors, and are seen in a variety of ways. For example, people from some ethnic group-ings are more likely to be self-employed, or may tend to work in certain occupations – some two-thirds of Chinese residents work in sales, distribution, hotels and restaurants; more than half of Indians and two-fifths of Paki-

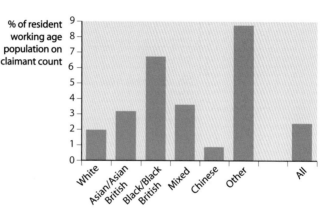

Figure 5.10 *Unemployment by ethnic group*

Source: ONS.

stanis and Bangladeshis are self-employed. This then has knock-on effects on earnings, to the extent that these vary between occupations and sectors. It is also apparent that unemployment rates vary between ethnic groupings, as can be seen in Figure 5.10.

International differences in productivity

Considering the UK economy in an international context, the relative cost of labour in different countries becomes important because this influences the relative competitiveness of UK goods in both overseas and domestic markets. In other words, the relative costs of production in different countries influence the prices that firms can charge. It thus becomes important to consider changes in **unit labour costs** over time, these being defined as the wages, salaries and other costs of using labour, divided by output per worker.

Key term

unit labour cost: wages, salaries and other costs of using labour, divided by output per worker

If unit labour costs in an economy rise more rapidly than in other countries, there will be a loss of competitiveness. Figure 5.11 compares annual changes in unit labour costs in the UK with changes in the member countries of the EU and with countries in the euro single currency area. This reveals that unit labour costs have grown more rapidly in the UK than elsewhere in the EU in recent years. If unit labour costs were to continue to grow more rapidly in the UK than in the EU then, ceteris paribus, this would imply a deterioration in the UK's competitive position.

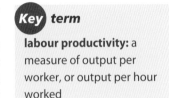

Key term

labour productivity: a measure of output per worker, or output per hour worked

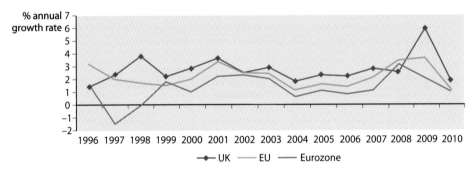

Figure 5.11 *Unit labour cost growth in the UK and EU, 1996–2010*

Source: OECD.

This in turn partly reflects different levels of productivity across countries. Productivity is a measure of productive efficiency: for example, **labour productivity** is output per unit of labour input. Different countries show appreciable differences in efficiency by this measure.

However, international comparisons of productivity are not straightforward, as measurements are subject to differences in data collection and differences in work practices. Figure 5.12 presents data for 2010 on GDP per head of population, expressed as index numbers, with the USA being the reference country and thus set to 100.

On this measure, the UK performs slightly better than Italy, France and Japan. As a measure of productivity levels, however, this is a misleading indicator. In particular, working hours are longer in the UK than in many other countries (especially within Europe), so in part, GDP per head reflects differences in the quantity of labour input. For this reason,

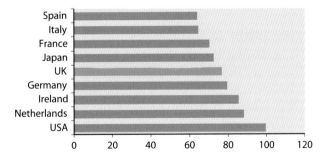

Figure 5.12 *GDP per head of population, selected countries, 2010 (USA = 100)*

Source: OECD.

GDP per hour worked is often seen as a more reliable indicator of relative productivity levels. This measure is graphed in Figure 5.13 and shows quite a different pattern. Indeed, on this basis both Ireland and the Netherlands show higher productivity than the USA, and the UK's performance is much more modest.

Figure 5.14 shows the growth rate of labour productivity in a range of countries since 1990. There is perhaps no consistent pattern over time here, although there are clearly periods in which productivity grew more rapidly in Europe than in the USA. However, it would appear that the US economy was more resilient in the recession that began in 2008.

It is also important to realise that labour productivity is not the only relevant measure, as countries may also differ in their use of capital. An alternative measure is obtained by dividing the quantity of output by the total input of all factors of production. This is known as **total factor productivity**. This is naturally more difficult to measure, as the measurement of capital stock is especially prone to error and misinterpretation. However, some estimates of multifactor productivity growth are shown in Figure 5.15.

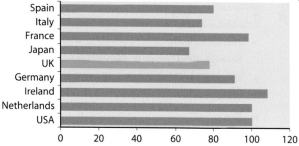

Figure 5.13 *GDP per hour worked, selected countries, 2010 (USA = 100)*

Source: OECD.

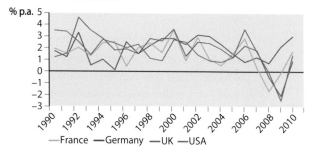

Figure 5.14 *Growth of labour productivity, selected countries, 1990–2010*

Source: OECD.

 Key term

total factor productivity: the average productivity of all factors, measured as the total output divided by the total amount of inputs used

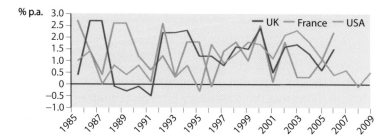

Figure 5.15 *Multifactor productivity growth, UK, France and USA, 1985–2009*

Source: OECD.

Summary

➤ Work and leisure are connected: when an individual takes a decision about how many hours to work, this then also determines how many hours are available for leisure activity.

➤ An additional hour spent at work is the opportunity cost of an hour's leisure — and vice versa.

➤ The overall economic activity rate has not altered very much in the UK in recent years, but there have been changes in the structure of employment between sectors.

➤ Service activity has increased as a proportion of employment, and manufacturing has declined.

➤ This may reflect changes in the pattern of consumer demand, and of specialisation between countries.

➤ Earnings have risen by more than prices in most years.

➤ There have been significant differences in movements of unit labour costs and labour productivity over time between the UK and other countries in the EU.

Exercise 5.2

Table 5.1 provides data on two labour productivity measures, based on the UK = 100. Discuss whether the UK's position has improved or deteriorated between 1991 and 2006. Explain your answer, and discuss why this might be important for the UK economy.

	GDP per worker						GDP per hour worked					
Year	France	Germany	Japan	UK	USA	G7	France	Germany	Japan	UK	USA	G7
1991	129	118	109	100	139	125	135	135	97	100	135	122
1994	122	115	99	100	134	120	127	130	91	100	126	116
1997	117	110	95	100	129	116	124	127	89	100	124	115
2000	115	105	91	100	128	114	123	122	85	100	119	110
2003	110	105	89	100	125	111	120	122	83	100	116	107
2006	110	100	90	100	128	111	117	117	84	100	119	107

Table 5.1 Labour productivity measures

Source: ONS.

Hours worked

An important dimension of the labour market is the number of hours that employees work per week. Figure 5.16 shows that this does vary a bit across countries, with full-time workers in the UK putting in more hours per week, on average, than workers in other countries in Europe. Thus in 2005, the average hours worked by full-time employees in the UK was 43.2, which is somewhat above the average for all EU countries, which was 41.8. In 2005, Norway showed the lowest average hours worked (39.4), and Iceland the highest (47.1).

In general, there has been a downward trend in average hours worked across many countries, partly influenced by EU legislation on the number of hours that workers are permitted to work. However, the changes have not been substantial.

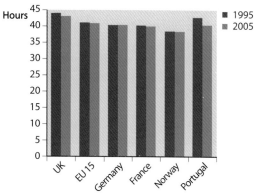

Figure 5.16 *Average hours worked, selected countries, 1995 and 2005, (full-time employees)*

Source: Eurostat.

Leisure

Although people in the UK are seen to work long hours compared with their European counterparts, it is still the case that the UK leisure industry is thriving. Indeed, it has been estimated that the leisure industry accounts for about 10% of the UK's total employment. Part of this industry caters to visiting tourists from overseas, but clearly the industry has become a key part of the economy.

The ways in which people spend their time outside work have seen some major changes in recent years, partly reflecting changes in technology that have revolutionised how people use their leisure time.

A survey carried out in 2005 under the auspices of the Office for National Statistics looked at how people spend their time. The summary results are shown in Figure 5.17. This reveals that leisure occupies the largest share of people's waking time – although housework and childcare come close for women.

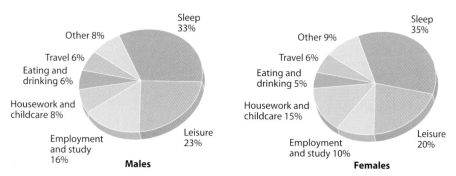

Figure 5.17 *Time spent on main activities, UK males and females, 2005*

Source: Time Use Survey (ONS).

Figure 5.18 shows how that leisure time is allocated between different activities, with watching television and video/DVD being the dominant form of leisure activity for both males and females. This accounts for more than half of leisure time. It would seem that social life and entertainment also occupy a large part of leisure time; hobbies, games and sport between them account for 15% of leisure time for males, and only 10% for females.

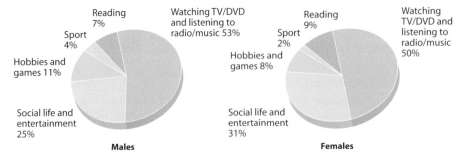

Figure 5.18 *Use of leisure time, UK males and females, 2005*

Source: Time Use Survey (ONS).

It is helpful to distinguish between different forms of leisure activity. First, there are activities that are *home based.* These include watching television or DVD, but also DIY and cooking for friends. The increased availability of home-based capital goods such as DVD players and computers may have affected the extent to which people spend their leisure time at home — certainly as compared with earlier generations.

A second category of leisure activities are those that are mainly *passive.* This category covers activities that are outside the home, but do not involve active participation. Such activities include going to the cinema or a football match, dining out at a restaurant and what is known as 'leisure shopping'.

Home-based activities take up the most amount of leisure time

Finally, there are *active* leisure activities, which involve active participation in some form of sporting activity, or visiting a theme park. As Figure 5.18 illustrates, such active leisure occupies a relatively small share of people's leisure time. Nonetheless, a majority of the adult population do participate in some form of sport, game or physical activity, according to the *General Household Survey*, as can be seen in Figure 5.19. This shows a clear relationship between active leisure participation and age — which is perhaps not surprising. It also shows something of a decline in such participation over time, especially between 1996/97 and 2002/03. This is especially marked among the younger age groups. For both males and females, the most popular activity included in this survey was walking.

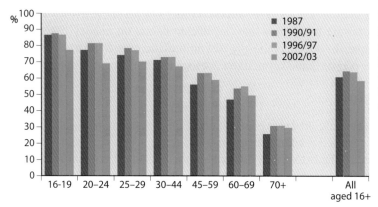

Figure 5.19 *Adult participation in a sport, game or physical activity, by age (Great Britain)*

Source: *Social Trends.*

Exercise 5.3

Keep a diary of your leisure activities over a period of a week, and analyse the proportions that are home based, passive and active. You might be able to persuade your parents to do the same, so that you can compare your pattern with theirs. Alternatively, compare your pattern with that shown in the data provided, or with your fellow students.

Leisure choices

Economic analysis provides some important insights into the way in which people take decisions about their leisure activities.

For example, people take decisions about how to allocate their time between work and leisure. This will partly reflect their personal preferences, but even at this level, the decision will depend upon an evaluation of the relative benefits and costs of time spent in work and leisure — a procedure embedded in the economic approach to decision making. Some people are in jobs that give them satisfaction, whereas others may wish to minimise the time spent at work. However, this is not the only influence on the decision about how much time to devote to work as opposed to leisure. The wage that a worker can earn in employment affects the trade-off between work and leisure, and can be seen as the opportunity cost of leisure. At a higher wage, an extra hour of leisure time carries a higher cost in terms of income forgone.

It is also worth noting that an additional hour spent at work provides additional income that can then be used to enhance the enjoyment of the remaining leisure time. This may encourage the use of more capital goods in the enjoyment of leisure. For example, it could be that a worker may choose to work extra hours in order to earn the income needed to buy DVDs that can be watched in the home, as an alternative to taking more time to visit the cinema. This all suggests that, if markets are to be able to allocate resources efficiently within a society, this must include efficiency in the leisure industry, and in the way in which labour markets operate to establish wage rates. The operation of other markets may also influence people's decisions about leisure. For

many people, the annual holiday is an important focus of leisure activity. Changes in the market for leisure travel may have significant effects on holiday destination choice — for example, the advent of the low-cost airlines has opened up a wider range of choice for many people. Some key markets are explored in the next chapter.

Health and leisure

A by-product of changing lifestyles is in the effect on a population's health. Recall Figure 5.19. This revealed a fall in participation in active sports and games among young age groups. To the extent that this reflects the increasing popularity of computer games and other passive activities, there could be implications for the future health of the population. Indeed, there is evidence of an increase in obesity, not only in the UK, but also in many other developed countries. This may have implications for the resources needed to provide healthcare in the future. To the extent that this is a problem that arises because of poor information or the existence of externalities, there may be a need for government intervention to mitigate the effects. This may explain the encouragement given to people to take part in some form of active leisure activity, or to adopt a healthier lifestyle.

Summary

➤ The number of hours worked by full-time employees in the UK has fallen since 1995, but average hours worked remains higher than in many other European countries.

➤ In spite of the long hours worked in the UK, the leisure industry has been thriving, accounting for about 10% of total employment.

➤ Leisure activity accounts for the largest share of people's waking time.

➤ Home-based leisure activity comprises a relatively large share of leisure activity undertaken by adults, and there has been something of a decline in participation in active leisure activities — sports and other physical activities.

➤ Economic analysis can help to explain these changes that have affected the leisure industry.

➤ A large-scale decline in participation in sporting and other physical activity may contribute to obesity and affect the long-term health of the population.

Exercise 5.4

The relative price of some leisure activities has changed significantly over the past 10–15 years. For example, the cost of home computers and access to the internet has fallen, as has the cost of DVD players and DVDs. Discuss how this relative price change has changed the pattern of leisure activity in the UK.

OCR A2 Economics

Chapter 6
Market structures and competitive behaviour in leisure markets

Part 1 of the book introduced the notion of market structure, and outlined its importance in enabling an allocation of resources that is good for society. It is important to see how this works in practice, and this chapter uses a number of case studies in order to evaluate how market structure has influenced the efficiency of resource allocation in the leisure sector.

Learning outcomes

After studying this chapter, you should:

> be familiar with the way in which market structure affects the efficiency of resource allocation in sections of the leisure sector

> understand the way in which the package holiday market operates as an oligopoly

> appreciate that firms in the package holiday business may face the threat of new entry from firms using the internet, thus affecting the contestability of the market

> be familiar with the way in which the market for television broadcasting has evolved over time, from monopoly to duopoly to oligopoly, becoming more competitive as technology has changed

> be aware of the importance of market structure in the market for spectator sports

> understand developments in the market for air travel, and the impact of the low-cost airlines

> appreciate the conditions under which price discrimination can be utilised by a firm in order to increase its profits

> be familiar with the way in which the theory of monopolistic competition can help in understanding the leisure sector

Markets in the leisure sector

It has been argued that the behaviour of firms is strongly influenced by the structure of the market in which they operate. This applies to the leisure sector, so it is important to explore how some key markets in this sector operate. A number of case studies are presented to look at different parts of the leisure sector. These case studies cover aspects of holiday and leisure travel, spectator sports, broadcasting and cinema admissions.

The market for package holidays in the UK

The market for package holidays is a significant part of the market for holidays in general. It is big business. In 2008, UK residents made 45.5 million holiday visits abroad, of which package holidays made up a large proportion. During the recession that followed, this number fell a little — to 38.5 million in 2009. This still represents a major change in habits over recent decades — in 1971, the number of holiday visits abroad was just 6.7 million. To what extent does the market operate efficiently? In order to evaluate efficiency, economic analysis suggests that a starting point is to examine the market structure.

The Association of British Travel Agents (ABTA) is an organisation that acts as a trade association for tour operators and travel agents in the UK. In 2011, ABTA claimed just under 1,500 members, with more than 6,000 travel agency offices. According to the ABTA website, between them, these accounted for 90% of UK-sold package holidays.

Superficially, the fact that there are more than 6,000 travel agency offices seems to suggest a competitive market, but this is misleading, as it is not only the number of offices that is important, but also the number of firms in the market, and the distribution of the business between them. In 2010, the largest three companies owned 25.8% of travel agent offices in the UK. With just three major operators dominating the market, it would be classified as an *oligopoly*. If the firms were to collude together in order to exploit their market power, this could have an adverse effect on allocative efficiency. A monopolist attempting to maximise profits would restrict output and raise price, thus pushing the market away from the point at which price is equal to marginal cost. However, the question is whether the firms do collude in this way, or whether there are other forces within the market that constrain or prevent them from exploiting their position.

One way in which firms in a market may be constrained is through the direct effects of regulation. The market for foreign package holidays has been investigated in the past by the Monopoly and Mergers Commission (now the Competition Commission). Investigations took place in the mid-1980s (reporting in 1986), and again in the late 1990s,

Thomas Cook is one of the three big companies that control the travel market

with a referral to the commission taking place in 1996. The 1986 report investigated allegations of what was, in effect, *resale price maintenance*. Resale price maintenance is where the producer of a good dictates the price at which it should be sold in the retail market – a practice that has been illegal for many years. The commission concluded that this was against the public interest, and outlawed the practice.

In the later investigation, the commission noted that at the time the largest three operators in the market accounted for around 50% of all foreign package holidays sold in 1996. In its report, the commission expressed concern about the degree of *vertical integration* in the market, particularly given that some of the ownership linkages between firms were not made clear to customers. Vertical integration is where a firm is involved in different stages of the production of a good or service. An example is that of First Choice Holidays. The commission pointed out that this firm was not only a tour operator, but also an airline (Air 2000), and for a period was also in a strategic alliance with Thomas Cook (travel agent). Consumers were not always aware that they were dealing with a firm that was involved at these different stages of the production process, which can affect the profit margins on particular holiday packages. However, while recommending greater transparency in the market, the commission did not condemn the operators outright. It did make a number of recommendations about certain practices, such as tying discounts to the purchase of insurance. But the commission concluded that 'we would characterise the travel trade as at present broadly competitive, and as having served the consumer well'.

The threat of investigation by the competition authorities may be one way of ensuring that operators in a market do not abuse their market position, but are there other forces at work that might influence firms? And how else might a judgement be reached as to the intensity of competition in a market?

One of the problems in evaluating a market is that, in general, it is not possible to observe marginal cost, so that it is not possible to check whether price is being set above marginal cost. An alternative might be to look at profits, and ask whether firms in a market seem to be making excessive profits. In the case of the travel companies, recent experience may not help in this respect. The substantial reduction in demand for foreign holidays following the terrorist attacks of 11 September 2001 in the USA created difficulties for many of the tour operators and travel agents, many of which posted sharp reductions in profits, or even losses. But this is not conclusive evidence that firms were not abusing their market power; it might just be a process of adjustment to lower demand for their products.

Perhaps more relevant is to examine the extent to which the market may be regarded as contestable. In other words, to what extent can the existing operators in the market rely on barriers to entry to protect them from hit-and-run entry, or to what extent is it possible for new firms to enter the market? If the market is contestable and open to entry by new firms, then it would not be possible for the existing firms to set prices at a level above average cost, as this would attract new competition.

The growth of the internet may be the key factor that determines the intensity of competition in the travel industry. The growing ability of consumers to by-pass the

local travel agent by making their own bookings online suggests that the travel market is highly contestable. It is now possible for a potential holidaymaker to find their flights, hotel accommodation, car rentals or hotel transfers from their PCs. This can be done either by booking direct with airlines and hotels, or by using one of the growing number of online firms, such as Expedia, the world's largest online travel agent.

The travel agents have thus had to respond to these new online entrants to their market. They have done so partly by themselves going online, and developing their own websites and online sales. They have also responded by looking for niche markets, offering specialist advice on long-haul holidays, adventure trips or skiing packages.

Offering specialist advice on skiing packages — a niche market for travel agents

The intensity of this competition is likely to be beneficial for consumers in terms of the prices that can be obtained for package holidays. Inevitably, there may also be dangers. For example, it may be that online purchase of the separate components of a holiday is more risky than buying from a travel agent backed by the code of conduct now issued by ABTA. Or it may be that the online companies themselves will go through a process of merger, acquisition and increasing concentration that may lead at some point to market power.

Exercise 6.1

Discuss the extent to which the growth of online sales of package holidays is influencing the range of destinations and variety of holidays on offer. Do you think that more regulation of online marketing is needed in order to protect consumer interests?

Television broadcasting

According to the 2005 Time Use Survey, watching either television or DVD/video occupies more than half of people's leisure time in the UK (see Figure 5.18). It is thus important to ensure that television broadcasting is being provided in an efficient manner. Again, whether this is the case depends partly on the market structure in the television broadcasting sector, which is likely to influence the behaviour of the enterprises engaged in this activity.

There are other aspects of broadcasting that affect the efficiency of the market. Indeed, there are three areas of potential market failure in the sector. A tendency to *concentration* (and hence imperfect competition) is one of these, but in addition, broadcasting has some aspects of a *public good*, and there may also be some *merit good* arguments.

Television broadcasting may be regarded as a public good because there is an extent to which it is non-rivalrous and non-exclusive. When a programme is broadcast, anyone with a television receiver can pick up the signal, so it is difficult to exclude people from

consuming the good. Furthermore, if one person watches the programme, this does not reduce the amount of it available for others to watch. You will remember from *AS Economics, Chapter 7* that these characteristics mean that public goods are under-provided in the absence of some form of government intervention. Partly for this reason, there has been government intervention in television broadcasting ever since transmissions first began. The BBC derives much of its income from the licence fee, which is one way of ensuring that people pay for the programmes that they watch. The situation has changed with technology in recent years, making it possible to exclude people from receiving some channels, and enabling firms to charge for particular programmes.

There is a view that television broadcasting has merit good characteristics, as it is believed that viewing habits can influence behaviour. Watching educational programmes may bring beneficial spillover effects, and may be regarded as a merit good. On the other hand, watching violent dramas may have the opposite effect, and encourage anti-social behaviour. In this case, we would regard some TV programmes as being demerit goods. These arguments have been used to justify government intervention to influence the content of programmes that are broadcast.

In terms of market structure, television broadcasting began as a *monopoly* (when only one BBC channel was available). ITV was granted a licence to broadcast in 1955, being funded through advertising revenue, so the market became a *duopoly*. As more terrestrial channels were launched, the market evolved into an *oligopoly*. The cost structure of television broadcasting encourages a relatively high degree of concentration. This is because the ratio of fixed to variable costs is very high, which in turn means that there are substantial economies of scale. The major costs arise in establishing the network of transmitters, and in making the programmes. The marginal cost entailed in transmitting the programmes is very small compared to these fixed costs.

Liz Barker presenting the BBC's long-standing children's programme, Blue Peter

How might the resulting market power be exploited by the firms involved? After all, the BBC does not control the size of its licence fee, and the commercial channels do not charge their customers directly. A danger of lack of competition is that firms may cut their costs, and thus may produce low-quality programmes, or only put out populist programmes that will attract audiences, and thus advertising revenue. But it might not provide the sorts of programme that the authorities would regard as meritorious.

The so-called digital revolution has made it possible for many other channels to become established, some of them available only on a subscription basis. This has affected the

barriers to entry, and enabled the market to be more contestable than before. In the UK, there are now more than 300 channels available. Some of these channels cater for niche markets, such as cookery, comedy or home improvement. Issues arising from the merit good argument remain, and clearly the authorities have a greater challenge to face in ensuring that what they see as an appropriate balance of programmes is broadcast, now that there are so many channels to deal with. As with any appeal to a merit good argument, there are bound to be differences between politicians and others about the extent to which the authorities should override consumer preferences.

The way that technology has developed to enable broadcasts to be restricted to subscribers or paying customers has enabled a number of new developments in this market. In particular, there are segments of the market where consumers are clearly prepared to pay a premium in order to view particular programmes. One obvious example of such a market segment is in sporting events, such as Premiership football and test cricket. These examples are discussed in the next section.

Exercise 6.2

Discuss the extent to which the authorities are justified in intervening to influence the sorts of programme that are being broadcast.

Spectator sports

Another important form of leisure activity is watching sport. This takes a wide variety of forms. Parents watch their children playing sport at the local sports centre, people attend sporting events, and there is plenty of 'live' sports action on television, both on the terrestrial channels and on specialist subscription channels such as Sky Sports.

As far as professional sporting events are concerned, there is some interlinkage between the markets. Ever since football matches were first televised, it has been argued that matches should not be shown 'live' at the traditional match time of Saturday at 3 p.m., as this was thought to affect attendance at the grounds. For Premiership and Championship clubs, gate receipts remain an important source of income, although television revenues have also become increasingly important in recent years. A lot of attention has been devoted to the earnings that footballers command in the Premiership. This issue is taken up in Chapter 7 (see page 114).

In terms of market structure, the way that the rights to televising events have become concentrated is an especially crucial area. In particular, BSkyB's position in this market has attracted considerable attention in relation to holding rights to televise live sporting events such as football and cricket. An important question is the extent to which BSkyB has monopoly power, and the extent to which it is able to exploit that market power at the expense of the viewers.

There is a specified list of events that are guaranteed to be shown on free-to-air terrestrial channels. This list includes the Olympics, the World Cup (football), the FA Cup Final, the Grand National and Wimbledon.

Test cricket was delisted in 1998 after lobbying from the England and Wales Cricket Board (ECB), which was keen to raise funds for investment. This enabled BSkyB to bid for exclusive rights to domestic test matches, in a deal that would remove cricket from the terrestrial channels from 2006 to 2009. A further review of the list was promised – but not until the switch-over to digital television has been completed.

Premiership football had fallen prey to Sky at a much earlier date. Sky won the rights to live Premiership football in 1992, and maintained its position until an auction that was held in May 2006. The auction was held following intervention by the European Commission, which had ruled that BSkyB's dominance of live Premiership football was acting against consumer interests. In the auction, six packages of matches were sold separately, four of which were bought by BSkyB, and the remaining two by the Irish pay-TV broadcaster Setanta. Within a week of the auction, BSkyB and Setanta reached a deal in respect of the pubs-and-clubs segment of the market. Under this agreement, Sky's corporate customers would get Setanta's sports channels bundled in to their monthly subscription. It would seem that monopoly had been replaced by a duopoly.

BSkyB's moves in these various sports markets were strategic, aiming to build up the number of subscribers by gaining control of these key market segments. From the perspective of BSkyB, this may be seen as an attempt to gain and consolidate entry into the television broadcasting market, which until the advent of satellite broadcasting had been an oligopoly controlled by the terrestrial channels via licensing agreements. Only by reaching a critical mass of subscribers would BSkyB be able to generate sufficient advertising revenue to become profitable.

The satellite station BSkyB gained a monopoly in the supply of certain televised live football and cricket matches

Chapter 8 will introduce another form of market structure – the monopsony. This covers the situation in which there is a single seller of a good. There may be elements of monopsony present in this market situation. The Premier League may be seen as a monopsony seller of the rights to live football – and the ECB of the rights to televise test cricket. By opening up to an auction and selling to the highest bidder, the Premier League gained funds to distribute to the Premiership clubs, and the ECB gained funds to invest in cricket. This is an example of a monopsony seller using its market power.

The evaluation of the effect of market structure in this situation is tricky. It could be argued that BSkyB has been able to use its market power to charge a high price to consumers for watching live football on television. However, if these matches were to be available on free-to-air television, it could be argued that this would damage match attendance and leave the football clubs struggling for revenue. The monopsony position of the Premier League has enabled it to channel revenue to the clubs, making the

Premiership one of the richest leagues in the world. Television revenues and audiences may be even more important in the case of test cricket.

The market situation was the subject of investigation by the UK's Competition Commission, which became involved in 1998 when BSkyB's proposed acquisition of Manchester United was referred by the secretary of state for trade and industry. The acquisition was prohibited on the grounds that it would reinforce the trend towards inequality of wealth between football clubs, and would give BSkyB additional influence over Premier League decisions relating to the organisation of football. However, this did not break the monopoly that BSkyB had over live Premiership broadcasts at that time.

After this, the European Commission became involved, and argued that BSkyB's exclusive right to televise live matches was in violation of European competition rules, as it was 'not in the interest of competition in the broadcasting market or the fans'. At the time, the Premier League agreed that after 2006 the tendering process would ensure that there were at least two television broadcasters of live Premiership matches. The commission intervened again in 2005 when it seemed that the Premier League was delaying matters, and the auction finally took place in April 2006.

Exercise 6.3

One advantage of the system that allowed BSkyB to gain a monopoly in the supply of televised live football and cricket matches is that this brought money into the respective sports, enabling investment in football clubs and cricket at grass-roots level. Discuss the extent to which consumers have benefited from satellite broadcasting of sporting activities.

The low-cost airlines

With the growth in the foreign package holiday market, air travel has come to be a key part of the leisure market. The face of air travel has changed dramatically since the appearance of the low-cost airlines, beginning with Southwestern in the USA (launched as long ago as 1971), followed by Ryanair in 1985 and easyJet in 1995. The model has now been copied by Air Asia and other airlines operating in southeast Asia.

This market provides an illustration of how intensified competition can affect the operation of markets. Before the advent of the low-cost airlines, the market for air travel was dominated by large national carriers, in many cases either state-run or heavily subsidised by governments. As time went by, these large airlines began to join together in strategic alliances that enabled them to work together yet maintain their individual characters. The market seemed to be consolidating and was effectively becoming more concentrated.

Deregulation provided an opening for changes in the market structure, by reducing the barriers to entry of new firms, especially in domestic and short-haul flights. In terms of holiday destinations, the changes opened up new possibilities for UK holidaymakers, whether for their annual vacations or for weekend city breaks.

In order to exploit that opening, the budget airlines needed a good understanding of economic analysis. Their success has been built on a thorough understanding of cost structures and recognition of the contestability of airlines, together with the judicious use of price discrimination.

Profits depend upon costs as well as revenue. EasyJet (not to mention other budget airlines, such as Ryanair and Flybe) undertook a close scrutiny of the structure of their costs. By focusing on each individual item of costs and looking for ways of cutting costs to a minimum, the budget airlines were able to achieve profitability.

In part, this has been connected with the understanding of demand. The budget airlines offer a 'no frills' approach, doing away with pre-assigned seats and pre-issued tickets, free in-flight catering, a separate business class and so on. They also fly to more remote locations, where airport charges are relatively low. But the savings go way beyond these conspicuous items.

In particular, the budget airlines have followed a pattern established by the Texas-based airline Southwestern, which set out four key rules. First, only fly one type of plane. This reduces maintenance costs and avoids the need to hold a wide range of spare parts. This is one source of potential economies of scale.

Second, drive down costs every year. This may be achieved while the airline is still expanding if there are economies of scale to be reaped. For example, it may be achieved by negotiating improved deals from suppliers — of fuel, insurance, etc.

Third, minimise the time that aircraft spend parked on the tarmac. The no frills and no tickets approach enables a much quicker turn-round of aircraft — which, after all, only earn money for the company when they are in the air. For example, an easyJet plane flying between Luton and Nice can make four round-trips per day — by spending only about half-an-hour on the tarmac at each end.

Fourth, do not try to sell anything except seats. Schemes that offer loyalty bonuses or air miles cost money to administer, and are more complicated than they are worth.

Following these rules and paying careful attention to the various forms of costs enabled the budget airlines to expand, to make profits and to transform air travel.

As far as price discrimination is concerned, easyJet operates a very simple fare structure based on supply and demand. The nature of the price structure is that passengers who book early pay the lowest prices, whereas those who book close to their travel time pay the highest prices.

EasyJet operates a simple fare structure based on supply and demand

You might expect that in a competitive market, the price structure would be the opposite. If prices follow costs, the marginal cost to easyJet of carrying an extra passenger is likely to be pretty low, so the flight could be filled up

by offering last-minute deals, with the price being driven close to marginal cost. But this is clearly not happening at easyJet, as the later a passenger books, the higher the price that they face.

This suggests that easyJet understands enough about the nature of demand to use price discrimination on its flights. People who book at the last minute are likely to be business travellers who need to fly urgently, perhaps for a business meeting or to clinch a deal. Such customers are likely to have low elasticity of demand, and thus be prepared to pay a higher price for their ticket. This is in contrast to those who can book well in advance, who are more likely to be people travelling for leisure — visiting relatives or going on holiday. For these travellers, the choice of when to fly is more flexible. This means there are more possible flights from which they can choose. And we know that when there are substitutes for a commodity, the price elasticity of demand is high. It is for these customers that easyJet can offer the low prices that we see being advertised. After all, at £20, it probably costs some customers more to get to the airport than it costs for the flight! It is this pricing policy that has revolutionised the leisure travel market.

So, easyJet can make use of this difference in demand elasticity to charge different prices to different customers, even if the product (the flight from London to Nice) is the same for all of them. Thus an understanding of demand is important for easyJet.

The entry of the budget airlines also caused the existing firms to reconsider the way in which they operate. Some reacted by setting up their own budget subsidiaries, with varying degrees of success. Others have had to accept that they need to focus on longer-haul flights.

The budget airlines case therefore provides another example of how competition can transform a market, and how contestability can affect firms' behaviour. Why can the airline business be regarded as contestable? After all, it might be argued that the set-up costs of establishing an airline are likely to be high, so it is difficult to claim that there are no sunk costs faced by firms. However, the key issue is that market conditions on particular routes may well encourage contestability. Once the airline is established, the costs of flying a new route are relatively low. There are bound to be some advertising costs, but otherwise an airline can switch aircraft to new routes quite quickly. It could then switch to other routes if profits were disappointing. In other words, hit-and-run entry is possible on particular routes. This may mean that existing airlines will not set prices at such levels that entry is attracted.

It is also worth noting that the low-cost airlines have flourished not only by taking customers away from the existing airlines, but also by tapping a new customer base. By offering low fares and easy accessibility, they have attracted passengers who would not otherwise have dreamed of flying, and opened up many new holiday destinations.

Exercise 6.4

Discuss ways in which price discrimination may be used by airlines.

Cinema admissions

Another significant part of the leisure market is the cinema. The year 1995 marked 100 years since the first cinema opened its doors to the public. At its peak in 1946, it is estimated that 80% of the UK population visited the cinema at least once during the year. You can see something of this in Figure 6.1, which shows annual cinema admissions since 1935. Patterns of leisure activity changed in the period after the Second World War. One of the major influences here was the spread of television, which had a significant impact on cinema admissions.

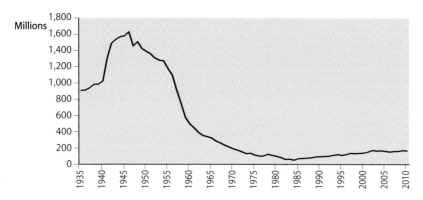

Figure 6.1 *Cinema admissions, 1935–2010*

Source: **www.cinemauk.org.uk/ukcinemasector**

The cinema market began to rally from the mid-1980s. In 1985 the first multiplex cinema opened in Milton Keynes, which allowed cinema goers more film choice. The revival was strengthened in more recent times as more screens went digital, and 3D films were launched. These innovations were needed for cinemas to begin to rebuild their audiences in the face of a changed market environment.

In terms of market structure, the cinema market looks highly concentrated in a number of dimensions. In the heyday of Hollywood, it is well known that the big studios dominated film production. This part of the market remains highly concentrated. Measured by box office takings, the top ten distributors in 2010 had a 94% share of the market in the UK and the Republic of Ireland. Indeed, the top five (Warner Bros, 20th Century Fox, Paramount, Walt Disney and Universal) took 73.2% of the market. However, there was also concentration amongst exhibitors. The top five exhibitors owned 75.5% of screens in the UK, with the top three (Odeon, Cineworld and Vue) owning 61.8%.

This degree of concentration may suggest oligopoly. However, it is important to re-member that there is no unique model of oligopoly, so it is not possible to say whether market failure will arise as a result of the concentration. For example, it could be argued that the extent to which the distributors are able to exercise market power as dominant sellers of the rights to show films may be counterbalanced by the fact that they are supplying to relatively few exhibitors. Technically, a market with a few buyers of a good is known as an **oligopsony**.

There are other reasons why it could be argued that market power for either distribu-tors or exhibitors will be limited. Cinemas operate in a wider market for leisure activity, so it is not possible to argue that there are no substitutes for cinema attendance. In the broader leisure market, cinemas must compete with other forms of activity that people engage in if they want a night out — dining at a restaurant, or watching sport, for ex-ample. In addition, cinemas need to compete with TV and other forms of indoor leisure activity. The impact that the spread of TV had on the cinema market has already been noted. It is also worth noting that the video market has been buoyant in recent years. The number of films sold on video increased by a factor of more than three between 1999 and 2008, and here again, improved technology has made watching films at home more attractive, with bigger and better TVs, DVDs and Blu-Ray. This provides competition for the exhibitors, although the distributors are involved in these markets as well.

In 2006, the Competition Commission investigated a proposed merger between Vue Entertainment Holdings (UK) Ltd and A3 Cinema Limited. The commission took the view that from a consumer perspective, the relevant market was local. Consumers would decide which film they wanted to view, and then look for the nearest cinema at which it was showing. The commission thus evaluated the effect of the merger on potential competition by checking whether there were cinemas to compete with Vue within a 20-minute drive time. In the case of Basingstoke, the commission found that Vue would own the only cinemas within a 20-minute drive time from Basingstoke, and they concluded that this would mean a substantial lessening of competition. In the case of Edinburgh, no such problem would arise. The commission also considered whether the increase in national markets would have a significant impact on Vue's negotiating position with its suppliers, such as screen advertising contractors, distributors and suppliers of food and drink for sale at the cinemas. Again, the impact was not expected to be great, and the merger was allowed to go ahead.

Monopolistic competition in the leisure sector

The theory of monopolistic competition describes a market with some features of monopoly and some features of perfect competition. Barriers to entry are low, so the market has many firms. However, firms in the market use product differentiation to influence consumers, and thus face downward-sloping demand curves.

If you look back at the analysis in Chapter 3, you will see that this form of market structure has implications for both productive and allocative efficiency. Firms produce at a level of output that is below that at which long-run average cost would reach the minimum, so there is not productive efficiency. Furthermore, price is set above marginal cost, so allocative efficiency is not achieved either.

A growing section of the leisure sector is food outlets. The number of restaurants and fast-food outlets has mushroomed in recent decades, and on many high streets in UK towns there is a proliferation of eating places and takeaways. This market seems highly contestable, as the set-up costs for starting a new restaurant or takeaway are relatively low. One of the characteristics of a market operating under monopolistic competition is the product differentiation that takes place. Each individual seller sets out to be different from its competitors. This is certainly a characteristic of the fast-food sector, where outlets offer different styles of cuisine – burgers, Indian, Chinese, Thai, Mexican and so on. Before condemning such a market as being damaging to consumers because of the effect on productive and allocative efficiency, it is worth being aware that this market offers consumers a wide range of choice for fast food. If they value this choice, then this should be seen as a benefit that arises because of the market structure.

Exercise 6.5

Discuss the factors that may have enabled large firms such as McDonald's, Burger King or KFC to become established as large firms in the fast-food sector alongside the many small competing firms.

Another part of the leisure sector that typifies monopolistic competition is local taxi markets. Count the local taxi companies in your local *Yellow Pages*. Again, firms may seek to differentiate their products through having a fleet livery, by advertising pre-booking only or by offering a limousine service. There may also be firms that specialise in longer-distance trips, say to airports.

Summary

➤ Market structure is important in determining whether allocative efficiency can be achieved.

➤ However, productive efficiency must also be taken into account.

➤ The package holiday market has become oligopolistic, with a few large firms dominating the market.

➤ However, the growth in the internet has meant that the market has become contestable, and the existing firms are facing intense competition from online entrants.

➤ Television broadcasting has also shown oligopolistic tendencies in the past, and given its characteristics as a public good and a merit good, there has been much government intervention and regulation.

➤ Again, changing technology has transformed the market and allowed greater competition among broadcasters.

➤ Spectator sport is another part of the leisure sector where the competition authorities have been active, particularly in relation to the growth of satellite broadcasting, where BSkyB has become a major player with a monopoly in certain areas.

➤ The low-cost airlines have transformed the market for air travel, making use of a thorough understanding of costs and the use of price discrimination.

➤ Cinemas constitute another significant segment of the leisure sector, and offer further insights into the effect of market structure.

➤ The leisure sector also offers examples of monopolistic competition in food outlets and taxi markets.

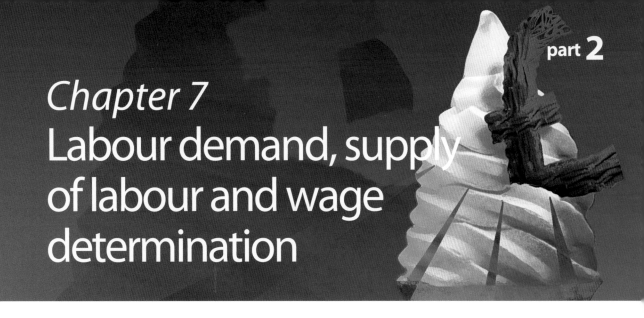

part **2**

Chapter 7
Labour demand, supply of labour and wage determination

The economic analysis of labour markets sheds light on a range of topical issues. How are wages determined? Differences in wages between people in different occupations and with different skills can be contentious. For example, why should Premiership footballers or pop stars earn such high wages compared with nurses or firefighters? This chapter begins by looking at the labour market as an application of demand and supply analysis.

Learning outcomes

After studying this chapter, you should:

➤ understand that the demand for labour is a derived demand
➤ be aware of the relationship between labour input and total and marginal physical product
➤ understand the concept of marginal revenue product
➤ be familiar with how a profit-maximising firm chooses the quantity of labour input to use in production
➤ be aware of the factors that influence the elasticity of demand for labour
➤ understand the decision of an individual worker as regards labour supply
➤ be aware of the choice made by the individual worker between work and leisure
➤ understand the reasons for earnings differentials between people working in different occupations and with different skills

Demand for labour

Firms are involved in production. They organise the factors of production in order to produce output. Labour is one of the key factors of production used by firms in this process, but notice that labour is valued not for its own sake, but for the output that it produces. In other words, the fundamental reason for firms to demand labour is for the revenue that can be obtained from selling the output that is produced by using labour.

The demand for labour is thus a **derived demand**, and understanding this is crucial for an analysis of the labour market.

To illustrate this, consider a firm that manufactures cricket bats. The firm hires labourers to operate the machinery that is used in production. However, the firm does not hire a labourer because he or she is a nice person. The firm aims to make profit by selling the cricket bats produced, and the labourer is needed because of the labour services that he or she provides. This notion of derived demand underpins the analysis of labour markets.

Chapter 1 introduced the notion of the short-run production function, showing the relationship between the quantity of labour input used and the quantity of output produced. Figure 7.1 should remind you of this. Here TPP_L is the **total physical product of labour**. As this is a short-run production function, capital cannot be varied: remember, this is how the short run is defined in this context.

The curve is drawn to show diminishing returns to labour. In other words, as labour input increases, the amount of additional output that is produced diminishes. This is because capital becomes relatively scarcer as the amount of labour increases without a corresponding increase in capital.

In examining the demand for labour, it is helpful to work with the **marginal physical product of labour**, which is the amount of additional output produced if the firm increases its labour input by 1 unit (e.g. adding 1 more person-hour), holding capital constant. This is in fact given by the slope of TPP_L. An example is shown in Figure 7.2. When labour input is relatively low, such as at L_0, the additional output

 Key *term*

derived demand: demand for a good not for its own sake, but for what it produces — for example, labour is demanded for the output that it produces

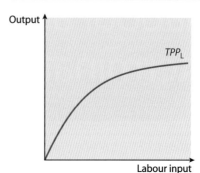

Figure 7.1 *A short-run production function*

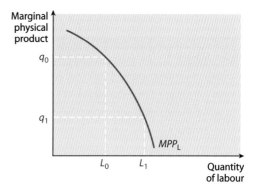

Figure 7.2 *The marginal physical product of labour*

 Key *term*

total physical product of labour (TPP_L): in the short run, the total amount of output produced at different levels of labour input with capital held fixed

marginal physical product of labour (MPP_L): the additional quantity of output produced by an additional unit of labour input

produced by an extra unit of labour is relatively high, at q_0, since the extra unit of labour has plenty of capital with which to work. However, as more labour is added,

the marginal physical product falls, so at L_1 labour the marginal physical product is only q_1.

What matters to the firm is the revenue that it will receive from selling the additional output produced. In considering the profit-maximising amount of labour to employ, therefore, the firm needs to consider the marginal physical product multiplied by the marginal revenue received from selling the extra output, which is known as the **marginal revenue product of labour** (MRP_L).

> **Key term**
>
> **marginal revenue product of labour** (MRP_L): the additional revenue received by a firm as it increases output by using an additional unit of labour input, i.e. the marginal physical product of labour multiplied by the marginal revenue received by the firm

If the firm is operating under perfect competition, then marginal revenue and price are the same and MRP_L is MPP_L multiplied by the price. However, if the firm faces a downward-sloping demand curve, it has to reduce the price of its product in order to sell the additional output. Marginal revenue is then lower than price, as the firm must lower the price on *all* of the output that it sells, not just on the last unit sold.

Consider a firm operating under perfect competition, and setting out to maximise profits. Figure 7.3 shows the marginal revenue product curve. The question to consider is how the firm chooses how much labour input to use. This decision is based partly on knowledge of the MRP_L, but it also depends on the cost of labour.

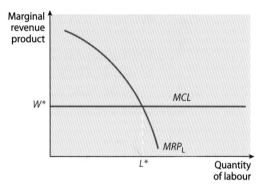

Figure 7.3 *The labour input decision of a profit-maximising firm under perfect competition*

The main cost of using labour is the wages paid to the workers. There may be other costs – hiring costs and so on – but these can be set aside for the moment. Assuming that the labour market is perfectly competitive, so that the firm cannot influence the market wage and can obtain as much labour as it wants at the going wage rate, the wage can be regarded as the *marginal cost of labour (MCL)*.

If the marginal revenue received by the firm from selling the extra output produced by extra labour (i.e. the MRP_L) is higher than the wage, then hiring more labour will add to profits. On the other hand, if the MRP_L is lower than the wage, then the firm is already hiring too much labour. Thus, it pays the firm to hire labour up to the point where the MRP_L is just equal to the wage. On Figure 7.3, if the wage is W^*, the firm is maximising profits at L^*. The MRP_L curve thus represents the firm's demand for labour curve. This approach is known as *marginal productivity theory.*

This profit-maximising condition can be written as:

wage = marginal revenue × marginal physical product of labour

which is the same as:

marginal revenue = wage/MPP_L [= marginal cost]

Remember that capital input is fixed for the firm in the short run, so the wage divided by the MPP_L is the firm's cost per unit of output at the margin. This shows that the profit-maximising condition is the same as that derived for a profit-maximising firm in Chapter 1: in other words, profit is maximised where marginal revenue equals marginal cost. This is just another way of looking at the firm's decision.

Exercise 7.1

Table 7.1 shows how the total physical product of labour varies with labour input for a firm operating under perfect competition in both product and labour markets. The price of the product is £5 and the wage rate is £30.

a   Calculate the marginal physical product of labour at each level of labour input.

b   Calculate the marginal revenue product of labour at each level of labour input.

c   Plot the MRP_L on a graph and identify the profit-maximising level of labour input.

d   Suppose that the firm faces fixed costs of £10. Calculate total revenue and total costs at each level of labour input, and check the profit-maximising level.

Labour input per period	Output (goods per period)
0	0
1	7
2	15
3	22
4	27
5	29

Table 7.1 A profit-maximising firm

Factors affecting the position of the demand for labour curve

There are a number of factors that determine the *position* of a firm's labour demand curve. First, anything that affects the marginal physical product of labour will also affect the MRP_L. For example, if a new technological advance raises the productivity of labour, it will also affect the position of the MRP_L. In Figure 7.4 you can see how the demand for labour would change if there were an increase in the marginal productivity of labour as a result of new technology. Initially demand is at MRP_{L0}, but the increased technology pushes the curve to MRP_{L1}. If the wage remains at W^*, the quantity of labour hired by the firm increases from L_0 to L_1. Similarly, in the long run, if a firm expands the size of its capital stock, this will also affect the demand for labour.

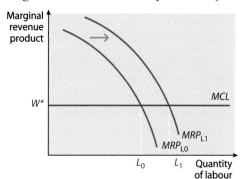

Figure 7.4 The effect of improved technology

As MRP_L is given by MPP_L multiplied by marginal revenue, any change in marginal revenue will also affect labour demand. In a perfectly competitive product market, this means that any change in the price of the product will also affect labour demand. For example, suppose there is a fall in demand for a firm's product, so that the equilibrium price falls. This will have a knock-on effect on the firm's demand for labour, as illustrated in Figure 7.5. Initially, the firm was demanding L_0 labour at the wage rate W^*, but the fall in demand for the product leads to a fall in marginal revenue product (even though the physical productivity of labour has not changed), from MRP_{L0} to MRP_{L1}. Only L_1 labour is now demanded at the wage rate W^*. This serves as a reminder that the demand for labour is a derived demand that is intimately bound up with the demand for the firm's product.

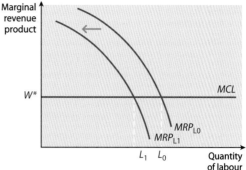

Figure 7.5 *The effect of a fall in the demand for a firm's product on the demand for labour*

A number of possible reasons could underlie a change in the price of a firm's product — it could reflect changes in the price of other goods, changes in consumer incomes or changes in consumer preferences. All of these indirectly affect the demand for labour.

Summary

➤ The demand for labour is a derived demand, as the firm wants labour not for its own sake, but for the output that it produces.

➤ In the short run, a firm faces diminishing returns to increases in labour input if capital is held constant.

➤ The marginal physical product of labour is the amount of output produced if the firm employs an additional unit of labour, keeping capital input fixed.

➤ The marginal revenue product of labour is the marginal physical product multiplied by marginal revenue.

➤ With perfect competition in the product market, marginal revenue and price are the same, but if the firm needs to reduce its price in order to sell additional units of output, then marginal revenue is smaller than price.

➤ A profit-maximising firm chooses labour input such that the marginal cost of labour is equal to the marginal revenue product of labour. This is equivalent to setting marginal revenue equal to marginal cost.

➤ The firm has a downward-sloping demand curve for labour, given by the marginal revenue product curve.

➤ The position of the firm's labour demand curve depends on those factors that influence the marginal physical product, such as technology and efficiency, but also on the price of the firm's product.

Elasticity of the demand for labour

In addition to the factors affecting the *position* of the demand for labour curve, it is also important to examine its *shape*. In particular, what factors affect the firm's elasticity of demand for labour with respect to changes in the wage rate? In other words, how sensitive is a firm's demand for labour to a change in the wage rate (the cost of labour)?

In studying AS economics, you will have been introduced to the influences on the price elasticity of demand, and identified the most important as being the availability of substitutes, the relative size of expenditure on a good in the overall budget and the time period over which the elasticity is measured (see *AS Economics, Chapter 4*). In looking at the elasticity of demand for labour, similar influences can be seen to be at work.

One significant influence on the elasticity of demand for labour is the extent to which other factors of production, such as capital, can be substituted for labour in the production process. If capital or some other factor can be readily substituted for labour, then an increase in the wage rate (ceteris paribus) will induce the firm to reduce its demand for labour by relatively more than if there were no substitute for labour. The extent to which labour and capital are substitutable varies between economic activities, depending on the technology of production, as there may be some sectors in which it is relatively easy for labour and capital to be substituted, and others in which it is quite difficult.

Second, the share of labour costs in the firm's total costs is important in determining the elasticity of demand for labour. In many service activities, labour is a highly significant share of total costs, so firms tend to be sensitive to changes in the cost of labour. However, in some capital-intensive manufacturing activity, labour may comprise a much smaller share of total production costs.

Whether capital can be substituted for labour varies, depending on the technology of production

Third, as was argued above, capital will tend to be inflexible in the short run. Therefore, if a firm faces an increase in wages, it may have little flexibility in substituting towards capital in the short run, so the demand for labour may be relatively inelastic. However, in the longer term, the firm will be able to adjust the factors of production towards a different overall balance. Therefore, the elasticity of demand for labour is likely to be higher in the long run than in the short run.

These three influences closely parallel the analysis of what affects the price elasticity of demand. However, as the demand for labour is a derived demand, there is an additional influence that must be taken into account: the price elasticity of demand for the product. The more price elastic is demand for the product, the more sensitive will the firm be to a change in the wage rate, as high elasticity of demand for the product limits the extent to which an increase in wage costs can be passed on to consumers in the form of higher prices.

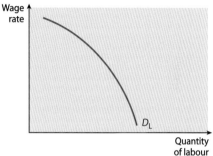

In order to derive an industry demand curve for labour, it is necessary to add up the quantities of labour that firms in that industry would want to demand at any wage rate, given the price of the product. As individual firms' demand curves are downward sloping, the industry demand curve will also slope downwards. In other words, more labour will be demanded at a lower wage rate, as shown in Figure 7.6.

Figure 7.6 *An industry demand for labour curve*

Summary

➤ The elasticity of demand for labour depends upon the degree to which capital may be substituted for labour in the production process.

➤ The share of labour in a firm's total costs will also affect the elasticity of demand for labour.

➤ Labour demand will tend to be more elastic in the long run than in the short run, as the firm needs time to adjust its production process following a change in market conditions.

➤ As the demand for labour is a derived demand, the elasticity of labour demand will also depend on the price elasticity of demand for the firm's product.

Exercise 7.2

Using diagrams, explain how each of the following will affect a firm's demand for labour:
a a fall in the selling price of the firm's product
b adoption of improved working practices that improve labour productivity
c an increase in the wage (in a situation where the firm must accept the wage as market determined)
d an increase in the demand for the firm's product

Labour supply

So far, labour supply has been considered only as it is perceived by a firm, and the assumption has been that the firm is in a perfectly competitive market for labour, and therefore cannot influence the 'price' of labour. Hence the firm sees the labour supply curve as being perfectly elastic, as drawn in Figure 7.3, where labour supply was described as *MCL*.

However, for the industry as a whole, labour supply is unlikely to be flat. Intuitively, you might expect to see an upward-sloping labour supply curve. The reason for this is that more people will tend to offer themselves for work when the wage is relatively high. However, this is only part of the background to the industry labour supply curve.

An increase in the wage rate paid to workers in an industry will have two effects. On the one hand, it will tend to attract more workers into that industry, thereby increasing labour supply. However, the change may also affect the supply decisions of workers already in that industry, and for existing workers an increase in the wage rate may have ambiguous effects.

Individual labour supply

Consider an individual worker who is deciding how many hours of labour to supply. Every choice comes with an *opportunity cost*, so if a worker chooses to take more leisure time, he or she is choosing to forgo income-earning opportunities. In other words, the wage rate can be seen as the opportunity cost of leisure. It is the income that the worker has to sacrifice in order to enjoy leisure time.

Now think about the likely effects of an increase in the wage rate. Such an increase raises the opportunity cost of leisure. This in turn has two effects. First, as leisure time is now more costly, there will be a substitution effect against leisure. In other words, workers will be motivated to work longer hours.

However, as the higher wage brings the worker a higher level of real income, a second effect comes into play, encouraging the consumption of more goods and services — including leisure, if it is assumed that leisure is a *normal good.*

Notice that these two effects work against each other. The substitution effect encourages workers to offer more labour at a higher wage because of the effect of the change in the opportunity cost of leisure. However, the real income effect encourages the worker to demand more leisure as a result of the increase in income. The net effect could go either way.

It might be argued that at relatively low wages the substitution effect will tend to be the stronger. However, as the wage continues to rise, the income effect may gradually become stronger, so that at some wage level the worker will choose to supply less labour and will demand more leisure. The individual labour supply curve will then be backward bending, as shown in Figure 7.7, where an increase in the wage rate above W^* induces the individual to supply fewer hours of work in order to enjoy more leisure time.

It is important to realise that decisions about labour supply may also be influenced by job satisfaction. A worker who finds his or her work to be satisfying may be prepared to accept a lower wage than a worker who really hates every minute spent at work. Indeed, firms may provide other **non-pecuniary benefits** – in other words, firms may provide benefits that are not fully reflected in wages. These are sometimes known as *fringe benefits.* This might include a subsidised canteen or other social facilities. It could also include in-work training, pension schemes or job security. If this is the case, then in choosing one job over another, workers may not only consider the wage rate, but the overall package offered by employers. In other words, by providing non-pecuniary benefits, firms may effectively shift the position of their labour supply curves, as workers will be prepared to supply more labour at any given wage rate. It may also be seen as a way in which firms can encourage loyalty, and thus hold on to workers when the job market is tight.

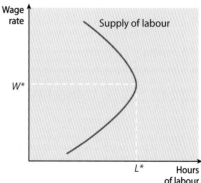

Figure 7.7 *A backward-bending individual labour supply curve*

Key term

non-pecuniary benefits: benefits offered to workers by firms that are not financial in nature

Industry labour supply

At industry level, the labour supply curve can be expected to be upward sloping. Although individual workers may display backward-bending supply curves, when workers in a market are aggregated, higher wages will induce people to join the market, either from outside the workforce altogether or from other industries where wages have not risen.

Summary

➤ For an individual worker, a choice needs to be made between income earned from working and leisure.

➤ The wage rate can be seen as the opportunity cost of leisure.

➤ An increase in the wage rate will encourage workers to substitute work for leisure through the substitution effect.

➤ However, there is also an income effect, which may mean that workers will demand more leisure at higher income levels.

➤ If the income effect dominates the substitution effect, then the individual labour supply curve may become backward bending.

➤ However, when aggregated to the industry level, higher wages will encourage more people into the industry such that the industry supply curve is not expected to be backward bending.

Labour market equilibrium

Bringing demand and supply curves together for an industry shows how the equilibrium wage is determined. Figure 7.8 shows a downward-sloping labour demand curve (D_L) based on marginal productivity theory, and an upward-sloping labour supply curve (S_L). Equilibrium is found at the intersection of demand and supply. If the wage is lower than W^* employers will not be able to fill all their vacancies, and will have to offer a higher wage to attract more workers. If the wage is higher than W^* there will be an excess supply of labour, and the wage will drift down until W^* is reached and equilibrium obtained.

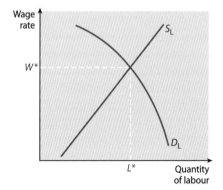

Figure 7.8 *Labour market equilibrium*

Comparative static analysis can be used to examine the effects of changes in market conditions. For instance, a change in the factors that determine the position of the labour demand curve will induce a movement of labour demand and an adjustment in the equilibrium wage. Suppose there is an increase in the demand

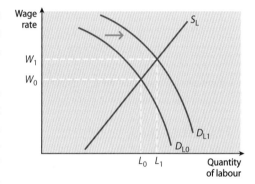

Figure 7.9 *An increase in the demand for labour*

for the firm's product. This will lead to a rightward shift in the demand for labour, say from D_{L0} to D_{L1} in Figure 7.9. This in turn will lead to a new market equilibrium, with the wage rising from W_0 to W_1.

This may not be the final equilibrium position, however. If the higher wages in this market now encourage workers to switch from other industries in which wages have not risen, this will lead to a longer-term shift to the right of the labour supply curve. In a free market, the shift will continue until wage differentials are no longer sufficient to encourage workers to transfer.

Exercise 7.3

Sketch a diagram to analyse the effects on labour market equilibrium if there is a fall in the selling price of a firm's product.

Summary

➤ Labour market equilibrium is found at the intersection of labour demand and labour supply.

➤ This determines the equilibrium wage rate for an industry.

➤ Comparative static analysis can be used to analyse the effects of changes in market conditions.

➤ Changes in relative wages between sectors may induce movement of workers between industries.

Labour markets

So far, the focus has been on the demand and supply of labour, sometimes seen through the eyes of a firm, sometimes through the eyes of a worker and sometimes looking at an industry labour market. It is important to realise that these are separate levels of analysis. In particular, there is no single labour market in an economy like the UK, any more than there is a single market for goods. In reality, there is a complex network of labour markets for people with different skills and for people in different occupations, and there are overlapping markets for labour corresponding to different product markets.

Transfer earnings and economic rent

Transfer earnings

Many factors of production have some flexibility about them, in the sense that they can be employed in a variety of alternative uses. A worker may be able to work in different occupations and industries; computers can be put to use in a wide range of activities. The decision to use a factor of production for one particular job rather than another carries an opportunity cost, which can be seen in terms of the next best alternative activity in which that factor could have been employed.

For example, consider a woman who chooses to work as a waitress because the pay is better than she could obtain as a shop assistant. By making this choice, she forgoes the opportunity to work at, say, John Lewis. The opportunity cost is seen in terms of this forgone alternative. If John Lewis were to raise its rates of pay in order to attract more staff, there would come a point where the waitress might reconsider her decision and decide to be a shop assistant after all, as the opportunity cost of being a waitress has risen.

The threshold at which this decision is taken leads to the definition of **transfer earnings**. Transfer earnings are defined in terms of the minimum payment that is required in order to keep a factor of production in its present use.

Economic rent

In a labour market, transfer earnings can be thought of as the minimum payment that will keep the marginal

Key *term*

transfer earnings: the minimum payment required to keep a factor of production in its present use

worker in his or her present occupation or sector. This payment will vary from worker to worker; moreover, where there is a market in which all workers receive the same pay for the same job, there will be some workers who receive a wage in excess of their transfer earnings. This excess of payment to a factor over and above what is required to keep it in its present use is known as **economic rent**.

Key term

economic rent: a payment received by a factor of production over and above what would be needed to keep it in its present use

The total payments to a factor can thus be divided between these two — part of the payment is transfer earnings, and the remainder is economic rent.

Probably the best way of explaining how a worker's earnings can be divided between transfer earnings and economic rent is through an appropriate diagram. Figure 7.10 illustrates the two concepts. In the labour market as drawn, firms' demand for labour is a downward-sloping function of the wage rate. Workers' supply of labour also depends on the wage rate, with workers being prepared to supply more labour to the labour market at higher wages. Equilibrium is the point at which demand equals supply, with wage rate W^* and quantity of labour L^*.

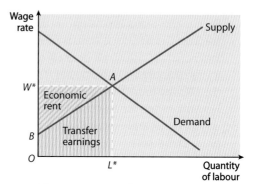

Figure 7.10 Transfer earnings and economic rent

Think about the nature of the labour supply curve. It reveals how much labour the workers are prepared to supply at any given wage rate. At the equilibrium wage rate W^*, there is a worker who is supplying labour at the margin. If the wage rate were to fall even slightly below W^*, the worker would withdraw from this labour market, perhaps to take alternative employment in another sector or occupation. In other words, the wage rate can be regarded as the transfer earnings of the marginal worker. A similar argument can be made about any point along the labour supply curve.

This means that the area under the supply curve up to the equilibrium point can be interpreted as the transfer earnings of workers in this labour market. In Figure 7.10 this is given by the area $OBAL^*$.

Total earnings are given by the wage rate multiplied by the quantity of labour supplied (here, area OW^*AL^*). Economic rent is thus that part of total earnings that is *not* transfer earnings. In Figure 7.10 this is the triangle BW^*A. The rationale is that this area represents the total excess that workers receive by being paid a wage (W^*) that is above the minimum required to keep them employed in this market.

If you think about it, you will see that this is similar to the notion of producer surplus, which is the difference between the price received by firms for a good or service and the price at which the firms would have been prepared to supply that good or service.

The balance between transfer earnings and economic rent

What determines the balance between the two aspects of total earnings? In this connection, the elasticity of supply of labour is of critical importance.

This can be seen by studying diagrams showing varying degrees of elasticity of supply. First, consider two extreme situations. Figure 7.11 shows a labour market in which supply is perfectly elastic. This implies that there is limitless supply of labour at the wage rate *W*. In this situation there is no economic rent to be gained from labour supply, and all earnings are transfer earnings. Any reduction of the wage below *W* will mean that all workers leave the market.

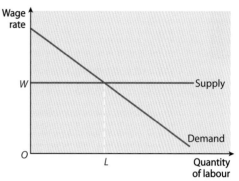

Figure 7.11 *Perfectly elastic labour supply*

Now consider Figure 7.12. Here labour supply is perfectly inelastic. There is a fixed amount of labour being supplied to the market and, whatever the wage rate, that amount of labour remains the same. Another way of looking at this is that there is no minimum payment needed to keep labour in its present use. Now the entire earnings of the factor are made up by economic rent (i.e. the area *OWAL*).

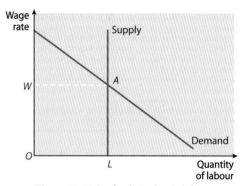

Figure 7.12 *Perfectly inelastic labour supply*

This illustrates how important the elasticity of labour supply is in determining the balance between transfer earnings and economic rent. The more inelastic supply is, the higher the proportion of total earnings that is made up of economic rent.

Surgeons and butchers: the importance of supply

Consider an example of differential earnings – say, surgeons and butchers. First think about the surgeons. Surgeons are in relatively inelastic supply, at least in the short run. The education required to become a surgeon is long and demanding, and is certainly essential for entry into the occupation. Furthermore, not everyone is cut out to become a surgeon, as this is a field that requires certain innate abilities and talents. This implies that the supply of surgeons is limited and does not vary a great deal with the wage rate. If this is the case, then the earnings of surgeons are largely made up of economic rent.

The situation may be reinforced by the fact that, once an individual has trained as a surgeon, there may be few alternative occupations to which, if disgruntled, he or she could transfer. There is a natural limit to how many surgeons there are, *and* to their willingness to exit from the market.

How about butchers? The training programme for butchers is less arduous than for surgeons, and a wider range of people is suitable for employment in this occupation. Labour supply for butchers is thus likely to be more elastic than for surgeons, and so economic rent will be relatively less important than in the previous case. If butchers were to receive high enough wages, more people would be attracted to the trade and wage rates would eventually fall.

In addition, there are other occupations into which butchers can transfer when they have had enough of cutting up all that meat: they might look to other sections of the catering sector, for example. This reinforces the relatively high elasticity of supply.

The importance of demand

Economic rent has been seen to be more important for surgeons than for butchers, but is this the whole story? The discussion so far has centred entirely on the supply side of the market. But demand is also important.

Indeed, it is the position of the demand curve when interacting with supply that determines the equilibrium wage rate in a labour market. It may well be that the supply of workers skilled in underwater basket weaving is strictly limited; but if there is no demand for underwater basket weavers then there is no scope for that skill to earn high economic rents. In the above example, it is the relatively strong demand for surgeons relative to their limited supply that leads to a relatively high equilibrium wage in the market.

Evaluation

This analysis can be applied to answer some questions that often appear about the labour market. In particular, why should the top footballers and pop stars be paid such high salaries, whereas valued professions such as nurses and firefighters are paid much less?

A footballer such as Wayne Rooney is valued because of the talent that he displays on the pitch, and because of his ability to bring in the crowds who want to see him play. This makes him a good revenue earner for his club, and reflects his high marginal productivity. In addition, his skills are rare — some would say unique. Wayne Rooney is thus in extremely limited supply. This combination of high marginal productivity and limited supply leads to a high equilibrium wage rate.

The talents of Wayne Rooney are in limited supply, which leads to a high equilibrium wage rate

For nurses and firefighters, society may value them highly in one sense – that they carry out a vital, and sometimes dangerous, occupation. However, they are not valued in the sense of displaying high marginal productivity. Furthermore, the supply is by no means as limited as in the case of top-class professional footballers. These factors taken together help to explain why there are such large differences in salaries between occupations. This is one example of how marginal productivity theory helps to explain features of the real world that non-economists often find puzzling.

Summary

➤ In a modern economy, there is a complex network of labour markets for workers with different skills, working in different occupations and industries.

➤ The total payments to a factor of production can be separated into transfer earnings and economic rent.

➤ Transfer earnings represent the minimum payment needed to keep a factor of production in its present use.

➤ Economic rent is a payment received by a factor of production over and above what would be needed to keep it in its present use.

➤ The balance between transfer earnings and economic rent depends critically on the elasticity of supply of a particular kind of labour.

➤ The position of the demand curve is also important.

Education and the labour market

The above discussion has highlighted the importance of education and training in influencing wage differentials between occupational groups. Education and training might be regarded as a form of *barrier to entry* into a labour market, affecting the elasticity of supply of labour. Because of differences in innate talents and abilities – not to mention personal inclinations – wage differentials can persist even in the long run in certain occupations. However, economists expect there to be some long-run equilibrium level of differential that reflects the preference and natural talent aspects of various occupations.

Changes in the pattern of consumer demand for goods over time will lead to changes in those equilibrium differentials. For example, during the computer revolution, when firms were increasing their use of computers at work and households were increasing their use of home computers, there was a need for more computer programmers to create the software that people wanted, and a need for more computer engineers to fix

During the computer revolution, firms increased their use of computers

the computers when they crashed. This meant that the wage differential for these workers increased. This in turn led to a proliferation of courses on offer to train or retrain people in these skills. Then, as the supply of such workers began to increase, so the wage differential narrowed.

This is what economists would expect to observe if the labour market is working effectively, with wages acting as signals to workers about what skills are in demand. It is part of the way in which a market system guides the allocation of resources.

Individual educational choices

In specific cases, such as that of computer programmers, you can see how individuals may respond to market signals. Word gets around that computer programmers are in high demand, and individual workers and job-seekers respond to that. However, not all education is geared so specifically towards such specific gaps in the market. How do individuals take decisions about education?

Such a decision can be regarded as an example of *cost–benefit analysis.* In trying to decide whether or not to undertake further education, an individual needs to balance the costs of such education against its benefits. One important consideration is that the costs tend to come in the short run, but the benefits only in the long run. Much of the discussion of student university tuition fees centres on this issue. Should students incur high debts now in the expectation of future higher earnings? Work through Exercise 7.4 to take this further.

Exercise 7.4

Suppose you are considering undertaking a university education. Compile a list of the benefits and the costs that you expect to encounter if you choose to do so. Discuss how you would go about balancing the benefits and costs, remembering that the timing of these needs to be taken into account.

In Exercise 7.4 you will have identified a range of benefits and costs. On the costs side are the direct costs in terms of tuition fees and living expenses, and there are also opportunity costs — the fact that you will have to delay the time when you start earning an income. But there are benefits to set against these costs, which may include the enjoyment you get from undertaking further study and the fact that university can be a great experience — that is, it can be a consumption good as well as an investment good. And, almost certainly, you have considered the fact that you can expect higher future earnings as a university graduate than as a non-graduate.

A recent study by the OECD investigated the relationship between education and earnings in a range of countries. Figure 7.13 presents some of the results, showing the differential in earnings between university graduates and those who left education

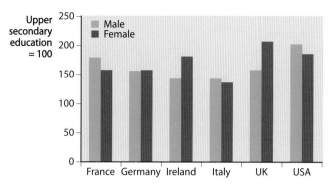

Figure 7.13 *Education and earnings*

Note: the graph shows average employment earnings of people with the equivalent of UK university undergraduate degrees relative to people with only secondary education.

Source: OECD.

at the end of secondary schooling. The data are expressed as index numbers, with earnings of secondary school leavers set equal to 100. Thus, for the UK, a male graduate earned 57% more than a secondary school leaver, whereas a female graduate earned 106% more. A study in *Labour Market Trends* in March 2003 also found that those leaving education at age 21 seem to experience around a 50% wage increase compared with those leaving education at 16; however, in that study there was no significant difference between men and women.

These data are a little difficult to interpret. They cannot be taken to mean that a university education necessarily increases the *productivity* of workers, because it may be that those who chose to undertake university education were naturally more able. This is the 'signalling' view of education — that the value of the degree is not so much what was learned during the programme of study as an indication that the person was capable of doing it. However, the fact that the returns to education are seen to vary across degree subjects suggests that employers do look for some value-added to emerge from university education. The evidence suggests that arts degrees have relatively little impact on average wages, whereas degrees in economics, management and law have large effects.

Degrees in law have a large impact on average wages

In spite of such evidence that lifetime earnings can be boosted by education, people may still demand too little education for the best interest of society, as was discussed in *AS Economics, Chapter 6*. This may be because there are *externality effects* associated with education. Although education has been shown to improve productivity, it has also been found that *groups* of educated workers are able to cooperate and work together so that collectively they are even more productive than they are as individuals. From this point of view, an individual worker may not perceive the full social benefit of higher education.

Figure 7.14 is a reminder of this argument. If marginal social benefit (*MSB*) is higher than marginal private benefit (*MPB*), there is a tendency for individuals to demand too little education, choosing to acquire Q_1 education rather than the amount Q^*, which is the best for society. This argument may be used to suggest that government should encourage people to undertake more education.

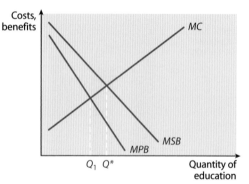

Figure 7.14 *Education as a positive consumption externality*

Summary

> Wage differentials may act as signals to guide potential workers in their demand for training and retraining.

> People demand education partly for the effect it will have on their future earnings potential.

> Externality effects may mean that people choose to demand less education than is desirable for society as a whole.

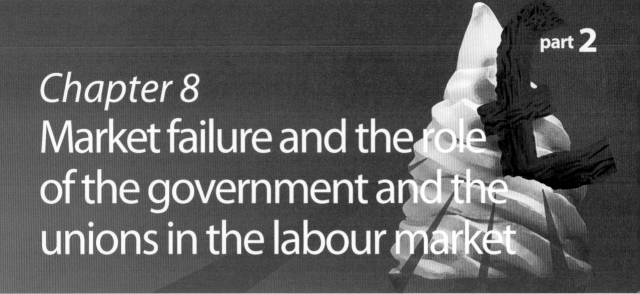

Chapter 8
Market failure and the role of the government and the unions in the labour market

Product markets do not always work perfectly. For example, a firm (or small group of firms) may come to dominate a market and use its market power to increase its supernormal profits to the detriment of the consumer. It has also been shown that some government interventions in product markets do not always have their intended effects. This chapter explores some of the ways in which imperfections can be manifest in labour markets. It also examines the extent to which legislation has been able to outlaw discrimination on the basis of ethnic origin or gender. The role of trade unions in a modern economy is also discussed.

Learning outcomes

After studying this chapter, you should:
- understand ways in which labour markets may be imperfect
- be aware of the operation of a labour market in which there is a monopsony buyer of labour
- be aware of ways in which governments may cause imperfections in labour markets through their interventions
- understand how unemployment may arise in a market
- understand the role of trade unions in the economy
- understand the effects of trade union activity on the labour market
- understand the nature and causes of inequality and evaluate measures to reduce inequality in the UK
- be able to discuss the implications of an ageing population

Market failure in labour markets

The previous chapter has described the operation of labour markets and the way in which equilibrium can be achieved. However, as with product markets, there are many ways in which labour markets may fail to achieve the most desirable results for society at large. Such market failure can occur on either the demand or the supply side of the market. On the demand side, it may be that employers — as the buyers of labour — have

market power that can be exploited at the expense of the workers. Alternatively, it may be that some employers act against the interests of some groups of workers relative to others through some form of discrimination in their hiring practices or wage-setting behaviour. On the supply side, there may be restrictions on the supply of some types of labour, or it may be that trade unions find themselves able to bid wages up to a level that is above the free market equilibrium.

On another level, the very existence of unemployment might be interpreted as indicating disequilibrium in the labour market — although there may also be reasons to expect there always to be some unemployment in a modern economy. Finally, there are some forms of government intervention that may have unintended effects on labour markets.

Monopsony

One type of market failure in a product market occurs when there is a single *seller* of a good: that is, a monopoly market. As you may recall, a firm with this sort of market dominance is able to restrict output,

 Key term

monopsony: a market in which there is a single buyer of a good, service or factor of production

and maximise profits by setting a higher price. A similar form of market power can occur on the other side of the market if there is a single *buyer* of a good, service or factor of production. Such a market is known as a **monopsony**.

In Chapter 7 it was assumed that firms in the labour market face perfect competition, and therefore must accept the market wage. However, suppose that one firm is the sole user of a particular type of labour, or is the dominant firm in a city or region, and thus is in a monopsony situation.

Such a monopsonist faces the market supply curve of labour directly, rather than simply accepting the equilibrium market wage. It views this supply curve as its average cost of labour because it shows the average wage rate that it would need to offer to obtain any given quantity of labour input.

Figure 8.1 shows a monopsonist's demand curve for labour, which is the marginal revenue product curve (MRP_L), and its supply curve of labour, seen by the firm as its average cost curve of labour (AC_L). If the market were perfectly competitive, equilibrium would be where supply equals demand, which would be with the firm using L^* labour at a wage rate W^*.

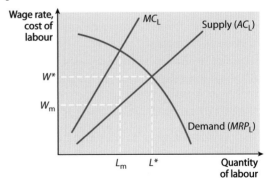

Figure 8.1 A monopsony buyer of labour

From the perspective of the monopsonist firm facing the supply curve directly, if at any point it wants to hire more labour, it has to offer a higher wage to encourage more workers to join the market — after all, that is what the AC_L curve tells it. However, the firm would then have to pay that higher wage to *all* its workers, so the *marginal cost* of hiring the extra worker is not just the wage paid to that worker, but the increased wage paid to all the other workers as well. So the marginal cost of labour curve (MC_L) can be added to the diagram.

If the monopsonist firm wants to maximise profit, it will hire labour up to the point where the marginal cost of labour is equal to the marginal revenue product of labour. Therefore it will use labour up to the level L_m, which is where $MC_L = MRP_L$. In order to entice workers to supply this amount of labour, the firm need pay only the wage W_m. (Remember that AC_L is the supply curve of labour.) You can see, therefore, that a profit-maximising monopsonist will use less labour, and pay a lower wage, than a firm operating under perfect competition. From society's perspective, this entails a cost, just as was seen in the comparison of monopoly and perfect competition in Chapter 2.

Exercise 8.1

Figure 8.2 shows a firm in a monopsonistic labour market.

a What would the wage rate be if this market were perfectly competitive, and how much labour would be employed?

b As a monopsony, what wage would the firm offer to its workers, and how much labour would it employ?

c Which area represents the employer's wage bill?

d What surplus does this generate for the firm?

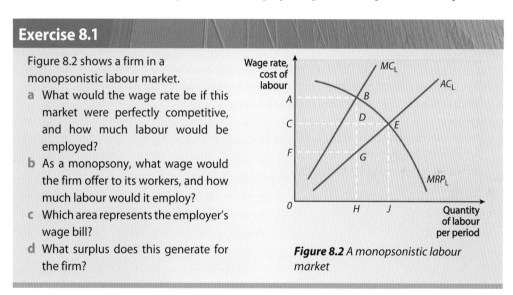

Figure 8.2 *A monopsonistic labour market*

Discrimination

In Chapter 7, it was explained that wage differentials across different labour markets within an economy such as the UK are to be expected because of differences in marginal productivity of different workers, and differences in economic rent and transfer earnings. However, the question often arises as to whether such economic analysis can explain all of the differentials in wages that can be observed. For example, consider Table 8.1.

These data point to differentials in pay and employment that require some investigation. There would seem to be a noticeable pay gap between women and men.

	Female/male pay gap (%)	Female/male part-time pay gap (%)	Ethnic employment gap (% points)
1975	36	34	n/a
1979	37	41	−1
1990	33	41	−7
1997	26	36	−9
2000	25	36	−9
2002	23	36	−9

Table 8.1
Wage differentials in the British economy

Source: Richard Dickens, Paul Gregg and Jonathan Wadsworth, 'The labour market under New Labour', *Economic Review*, September 2003.

For full-time workers this has narrowed since 1975, but for part-time workers it has not. It also appears that employment opportunities for ethnic minority groups have worsened since 1975 – in spite of legislation that has increasingly tried to ensure equal opportunities for all. It is important to explore the extent to which these differences can be explained by economic analysis, and the extent to which they reflect discrimination in pay or employment opportunities.

The mere fact that there is inequality does not prove that there is discrimination. You have seen the way in which education and training affects earnings, so differentials between different groups of people may reflect the different educational choices made by those different groups. The gender gap may also reflect the fact that childcare responsibilities interrupt the working lives of many women. This is important in terms of human capital and the build-up of experience and seniority. The increasing introduction of crèche facilities by many firms is reducing the extent of this contribution to the earnings gap, but it has not eliminated it. In addition, there have been changes in social attitudes towards female education beyond the age of 16. When girls were expected to become homemakers, education beyond 16 was not

The narrowing of the gender pay gap is partly a result of changing social attitudes

INGRAM

highly valued, so there were generations of women who missed out on education, and consequently found themselves disadvantaged in the labour market. Although attitudes have changed, such effects take a long time to work their way through the system.

Summary

➤ A market in which there is a single buyer of a good, service or factor of production is known as a monopsony market.

➤ A monopsony buyer of labour will employ less labour at a lower wage than if the market is perfectly competitive.

➤ Wage differentials and employment conditions are seen to vary between males and females and between ethnic groups, and only part of the variance can be explained by economic analysis, suggesting there may be discrimination.

Unemployment

In AS economics, unemployment was discussed at a *macroeconomic* level, as one of the key measures of an economy's overall performance (see *AS Economics, Chapter 13*). In that context a number of different causes of unemployment were identified.

Frictional unemployment was seen as arising when workers switch between jobs. This is a purely transitional phenomenon, and is necessary if the labour market is to be flexible in allowing people to transfer between firms or industries. When retraining is needed to ease the transition, the unemployment may be longer term: for example, when some sectors are declining and others are expanding, workers may need to be re-skilled in order to make the transfer. This is known as *structural unemployment*. It was also pointed out that in the macroeconomic context there may be a state of *demand-deficient unemployment*, in which aggregate demand in the economy is insufficient for the economy to reach full employment.

In a *microeconomic* context, unemployment might be seen from a different angle. While some frictional unemployment cannot be avoided, structural unemployment can be regarded as an indicator of some inflexibility in labour markets, slowing the process by which workers can move from one job to another.

One cause of structural unemployment may be that firms are not providing sufficient training to ensure a smooth transition. On-the-job training is an important way to enable workers to gain the skills that will make them more productive in the future. When firms are taking employment decisions, they are concerned not only with today's marginal revenue product of workers, but with the longer-term perspective.

Providing training is costly to a firm, however, so it will need some assurance that it will be able to reap the benefits at a later date in the form of higher productivity. It may also be aware that firms choosing not to provide training may be able to poach

its newly trained workers without having incurred the costs of the training. In other words, there is a potential *free-rider* problem here.

There may be some skills that are useful only within the firm. Such *firm-specific* skills do not pose quite the same problems. However, for generic transferable skills there is an incentive for firms to underprovide training. Some government intervention may therefore be needed to rectify this situation.

Unemployment could also arise where some people choose not to work simply because unemployment benefit is set at such a level that they are better off on benefits than accepting a low-paid job. This is an area where the government has to maintain a careful balance in policy. On the one hand, it may be seen as important to provide protection for vulnerable people who are unable to obtain

Key term

unemployment trap: a situation in which people choose to be unemployed because the level of unemployment benefit is high relative to the wage available in low-paid occupations

employment. On the other hand, if benefits are set at too generous a level, people may opt for unemployment rather than low-paid jobs. This is sometimes known as the **unemployment trap**. Unemployment that results from this is *voluntary unemployment*, in the sense that people are choosing to be unemployed because of the incentives that face them. To counter this, the government needs to ensure that 'work pays'.

Disequilibrium unemployment

One important potential cause of unemployment is disequilibrium in a labour market. Some examples of this have already been given. A wage set at a level that is above the equilibrium rate can cause unemployment in a labour market.

This is shown in Figure 8.3 where, given the demand curve D^*, the equilibrium wage is at W^*, with labour employed up to L^*. With the wage held above the equilibrium rate, at W_1, the supply of labour (S_1) exceeds the quantity of labour that firms are prepared to hire (D_1), and the difference ($S_1 - D_1$) is unemployment — the number of workers who would like a job at the going wage rate, but are unable to find a job.

This could occur for a number of reasons. In some circumstances the introduction of a minimum wage could have this effect. Another possibility is that a trade union is able to negotiate a wage that is higher than the equilibrium rate. These will be analysed shortly.

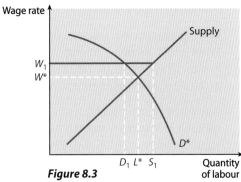

Figure 8.3
Disequilibrium unemployment

Disequilibrium unemployment could also happen where there is inflexibility in the market. For example, suppose that a firm experiences a fall in the demand for its product. As the price of the product falls, so the marginal revenue product of labour falls, and the firm would want to move to a lower employment level and pay lower wages. This

is shown in Figure 8.4. If previously the demand for labour was at D_0 then W_0 would have been the equilibrium wage rate, and employment would have been L_0, with no unemployment. When the demand for labour falls to D_1, there would be a new potential equilibrium with the wage at W^* and employment L^*. However, if the market is sluggish to adjust, perhaps because there is resistance to lowering wages from W_0 to W^*, then this will cause unemployment. In other words, with the wage remaining at W_0, workers continue to try to supply L_0 labour, but firms will only demand L_1, and the difference is unemployment. This situation of sticky wage adjustment is thus another cause of unemployment.

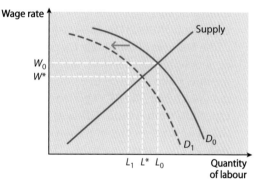

Figure 8.4 Inflexibility in wage adjustment

Labour mobility

A further reason for labour market inflexibility is that workers are not perfectly mobile. Mobility here can be seen in two important dimensions. First, there may be geographic immobility, where workers may be reluctant to move to a new region in search of appropriate employment. Second, there may be immobility between occupations. Both sorts of immobility can hinder the free operation of labour markets.

Geographic mobility

There are a number of reasons that help to explain why workers may not be freely mobile between different parts of the country. This will cause problems for the labour market if the available jobs and the available workers are not located in the same area. A key issue involves the costs that are entailed in moving to a new job in a new region. These could be considerable in social terms – people do not like to move away from their friends and relatives, or to leave the area that they know or where their favourite football team plays. Parents may not wish to disrupt their children's education. However, there are also strong economic considerations.

The relatively high rate of owner-occupied housing in the UK means that workers who are owner-occupiers may need a strong inducement to move to another part of the country in search of jobs. For council house tenants, too, it may be quite difficult to relocate to a different area for employment purposes because they will have to return to the bottom of the waiting list for housing. Differences in house prices in different parts of the country further add to the problem of matching workers to jobs.

There may also be information problems, in that it may be more difficult to find out about job availability in other areas. The internet may have reduced the costs of job search to some extent, but it is still easier to find jobs in the local area, where the reputation of firms is better known to locals. Where both partners in a relationship are working, this may also make it more difficult to find jobs further afield, and there is some evidence that females tend to be less mobile geographically than males.

International mobility of labour has increased in recent years, especially since the expansion of the EU in 2004, with the addition of ten new member countries. One of the features of the Single Market measures of 1992 was to allow free movement of people, goods, services and capital within the EU. Not all of the existing EU members allowed free movement of labour from the new members, but Britain did. As a result, the UK experienced large waves of migration from eastern Europe, especially from Poland. This was partly a response to the wage differential between the countries. As the marginal product of labour was higher in the UK than in Poland and other countries, this also meant that wages were relatively high. This wage differential thus acted as an incentive for workers to move to the UK. However, as time has gone by, this differential has narrowed, and the flows of workers have slowed.

Exercise 8.2

Draw two labour market diagrams to represent the demand and supply of labour in the UK and Poland before the EU expansion. Show on the diagrams how the two markets would adjust to a flow of workers from Poland to the UK.

Occupational mobility

The difficulty that people face in moving between occupations is an important source of labour market inflexibility, and may result in structural unemployment. Over time, it is to be expected that the pattern of consumer demand will change, and if the pattern of economic activity is to change in response, it is important that some sectors of the economy decline to enable others to expand. As the UK economy has moved away from manufacturing towards service sector activities, people have needed to be occupationally mobile to find work.

There are costs involved for workers switching between occupations. A displaced farm worker may not be able to find work as a ballet dancer without some degree of retraining! As explained earlier, firms may be expected to underprovide training to their workers because of the free-rider problem. There may therefore be a need for some government intervention to ensure that training is provided in order to combat the problem of structural unemployment and to facilitate occupational mobility.

As with geographic mobility, another factor that may impede occupational mobility is the question of information. Workers may not have enough information to enable them to judge the benefits from occupational mobility. For example, they may not be aware of their aptitude for different occupations, or the extent to which they may gain job satisfaction from a job that they have not tried. These arguments do not apply only to workers displaced by structural change in the economy. They are equally valid for workers who are in jobs that may not necessarily be the best ones for them.

Summary

➤ Unemployment arises for a number of reasons at the microeconomic level.

➤ Structural unemployment, arising from changes in the structure of economic activity within an economy, may reflect inflexibility in a labour market, which slows the process by which workers move from declining into expanding sectors.

➤ Firms may underprovide training in transferable skills because of a possible free-rider effect.

➤ Unemployment in a market may arise if wages are held above the equilibrium level — because of trade union action, a minimum wage or sluggish adjustment to a fall in demand.

➤ Geographic immobility may impede the operations of the labour market, if workers are not readily able to move between different parts of the country.

➤ Occupational immobility may also contribute to the inflexibility of the labour market.

Effects of government intervention

Labour markets can be a source of politically sensitive issues. Unemployment has been a prominent indicator of the performance of the economy, and there has been an increasing concern in recent years with issues of health and safety and with ensuring that workers are not exploited by their employers. This has induced governments to introduce a number of measures to provide the institutional setting for the operation of labour markets. However, such measures do not always have their intended effects.

Minimum wage

In its manifesto published before the 1997 election, the Labour Party committed itself to the establishment of the National **Minimum Wage** (NMW). This would be the first time that such a measure had been used in the UK on a nationwide basis, although minimum wages had sometimes been set in particular industries.

 Key term

minimum wage: legislation under which firms are not allowed to pay a wage below some threshold level set by the government

After the election, a Low Pay Commission was set up to oversee the implementation of the policy, which came into force in April 1999. Initially the NMW was set at £3.60 per hour for those aged 22 and over, and £3 for those aged 18–21. The rates are adjusted annually. From 1 October 2011 the rates were £6.08 for those aged 21 and over and £4.98 for those aged 18–20 (known as the 'development rate'). A minimum wage of £3.68 per hour applied to 16- and 17-year-olds.

The objectives of the minimum wage policy are threefold. First, it is intended to protect workers against exploitation by the small minority of bad employers. Second, it aims to improve incentives to work by ensuring that 'work pays', thereby tackling the problem of voluntary unemployment. Third, it aims to alleviate poverty by raising the living standards of the poorest groups in society.

McDonald's argued that it was already paying above the minimum wage

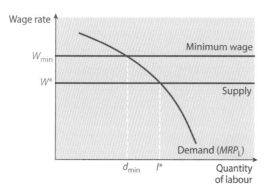

Figure 8.5 *The effect of a minimum wage on a firm in a perfectly competitive labour market*

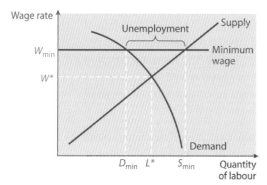

Figure 8.6 *The effect of a minimum wage in a perfectly competitive labour market*

The policy has been a contentious one, with critics claiming that it meets none of these objectives. It has been argued that the minority of bad employees can still find ways of exploiting their workers: for example, by paying them on a piecework rate so that there is no set wage per hour. Another criticism is that the policy is too indiscriminate to tackle poverty, and that a more sharply focused policy is needed for this purpose. For example, many of the workers receiving the NMW may not in fact belong to poor households, but may be women working part time whose partners are also in employment. But perhaps most contentious of all is the argument that, far from providing a supply-side solution to some unemployment, a National Minimum Wage is causing an increase in unemployment because of its effects on the demand for labour.

First, consider a firm operating in a perfectly competitive market, so that it has to accept the wage that is set in the overall market of which it is a part. In Figure 8.5 the firm's demand curve is represented by its marginal revenue product curve (MRP_L), and in a free market it must accept the equilibrium wage W^*. It thus uses labour up to l^*.

If the government now steps in and imposes a minimum wage, so that the firm cannot set a wage below W_{min}, it will reduce its labour usage to d_{min}, since it will not be profitable to employ labour beyond this point.

This effect will be similar for all the other firms in the market, and the results of this can be seen in Figure 8.6. Now the demand curve is the combined demand of all the firms in the market, and the supply curve of labour is shown as upward sloping, as it is the market supply curve. In free market equilibrium the combined demand of firms in the market is L^*, and W^* emerges as the equilibrium wage rate.

When the government sets the minimum wage at W_{min}, all firms react by reducing their demand for labour at the higher wage. Their combined

demand is now D_{min}, but the supply of labour is S_{min}. The difference between these $(S_{min} - D_{min})$ is unemployment. Furthermore, it is involuntary unemployment – these workers would like to work at the going wage rate, but cannot find a job.

Notice that there are two effects at work. Some workers who were formerly employed have lost their jobs – there are $L^* - D_{min}$ of these. In addition, however, the incentive to work is now improved (this was part of the policy objective, remember?), so there are now an additional $S_{min} - L^*$ workers wanting to take employment at the going wage rate. Thus, unemployment has increased for two reasons.

It is not always the case that the introduction of a minimum wage leads to an increase in unemployment. For example, in the market depicted in Figure 8.7 the minimum wage has been set below the equilibrium level, so will have no effect on firms in the market, which will continue to pay W^* and employ L^* workers. At the time of the introduction of the NMW, McDonald's argued that it was in fact already paying a wage above the minimum rate set.

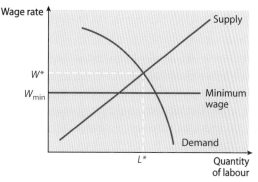

Figure 8.7 *A non-binding minimum wage in a perfectly competitive labour market*

This is not the only situation in which a minimum wage would *not* lead to unemployment. Suppose that the labour market in question has a monopsony buyer of labour. The firm's situation is shown in Figure 8.8. In the absence of a minimum wage, the firm sets its marginal cost of labour equal to its marginal revenue product, hiring L_0 labour at a wage W_0. A minimum wage introduced at the level W_{min} means that the firm now hires labour up to the point where the wage is equal to the marginal revenue product and, as drawn in Figure 8.8, this takes the market back to the perfectly competitive outcome.

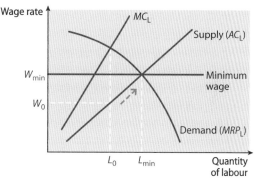

Figure 8.8 *A minimum wage with a monopsony buyer of labour*

Notice that the authorities would have to be very knowledgeable to set the minimum wage at exactly the right level to produce this outcome. However, any wage between W_0 and W_{min} will encourage the firm to increase its employment to some extent as the policy reduces its market power. Of course, setting the minimum wage above the competitive equilibrium level will again lead to some unemployment. Thus, it is critical to set the wage at the right level if the policy is to succeed in its objectives.

It is also important to realise that there is not just a single labour market in the UK. In fact, it could be questioned whether a single minimum wage set across the whole country could be effective, as it would 'bite' in different ways in different markets. For example, wage levels vary across the regions of the UK, and it must be questioned whether the same minimum wage could be as effective in, say, London as in Northern Ireland or the north of England.

Health and safety regulation

The government intervenes in the labour market through a range of measures designed to improve safety standards in the workplace.

Such regulation can impinge quite heavily on labour markets. One example is the EU Working Time Directive. This aims to protect the health and safety of workers in the European Union by imposing regulations in relation to working hours, rest periods, annual leave and working arrangements for night workers. The legislation came into effect in the UK in October 1998. Exceptions were made for junior doctors in training, for whom the directive was to be phased in gradually. There are some other workers who have signed contracts opting out of the directive. The UK implemented the 48-hour week later than countries elsewhere in Europe because of a special dispensation. Countries elsewhere complained about this, arguing that it gave UK firms an unfair competitive advantage. This seems to suggest that the directive does indeed have an effect on the labour market.

Health and safety measures increase costs for many industries

The effect of these health and safety measures has been to raise the costs to firms of hiring labour. In the case of the Working Time Directive, firms may have to spread the same amount of work over a greater number of workers, and as there are some fixed hiring costs, this raises the cost of labour. Similarly, if the firm has to spend more on ensuring safety, it adds to the firms' costs.

Figure 8.9 illustrates one way of viewing the situation. It shows a perfectly competitive labour market for an industry as a whole

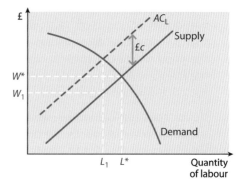

Figure 8.9 The effect of a health and safety regulation in a perfectly competitive market

rather than an individual firm. Without regulation, the market reaches equilibrium with labour employed up to L^* at a wage of W^*. Suppose a health and safety regulation is introduced that adds a constant amount (of £c) to firms' cost per unit of labour employed. Firms then find that the average cost of labour is higher by £c – shown as AC_L in the diagram. They will thus employ labour up to the point where the average cost of labour is equal to the marginal revenue product. (Remember that this is a perfectly competitive labour market, so it is the average cost of labour that is significant in the market: each individual firm perceives this as its marginal cost.) This is at the quantity of labour L_1, and wage is given by W_1, which is the wage that attracts L_1 workers into the market.

The monopsony market could be analysed in a similar fashion, but the effects are comparable – there is a reduction in the amount of labour employed and a fall in the wage rate.

This sort of intervention can be justified by appealing to a merit good argument (which was discussed in *AS Economics, Chapter 7*), which claims that the government knows better than workers what is good for them. Thus, individual workers' decisions about labour supply do not take health and safety sufficiently into account, and the regulation that adds to firms' costs is a way of protecting the workers, given that firms have an incentive to skimp on health and safety in order to keep costs down.

As with other policies, the judgement of the degree of regulation that is required is a difficult one to get right. If governments misjudge the amount of protection that workers need and set c too high, this could lead to lower employment than is optimal.

Some health and safety issues arise from externality effects. For example, firms transporting toxic or other dangerous substances may not face the full costs of their activities because they do not have the incentive to control the risk of affecting individuals. Regulation to enforce the appropriate transportation of such substances is a way of internalising such an externality.

Exercise 8.3

Use Figure 8.10 to explain how the externality effect in the paragraph above comes about.

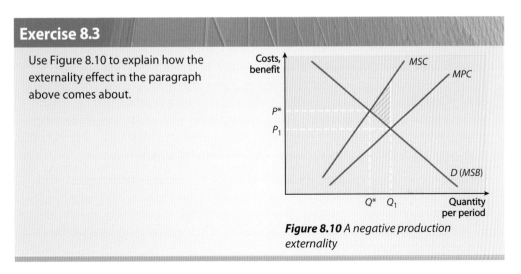

Figure 8.10 *A negative production externality*

Summary

➤ Governments have intervened in labour markets to protect low-paid workers, but policies need to be implemented with care because of possible unintended side-effects.

➤ The Labour government under Tony Blair introduced the National Minimum Wage in 1999.

➤ In a perfectly competitive labour market, a minimum wage that raises the wage rate above its equilibrium value may lead to an increase in unemployment.

➤ This is partly because firms reduce their demand for labour, but it also reflects an increased labour supply, as the higher wage is an incentive for more workers to join the market.

➤ A minimum wage that is set below the equilibrium wage will not be binding.

➤ A minimum wage established in a monopsony market may have the effect of raising employment.

➤ Health and safety legislation may help to protect workers, and may be interpreted as an example of a merit good.

➤ However, it adds to firms' costs, so may reduce employment.

➤ It is thus important to keep health and safety in perspective, and not overprotect at the expense of lower employment levels.

Trade unions

Trade unions are associations of workers that negotiate with employers on pay and working conditions. Guilds of craftsmen existed in Europe in the Middle Ages, but the formation of workers' trade unions did not become legal in the UK until 1824. In the period following the Second World War, about 40% of the labour force in the UK were members of a trade union. This percentage increased during the 1970s, peaking at about 50%, but since 1980 there has been a steady decline to below 30%.

 Key term

trade union: an organisation of workers that negotiates with employers on behalf of its members

Trade unions have three major objectives: wage bargaining, the improvement of working conditions, and security of employment for their members. In exploring the effect of the unions on a labour market, it is important to establish whether the unions are in a position to exploit market power and interfere with the proper functioning of the labour market, and also whether they are a necessary balance to the power of employers and thus necessary to protect workers from being exploited.

There have been some changes in the way in which trade unions have engaged with bargaining with employers in recent years, with a stronger focus on local agreements and on performance-related pay. In terms of marginal productivity theory, this emphasis on performance makes intuitive sense, as it strengthens the links between workers' productivity and their pay.

There are two ways in which a trade union may seek to affect labour market equilibrium. On the one hand, it may limit the supply of workers into an occupation or industry. On the other hand, it may negotiate successfully for higher wages for its members. It turns out that these two possible strategies have similar effects on market equilibrium.

Restricting labour supply

Figure 8.11 shows the situation facing a firm, with a demand curve for labour based on marginal productivity theory. The average going wage in the economy is given by W^*, so if the firm can obtain workers at that wage, it is prepared to employ up to L_0 labour.

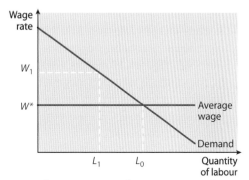

Figure 8.11 A trade union restricts the supply of labour

However, if the firm faces a trade union that is limiting the amount of labour available to just L_1, then the union will be able to push the wage up to W_1. This might happen where there is a *closed shop*: in other words, where a firm can employ only those workers who are members of the union. A closed shop allows the union to control how many workers are registered members, and therefore eligible to work in the occupation.

In this situation the union is effectively trading off higher wages for its members against a lower level of employment. The union members who are in work are better off – but those who would have been prepared to work at the lower wage of W^* either are unemployed or have to look elsewhere for jobs. If they are unemployed, this imposes a cost on society. If they are working in a second-choice occupation or industry, this may also impose a social cost, in the sense that they may not be working to their full potential.

The extent of the trade-off depends crucially on the elasticity of demand for labour, as you can see in Figure 8.12. When the demand for labour is relatively more elastic, as shown by D_{L0}, the wage paid by the firm increases to W_0, whereas with the relatively more inelastic demand for labour D_{L1} the wage increases by much more, to W_1.

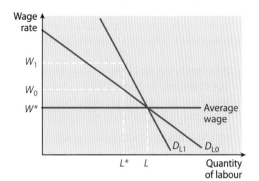

Figure 8.12 The importance of the elasticity of demand for labour

This makes good intuitive sense. The previous chapter explained that the elasticity of demand would be low in situations where a firm could not readily substitute capital for labour, where labour formed a small share of total costs, and where the price elasticity of demand for the firm's product was relatively inelastic. If the firm cannot readily substitute capital for labour, the union has a relatively strong

bargaining position. If labour costs are a small part of total costs, the firm may be ready to concede a wage increase, as it will have limited overall impact. If the demand for the product is price inelastic, the firm may be able to pass the wage increase on in the form of a higher price for the product without losing large volumes of sales. Thus, these factors improve the union's ability to negotiate a good deal with the employer.

Negotiating wages

A trade union's foremost function can be regarded as negotiating higher wages for its members. Figure 8.13 depicts this situation. In the absence of union negotiation, the equilibrium for the firm is where demand and supply intersect, so the firm hires L_e labour at a wage of W_e.

If the trade union negotiates a wage of W^*, such that the firm cannot hire any labour below that level, this alters the labour supply curve, as shown by the kinked red line. The firm now employs only L^* labour

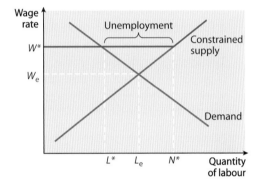

Figure 8.13 *A trade union fixes the wage*

at this wage. So, again, the effect is that the union negotiations result in a trade-off between the amount of labour hired and the wage rate. When the wage is at W^*, unemployment is shown on Figure 8.13 as $N^* - L^*$.

The elasticity of demand for labour again affects the outcome, as shown in Figure 8.14. This time, with the relatively more inelastic demand curve D_{L1}, the effect on the quantity of labour employed (falls from L_e to L^{**}) is much less than when demand is relatively more elastic (falls from L_e to L^*).

From the point of view of allocative efficiency, the problem is that trade union intervention in the market may prevent wages from acting as reliable signals to workers and firms, and therefore may lead to a sub-optimal allocation of resources.

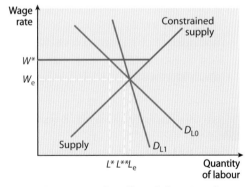

Figure 8.14 *The effect of elasticity of demand for labour when the union fixes the wage*

Job security

One possible effect of trade union involvement in a firm is that workers will have more job security: in other words, they may become less likely to lose their jobs with the union there to protect their interests.

From the firm's point of view, there may be a positive side to this. If workers feel secure in their jobs, they may be more productive, or more prepared to accept changes in working practices that enable an improvement in productivity.

For this reason, it can be argued that in some situations the presence of a trade union may be beneficial in terms of a firm's efficiency. Indeed, the union may sometimes take over functions that would otherwise be part of the responsibility of the firm's human resource department.

Labour market flexibility

One of the most telling criticisms of trade unions has been that they have affected the degree of flexibility of the labour market. The most obvious manifestation of this is that their actions limit the entry of workers into a market.

This may happen in any firm, where existing workers have better access to information about how the firm is operating, or about forthcoming job vacancies, and so can make sure that their own positions can be safeguarded against newcomers. This is sometimes known as the *insider–outsider* phenomenon. Its effect is strengthened and institutionalised by the presence of a trade union, or by professional bodies such as the Royal College of Surgeons.

This and other barriers to entry erected by a trade union can limit the effectiveness and flexibility of labour markets by making it more difficult for firms to adapt to changing market conditions.

Summary

- Trade unions exist to negotiate for their members on pay, working conditions and job security.
- If trade unions restrict labour supply, or negotiate wages that are above the market equilibrium, the net effect is a trade-off between wages and employment.
- Those who remain in work receive higher pay, but at the expense of other workers who either have become unemployed or work in second-choice occupations or industries.
- However, by improving job security, unions may make workers more prepared to accept changes in working practices that lead to productivity gains.
- Barriers to the entry and exit of workers may reduce firms' flexibility to adapt to changing market conditions.
- If a monopsony firm is faced by a trade union acting as a monopoly provider of labour, the firm's ability to reduce employment and lower wages will be limited.
- The final outcome in such a market will depend upon the relative bargaining power of the employer and the union.

Flexibility and unemployment

Measuring unemployment is a key way of trying to evaluate whether labour markets are operating effectively. Large-scale unemployment suggests that a society is failing to use its resources efficiently, and is operating *within* its production possibility frontier; by reallocating resources within the economy, and thus moving to the frontier, society as a whole can be made better off.

Some of the explanations that have been advanced for unemployment suggest that there is a transitional element: in other words, that unemployment can occur because the market is sluggish in adjusting to equilibrium, or that workers are unemployed because they do not have the right mix of skills that employers are seeking.

The more flexible labour markets are, the more rapidly such unemployment will subside as equilibrium is reached. Thus, an important set of policies to examine are those that will improve the flexibility with which labour markets can adjust towards equilibrium. It has been claimed that the degree of flexibility of markets is important in explaining differences in observed unemployment rates between countries, which is an issue that will be discussed later in the chapter.

The benefits of flexibility go beyond the labour market itself. If a labour market does not adjust readily, it will slow the whole process of changing resource allocation, and this in turn will slow the process of economic growth, which may be seen as a prime long-term aim of economic policy.

It may not be straightforward to identify when full employment has been reached. Some unemployment cannot be avoided, and will exist even when the labour market is in equilibrium.

The flexibility of labour markets affects the number of people looking for work and their ability to find jobs

Unemployment in the UK

The overall unemployment rate in the UK since 1971 is presented in Figure 8.15, using the claimant count measurement method. This counts the number of people claiming unemployment benefit each month. It was briefly introduced in *AS Economics*,

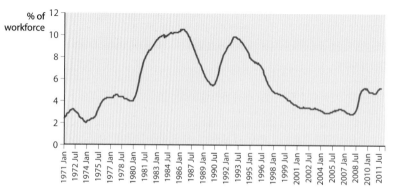

Figure 8.15
Unemployment in the UK, 1971–2011 (claimant count)

Source: ONS.

OCR A2 Economics

Chapter 9, and provides a useful picture of how unemployment has varied through time. Although the ILO method of measuring unemployment is more useful in many ways, the claimant count data are available over a longer period of time.

The large swings in unemployment that are visible on the graph are due to a number of causes. The large increase in the early 1980s reflected in part a change in the emphasis of economic policy. There was a new determination to bring inflation under control using monetary policy whereas in earlier periods the government had been more concerned about achieving full employment. However, other things were happening as well. North Sea Oil came on stream just before the second oil price crisis of 1979–80, a net effect of which was a loss in competitiveness of UK goods, which led to a decline in the manufacturing sector in the 1980s. There were also changes in the demographic structure of the population, which will be taken up at the end of the chapter.

The reduction in unemployment in the late 1980s was associated with what has come to be known as the 'Lawson boom', a period of relatively loose monetary policy that was followed by a severe recession in which unemployment rose again. But perhaps the most striking aspect of Figure 8.15 is the period since 1993, which showed a steady decline in the unemployment rate and a much steadier pattern, at least until the end of 2008 when recession began to bite and unemployment started to increase again. However, you can see that the unemployment rate seemed to stabilise close to 5% by the end of 2011, which is considerably lower than the peak experienced in previous recessionary periods.

Figure 8.16 focuses on a different aspect of unemployment. Economists have argued that some unemployment is by its nature transitional, a feature of the adjustment process of the economy. In this context it is useful to examine the extent to which there is long-term unemployment. Figure 8.16 shows the percentage of the unemployed who have been unemployed for more than a year.

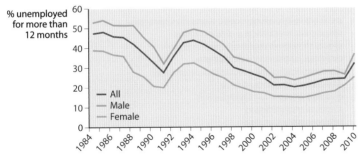

Figure 8.16
The long-term unemployed in the UK, 1984–2010

Notes: data relate to the spring of each year. The long-term unemployed are those who have been without work for a year or more.

Source: ONS.

The overall picture shows that there has been a large decline in long-term unemployment, from nearly 50% in 1984 to only just over 20% in the spring of 2005. This might be interpreted as an encouraging sign for the economy, indicating that most unemployment is relatively short term in nature. Indeed, taking this figure together with the previous one, which showed such a large decline in overall unemployment, it might be concluded that the economy was not far from a full-employment position at this time.

Notice that there is a difference between male and female workers in these data, indicating that the majority of long-term unemployed workers are male. There is also an age effect in the data, which is shown in Figure 8.17. This focuses just on the years 1993 and 2010, and shows that long-term unemployment is more prevalent among older workers. There has clearly been a substantial improvement in all age groups, but the decline has been much more marked for younger workers. This may partly reflect the greater difficulty that older workers find in switching occupations, but it may also be associated with the training schemes for younger workers that have been introduced in recent years, which will be discussed shortly.

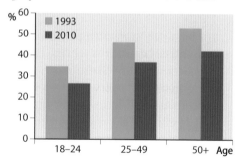

Figure 8.17 *Long-term unemployed as a percentage of all unemployed in the UK by age groups, 1993 and 2010*

Source: ONS.

The relatively low proportion of long-term unemployed highlights the fact that unemployment is a dynamic variable. It is easy to fall into the trap of thinking of the unemployed as being a pool of people unable to get work. However, in any period there are always people becoming unemployed, and others obtaining jobs. In a typical year more people get jobs, and more become unemployed, than the average number of people who are unemployed at any one time.

It is also important to remember that there are substantial regional variations in unemployment rates across the UK. Figure 8.18 shows the picture in 2010. The percentage rate varies from about 3% in the South West and the South East to 6% or more in the North East and Northern Ireland.

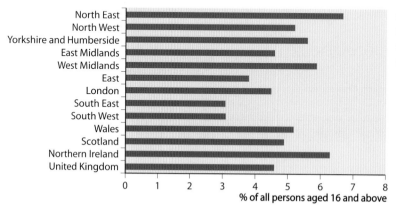

Figure 8.18 *Unemployment in the regions of the UK, 2010*

In part, the variation in unemployment rates between regions reflects the differing pattern of economic activity across the country. If a region happens to have a concentration of employment in a declining industry, it will tend to display higher unemployment rates because labour is not perfectly mobile and unemployed workers

may find that there are no available jobs in their area, but may still be reluctant to move.

Figure 8.19 compares unemployment in the UK with that of selected other countries. One prominent feature of this graph is that the continuous decline in the unemployment rate that the UK enjoyed after 1993 has not been shared by the other countries shown — or by the euro area countries as a whole. Indeed, it would appear that France and Germany in this period converged on a relatively high unemployment rate, whereas the UK steadied at a lower rate. The pattern is most striking for Germany, which enjoyed a much lower unemployment rate in the 1980s and early 1990s, but has since shown a weaker performance. This may partly reflect the difficulty experienced after the reunification of West and East Germany in the 1990s, beginning with the destruction of the Berlin Wall in 1989, which has undoubtedly affected Germany's unemployment rate. However, unemployment in the UK rose steeply in the recession of 2008–10, overtaking France.

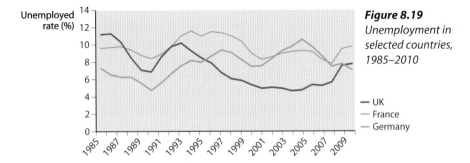

Figure 8.19
Unemployment in selected countries, 1985–2010

Exercise 8.4

Table 8.2 provides data on unemployment in the regions of the UK in 1992 and 2005.

For each region and each year, calculate an index number for unemployment in the region based on the UK = 100. (If you need to be reminded about how to calculate index numbers, it was discussed in *AS Economics, Chapter 9*.)

Use your results to identify which regions have experienced the greatest and least changes in the unemployment rate relative to the national average. Discuss the reasons for these results.

Region	Spring 1992	Spring 2005
UK	**9.7**	**4.7**
North East	11.8	6.4
North West	10.0	4.5
Yorkshire & Humberside	10.1	4.8
East Midlands	8.8	4.4
West Midlands	10.6	4.5
East	7.7	3.8
London	12.0	7.0
South East	7.8	3.7
South West	9.1	3.3
Wales	8.9	4.5
Scotland	9.5	5.6
Northern Ireland	12.1	4.9

Table 8.2 *Unemployment in UK regions, 1992 and 2005*

Source: ONS.

Summary

➤ Unemployment has shown quite wide variations through time in the UK, but declined steadily between 1993 and 2005; unemployment began to rise again in late 2008/early 2009.

➤ The proportion of unemployed workers who have been unemployed for more than a year also showed an appreciable decline.

➤ There are significant variations in unemployment rates across the regions of the UK, but the pattern of the differences altered during the 1990s.

Policies to promote flexibility

What makes for a flexible labour market? At the microeconomic level, where a prime concern is with achieving a good allocation of resources for society, the issue is whether workers can transfer readily between activities to allow resource allocation to change through time. This requires a number of conditions to be met. Workers need to have information about what jobs are available (and, perhaps, where those jobs are available), and what skills are needed for those jobs. Employers need to be able to identify workers with the skills and talents that they need. If workers cannot find the jobs that are available, or do not have the appropriate skills to undertake those jobs, the market will not function smoothly. Similarly, if employers cannot identify the workers with the skills that they need, that too will impede the working of the market.

Arguably, the problem has become acute in recent years, with a change in the balance of jobs between skilled and unskilled workers. As the economy gears up to more hi-tech activities, and low-skill jobs are outsourced or relocated to other countries, the need for workers to acquire the right skills becomes ever more pressing.

The New Deal

An important policy launched by the new Labour government in 1997 was a package of policy measures known as the New Deal, which was aimed at reducing long-term unemployment. Figures 8.16 and 8.17 certainly suggest that long-term unemployment has declined, but it cannot be assumed that this reflects the impact of the New Deal alone. After all, other aspects of the economy have improved in the same period, contributing to an overall fall in the unemployment rate.

The New Deal measures were aimed at three age groups – the groups shown in Figure 8.17. Young people aged 18–24 years old who had been unemployed for a period of more than 6 months would be assigned a personal adviser to provide them with information about available jobs and contacts with potential employers. If they were still without a job after a further 4 months, they would either enter a year of full-time education or training, or take up a job with the voluntary sector for 6 months or the environmental task force; or they would go into subsidised employment which would include on-the-job training. Similar targeted programmes were provided for the older age groups.

Notice that such measures are designed to improve the flexibility of the labour market, by providing unemployed workers with information and skills training. Furthermore, employers receive a subsidy to take on workers, who can then be observed in the workplace, which provides a better insight into their potential than any interview or other screening process.

A survey published in *Labour Market Trends* in 2007 indicated that nine out of ten employers in the survey provided at least some of their employees with job-related training. Figure 8.20 indicates that a relatively high percentage of employees received such training, especially in the younger age groups.

Figure 8.20 *Employees receiving job-related training, winter 2007*

* 59 for women, 64 for men.

Source: ONS.

Trade union reform

A further question concerns the extent to which the trade unions have affected the operation of labour markets. By negotiating for a wage that is above the equilibrium level, trade unions may trade off higher wages for lower levels of employment. The potential disruption caused by strike action can also impede the workings of a labour market.

Some indication of this disruption can be seen in Figure 8.21. Clearly, compared with the 1970s and 1980s, the amount of disruption through strikes in recent years has been very low. However, even the 1979 figure pales into insignificance besides the 162 million working days lost in the General Strike of 1926; but, in fact, the 1970s and 1980s were a tempestuous period, in which trade union action severely disrupted UK industry. So why has life become so much quieter?

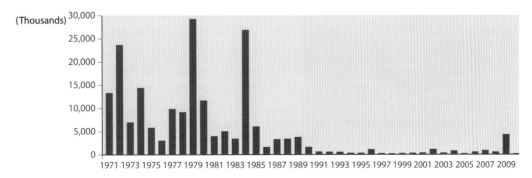

Figure 8.21 *Working days lost in the UK through industrial action, 1971–2010*

Source: ONS.

It was perhaps no surprise that unions should have worked hard to protect their members during the 1980s, when unemployment was soaring and the Thatcher government was determined to control inflation — including inflation of wages. Legislation was introduced in the early 1980s to begin to reform the trade unions, and after the highly disruptive miners' strike ended in 1985, the government introduced a number of further reforms designed to curb the power of the trade unions, making it more difficult for them to call rapid strike action. For example, secret ballots were to be required before strike action could be taken. This may help to explain why trade union membership has been in decline since the 1980s. By weakening the power of trade unions in this way, some labour market inflexibility has been removed.

Another factor may have been changes in the structure of economic activity during this period. Manufacturing employment was falling, whereas the service sectors were expanding. Traditionally, union membership has been higher among workers in the manufacturing sector than in services.

Regional policy

There have always been differences in average incomes and in unemployment rates between the various regions of the UK. In broad terms, there are two possible responses to this — either persuade workers to move to regions where there are more jobs, or persuade the firms to move to areas where labour is plentiful. Each of these solutions poses problems. Housing markets limit the mobility of workers, and it is costly for firms to relocate their activities.

The regions most affected in the past have been those that specialised in industries that subsequently went into decline: for example, coal mining areas or towns and regions dominated by cotton mills. In a broad context, it is desirable for the economy to undergo structural change as the pattern of international comparative advantage changes, but it is painful during the transition period. Thus, successive governments have implemented regional policies to try to cope with the problems experienced in areas of high unemployment.

At the same time, the booming regions can be affected because of the opposite problem — a shortage of labour. Thus, measures have been taken to encourage firms to consider relocating to regions where labour is available. This included leading by example, with some civil service functions being moved out of London.

Middlesbrough — one of the areas of the country with a high concentration of heavy industry and manufacturing that has experienced economic decline

EU funding has helped in this regard, with Scotland, Wales and Northern Ireland all qualifying for grants. Since 1999, the Regional Development Agencies set up by the Labour government have been given responsibility for promoting economic development in their regions. There are eight of these agencies covering the country. Although differentials have narrowed in recent years, it is difficult to know how much of this narrowing can be attributed to the success of regional policy. It has also been pointed out that there are some areas that have been receiving regional aid for more than 70 years, but are still disadvantaged, so it is difficult to argue that regional policy has had outstanding success.

Technology and unemployment

One of the greatest fallacies perpetuated by non-economists is that technology destroys jobs. Bands of labourers known as Luddites rioted between 1811 and 1816, destroying textile machines, which they blamed for high unemployment and low wages. In the twenty-first century there is a strong lobbying group in the USA arguing that outsourcing and cheap labour in China are destroying US jobs.

In fact, new technology and an expansion in the capital stock should have beneficial effects — so long as labour markets are sufficiently flexible. Consider a market in which new technology is introduced. If firms in an industry invest in technology and expand the capital stock, this affects the marginal revenue product of labour and hence the demand for labour, as shown in Figure 8.22, where demand shifts from D_1 to D_2. In this market, the effect is to raise the wage rate from W_1 to W_2 and the employment level from L_1 to L_2.

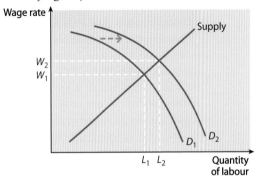

Figure 8.22 An increase in capital

However, it is important to look beyond what happens in a single market, as the argument is that it is all very well expanding employment in the technology sector — but what about the old industries that are in decline? Suppose the new industries absorb less labour than is discarded by the old declining industries? After all, if the effect of technology is to allow call centres to create jobs in India at the expense of the USA or the UK, does this not harm employment in those countries?

The counter-argument to this lies in the notion of the gains from specialisation introduced in *AS Economics, Chapter 1*. This argues that countries can gain from international trade through specialising in certain activities. Setting up call centres in India frees UK workers to work in sectors in which the UK has a comparative advantage, with the result that the UK can import (and thus consume) more labour-intensive goods than before.

There is one proviso, of course. It is important that the workers released from the declining sectors have (or can obtain) the skills that are needed for them to be absorbed

Technology has often been blamed for taking away jobs

into the expanding sectors. This recalls the question of whether the labour market is sufficiently flexible to allow the structure of economic activity to adapt to changes in the pattern of comparative advantage. However, it also serves as a reminder that policy should be aimed at enabling that flexibility, and not at introducing protectionist measures to reduce trade, which would be damaging overall for the economy.

Exercise 8.5

For each of the following situations, sketch a demand and supply diagram for a labour market to analyse the effects on the wage rate and employment level.

a An increase in the rate of immigration of people into the country.

b A reduction in the rate of the Jobseekers' Allowance.

c An improvement in technology that raises labour productivity.

d A new health and safety regulation to safeguard workers against industrial injury.

e An increase in the number of old people as a percentage of the population.

Summary

➤ An important factor influencing the rate of unemployment is the degree of flexibility in labour markets.

➤ The New Deal was a package of measures introduced with the objective of reducing long-term unemployment, through providing information to jobseekers and training.

➤ Trade union reforms were introduced during the 1980s and have contributed to flexibility in labour markets.

➤ Regional policy has attempted to reduce the differentials in unemployment rates between the regions of the UK.

➤ The Social Chapter has attempted to harmonise labour market policies across the EU. In some cases, this may have reduced the flexibility of labour markets in the interest of worker protection.

➤ Adjustment in labour markets is needed in order to cope with the changing international pattern of specialisation.

Inequality and poverty

All societies are characterised by some inequality — and some poverty. Although the two are related, they are not the same. Indeed, poverty might be regarded as one aspect of inequality.

If there is a wide gap between the richest and poorest households, it is important to evaluate just how poor are those poorest households, and whether they should be regarded as being 'in poverty'. This requires a definition of poverty.

One approach is to define a basket of goods and services that is regarded as being the minimum required to support human life. Households that are seen to have income that falls short of allowing them to purchase that basic bundle of goods would be regarded as being in **absolute poverty**.

Poverty can also be defined in *relative* terms. If a household has insufficient income for the members of the household to participate in the normal social life of the country, then they are said to be in **relative poverty**. This is also defined in terms of a poverty line. The line is defined as 50% of the median adjusted household disposable income (the median is income of the middle-ranked household).

 Key term

absolute poverty: situation of a household whose income is insufficient to purchase the minimum bundle of goods and services needed for survival

relative poverty: situation in which household income falls below 50% of median adjusted household income

The percentage falling below the poverty line is not a totally reliable measure, as it is also important to know *how far* below the poverty line households are falling. Thus the income gap (the distance between household income and the poverty line) is useful to measure the intensity of poverty as well as its incidence.

Inequality is a broader concept, as it relates to the overall distribution of income and wealth within society. Measuring inequality provides a substantial challenge, as it requires data on income at the household level across the country. One measure is to look at the ratio of the richest 10% of households to the poorest 10%. For example, the

richest 10% of households in the UK earn 10.5 times as much as the poorest 10%; in the USA this ratio is 16.9.

Causes of inequality and poverty

Inequality arises through a variety of factors, some relating to the operation of the labour market, some reflecting patterns in the ownership of assets, and some arising from the actions of governments.

Labour market explanations

This part of the book has set out a number of ways in which the labour market is expected to give rise to inequalities in earnings. This arises from demand and supply conditions in labour markets, which respond to changes in the pattern of consumer demand for goods and services, and changes in international comparative advantage between countries. Furthermore, differences in the balance between economic rent and transfer earnings between different occupations and economic sectors reinforce income inequalities.

However, a by-product of changes in the structure of the economy may be rising inequality between certain groups in society. For example, if there is a change in the structure of employment away from unskilled jobs towards occupations that require a higher level of skills and qualifications, then this could lead to an increase in inequality, with those workers who lack the skills to adapt to changing labour market conditions being disadvantaged by the changes taking place. In other words, if the premium that employers are prepared to pay in order to hire skilled or well-qualified workers rises as a result of changing technology in the workplace, then those without those skills are likely to suffer.

The decline in the power of the trade unions may have contributed to the situation, as low-paid workers may find that their unions are less likely to be able to offer employment protection. It has been argued that this is a *good* thing if it increases the flexibility of the labour market. However, again a balance is needed between worker protection and having free and flexible markets.

Ownership of assets

Perhaps the most obvious way in which the ownership of assets influences inequality and its changes through time is through inheritance. When wealth accumulates in a family over time, and is then passed down to succeeding generations, this generates a source of inequality that does not arise from the current state of the economy or the operations of markets.

It is important to be aware that income and wealth are not the same. Income is a 'flow' that households receive each period, whereas wealth is a 'stock', being the accumulation of assets that a household owns. Wealth is considerably less evenly distributed than income. In 2001, the most wealthy 1% of households in the UK owned 23% of the marketable wealth (33% if we take out the value of dwellings), and the most wealthy 50% of households owned 95% of marketable wealth.

Notice, however, that although wealth and income are not the same thing, inequality in wealth can also lead to inequality in income, as wealth (the ownership of assets) leads to an income flow, from rents and profits, which then feeds back into an income stream.

A significant change in the pattern of ownership of assets in recent decades has been the rise in home ownership and the rise in house prices. For those who continue to rent their homes, and in particular for those who rent council housing, this is a significant source of rising inequality.

Demographic change

A feature of many developed countries in recent years has been a change in the age structure of the population. Improved medical drugs and treatments have meant that people are living longer, and this has combined with low fertility rates to bring about an increase in the proportion of the population who are in the older age groups. This has put pressure on the provision of pensions, and increased the vulnerability of this group in society. State pensions have been funded primarily by the contributions of those in work, but if the number of people of working age falls as a proportion of the whole population, then this funding stream comes under pressure.

Government intervention

There are a number of ways in which government intervention influences the distribution of income in a society, although not all of these interventions are expressly intended to do so. Most prominent is the range of transfer payments and taxation that have been implemented. Another example is the minimum wage legislation discussed earlier, which was also intended to protect the poor.

The overall effect of these measures has a large effect on income distribution. For example, in 2009/10 the 'original income' of the top quintile of households in the UK was about 16 times greater than for those in the bottom quintile (original income is income before any adjustment is made for the effect of taxation or benefits). After adjusting for benefits and taxes, the ratio of top to bottom quintile fell to about four to one.

Benefits

There are two forms of benefit that households can receive that help to equalise the income distribution. First, there are various types of *cash benefits*, such as income support, child benefit, incapacity benefit and working families tax credit. These benefits are designed to protect families in certain circumstances whose income would otherwise be very low. Second, there are *benefits in kind*, such as health and education. These benefits accrue to individual households depending on the number of members of the household and their age and gender.

Of these benefits, the cash benefits are far more important in influencing the distribution of income. For the lowest quintile in 2009/10, such benefits made up nearly 60% of gross income, and were also significant for the second quintile.

Taxation

Direct taxes (taxes on incomes) tend to be progressive. In other words, higher income groups pay tax at a higher rate. In 2009/10, the richest 20% of households paid 24.4% of their gross income in direct taxes, compared with only 10.2% in the poorest 20%.

In the UK, the main direct taxes are income tax, corporation tax (paid by firms on profits), capital gains tax (paid by individuals who sell assets at a profit), inheritance tax and petroleum revenue tax (paid by firms operating in the North Sea). There is also the council tax, collected by local authorities.

With a tax such as income tax, its progressive nature is reflected in the way that the percentage rates payable increase as an individual moves into higher income ranges. In other words, the **marginal tax rate** increases as income increases. The progressive nature of the tax ensures that it does indeed contribute to reducing inequality in the income distribution — although its effects are less than the cash benefits discussed earlier.

> **Key term**
>
> **direct tax**: a tax levied directly on income
>
> **indirect tax**: a tax on expenditure, e.g. VAT
>
> **marginal tax rate**: tax on additional income, defined as the change in tax payments divided by the change in taxable income
>
> **progressive tax**: a tax in which the marginal rate rises with income
>
> **regressive tax**: a tax bearing more heavily on the relatively poorer members of society

The effect of **indirect taxes** can sometimes be **regressive**: in other words, indirect taxes may impinge more heavily on lower-income households. Indirect taxes are taxes that are paid on items of expenditure, rather than on income.

An example of an indirect tax is value-added tax (VAT), which is charged on most goods and services sold in the UK. However, there are also tobacco taxes, excise duties on alcohol and oil duties. These specific taxes are levied per unit sold.

An indirect tax could be regressive where a product is consumed by a higher proportion of low-income households — for example, evidence suggests that a higher proportion of unskilled workers smoke cigarettes than professional groups. If expenditure on the product is a higher proportion of income of low-paid workers than it is for the rich, then a tax on the product will fall more heavily on the poor than on the rich.

The balance of taxation

The balance of taxation between direct and indirect taxes is thus an important aspect of the government's redistributive policy. A switch in the balance from direct to indirect taxes will tend to increase inequality.

There may be reasons why such a switch might be seen as desirable. When Margaret Thatcher came to power in 1979, one of the first actions of her government was to do just that — to increase indirect taxes and introduce cuts to income tax. An important part of the rationale was that high marginal tax rates on income can have a disincentive effect. An important part of the rationale for this policy was the disincentive effects of high marginal tax rates. If an individual is aware that providing additional work will produce low rewards because a high proportion of the income earned will be taxed away, then there is little incentive to put in those extra hours. The converse of this is that a reduction in income tax could induce more work if this improves the return on additional effort.

This reminds us yet again of the need for a balanced policy that recognises that some redistribution of income is needed to protect the vulnerable, but that also recognises the disincentive effects of over-taxing the better-off.

Pensions policy

It has become clear that action is needed on pensions to cope with the changing demographic structure. The Pensions Commission has recommended a three-pronged approach to this. One approach is to encourage higher private saving, in order to reduce the extent to which individuals have to depend on the state pension. The second strand is to make the basic state pension more universal and flat-rate, and to index to earnings rather than prices. Finally, consideration is being given to raising the age at which the state pension is payable, and to encourage later retirement. More discussion can be found in the article 'The "problem" of an ageing population' by Gemma Tatlow (*Economic Review*, September 2006).

Summary

➤ Some degree of inequality in income and wealth is present in every society.

➤ Absolute poverty measures whether individuals or households have sufficient resources to maintain a reasonable life.

➤ Relative poverty measures whether individuals or households are able to participate in the life of the country in which they live: this is calculated as 50% of median adjusted household disposable income.

➤ Inequality arises from a range of factors.

➤ The distribution of wealth is strongly influenced by the pattern of inheritance, but in recent years changing patterns of home ownership, coupled with rises in house prices, have also been significant.

➤ The natural operation of labour markets gives rise to some inequality in income.

➤ Government action influences the pattern of income distribution, with the net effect being a reduction in inequality.

➤ Most effective in this is the provision of cash benefits to low-income households.

Transport economics

Part 3

Chapter 9
Transport, transport trends and the economy

This part of the book examines the economics of transport. This is an important sector in any economy, as the efficiency and coverage of the transport sector is crucial for individuals, who need to move between locations for work and leisure, and for businesses, which need to transport their products — both inputs and outputs. As the economy expands and real incomes rise, it is to be expected that there will be changes in the demand for transport and, perhaps, changes in the pattern of that demand between alternative modes of travel. It is also important to be aware that there has been considerable technological change in recent decades that will inevitably have had an impact on the transport sector. This part of the book examines these aspects of the development of the transport sector, and the role of government in responding to potential areas of market failure.

Learning outcomes

After studying this chapter, you should:
- ▶ appreciate the significance of the transport sector in the operation of the economy
- ▶ understand that the demand for transport is a derived demand
- ▶ be aware of the nature of the market for transport
- ▶ be familiar with the characteristics of transport modes
- ▶ be aware of recent trends in the UK transport sector

The nature of transport

According to the *Oxford English Dictionary*, to **transport** is to 'take (persons, goods, troops, baggage etc.) from one place to another'. This might be a simple definition, but it provides a context for discussing transport economics, which deals with the economic analysis surrounding transportation, with a particular focus on the transportation of persons and goods. Such transportation is of critical importance for the

Key term

transport: process of moving people or goods from one place to another

modern economy. People need to move around as part of everyday life, for shopping, for leisure and for travel to work. Businesses need to move goods around as part of their production process. This includes bringing materials and other production inputs in, and also sending out finished products into the distribution system.

It is important to be aware that intimately bound up with the provision of transport services is the need for the provision of **transport infrastructure**. Buses need roads, trains need track, ships need ports.

Improvements in transport and storage mean fruit and vegetables can be imported into the UK from far afield

It is clear that it would be ridiculous to expect every bus company and taxi firm to build its own roads, so a key part of any transport system is the necessity to provide the infrastructure that firms need to be there if they are to be able to deliver transport services.

Recent decades have seen the rise of **globalisation** — a process by which firms are increasingly operating in global markets, rather than just functioning within the domestic economy. Transportation becomes even more important in this context, and recent technological change in the transport (and communications) sector has greatly contributed to the process of globalisation. Transport enables the world's economies to become more closely integrated. For example, it makes it possible for multinational corporations to take advantage of differing cost conditions in different parts of the globe. Improvements in transport and storage have enabled even fruit and vegetables to be imported into countries like the UK from far afield. You can see evidence of this in your local supermarket by checking out the country of origin of some of the products on sale.

An important point to notice at the outset is that the demand for transport is a **derived demand**. People and businesses demand transport not for its own sake, but because of the services that it provides. Some people might· enjoy travel for its own sake, but in general the demand for transport is

Key *term*

transport infrastructure: the permanent installations such as roads, railway track, airports and port facilities that are needed for firms to be able to provide transport services

globalisation: a process by which the world's economies are becoming more closely integrated

derived demand: demand for a good or service not for its own sake, but for what it produces

indirect. A firm may demand transport in order to deliver its product to the market, or an individual may demand transport in order to get to the office or the shops. This must be borne in mind when undertaking economic analysis of the demand for transport. Another example of derived demand is a firm's demand for labour: firms demand labour not for its own sake, but for the output that it produces.

The supply side of the transport market is also important, of course. Chapter 2 explained that **allocative efficiency** is important for society. In the context of the market for transport, it is important to examine whether the market operates effectively to provide the quantity, range and quality of transport services that people and firms wish to consume. In other words, is the price of transportation services equal to marginal cost across the sector? Chapters 10 and 11 will explore this issue, which depends on the structure of the various markets for transport. Transport offers some interesting examples of how markets operate. We will discuss, in particular, the market for bus travel and the emergence of the low-cost airlines, which have revolutionised air travel.

Key term

allocative efficiency: achieved when society is producing an appropriate bundle of goods relative to consumer preferences

The role of government has also been important, as the transport sector has been characterised by many examples of externalities. Issues of congestion and the pollution caused by vehicle emissions are well-known examples of externalities, which were discussed in *AS Economics, Chapter 6.* Issues relating to deregulation and privatisation have also typified the transport sector in recent decades. These will be discussed in Chapters 11 and 12.

As already discussed, the delivery of transportation services occurs in two phases. First, the delivery depends crucially on the availability of infrastructure. In order to provide road transport, there is a need for roads; a rail service requires track, and so on. The second phase is the provision of transport through various modes. For example, road transport can be in the form of private cars, buses and coaches, motor cycles and so on. The distinction between the two phases is significant because the first phase has typically involved government intervention, whereas the second phase has primarily been provided within private markets. The provision of infrastructure poses particular economic problems and requires careful evaluation of direct and indirect costs and benefits. Cost–benefit analysis in the context of transportation will be discussed in Chapter 12.

There is a major coordination problem here. There are many decisions being made by different agents, all of which are interrelated. This is further complicated by the fact that decisions about infrastructure take so long to come into effect. Decisions being taken today will affect the structure and efficiency of the transport system far into the future. An extreme example is the Channel Tunnel. The first recorded suggestion for a

tunnel linking England and France was made in 1802, and work actually commenced in 1881, only to be abandoned 2 years later. In more modern times, the English and French governments agreed to have another go at building a tunnel in 1973, but plans were again shelved. More studies were commissioned in the 1980s, work finally commenced in 1987 and the Tunnel was completed in 1994 (2 years late). Thus the period that elapsed between planning the infrastructure and it coming into operation was an extended one. This may be an extreme example, but it illustrates some of the problems in coordinating decisions.

Modes of transport

The market for transportation services encompasses a variety of modes of transport that need to be considered in any economic analysis of the sector. These modes include rail, road, air and water — and, in addition, there are some categories of goods that can be transported through pipelines. The balance between the various modes of transport has changed over time, partly reflecting changes in technology, but also in response to changes in real incomes and consumer preferences. Within each mode, there may be several forms of transport available. For example, road traffic covers not only cars, but also motorcycles, buses and coaches, light vans, heavy goods vehicles (HGVs) and pedal cycles.

The various modes have different economic characteristics. It might be argued that road transport has more flexibility than some other modes, as it is less constrained by specific infrastructure than the railways or canal network. On the other hand, rail transport has advantages in its ability to carry in bulk at relatively high speed. Air travel is clearly advantageous for long-distance travel, but also requires substantial infrastructure in the form of airports and air traffic control systems. Air travel remains the best way of visiting Australia, but you would not consider flying to the local shops!

Exercise 9.1

Discuss the relative merits of the major modes of transport (road, rail, air, water and pipeline) in respect of the following characteristics:

a   carrying capacity

b   flexibility of origin and destination

c   the need for infrastructure

d   ability to carry a wide variety of goods

e   the need for security

f   speed of transport

part 3

Passenger traffic

Figure 9.1 shows the changing pattern of passenger transport since 1971. The index shown in the figure is calculated on the basis of comparing billion passenger kilometres in each of the years with the level that was shown in 1971. Thus for all modes, there was an increase of about 90% between 1971 and 2009 (i.e. the value of the index in 2009 was 190.2). Passenger kilometres by air increased by 400% in the same period. In contrast, kilometres travelled by bus and coach fell by nearly 40%. A striking feature of the figure is the increase in air travel, which may in part be associated with the arrival of the low-cost airlines. However, you can see that the increase steadied out during the 2000s.

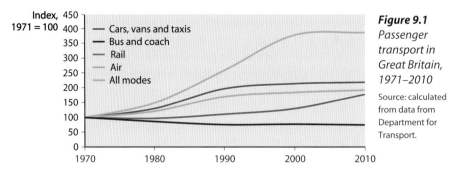

Figure 9.1 Passenger transport in Great Britain, 1971–2010

Source: calculated from data from Department for Transport.

As far as domestic transport is concerned, road traffic is the most used form of domestic transport, whether measured by the number of journeys undertaken or the average annual distance covered. Figure 9.2 shows index numbers comparing the average annual distance covered by people using various modes of transport relative to the distance covered by car. It shows, for example, that the average distance covered by rail or tube (per person per year) was 8.3% of that covered by car in 1985/86, and 9.6% in 2009. Studying these data, you will see that apart from rail all modes fell relative to car travel between 1985/86 and 2009.

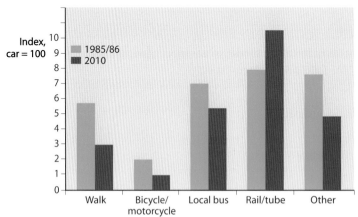

Figure 9.2 Average annual distance travelled in Great Britain by mode, 1985/86 and 2009

Source: Department for Transport.

This impression is reinforced by Figure 9.3, which shows the number of 'vehicle kilometres' travelled by car and by other modes of road traffic each year between 1980 and 2010. Note that to measure the usage of any form of transport, two common methods are used. One is to measure the distance travelled by a vehicle in a year

OCR A2 Economics

(a vehicle kilometre); an alternative is to measure the distance travelled by vehicle occupants (passenger kilometres, or tonne kilometres in the case of freight). Using passenger kilometres makes a lot of sense if the aim is to compare the efficiency of alternative modes of transport. For example, consider a journey between London and Newcastle. A train can obviously carry more passengers than a private car, so measuring just in terms of vehicle kilometres would be highly misleading, whereas measuring in terms of passenger kilometres is much more meaningful.

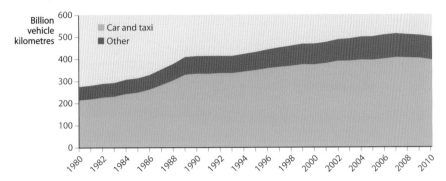

Figure 9.3 *Road traffic in Great Britain by transport mode, 1980–2010*

Note: data for 1993 onwards are not directly comparable with earlier data.

Source: Department for Transport.

Figure 9.3 shows a steady expansion in car kilometres throughout most of the period until the recession of 2008, but relatively little expansion in the other modes of road transport. This is probably what one would expect from economic analysis. This period was one of generally rising real incomes (until the recession), and it could be argued that car transport is likely to display a strong positive income elasticity of demand, whereas, for example, bus travel is likely to have a low — and perhaps negative — income elasticity of demand. In other words, bus travel could be seen as an example of an inferior good, so with rising real incomes it would be expected that the pattern of demand would switch away from bus travel towards the use of private cars. On the other hand, it may be that the demand for bus travel depends on other factors as well, such as the reliability of the service provided, and the amount of congestion on the roads.

A common method of measuring transport usage is by passenger kilometres

Figure 9.4 shows the pattern of non-car road traffic by mode over the same period, again measured in vehicle kilometres. The data are shown as index numbers, based on

1980 = 100, in order to demonstrate the changes in the pattern that have been taking place over time. The strongest growth was in the use of light vans, where the number of vehicle kilometres more than doubled between 1980 and 2010. The use of buses and coaches also increased, by a relatively modest 45% over the period. However, there was a fall in the use of pedal cycles (down by 4%) and motorcycles (down by 40%).

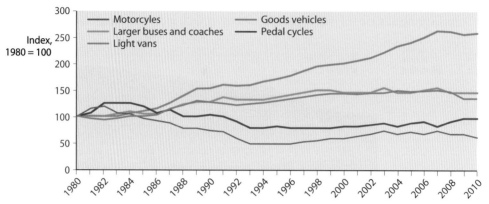

Figure 9.4 *Non-car road traffic by transport mode, 1980–2010*

Source: Department for Transport.

To what extent are the trends in road traffic associated with changes in real incomes? One way to explore this question is to look at changes in road traffic relative to changes in real GDP. Figure 9.5 presents some data on this issue. It shows indexes of road traffic and real GDP based on 1980 = 100. Until about 1990 it seems that road traffic and real GDP rose together. There was then a period in which real GDP flattened out, with road traffic continuing to grow for a couple of years until it also flattened out. Real GDP then caught up and the two series converged towards the end of the period. The fact that the demand for transport has risen with changes in real income could suggest that transport is a normal good, whereas the fall in the usage of motorcycles (especially during the 1980s and early 1990s) might suggest that motorcycle transport could be seen as an inferior good. In other words, as real incomes rise, consumers tend to switch from motorcycles to cars. Also apparent in the figure is the way that real GDP dipped in the recession towards the end of the period: accompanied by a fall in road traffic.

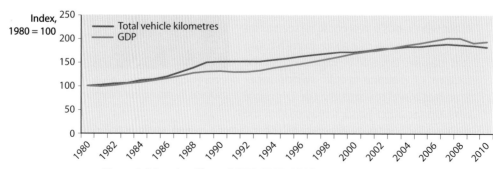

Figure 9.5 *Road traffic and GDP, 1980–2010*

Sources: Department for Transport, ONS.

The use of pedal cycles has fallen over the last two decades

However, the data suggest that the relationship between traffic and income is not a straightforward one. This is what is to be expected, given that in real life it cannot be expected that a ceteris paribus assumption will hold true. In particular, consumers may also respond to changes in the real cost of transport. The theory of demand suggests that the demand for a good depends upon the price of the good and the prices of other goods as well as upon consumer incomes and preferences. This holds for the demand for transport as much as for any other good.

Figure 9.6 shows how relative prices of different modes of passenger transport have changed since 1996. Here again, an index is used to show these relative (or real) prices. These index numbers are based on components of the consumer price index (CPI), in which for any given year, the price of passenger transport is expressed as a percentage of the all items index, but all based on 1996 = 100. What this shows is that road transport has become steadily more expensive over the years, with the price rising by more than the CPI for all items. On the other hand, the relative price of air travel fell after 2001, only to increase again towards the end of the 2000s. The relative price of air travel was about 10% higher above the CPI in 2010 than in 1996, but still low relative to other modes of transport.

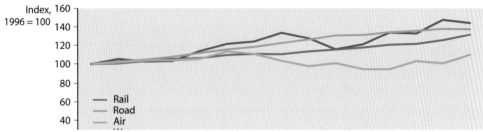

Figure 9.6 *The real price of passenger transport in Great Britain by mode, 1996–2010*

Source: calculated from ONS data.

Freight traffic

Figure 9.7 summarises the movement of domestic freight according to mode of transport, again showing data between 1980 and 2009. In terms of tonne kilometres, road transport again dominates the scene, although it would appear that shipping of goods is also significant. The data here include both coastal shipping and internal waterways. Rail is seen to carry a relatively small proportion of total freight, with something of an increase since the mid-1990s. The dip in road freight in the recession of the late 2000s is very evident in this figure.

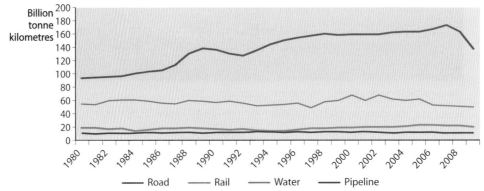

Figure 9.7 *Domestic freight transport in Great Britain by transport mode, 1980–2009*

Source: Department for Transport.

In interpreting these data it is important to be aware of the average length of journeys, which varies substantially between the transport modes. Figure 9.8 clearly shows that the average length of domestic haul for freight carried by water was significantly greater than for other modes of transport. This is likely to reflect the cost structure of the mode. It pays to transport freight by sea for long distances because of the relatively high loading costs compared with loading an HGV. In other words, there may be economies of scale

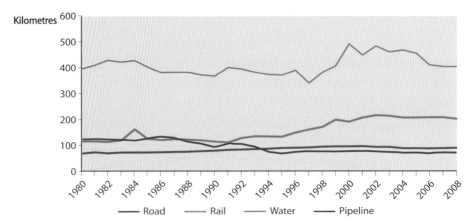

Figure 9.8 *Average length of domestic haul in Great Britain by transport mode, 1980–2008*

Source: Department for Transport.

(distance) involved here. A similar argument might apply in the case of rail freight transport. The graph reveals that there has been an appreciable increase in the average length of haul by rail, suggesting that rail is competing better for long-haul freight as opposed to short haul, where it would be expected that road transport would have an advantage because of its flexibility.

For businesses, some use of road transport is inevitable. Rail and water transport may have advantages for long-haul transport, but delivery to individual factories or sales outlets requires an element of road transportation. There are few factories that can have their own rail terminal.

The need to transport raw materials or finished products may have a strong influence on the location decision of firms. If the materials used in the production process are bulky or heavy relative to the output produced by a firm, it may choose to locate where the materials can be conveniently brought in. On the other hand, if the firm's product is fragile or otherwise difficult to transport, the firm may prefer to be located close to its market.

Thus the nature of the transportation needs of a firm may have important repercussions for location decisions. Modern industry is less prone to these influences, but location decisions in the past continue to influence the present pattern of activity.

The UK shows a similar modal split of passenger travel as in the EU as a whole, as shown in Figure 9.9. This pattern has changed very little over the past 20 years, although changes have been visible in some countries. For example, the use of passenger cars in Greece has increased substantially as real incomes have risen, while the share of passenger transport by coaches and buses has fallen. We might expect this sort of pattern if bus travel is an inferior good from the vantage point of people in Greece.

The pattern of freight transport across Europe varies much more, which is shown by Figure 9.10. This naturally reflects the availability of appropriate

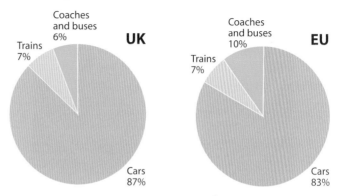

Figure 9.9 *Modal split of passenger non-air transport, 2008*
Source: Eurostat.

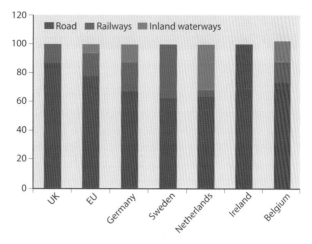

Figure 9.10 *Modal split of freight transport, 2009*
Source: Eurostat.

infrastructure in different countries. For example, It is not surprising to find that inland waterways are significantly more important for freight in the Netherlands and in Belgium, whereas road dominates in the UK and Ireland.

Forecasting transport needs

The two-phase nature of the delivery of transport services means that it is very important to be able to forecast the future demand for transport. The provision of infrastructure requires careful future planning, given the time that it takes to build new roads or construct new port facilities. The nature of the demand for transport makes such forecasting a difficult undertaking. This is partly because the provision of infrastructure may itself influence demand. For example, there has been considerable debate about the effect of road building and improvement schemes. It has been argued that road improvements have the effect of increasing the amount of traffic on the roads, rather than reducing congestion.

The fact that much of the transport infrastructure is publicly provided means that such forecasting is an integral part of the process – and it also means that the authorities need a way of taking externalities into account when formulating a transport strategy. There also needs to be careful coordination of transport planning, given the interactions between the demands for different modes of transport. For example, decisions taken now about improvements to the rail network may have implications for the future demand for road transport, and hence for the present need to invest in the road system.

Rail transport has advantages for long-haul transport

Forecasting of transport needs can only be undertaken with an understanding of the economic processes at work. Such an understanding needs to encompass both the demand and supply sides of the market for transport, and needs to be able to take into account the potential interactions between different transport markets. The demand for transportation services is likely to change over time as real incomes change, and as relative prices move. The supply of transportation services will be influenced by the way that markets evolve through time, and by advances in technology that may bring about changes in the relative importance of different modes of travel.

As an illustration, Figure 9.11 shows some forecasts of traffic volume made by the Department of Transport in 1997. These relate to billion vehicle kilometres travelled

by car (including taxis). The graph shows the actual data up to 1996, and then the forecasts up to 2031. Given that there is considerable uncertainty about the forecasts, three variants are shown. The 'Central' forecast represents the most likely scenario, and the 'High' and 'Low' forecasts represent alternative forecasts based on different assumptions. In producing these forecasts, assumptions had to be made about key influences on traffic, such as the rate of increase of real incomes (GDP), changes in fuel prices and in fuel efficiency, the road network, policies on rail and bus services, and so on. With so many assumptions, you should not be surprised at the range in the forecasts, which naturally becomes wider the further the forecasts extend into the future.

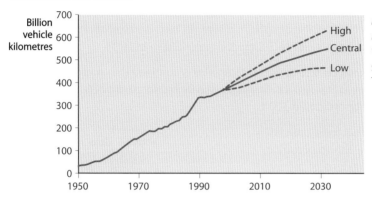

Figure 9.11
Forecasting traffic volume

Source: Department for Transport.

Exercise 9.2

Suppose you were set the task of forecasting the volume of road traffic over the next 25 years. Discuss why you would need to take into account the investment plans for the rail network. Identify other factors that would affect your forecasts.

Paying for transportation services

A strong reason for public provision of transport services in the past has been that transport infrastructure has some of the characteristics of a public good. Recall from *AS Economics, Chapter 7* that a public good is one which is non-rivalrous and non-excludable. In other words, the consumption of a good by one person does not prevent others from also consuming the good, and consumers cannot be excluded from consuming the good. Many roads can be seen to have these characteristics. There is only rivalry in consumption when the road becomes congested, and it is difficult to exclude people from using the road — at least while maintaining a flow of traffic. There are some situations in which it does become possible to charge for road use — as witness the M6 toll road and the London Congestion Charge. However, extending such schemes to a wider range of roads is difficult. In other words, roads may be seen as quasi-public goods. Chapter 12 returns to this issue to examine the economic arguments concerning road pricing and the imposition of user charges.

Exercise 9.3

Explain why a road system may be regarded as a public good. If necessary, refer back to *AS Economics, Chapter 7.*

The importance of the transport sector in the economy

The transport sector is a significant sector as far as the overall economy is concerned. In 2011, it accounted for 4.8% of total employment in the UK. This proportion has remained stable over time, having been 4.8% in 1978. As far as households' budgets are concerned, expenditure on transport in real terms has risen substantially, reaching £77.80 in 2008. This represents 16.5% of total expenditure in 2008.

The division of this expenditure between categories is dominated by motoring expenditure, as can be seen in Figure 9.12. Motoring accounted for about 80% of household expenditure on transport in mid-2011.

It might be argued that these data fail to do full justice to the importance of transport in a modern economy. In other words, the importance of transport goes beyond its ability to employ people and to occupy part of every household's budget. This is because of its pivotal importance to both businesses and households. The economics of transport provision is thus an important area of study. If resources are not well allocated in this sector, it will have repercussions across the whole economy.

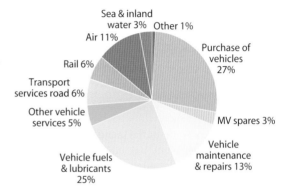

Figure 9.12 *Household expenditure on transport, quarter 2, 2011*
Source: ONS.

The transport sector is seen to be especially critical in the context of international trade. Once countries begin to specialise in the production of certain goods, and want to trade these with other countries, transport becomes of central importance. Such specialisation is important if producers are to reach a sufficiently large market to be able to take full advantage of economies of scale in production. This may be hindered if the transport system is inefficient. Indeed, try to imagine a world in which goods cannot be transported from one country — or from one region — to another. Each country would need to produce all the goods and services that its residents wished to consume. This would be highly inefficient, and would limit the range of commodities that could be consumed.

Summary

➤ Transport involves the movement of people and goods from one place to another, and is a vital part of a modern economy.

➤ The demand for transport is a derived demand, in the sense that it is demanded not for its own sake, but for the services it provides.

➤ The supply of transportation services in the past has come from a mixture of public and private sector provision.

➤ The provision of appropriate infrastructure for the transport sector may require some government intervention to the extent that it involves public good aspects.

➤ The market for transport covers a range of different modes, each of which may be suitable for particular segments of the market, although the modes may compete with each other in some areas.

➤ Road traffic is the most important mode of passenger transport, whether measured by the number of journeys undertaken or by the distance covered.

➤ There has been a substantial increase in the volume of car traffic in the last 25 years, but relatively little expansion of other modes of road transport.

➤ Road transport is also the most important form of freight transport, although transport by water (coastal shipping and internal waterways) remains important, especially for long hauls.

➤ Economic analysis is an integral part of attempts to forecast future transport needs.

➤ The transport sector is vital to the functioning of a modern economy.

Chapter 10
Market structures and competitive behaviour in transport markets

Part 1 of the book introduced the notion of market structure, and outlined its importance in enabling an allocation of resources that is good for society. It is important to see how this works in practice, and this chapter presents an evaluation of how market structure has influenced the allocation of resources in the transport sector.

Learning outcomes

After studying this chapter, you should:
- ➤ be aware of the issues surrounding the privatisation of the rail industry, and the need to balance efficiency gains against the maintenance of safety standards
- ➤ be familiar with changes in the market for bus transport in the UK as an example of how market structure can evolve over time
- ➤ understand how contestability may inhibit firms' behaviour in the context of low-cost airlines
- ➤ be familiar with the notion of a natural monopoly, and appreciate the extent to which the Channel Tunnel may be seen as an example of this
- ➤ understand what is meant by deregulation and franchising
- ➤ be able to evaluate the impact of deregulation in transport markets

Nationalisation or privatisation?

A particular issue in the transport sector has concerned the degree of public ownership that is appropriate. In the aftermath of the Second World War many enterprises operating in markets that were natural monopolies were nationalised. The transport sector was among the first to go through this process, whereby enterprises were taken into state ownership.

 Key term

nationalisation: a process whereby an enterprise is taken into state ownership

The main arguments for nationalisation concern productive and allocative efficiency. Figure 10.1 shows a natural monopoly, the key feature of which is that long-run average cost (*LAC*) is declining right up to the limit of market demand. If such a market

is operated as a profit-maximising private monopoly, then the firm chooses output Q_m, where marginal cost equals marginal revenue. The price that clears the market is then at P_m. From society's point of view, this is inefficient in terms of both productive and allocative efficiency. The firm is operating at relatively high average cost — that is, it is not fully exploiting the available economies of scale, so does not achieve productive efficiency. Furthermore, the firm sets a price that is substantially above marginal cost, so allocative efficiency is not achieved.

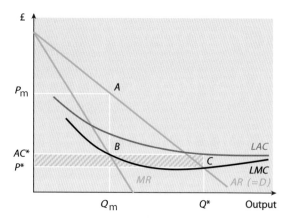

Figure 10.1 *A natural monopoly*

One option for the authorities would be to regulate the market, and to force the firm to set a price equal to marginal cost. This would be at Q^*, with price set at P^*. This is problematic, because this forces the firm to set a price that is below long-run average cost, so it would be forced to make a loss in the long term, given by the shaded area in Figure 10.1. This is not a viable situation, and the authorities could only enable the firm to operate by providing a subsidy.

Another argument for nationalisation was based on the presence of externalities in transport markets. In particular, it was argued that the railways provided a social service by ensuring that otherwise remote communities were not isolated. In other words, marginal social benefits from some routes exceeded marginal private benefits. A profit-maximising private firm would not find it profitable to maintain such routes, whereas a publicly-owned enterprise could cross-subsidise such services.

In time, some flaws in this approach began to become apparent. The whole basis under which nationalised enterprises operated required continuing subsidies. It was seen that this meant higher government borrowing than would otherwise have been needed. In addition, it was argued that the managers of subsidised public enterprises had no real incentive to achieve high efficiency, and it was perceived that many state enterprises were characterised by X-inefficiency.

In the 1980s, the then prime minister, Margaret Thatcher, embarked on a programme of **privatisation**, transferring many state-owned enterprises into the private sector, including a number in the transport sector.

Key **term**

privatisation: a process whereby an enterprise is transferred from public into private ownership

The main objectives of privatisation were to counter the flaws outlined above. By withdrawing subsidies and making managers accountable to shareholders, it was hoped to eliminate the X-inefficiency that had built up over the years. As a by-

product, the process of selling off these enterprises would expand share ownership — a separate objective of the government. It would also reduce the need for government borrowing. In order to prevent enterprises from abusing their market position, official regulators were established to monitor the process. One of the steps taken by regulators was to give targets for productivity gains, in that prices were required to rise more slowly than the retail price index. In addition, where possible, competition was encouraged, this being seen as another way of giving managers good incentives to be efficient.

Deregulation and the market for bus transport in the UK

One market that was part of the privatisation drive was the bus sector. For many years the UK market for bus transport was highly regulated. Local authorities had responsibility for bus transport in their areas, and bus routes between cities in England and Wales were served by a nationalised monopoly company — the National Bus Company, created under the Transport Act of 1968. A second company controlled routes in Scotland. Market forces were thus overridden by local regulation and planning.

During the 1980s, the market (except in London) was deregulated as part of Margaret Thatcher's privatisation drive, in which many industries that had previously been state operated were sold into private hands. In the case of bus transport, the National Bus Company was broken into 72 separate companies in 1986, with no single buyer being allowed to purchase more than three of these companies, and buyers being prohibited from owning companies that operated in contiguous areas.

The fundamental idea behind this move to withdraw government from direct intervention in these markets was to stimulate competition among firms. It had been argued that one characteristic of state-owned enterprises was X-inefficiency. Managers of such enterprises were seen to be inadequately monitored, and faced no great incentive to improve efficiency. In the absence of competition, complacency would creep in, and production would no longer take place at minimum cost. By allowing and encouraging competition — or by making managers accountable to private shareholders — it was argued that X-inefficiency would be eliminated and productivity improved.

An important effect of deregulation was seen in relation to barriers to entry. With a deregulated market, entry was no longer tightly controlled, and as long as a firm could meet the safety requirements, it could set up in business.

In the case of bus transport, deregulation at first seemed to affect the market in the way that had been expected. During the early part of this period, many small bus companies sprang up, and there was intense competition between them. It seemed that perfect competition could become a reality. In particular, it was argued that barriers to entry were so low that competition would be assured, and that the bus market should be regarded as highly contestable. Prices were being driven down towards marginal cost, and consumers reaped the benefit.

As time went by, however, it became apparent that some bus companies were beginning to grow, and others were going out of business. Gradually the market was becoming more concentrated, as revealed by data published by the Competition Commission (formerly the Monopolies and Mergers Commission). In 1989, the largest firm in the bus industry was Stagecoach, with just 3.9% of the UK industry by turnover. At this time, the largest 9 companies accounted for just 12.8% of the market. This changed rapidly over the following 5 years, by the end of which Stagecoach had increased its share to 13.4%, and the top 9 firms accounted for 56% of the UK market. The process of merger and acquisition continued after that time, and by 2003 the top four firms in the market accounted for more than 60% of the market. The shares are shown in Figure 10.2.

However, these data may understate the extent of market power held by the largest firms. This is because not all of the large firms are equally active in the regions. In other words, some firms concentrate their activities in certain areas of the country, and may become dominant in particular local markets. An example of market shares in a local market is given in Figure 10.3, which shows the situation in the bus market in west central Scotland in 2003. The Office of Fair Trading (OFT) argued that many local markets were likely to be even more concentrated than this, as the 'big four' had tended to focus their strength in particular areas.

One reason for this level of concentration might be the existence of some economies of scale. It might be that bus manufacturers could be persuaded to give discounts on bulk orders for new buses, or perhaps there are economies of scale in servicing and maintaining a large fleet of vehicles. These would enable the larger bus companies to undercut smaller providers.

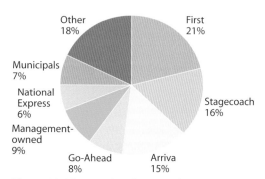

Figure 10.2 *Bus market shares in the UK, 2003*

Source: Bus Industry Monitor, 2003.

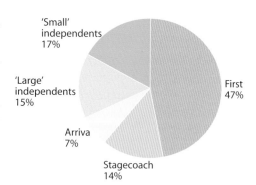

Figure 10.3 *Bus market shares in west central Scotland, 2003*

Notes: 'large' independents are operators with a market share of 1% or over; 'small' independents are companies with a market share of less than 1%.

Source: Strathclyde Partnership for Transport.

It seems clear that some of the larger bus companies did indeed achieve economies of scale, since they claimed this as a defence in investigations carried out by the OFT and the Competition Commission. It also seems to be the case that companies were prepared to use their power to increase their market share, and a number of investigations were triggered by

Large bus companies such as Stagecoach achieved economies of scale which allowed them to undercut smaller providers

accusations of anti-competitive behaviour by bus companies. For example, it was alleged that one large bus company seeking entry into a new market would get hold of competitors' timetables, and then send along a free bus service to poach all the passengers.

Such *predatory pricing* rarely benefits consumers in the long run. Once competitors have been forced out of the market, the predator firm can then raise price (and restrict output) so as to increase profits. This helps to explain why the OFT has kept a close eye on the bus industry as it has evolved over the last 20 years.

In 1995 the takeover by Stagecoach of Ayrshire Bus prompted an investigation by the Monopolies and Mergers Commission. This case highlighted an important aspect of the influence of market structure on consumer welfare: namely, that there is a potential trade-off between productive and allocative efficiency. By gaining market power, a firm may be able to increase its profits by charging a price above marginal cost, which is damaging in terms of allocative efficiency. On the other hand, by tapping into economies of scale, it improves productive efficiency, which may lead to prices being lower than they would otherwise have been.

Another aspect of Stagecoach's operations (and those of other large bus companies) is an involvement in rail transport. By coordinating its rail and bus services — for example, through timetabling — the company may again be able to make life difficult for competitors. However, it may be argued that, although allocative efficiency may suffer from this practice, productive efficiency improves.

A key question in all of this is the extent to which a bus company on a particular route has sufficient market power to maintain price at such a level as to make supernormal profits. The *sunk costs* involved for another bus company to start serving a new route may be relatively low. This suggests that a bus company that consistently makes supernormal profits on a route is likely to be vulnerable to hit-and-run competition. In other words, if a market for bus transport is contestable, the existing firm may choose not to set price at a level that generates high profits

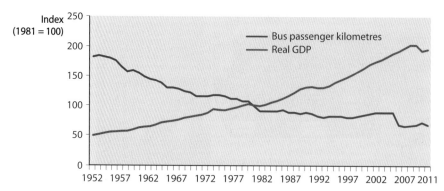

Figure 10.4 *Passenger kilometres by bus and real GDP, 1952–2011*

and attracts the entry of new firms. The market would then behave very much as if it were perfectly competitive – at least in terms of pricing. However, it would seem that this has not always been the case.

It is also important to be aware that this is a shrinking market. Figure 10.4 shows how the number of passenger kilometres has declined steadily since 1950, using index numbers based on 1981 = 100. You can see that this decline took place against a backdrop of steadily rising real GDP. It might be expected that firms would have less scope for using market power when overall demand is in decline.

To summarise the situation in the bus industry, it evolved fairly rapidly after deregulation. Having been a tightly regulated sector, it was transformed initially into a state of monopolistic competition, but then went through a process of merger and acquisition, becoming an oligopoly. The monitoring activities of the competition authorities and the potential contestability of markets may have prevented firms from fully exploiting their market positions at the expense of consumers. However, it is very difficult to come to an overall judgement on the effectiveness of privatisation in this market, as it is impossible to evaluate what the market would have been like had there not been deregulation and privatisation.

Exercise 10.1

Visit the website of the Office of Fair Trading (**www.oft.gov.uk**) and find out whether there have been any recent merger cases involving bus transport operators. Discuss the extent to which contestability offers protection to consumers.

Regulation and the market for bus transport in London

The Transport Act of 1985 triggered the deregulation of bus services in the UK – except in London and Northern Ireland. It was intended that eventually the market for bus travel in London would also be deregulated, and moves towards this were

OCR A2 Economics

implemented. However, deregulation was postponed until after the general election in 1997. The incoming Labour government did not go ahead with deregulation, and instead reintroduced a strategic governing authority for London. Transport for London (TfL) was launched in July 2000, replacing London Transport. TfL has responsibility for public transport within the London area, including buses and the Underground – not to mention the Congestion Charge, which will be discussed in Chapter 11. This is all set in the context of the Mayor's Transport Strategy.

Although London was exempt from deregulation under the 1985 Act, changes were introduced at that time. In particular, private bus companies could tender for bus routes within London in an open market, but London Transport continued to fix prices and co-ordinate the network. Under TfL, regulation has been extended to cover a number of aspects of service quality, as well as having close co-ordination of the network, and competitive tendering for individual routes. The success of TfL has led to calls for bus services elsewhere to be re-regulated.

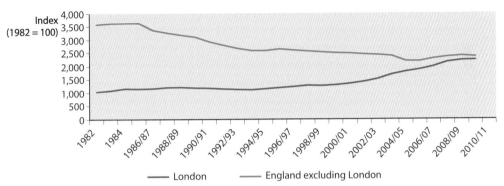

Figure 10.5 *Bus journeys undertaken, 1982–2010*

The success can partly be seen in the number of bus journeys undertaken in London compared with elsewhere. Figure 10.5 shows something of this. You can see that the number of passenger journeys in London has increased steadily – especially during the 2000s. By contrast, in the rest of England there has been a steady decline in the number of journeys undertaken.

TfL claims to operate about 7,500 buses, serving 6 million passengers on a typical weekday, covering 19,500 bus stops on 700 different routes in the London area. More than 100 of these routes run 24 hours a day, 7 days a week.

So what are the benefits of regulation in the context of London?

One obvious point to make is that this is a complex network of routes over a large area. Allowing completely free competition between companies might mean that bus companies would focus on the most profitable routes, leaving some routes not being served. It is worth noting in this context that TfL claims that 90% of London residents live within 400 metres of a bus stop. Some degree of regulation is needed to ensure that this remains the case. Regulation thus provides co-ordination between service

providers — and also between modes of transport, given that TfL also controls the Underground system and influences the pattern of car usage through the Congestion Charge. This ability to produce an integrated plan for transport is an important aspect of TfL's role.

TfL is also able to impose and monitor quality standards in terms of services (such as waiting times), safety, driver quality, emissions (important for the environment) and provision for wheelchair users.

Privatisation and the railways

Another part of the transport sector that went through a process of privatisation is the railways. As with other privatisations, the government hoped to achieve a number of objectives by this process. One objective was to improve efficiency, as it was argued that the managers of state-owned enterprises faced weak incentives to achieve productive efficiency. If an element of competition could be introduced, and if managers could be made accountable to shareholders, it was thought that this should lead to a reduction in X-inefficiency and an overall improvement in welfare. At the time that rail privatisation was being discussed in the early 1990s, there was also a concern about the financing of the rail system, with an escalating need for public subsidies. The Serpell Report, which examined the industry, argued that safety targets had been excessively high, and suggested that there could be some relaxation of maintenance standards.

It was initially envisaged that train operations should be privatised, but that network provision would remain in the hands of the public sector. However, in the event, both train and network operations were privatised in 1996. As far as the network operations were concerned, it was intended that efficiency improvements and maintenance cost reductions would be achieved through a process of contracting out. As far as the train operators were concerned, it was hoped that competition between operators would stimulate efficiency gains.

The process by which rail services were privatised was through a system of **franchising**. Firms were able to take responsibility for operating trains on particular routes for a given period. There were 25 such passenger franchises, divided between a number of train operating companies.

 Key *term*

franchising: under rail privatisation, a situation in which a firm is given the right to operate a particular service for a stated period

However, for many routes the outcome was that a single operator emerged, so that competition was less intense than had been hoped. In part, this reflected the franchising system that had been adopted, which meant that train operating companies effectively operated as monopolies on their routes, although they may have faced competition on some overlapping routes. Furthermore, as time went by, some consolidation of firms took place, and some bus operators began to move into the rail sector. Figure

It was argued that privatisation of the railways would lead to an improvement in efficiency

10.6 shows the national market shares among train operators in 2010/11. By this time, the largest three firms were supplying about 68% of the market in terms of the number of passenger journeys, and 66% of passenger kilometres, so even on a national scale, concentration was high. The fact that some companies were sole operators on individual routes suggests that competition is likely to be limited. In the context of a broader transport market, it is also potentially significant that some of the large suppliers of rail transport are also important providers in the bus market.

In terms of carrying freight, the market was even more concentrated, with the largest company (DB Schenker) carrying an estimated 62% of the rail freight market in the UK in 2010 and running more than 800 trains per day. However, given that there is strong competition from road haulage, the lack of competition in the rail sector may not be a major concern, particularly as substantial economies of scale are available.

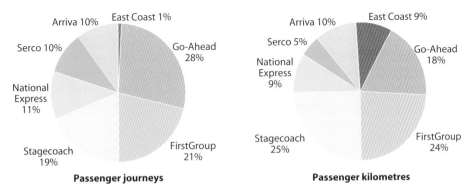

Figure 10.6 *Market shares of train operating companies, 2010/11*

Source: Department for Transport.

One of the most contentious parts of the rail market since privatisation has been the development and maintenance of the network. After privatisation, Railtrack became the monopoly owner of railway infrastructure. This includes track, signalling, stations, depots, bridges, tunnels, level crossings, viaducts and so on. A high-profile fatal train crash at Hatfield in 2000, resulting from a fault in the track, brought Railtrack under the spotlight and in 2002 it was replaced by Network Rail. Network Rail is a company 'limited by guarantee', which means that it is a private organisation operating as a commercial enterprise, but with no shareholders and hence no requirement to pay dividends. Any profits are reinvested to maintain and upgrade the rail infrastructure.

Figure 10.7 shows the level of investment in rolling stock (vehicles) and rail infrastructure since 1985. This seems to show that investment in infrastructure began to increase after privatisation, accelerating towards the end of the period shown. Investment in rolling stock seemed to dip after privatisation, but then began to pick up again.

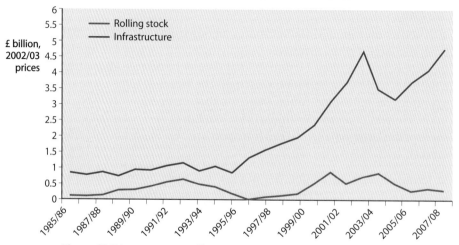

Figure 10.7 *Investment in rolling stock and rail infrastructure, 1985–2009*
Source: Department for Transport.

The overall regulation and planning of the rail industry has also gone through a process of change. On privatisation, responsibility for monitoring market structure was given to the Office of the Rail Regulator, whose brief involved 'the regulation of the monopoly and dominant elements of the railways with particular focus on the rail network infrastructure operator'. From the point of view of economic analysis, one danger is that a monopoly operator would choose to maximise profits by setting prices high and restricting output, but equally there is a concern that profits would be increased at the expense of safety or service standards.

The Transport Act of 2000 introduced further changes, launching the Strategic Rail Authority (SRA) to promote better use of the railways within an integrated transport policy. The SRA itself was wound up in 2005, and its functions subsumed into the Department for Transport (Rail Group). Another reorganisation of functions in 2004 saw the establishment of a new Office of Rail Regulation (ORR) as a combined safety and economic regulator.

The need to achieve such a variety of objectives makes it difficult to evaluate the extent to which rail privatisation has been successful. The original aims of privatisation were to achieve efficiency gains and to reduce maintenance costs. However, the fact that privatisation took place in a context where investment in infrastructure had been neglected over a period of years complicates the analysis. There are also clear costs for society if efficiency gains compromise safety standards. In the early part of the twenty-first century it would seem that the industry is beginning to improve. Time alone will tell whether the rail system will be able to play its full part within an integrated transport system in the future. The significance of this will be discussed in Chapter 12.

Price discrimination

From an economic point of view, one interesting aspect of the rail industry is the extensive use of *price discrimination*. This is a process by which a firm is able to charge a different price to different customers for the same good (see Chapter 3). In the context of the railways, the most obvious example of price discrimination is the difference between peak and off-peak fares.

The practice is made possible because those who need to use the railways in order to travel to work have to travel at certain times of day, and have less elastic demand than those who can travel at any time of day, perhaps for leisure trips, shopping, etc. A monopoly operator is thus able to charge commuters travelling in peak periods a higher price, as they are less sensitive to price – or have less choice about when to travel.

Passengers who have to pay the higher prices may well see this as exploitative behaviour by the monopolist. However, there may be situations in which a firm would not be able to remain in business without the possibility of price discrimination. For example, consider Figure 10.8. Here, the firm faces average costs that are always above demand (*AR*). Setting marginal cost equal to marginal revenue suggests that the profit-maximising level of output is q_m, but if the firm chooses to produce this output, and sets a price at p_m, the result

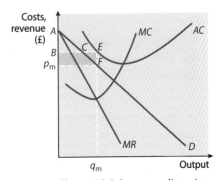

Figure 10.8 A monopolist using price discrimination

is a loss (given by the shaded area), as average cost exceeds average revenue. Such a situation is not sustainable in the long run.

However, if the firm is able to use price discrimination, it may be possible to remain profitable by tapping the consumer surplus of some groups of customers. For example, if the firm can operate perfect price discrimination, it could acquire the area of consumer surplus *ABC* as profit to set against the area *CEF* of losses. One of the tasks of the regulator may be to make sure that this practice is not over-exploited by the train operators.

The low-cost airlines

With the growth in the foreign package holiday market, air travel has come to be a key part of the leisure market, as well as being critical in terms of transport. The face of air travel has changed dramatically since the appearance of the low-cost airlines, beginning with Southwestern in the USA (launched as long ago as 1971), followed by Ryanair in 1985 and easyJet in 1995. The model was later copied by Air Asia and other airlines operating in southeast Asia.

This market provides an illustration of how intensified competition can affect the operation of markets. Before the advent of the low-cost airlines, the market for air travel was dominated by large national carriers, in many cases either state-run or heavily subsidised by governments. As time went by, these large airlines began to join together in strategic alliances that enabled them to work together yet maintain their individual characters. The market seemed to be consolidating and was effectively becoming more concentrated.

Deregulation provided an opening for changes in the market structure, by reducing the barriers to entry of new firms. However, in order to exploit that opening, the budget airlines needed a good understanding of economic analysis. Their success has been built on a thorough understanding of cost structures and a recognition of the contestability of airlines, together with the judicious use of price discrimination.

Profits depend upon costs as well as revenue. EasyJet (not to mention other budget airlines, such as Ryanair and Flybe) have taken a close look at the structure of costs. Figure 10.9 shows a detailed breakdown of the costs of a typical easyJet flight. By focusing on each individual item of costs and looking for ways of cutting costs to a minimum, the budget airlines have been able to achieve profitability.

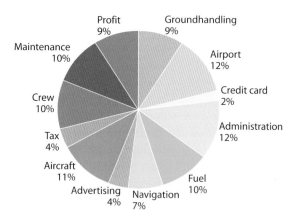

Figure 10.9 *The cost of an easyJet flight*

Source: *Guardian*, 20 August 2003.

In part, this has been connected with the understanding of demand. The budget airlines offer a 'no frills' approach, doing away with pre-assigned seats and pre-issued tickets, free in-flight catering, a separate business class and so on. They also use more

remote airports, where charges are relatively low. But the savings go way beyond these conspicuous items.

In particular, the budget airlines have followed a pattern established by the Texas-based airline Southwestern, which sets out four key rules.

First, only fly one type of plane. This reduces maintenance costs and avoids the need to hold a wide range of spare parts. This is one source of potential economies of scale.

Second, drive down costs every year. This may be achieved while the airline is still expanding if there are economies of scale to be reaped. For example, it may be achieved by negotiating improved deals from suppliers – of fuel, insurance, etc.

Third, minimise the time that aircraft spend parked on the tarmac. The no frills and no tickets approach enables a much quicker turn-round of aircraft – which, after all, only earn money for the company when they are in the air. For example, an easyJet plane flying between Luton and Nice can make four round-trips per day – by spending only about half-an-hour on the tarmac at each end.

Fourth, do not try to sell anything except seats. Schemes that offer loyalty bonuses or air miles cost money to administer, and are more complicated than they are worth.

Following these rules, and paying careful attention to the various forms of costs identified in Figure 10.9 has enabled the budget airlines to expand, to make profits (9% in the diagram), and to transform air travel.

As far as price discrimination is concerned, easyJet says on its website that it 'operates a very simple fare structure...based on supply and demand'. The nature of the price structure is that passengers who book early pay the lowest prices, whereas those who book close to their travel time pay the highest prices. Figure 10.10 (based on information in an article in the *Guardian*) shows that on a particular flight from Luton to Nice on 20 August 2003, the prices paid by passengers varied from just £20 to about £140.

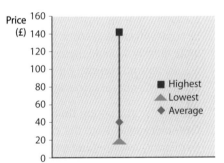

Figure 10.10 *Prices paid on an easyJet flight*

Source: *Guardian*, 20 August 2003.

You might expect that in a competitive market, the price structure would be the opposite. If prices follow costs, the marginal cost to easyJet of carrying an extra passenger is likely to be pretty low, so the flight could be filled up by offering last-minute deals, with the price being driven close to marginal cost. But this is clearly not happening at easyJet, as the later a passenger books, the higher the price that they face.

This suggests that easyJet understands enough about the nature of demand to use price discrimination on its flights. People who book at the last minute are likely to be business travellers who need to fly urgently, perhaps for a business meeting or to clinch a deal. Such customers are likely to have low elasticity of demand, and thus be

prepared to pay a higher price for their ticket. This is in contrast to those who can book well in advance, who are more likely to be people travelling for pleasure — visiting relatives or going on holiday. For these travellers, the choice of when to fly is more flexible. This means there are more possible flights from which they can choose. And we know that when there are substitutes for a commodity, the price elasticity of demand is high. It is for these customers that easyJet can offer the low prices that we see being advertised. After all, at £20, it probably costs some customers more to get to the airport than it costs for the flight!

So, easyJet can make use of this difference in demand elasticity to charge different prices to different customers, even if the product (the flight from London to Nice) is the same for all of them. Thus an understanding of demand is important for easyJet.

The entry of the budget airlines also caused the existing firms to reconsider the way in which they operate. Some reacted by setting up their own budget subsidiaries, with varying degrees of success. Others have had to accept that they need to focus on longer-haul flights.

The budget airlines case therefore provides another example of how competition can transform a market, and how contestability can affect firms' behaviour. Why can the airline business be regarded as contestable? After all, it might be argued that the set-up costs of establishing an airline are likely to be high, so it is difficult to claim that there are no sunk costs faced by firms. However, the key issue is that market conditions on particular routes may well encourage contestability. Once the airline is established, the costs of flying a new route are relatively low. There are bound to be some advertising costs, but otherwise an airline can switch aircraft to new routes quite quickly. It could then switch to other routes if profits were disappointing. In other words, hit-and-run entry is possible on particular routes. This may mean that existing airlines will not set prices at such levels that entry is attracted.

It is also worth noting that the low-cost airlines have flourished not only by taking customers away from the existing airlines, but also by tapping a new customer base. By offering low fares and easy accessibility, they have attracted passengers who would not otherwise have dreamed of flying.

Exercise 10.3

Discuss ways in which price discrimination may be used by airlines.

The Channel Tunnel — a natural monopoly?

Earlier in the chapter it was pointed out that some markets may result in a *natural monopoly*, mainly because of the structure of their costs. The argument was illustrated by Figure 10.1.

This situation may arise where there are large fixed (or set-up) costs, but relatively low variable costs. One example might be an underground railway system in a city. There are large set-up costs involved in building the rail network and buying the rolling stock, but very low variable costs, in the sense that the cost of carrying one additional passenger is very low indeed.

At first glance, it might be thought that the Channel Tunnel is rather similar. The construction and other fixed costs of building the tunnel are very high indeed compared with the marginal cost of transporting one additional passenger through it. Furthermore, there is only one Channel Tunnel (and only likely to be), so is this not a good example of a natural monopoly?

If this were the case, then concern might arise if the tunnel operator was able to charge a monopoly price in order to maximise profits. This would entail some allocative inefficiency, as the price would be set above marginal cost.

One response to this could be for the authorities to regulate the market, and require the firm to set a price that was equal to marginal cost — that is, the price that would ensure allocative efficiency. The problem here is that this forces the firm to make losses.

The question that then arises is whether it is likely that the Channel Tunnel operator will have the power to exploit its market position. Strictly speaking, there is no question of contestability here. It is not possible for a second tunnel to be set up to provide hit-and-run entry, especially given the sunk costs that would be involved.

However, this does not mean that the Channel Tunnel does not face competition. The cross-Channel ferry companies provide stiff competition for the tunnel, and may prevent it from exercising its market power. The Channel Tunnel may perhaps never be forced to set a price as low as marginal cost, but setting a price much above average cost would probably invoke a price response from the ferries.

The cross-Channel routes may thus be regarded as an *oligopoly* market, in which the tunnel and the ferry companies will set price having some regard to the actions and likely reactions of the other operators in the market.

Notice that the market interactions work in both directions. In recent years, there has been some consolidation among the ferry operators, through a process of merger and acquisition. This has triggered a number of investigations by the OFT and the Competition Commission. In reaching their judgements, the effect on the ferry companies of competition from the Channel Tunnel has been an influential factor.

Cross-Channel ferry companies operate in an oligopoly market with the Channel Tunnel

Exercise 10.4

Discuss the extent to which the rail route between London and Edinburgh may be seen as a potential monopoly situation.

Monopoly — BAA plc

In 1987 the British Airports Authority was privatised and BAA plc was established. The firm was responsible for the airports that had previously been under the aegis of the previous authority — namely, the three London airports (Heathrow, Gatwick and Stansted), plus airports in Scotland (Aberdeen, Edinburgh, Glasgow and Prestwick). Prestwick was sold in 1991 and Southampton was acquired in 1990. This meant that BAA plc had an effective monopoly on flights in and out of London and a stranglehold on flights in and out of Scotland.

One of the objectives in setting up BAA plc was to have a single enterprise that would be able to take strategic decisions to plan ahead, and to provide the airport capacity needed to meet the expected growth in demand. In addition, it was hoped that the provision of the infrastructure needed for air travel would help to encourage competition among the airlines providing the transport services.

In the event, things did not work out well, and after 20 years of operation, BAA plc was seen to have failed to provide sufficient capacity to meet demand in the South East region. There was also mounting criticism of the way that BAA was managing its airports — especially Heathrow. In March 2007, the OFT referred the case to the Competition Commission for investigation under the Enterprise Act 2002. The brief for the investigation was

> ...to investigate whether any feature, or combination of features, of the market or markets for airport services in the UK as exist in connection with the supply of airport services by BAA Limited prevents, restricts or distorts competition in connection with the supply or acquisition of any goods or services in the UK or a part of the UK. If so there is an 'adverse effect on competition'.

> (Competition Commission, 2008)

In terms of market share, it was clear that BAA was in a very strong position. The CC noted that its seven airports accounted for more than 60% of all passengers using UK airports. In the southeast, Heathrow, Gatwick, Stansted and Southampton between them accounted for 90% of air passengers; in Scotland, 84% of air passengers were accounted for by Edinburgh, Glasgow and Aberdeen. The key issue is whether this market position was damaging competition, and hence working against consumer interests.

An important aspect of this is whether there is scope for competition between airports, and what effect such competition would have on the nature and quality of service that would be offered. In order to approach this question, the CC looked at

CHARLES BOWMAN/ALAMY

Terminal 5 at Heathrow — BAA plc had an effective monopoly on flights in and out of London

evidence relating to non-BAA airports that could be regarded as being in potential competition with each other — for example, Birmingham International Airport and East Midlands Airport, Cardiff International Airport and Bristol International Airport and other combinations. Some evidence was found that suggested that there could be competition between airports — in particular, in relation to the low-cost airlines. However, competition is most likely where there is spare capacity — which is not the case for Heathrow and Gatwick.

Competition also requires there to be the potential for substitution in demand. In other words, there needs to be some overlap in the potential catchment area for competing airports. In relations to BAA's airports in Scotland, it was found that there was some overlap in catchment between Glasgow and Edinburgh — but not with Aberdeen. In the South East, there was little evidence of competition between BAA's London airports and non-BAA airports (apart from some competition between Southampton and Bournemouth). However, there was significant overlap in the catchment areas of these airports, suggesting the possibility of some competition (subject to capacity constraints).

The CC came to the view that the shortage of capacity in the South East had partly arisen from the common ownership of the three BAA London airports, and that had these airports been under separate ownership, the incentives to expand capacity and improve the quality of service being offered would have been higher.

Having concluded that there was evidence that the market structure was having an adverse effect on competition, the CC in its provisional findings recommended that BAA should sell two of its three airports in the South East, and should not be allowed to continue to own airports in both Glasgow and Edinburgh. The CC reinforced this in March 2009 by ruling that BAA should sell Gatwick, Stansted and either Glasgow or Edinburgh. Subsequently, BAA sold Gatwick but appealed

against the ruling that it should also sell Stansted and Glasgow or Edinburgh. In July 2011 the CC reiterated this ruling after the Supreme Court refused BAA permission to appeal further.

Duopoly — Boeing and Airbus

At first glance, aircraft manufacture seems another potential natural monopoly — again because of its cost structure. The key issue for aircraft manufacture lies in the enormous cost of research and development (R&D), besides which the marginal cost of producing an additional aircraft is relatively minor. And yet, the market is effectively a *duopoly*, with Boeing and Airbus being the only effective global competitors.

This market has triggered much transatlantic debate and contention. Boeing, the US producer, has accused European governments of unfairly subsidising Airbus's R&D programme. In return, Airbus has responded by pointing to the benefits that Boeing has received from the US military research programme.

Without being drawn into this debate, the net effect of the interventions has been to create a duopoly situation in which Boeing and Airbus appear to compete aggressively for market share. This probably means better allocative efficiency than if one of the firms were able to dominate the global market. Ultimately, air travellers benefit from this.

Monopolistic competition in road transport

The theory of monopolistic competition describes a market with some features of monopoly and some features of perfect competition. Entry barriers are low, so the market has many firms. However, firms in the market use product differentiation to influence consumers, and thus face downward-sloping demand curves.

If you look back at the analysis in Chapter 3, you will see that this form of market structure has implications for both productive and allocative efficiency. Firms produce at a level of output below that at which long-run average cost would reach the minimum, so there is not productive efficiency. Furthermore, price is set above marginal cost, so allocative efficiency is not achieved either.

Take a drive along a motorway or trunk road in the UK, and observe the heavy goods vehicles (HGVs) and smaller vans that you pass. You will see HGVs and vans in a wide variety of liveries, from a wide range of countries and carrying a wide diversity of loads.

This is a market characterised by many competing firms, many of which operate in niche markets. Firms try to differentiate their offering by carrying particular categories of products — building materials, perhaps, or electronic goods. Some may trade between certain destinations. They advertise by broadcasting these specialisms on their vehicles, in the *Yellow Pages* or on the internet.

Another part of the road transport market that may typify monopolistic competition is local taxi markets. Count the local taxi companies in your local *Yellow Pages*. Again, firms may seek to differentiate their products through having a fleet livery, by advertising pre-booking only or by offering a limousine service. There may also be firms that specialise in longer-distance trips, say to airports.

chapter 10

Summary

➤ Market structure is important in determining whether allocative efficiency can be achieved.

➤ However, productive efficiency must also be taken into account.

➤ After deregulation, the market for bus transport in the UK went through a process of evolution from monopolistic competition to oligopoly.

➤ Rail privatisation was introduced to promote greater productive efficiency, but it has taken many years for the industry to settle down.

➤ The low-cost airlines have transformed the market for air travel, using price discrimination and a thorough understanding of costs.

➤ The Channel Tunnel offers an example of a natural monopoly, but it cannot ignore competition from the ferry companies.

➤ The transport sector also offers examples of duopoly (Boeing and Airbus) and monopolistic competition in road haulage.

Chapter 11
Market failure and the role of intervention in transport markets

Transport markets can be affected by market failure, which can have a substantial impact on the effective delivery of transport services and have repercussions for other sectors in the economy and on people's wellbeing. The impact of externalities is particularly important in the transport sector, and in this chapter we will examine the various ways in which market failure needs to be recognised.

Learning outcomes

After studying this chapter, you should:
- be aware of the importance of externalities in the transport sector and be able to discuss how these may be tackled through regulation and taxation
- understand the meaning and rationale of the hypothecation of taxation
- appreciate the importance of environmental issues in the transport sector
- be able to evaluate transport policy in its treatment of environmental issues
- be aware of why policy may be needed in order to ensure that adequate health and safety standards are maintained
- understand how market failure is relevant to the problem of traffic congestion and evaluate the policy options for tackling this issue
- be familiar with the European context in which transport policy in the UK and other EU member states operates
- understand what is meant by user charging and road pricing, and analyse and evaluate their economic basis
- be able to compare the experience of the UK with that of other countries

Market failure and transport

Earlier chapters have highlighted the fact that market failure is significant in the transport sector, arising in a number of guises. A problem that arises when the government attempts to rectify market failure is that there are some situations in which the remedy is worse than the disease. Well-intended government intervention can sometimes have distortionary effects on resource allocation that leave society no

better off – or even worse off. It is important to be aware of this and to try to guard against it when designing policy measures. This chapter begins with a reminder of key areas of market failure that can affect the transport sector.

Externalities

An important form of market failure that is prevalent in transport markets is externalities. Externalities arise in situations where there are costs or benefits associated with a transaction that are not fully reflected in market prices. This could lead to a situation in which, for example, social costs exceed private costs. This causes allocative inefficiency, as the decisions made by private firms or individuals will not correspond to what is best for society as a whole. For example, if a firm uses a fleet of trucks to transport freight around the country and these trucks have been poorly maintained, so they give off noxious fumes, this imposes costs on other road users – or people who live close to the roads. However, the firm will not need to face up to the full cost of its activities unless forced to do so by policy.

Another example of externalities in the transport sector is where new infrastructure, such as a new road or rail link, entails damage to the environment. Such damage must be factored into the cost–benefit appraisal of any major scheme for transport infrastructure, which will be discussed in Chapter 12. The policy issue here is to achieve balance in the long-term operations of the transport sector.

Information and health and safety

Information failure can be a significant source of market failure, especially where some participants in a market have better information than others. One area in which this is relevant in the transport sector is in relation to the merit good argument, where it can be argued that the government is more able to take a long-term view of the transport market, and has better information about how the future balance of transport could be shaped than enterprises in the private sector, or those responsible for managing public enterprises in a particular part of the transport sector. It could also be argued that the government has broader information, so is able to undertake a coordinating role between the competing transport modes. This will be discussed in Chapter 12.

Another merit good argument relates to health and safety regulations. Individual workers may take decisions about their supply of labour that do not adequately recognise health and safety issues. The authorities have better information about health and safety and thus impose regulations on firms to safeguard workers' interests. This imposes costs on firms, and may have the effect of reducing the demand for labour – but in the best interests of the workers who *are* employed. However, it is clearly important to reach an appropriate balance between ensuring the health and safety of workers and maintaining employment.

In the transport sector, health and safety issues also arise in the context of passengers. This has been contentious for the railways since privatisation. The privatised rail sector was given productivity targets to meet. The danger then

The rail crash at Ladbroke Grove, October 1999; safety on the railways remains a contentious issue

was that those targets would be met at the expense of safety. Again, some form of regulation to avoid this danger is important.

Public goods

Transport infrastructure may be seen to have some of the characteristics of a public good, which means that some form of public intervention will be needed to ensure that sufficient infrastructure is provided. The provision and maintenance of roads, street lighting and road signage comes into this category. In the absence of intervention, too little of such goods would be provided, as the free-rider problem makes it impossible to charge users for their consumption of street lighting or road signs. For some stretches of road, or some sections of the road network, some form of user charging may be possible. This will be discussed later in the chapter.

Exercise 11.1

Identify the form of market failure that is potentially present in each of the following situations, and comment on the likely consequences for society in the absence of intervention by the authorities.

a   a motorway services area

b   the provision of road signs

c   spillage from an oil tanker close to a tourist beach

d   the provision of safety belts in coaches

e   motorway maintenance

part 3

Taxation and regulation of transport

Given that these various forms of market failure are likely to distort the pattern of resource allocation in the transport sector, how can the authorities seek to improve matters? In a particular market, there are usually two main possibilities. First, taxes can be used to influence the price of a good or service, and thus influence the market equilibrium. Second, some form of direct regulation or control can be used to influence the market outcome.

Consider the case of externalities. Externalities arise in situations where there are items of cost or benefit associated with transactions that are not reflected in market prices. In these circumstances, a free market will not lead to an optimum allocation of resources. In order to deal with such market situations, one approach is to bring those externalities into the market mechanism — a process known as **internalising an externality**. For example, in the case of pollution, this principle would entail forcing polluting firms to face the full social cost of their production activities. This is sometimes known as the **polluter pays principle**.

 Key term

internalising an externality: an attempt to deal with an externality by bringing an external cost or benefit into the price system

polluter pays principle: the principle that the cost of pollution should be borne by whoever is responsible for that pollution

Pollution

Figure 11.1 illustrates a negative production externality such as air pollution. It shows a market for freight transportation by road. Let us suppose that firms in this market use trucks that emit fumes, thus imposing costs on society that the firms do not face. In other words, the marginal private costs faced by the firms are less than the marginal social costs that are inflicted on society. Firms in this market would choose to transport freight up to the point Q_1 and charge a price of P_1. At this point, marginal social benefit is below the marginal cost of transporting goods,

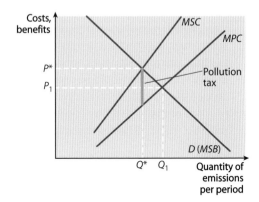

Figure 11.1 *Tackling pollution using taxation*

and it can be claimed that 'too much' freight is being transported. Society would be better off at Q^*, with a price charged at P^*.

One point to notice here is that this optimum position is not characterised by *zero* pollution. In other words, from society's point of view, it pays to abate pollution only up to the level where the marginal benefit of reducing pollution is matched by the marginal cost of doing so. Reducing pollution to zero would be too costly.

However, how could society reach the optimum position at Q^*? In line with the principle that the polluter should pay, one approach would be to impose a tax on firms such that they faced the full cost of their actions. In Figure 11.1, if firms are required to pay a tax equivalent to the vertical distance between marginal private cost (*MPC*) and marginal social cost (*MSC*), they would choose to produce at Q^*, paying a tax equal to the green line on the diagram.

An alternative way of looking at this question is to draw a diagram that shows the marginal benefit and marginal cost of emissions reduction. This is done in Figure 11.2. Here, *MB* represents the marginal social benefits from reducing emissions, and *MC* the marginal costs of reducing emissions. The optimum amount of reduction is found where marginal benefit equals marginal cost, at e^*. Up to this point, the marginal benefit to society of reducing emissions exceeds the marginal cost of so doing, so it is in the interest of society

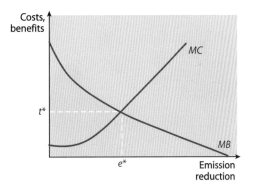

Figure 11.2 *Reducing emission of toxic fumes*

to reduce pollution. However, beyond that point the marginal cost of reducing the amount of pollution exceeds the benefits that accrue, so society would be worse off. Setting a tax equal to t^* in Figure 11.2 will induce firms to undertake the appropriate amount of emission reduction.

However, this is not the only way of reaching the objective. Figure 11.2 suggests that there is another possibility: namely, to set environmental standards and to prohibit emissions beyond e^*. This amounts to the control of quantity rather than price. If the government has full information about marginal costs and marginal benefits, the two policies will produce the equivalent result.

Either of the approaches outlined above is fine, *if* the authorities have full information about marginal costs and benefits. But how likely is this? In fact, the measurement of both marginal benefits and marginal costs is fraught with difficulties.

We cannot measure the marginal social benefits of reducing pollution with any degree of precision. There are many different factors to be taken into consideration. It may be argued that there are significant gains to be made in terms of improved health and lower death rates if pollution can be reduced. Quantifying this is not straightforward, however, even if we could come to a valuation of the saving in resources devoted to future healthcare. There may also be considerations in terms of direct improvements to the quality of life of members of society. In addition, there is the question of whether to take into account international effects when formulating domestic policy, and of choosing an appropriate discount rate for evaluating benefits that will be received in the future. The environmentalist and the industrialist may well arrive at different evaluations of the benefits of controlling pollution.

Pollution by motor vehicles is regulated by the government

The measurement of costs may also be problematic. For example, it is likely that there will be differences in efficiency between firms. Those using modern trucks may face lower costs than those using relatively old vehicles. Do the authorities try to set a tax that is specific to each firm to take such differences into account? If they do not and set a flat-rate tax, then the incentives may be inappropriate. This would mean that a firm using modern trucks would face the same tax as one using old vehicles. The firm using new capital would then tend to produce too little output relative to those using older, less efficient capital.

In practice, the government has chosen to address this problem of traffic fumes through regulation rather than taxation. Part of the annual MoT test of all vehicles entails measuring the fumes emitted, which must come within certain limits set by legislation. Otherwise the vehicle will fail its MoT test and not be permitted on the roads.

Although the discussion so far has focused on pollution, this is by no means the only form of externality associated with the transport sector. Other by-products of transportation may include noise, blight and stress. These are also externalities, in the sense that people incur costs as a result of transportation that are not included in market prices.

Noise pollution has also been identified as a significant externality that the transport sector imposes on society. The European Commission has claimed that environmental noise caused by traffic is 'one of the main local environmental problems in Europe', and that 'around 20 percent of the Union's population or close on 80 million people suffer from noise levels that scientists and health experts consider to be unacceptable' (**ec.europa.eu/environment/noise/greenpap.htm**). Of particular relevance in this context is the noise caused by road and rail traffic. People living near busy roads or rail routes, or on the flight paths of airports suffer from the noise produced by cars, trains and aircraft. It may even be that they incur the additional expense of installing double glazing in order to mitigate the effects of the noise.

The siting of new roads and rail routes has been contentious. For example, in May 2010 the government confirmed its commitment to the proposal to build a new high-speed rail network linking London with Birmingham, Manchester and Leeds, with stops in the East

Midlands and South Yorkshire. Consultation on this closed in July 2011, Campaigners formed pressure groups (such as StopHS2) to object to the scheme, arguing that the environmental impact had not been adequately assessed. The Woodland Trust claimed that the route would cause direct damage to at least 21 ancient woodlands along the route, and affect another 27 ancient woods within 200 metres of the proposed lines. This is an example of blight — irreversible damage done to the countryside as a result of the new railway lines. The claim here is that there is an externality effect that involves damage to the national heritage, for the benefit of allowing a relatively small number of people to travel from London to Birmingham a bit quicker than they can at present. Similar protests ensue around many new road projects.

It is also argued that as traffic increases through time, there are associated increases in stress levels, both of those travelling and of those living near the increasingly busy roads. For example, as congestion mounts, drivers find themselves more often in traffic jams, thus experiencing stress, which affects their quality of life. It may also be that as traffic increases, so does the probability of being involved in an accident. Furthermore, accidents can affect innocent bystanders as well as those directly involved in the accident. All of these things represent externality effects that are not taken into account in decisions about using transportation.

Evaluation

For any intervention by the government, care is needed to ensure that taxes or regulations have their intended effects. In other words, it is important to guard against the possibility of government failure. If taxes are set at too high (or too low) a level, or if regulations are too stringent (or too loose), the best result for society in terms of resource allocation will not be achieved. Furthermore, it is important to remember that markets are interconnected, so intervention in one market may have knock-on effects on resource allocation elsewhere.

A key problem comes in determining the appropriate level at which a tax should be set in order to counter the effects of an externality. This is because the tax needs to reflect the additional social cost that is being inflicted on society — and this is very difficult to calculate in many cases. You might perhaps argue that the extent to which people are prepared to pay to install double glazing in order to counter noise pollution could be a measure of the impact of noise — but this cannot be the whole answer. In some other instances, it could be even more difficult to find an agreed measurement. For example, how could we put a value on the increased probability of being involved in a traffic accident? Some of these issues will be considered in Chapter 12 when we will discuss the use of cost–benefit analysis.

Exercise 11.2

Discuss approaches that could be adopted to limit noise pollution.

Hypothecation

Within the transport sector, a contentious issue has been the level of duties levied on petrol and diesel, and road taxes. Motorists have claimed that they are being unfairly treated by heavy duties and high road taxes — not to mention the fines imposed when drivers are caught on speed cameras. Such arguments lead towards the notion of **hypothecation**.

 term

hypothecation: in the context of the transport sector, the principle that revenues raised from taxing transport should be used to improve the transport system

Literally speaking, 'hypothecation' comes from the phrase 'hypothetical dedication'. In the transport arena, what this means is that revenues raised from the taxation of transport should be dedicated to expenditures that are concerned with transportation. For example, the revenues from gasoline tax in the USA are dedicated to the funding of transportation infrastructure.

Another example of hypothecation is the London Congestion Charge, where it was agreed that any net revenues raised by the scheme would be ploughed back into improving London's transport network. This is seen as one way of enabling improvements to public transport systems and traffic management, with private road users footing the bill. As a way of making charges politically acceptable to those who pay them, hypothecation may be an effective device. However, does it make sense in terms of economic analysis? If there are significant externalities associated with private motoring that affect other aspects of the economy, then there is a case for taxing motorists more heavily, and for using some of the revenues to correct for other distortions of resource allocation: for example, in remedying environmental damage.

Exercise 11.3

Singapore has, for many years, imposed a range of financial instruments on motorists. These have included heavy customs duties and other charges for people wanting to put a new car on to Singapore's roads; there are also charges for taking a car into the Central Business District. The revenues raised from these measures have enabled the Singapore government to make substantial improvements to the road infrastructure in the city. Explain how this illustrates the principle of hypothecation.

Transport and the environment

In formulating a vision of the future pattern of transport in the UK, the environment is seen to be a central concern. For example, there is a major concern about the emission of greenhouse gases from private motoring, which suggests that car usage needs to be managed, rather than being allowed to continue to expand in line with demand. This requires greater encouragement to use public transport, or a shift towards more fuel-efficient cars. However, individual consumers will not switch towards public transport unless its quality can be improved — which then requires investment to bring about those improvements and make public transport a more attractive alternative.

One way of encouraging more use of public transport might be through a subsidy. Figure 11.3 shows how this might work. Here, S_0 represents the supply curve in the absence of a subsidy, so that with demand at D, the market equilibrium is with price P_0 and quantity of bus journeys Q_0. If the authorities introduce a subsidy of an amount BC, this encourages the bus companies to supply more bus journeys at any given price, so the effective supply curve is now S_1, and the equilibrium moves to a lower price P_1 and higher quantity Q_1.

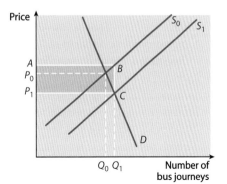

Figure 11.3 A subsidy to bus companies

How effective is such a policy likely to be? Figure 11.3 was drawn with the demand curve relatively steep. This is probably realistic to some degree, as the demand for bus journeys is probably not too sensitive to price, so a subsidy has relatively little impact on the number of bus journeys undertaken. In addition, the cost to the authorities is relatively high. It is shown by the shaded area ($ABCP_1$) in Figure 11.3. This seems to suggest that the use of subsidies will be expensive and ineffective. This will be reinforced if increases in the real income of consumers cause the demand curve to shift to the left over time — in other words, if bus journeys can be regarded as an inferior good — which again seems a reasonable assumption.

In evaluating such a policy measure, it is important to realise that the benefits from encouraging more bus travel may go beyond the individual market. If the demand for bus journeys is inelastic, this makes subsidies relatively expensive. Nonetheless, in combination with measures to discourage private motor vehicles (reducing the number of city-centre parking spaces, introducing bus lanes and so on), subsidies can be an effective way of changing people's attitudes towards transport modes.

There may also be a case for subsidising rural bus travel, where there are communities that would otherwise be isolated. In other words, subsidies for bus travel may contribute to social inclusion of rural communities where bus routes might prove unprofitable for the private sector in the absence of some form of subsidy. The Rural Bus Subsidy Grant and Rural Bus Challenge policies were introduced in 1998. An evaluation undertaken for the Department for Transport after 5 years of operation suggested that these measures had been successful in meeting their objectives.

The rural subsidies apart, subsidies have not been widely used as a way of encouraging more usage of buses and coaches. Such subsidies as have been provided tend to be aimed at rather different targets — for example, bus passes for the elderly, which are intended to provide protection for vulnerable individuals, rather than as part of a transport policy.

Sustainability in transport

An important consideration in considering the impact of transport on the environment is the question of **sustainability**. Concern for the environment has become a prominent and contentious issue in recent decades, nowhere more than in relation to transport. This means moving towards a future pattern of transportation that will not damage prospects for future generations. For example, it could be argued that a sustainable transport system would see more freight being shifted from road towards rail, given its lower rate of CO_2 emissions as compared with road transport. The data also suggest that gains could be made by switching individual journeys away from private cars, which remain the most polluting mode of transport.

Exercise 11.4

Discuss why some modes of transport may be more sustainable than others.

Safeguarding the environment has been seen as critical, partly because of its direct impact on the quality of life. People gain utility from living in or visiting a pleasant environment — or even just from knowing that such areas exist.

 Key term

sustainable transport development: an approach to planning the transport system which ensures that present needs can be met without compromising the ability of future generations to meet their transport needs

We have already seen that important externality effects arise in relation to the environment. The threat of global warming raises issues about the importance of safeguarding the environment for the benefit of future generations as well as people living today. In terms of economic analysis, this is tantamount to arguing that there are externality effects that may cross national borders, or that may cross generations. Decisions taken today that affect the environment may have repercussions for other nations, or for future generations, which are not reflected in market prices. It is especially difficult to tackle these transnational externality effects, as it requires coordinated action across countries. No individual country has an incentive to take action unless it can be sure that other countries will do the same. For example, if the UK introduces stringent measures to restrict pollution emitted by road hauliers, this has the effect of raising their costs — perhaps they are forced to introduce cleaner engines or maintain their vehicles more frequently. This puts UK firms at a competitive disadvantage relative to other firms. Given the importance of trade within Europe as globalisation proceeds, this may have a serious impact on British firms. The UK government will therefore face pressure from firms to allow them to compete on equal terms with their European neighbours.

For these sorts of reasons, a UK transport policy must take into account the broader European perspective, and there is a need to coordinate across countries in the European Union.

It is important to note that different modes of transport have different implications for the environment. For example, this helps to explain why the 2004 White Paper included a clause about the need to encourage walking and cycling for local trips. The use of cars for short journeys is seen as especially damaging from an environmental perspective. Yet another spin-off is that walking and cycling are seen to be beneficial from a health perspective, and with a growing problem of obesity affecting people in the UK, a transport system that discourages people from taking physical activity may have long-term effects on the health service.

The difference in greenhouse gas emissions between the various types of transport is seen clearly in Figure 11.4. The vast majority of emissions emanate from road traffic – cars, heavy goods vehicles and light vans. Other forms of transport contribute far less towards greenhouse gases, notably the rail network. This would seem to have clear implications for transport policy, in the sense that rail, bus and coach modes have a much smaller carbon footprint.

In order to achieve a sustainable transport policy, there must be two themes. First, it is important to use policy to influence the future demand for transport overall. Second, it is important for policy to shape the pattern of transportation between the modes, by encouraging less use of road transport as well as encouraging more sustainable modes of transport, such as rail, bus, cycling and walking.

A UK transport policy must take into account the broader European perspective

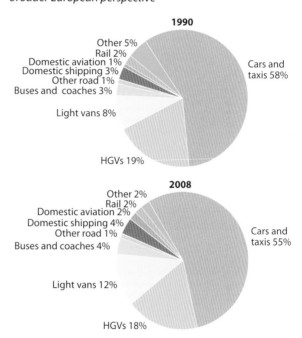

1990

Other 5%
Rail 2%
Domestic aviation 1%
Domestic shipping 3%
Other road 1%
Buses and coaches 3%
Light vans 8%
HGVs 19%
Cars and taxis 58%

2008

Other 2%
Rail 2%
Domestic aviation 2%
Domestic shipping 4%
Other road 1%
Buses and coaches 4%
Light vans 12%
HGVs 18%
Cars and taxis 55%

Figure 11.4 *Greenhouse gas emissions from different types of transport, 1990 and 2008*

Source: Department for Transport.

European transport policy

Concern for the environment has also been a central focus of European transport policy, which is overlaid on the policies of member countries of the EU. For example, in July 2008 the European Commission (EC) set out a series of proposals that were submitted to the European Parliament and the Council entitled 'Greening Transport'

(ec.europa.eu/transport/greening/index_en.htm). These provide a useful summary of European attitudes towards this important issue, and are intended to be seen as complementary to the policies adopted by countries in the EU.

As outlined earlier in the chapter, economic policy that is designed to combat failure in a particular market can operate in one of two ways. One way is to use taxes or other methods to ensure that the prices that are faced by market participants (whether producers or consumers) reflect the true costs of an economic activity, including external costs and benefits. The second way is to use direct regulation to bring about the desired results. European policy on transport attempts to use a combination of the two approaches.

Getting the prices right

One central theme of European policy reflects the importance of ensuring that the external costs of transport are internalised — that is, the external costs should be reflected in market prices. The principle of **subsidiarity** limits the actions that can be taken at European level.

 term

subsidiarity: the principle that decisions should be taken as closely as possible to the citizen

The idea of subsidiarity is that decisions should be taken as closely as possible to the citizen. This means that action should only be taken at the EU level if it is shown to be more effective than action taken at national, regional or local level. In relation to transport policy, if the EC were to impose a system of congestion charges in a particular city within a member state, this would be seen as contravening the principle of subsidiarity.

This principle of subsidiarity prevents the EC from taking action to impose taxes or other charges that affect private transport. However, the EC has imposed emission standards for heavy goods vehicles, and encourages member states to implement differentiated charging systems to improve the efficiency of road freight transport. It is important to be aware that the external costs of road freight are not only seen in relation to climate change, but also affect wear and tear on the infrastructure, congestion and noise pollution.

The EC has also undertaken research and development in order to provide a framework that will better identify the real costs of transport, so that variable charges can be imposed by member states according to local air and noise pollution. Further to this, the EC is proposing a common and transparent method to be used to calculate external costs. The proposal also supports the idea of hypothecation, by insisting that any revenues raised should be earmarked for reducing the environmental impact of transportation.

Another important area of European policy designed to combat climate change is the Emissions Trading System (ETS), which was launched in 2005. The EU ETS is the world's largest company-level 'cap-and-trade' system for trading in emissions of carbon dioxide (pollution permit schemes were discussed in *AS Economics, Chapter 6*). Although the focus in the early years of the ETS was on big industrial emitters of

carbon dioxide, the EC is aware that the transport sector was responsible for about 19% of emissions in 2005, and airlines join the scheme in 2012.

Although the EC does not attempt to dictate precise pricing rules for member states, what it has done is to set minimum tax levels for motor fuels to which all member nations must adhere — although they may, of course, choose to set taxes on fuels at higher levels.

Regulatory instruments

As with the pricing instruments, the EC does not attempt to impose regulation across the whole of the EU. However, it operates by setting thresholds that all member states must follow. One example of such regulation is that the EC has established standards that set permitted emission levels for all new vehicles produced in the EU — both for road vehicles and for some other types of transport, such as vessels and recreational craft. Standards are also imposed that set the maximum levels of certain pollutants that are permitted in fuels (e.g. lead in petrol). Furthermore, all new infrastructure projects are subject to rules on environmental assessment.

By these sorts of measures the EC is attempting to establish a common framework within which the transport policies of individual member states of the EU can be partially coordinated.

Exercise 11.5

Discuss the advantages and disadvantages of a two-tier transport policy in which the EC sets basic standards to which countries must comply, but in which countries can also implement their own policies.

Congestion and road pricing

With the introduction of the congestion charge in parts of central London, the London authorities have been attempting to tackle congestion. When traffic on the roads reaches a certain volume, congestion imposes heavy costs on road users. This is another example of an externality.

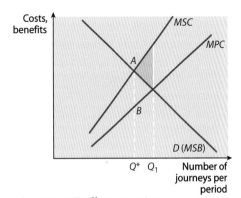

Figure 11.5 Traffic congestion

Figure 11.5 illustrates the situation. Suppose that D (MSB) represents the demand curve for car journeys along a particular stretch of road. When deciding whether to undertake a journey, a driver will balance the marginal benefit gained from making the journey against the marginal cost that he or she faces. This is given by MPC — the marginal private cost of undertaking journeys. When the road is congested, a motorist who decides to undertake the journey adds

to the congestion and slows the traffic. The *MPC* curve incorporates the cost to the motorist of joining a congested road, and the chosen number of journeys will be at Q_1.

However, in adding to the congestion, the motorist not only suffers the costs of congestion, but also imposes some marginal increase in costs on all other users of the road, as everyone suffers from slower journeys as a result of the extra congestion. Thus the marginal social cost (*MSC*) of undertaking journeys is higher than the cost faced by any individual motorist. *MSC* is therefore shown to be higher than *MPC*. Society would be better off with lower congestion if the number of journeys were limited to Q^*, where marginal social benefit equals marginal social cost.

The extent of the welfare loss that society endures as a direct result of the congestion is given by the shaded area in Figure 11.5. This measures the extent to which marginal social cost exceeds marginal private cost between Q^* and Q_1. One possible remedy is to impose a tax on journeys undertaken. Such a tax would need to be set at a level that reflected the difference between marginal social cost and marginal private cost — at Q^*, this is the distance *AB*. This policy forces motorists to face the social cost of their actions, so that they will choose to be at Q^*.

It could be argued that the full social cost of congestion goes beyond the direct effects arising from the externality. There are broader issues to be considered that cannot readily be quantified as part of the social cost of congestion. This comes back to the issue raised earlier that the existence of an efficient and well-functioning transport system is important to ensuring the smooth functioning of other markets, and for maintaining the competitiveness of domestic firms that are competing in international markets. If the transport system grinds to a halt because of congestion, it is not just the people stuck in the traffic jam who bear the costs. The economy at large may also suffer.

An important issue here concerns the practicality of road taxes. The first attempt at road pricing was in Singapore in the mid-1970s. The Singapore government was concerned to prevent the build-up of traffic congestion in the central business district (CBD). It thus introduced a charge that had to be paid by all vehicles entering the CBD during peak periods. This was quite costly to implement given the technology available, as the only way of monitoring the policy was to have individuals located at all entry points into the CBD watching for cars that were not displaying a current ticket entitling them to enter the district. As technology has improved, so Singapore has switched to a system of electronic road pricing, whereby all cars have to be fitted with an electronic device that is triggered every time a vehicle enters a restricted section of road. The driver is then automatically charged. Such a system

The congestion charge helps to keep an efficient flow of traffic in central London

can be made very flexible, allowing charges to be varied according to the degree of congestion that is currently occurring.

The London Congestion Charge operates on a similar basis, with motorists having to pay a fixed charge for entering a specified area within Central London. When Singapore began its scheme, it had an important advantage — it is relatively compact, with relatively few entry points into the CBD. (Singapore is approximately the size of the Isle of Wight and in 2010 had a population of just over 5 million, so you can understand why it should be worried about the possible effects of congestion.) Some indication of the effectiveness of the London Congestion Charge can be seen in Figure 11.6, which shows the number of people entering Central London during the morning peak period, expressed as an index based on 1996. You can see how the balance between public and personal transport has changed in recent years.

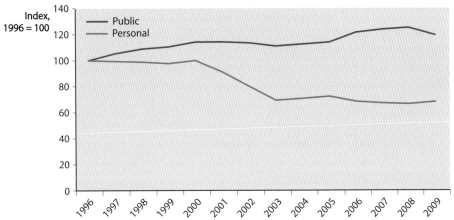

Figure 11.6 *People entering Central London during the morning peak*

Source: Department for Transport.

It is also possible to levy charges for specific stretches of road in the form of tolls. The Severn Bridge and the M6 Toll Road are examples of this. Such charges tend to be used quite sparingly, as there is a danger of slowing the traffic so much in order to collect the fees that nothing is gained in terms of easing congestion — although tolls may allow private companies to recoup the construction and maintenance costs of the road. Technology has again made life a bit easier, at least for regular users, who can be charged automatically using an electronic device. For example, such a system is in place for the tunnels that join Hong Kong Island to Kowloon, which carry enormous traffic flows every day. Similar toll arrangements apply on many motorways in Europe.

Evaluation

In addition to its charge for entering the CBD, Singapore has for many years operated a scheme whereby anyone wanting to buy a car must obtain a Certificate of Entitlement (CoE). These CoEs are auctioned every month, and for many years were being sold at prices that far exceeded the price of a car. The policy enabled the Singapore authorities to regulate strictly the number of cars that were allowed in the country. However,

such a policy is not well targeted, as it is not car ownership that needs to be controlled, but car usage. A road-pricing scheme is thus superior to a tax on car ownership for tackling road congestion. A tax on petrol or diesel is also relatively ineffective, as duty on petrol has to be paid whether the motorist is going to drive on a congested street in the city centre or a crowded motorway — or whether that motorist is using rural roads, where the issue of congestion does not arise.

This is an important aspect of the congestion issue. Not all drivers impose the same congestion costs on others. The extent to which this happens depends upon which roads a motorist uses, and at what time of day. This makes policy design tricky. For example, consider Figure 11.7, which shows the demand for journeys on an urban road. For much of the time, demand is relatively low, at D_{low}. In this situation, there is no congestion, and marginal private and social costs coincide, so there is no need for any intervention. However, at other times of day, demand may be higher so that traffic begins to build up. When demand reaches D_{medium}, there is some congestion, and a small tax is needed in order that motorists face the social cost of their journeys — this is given by the distance XY. However, in peak times, when traffic becomes heavy (demand is D_{peak}), congestion becomes greater, and the difference between marginal social costs and marginal private costs requires a much larger tax (AB).

Similarly, the demand for journeys in different parts of the national road network varies substantially. There are roads in rural areas that never experience congestion, and there are roads in some urban areas that never seem to be free of it. The nature of traffic flows on the inter-urban motorways — or on the M25 — may be different again.

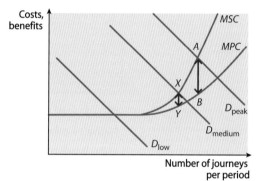

Figure 11.7 *Finding the right tax when demand varies*

Thus road pricing needs to be a very flexible tool if it is truly to target congestion when and where it happens. However, it is clearly more targeted than a general tax on petrol, which treats every mile travelled as being equivalent — except insofar as congestion affects fuel consumption.

In general, user charges tend to be favoured by economic analysis because if people do not have to take account of both private and social costs when taking decisions, they will tend to make decisions that are not in the best interests of society as a whole. Transport policy provides many good examples of how this works out in the real world.

Summary

> Market failure affects the transport sector in various ways, including imperfect competition, externalities, information failure and public goods provision.

> In order to deal with market failure, the government can intervene by using taxation and/or regulation to achieve a better outcome for society.

OCR A2 Economics

➤ Pollution is an example of an externality, and can be tackled through taxation or through direct control of emissions.

➤ It has been argued that the revenues raised through the taxation of transport should be dedicated to transport-related expenditures. This principle is known as hypothecation.

➤ Issues also arise in relation to ensuring health and safety standards, reflecting a merit good argument.

➤ In formulating a vision of the future of the transport sector, it is important to aim for sustainable transport development, particularly in terms of safeguarding the environment for future generations.

➤ In addition to domestic transport policy, the UK and other EU countries operate within a framework of European regulations and standards.

➤ Congestion on the roads is another example of externalities. This may be tackled through the use of road pricing or by imposing tolls for the use of certain stretches of road.

Exercise 11.6

Discuss the arguments for and against introducing road pricing in your own town or city. How else could the local authority seek to control congestion?

Chapter 12
Transport economics and government policy

The transport sector is critical to the operation of the economy, and it is important to analyse the way in which resources are allocated within the transport sector, as well as between transport and the rest of the economy. This analysis goes beyond the issues of market failure that were raised in the previous chapter.

Learning outcomes

After studying this chapter, you should:

➤ understand and be able to evaluate the objectives of transport policy

➤ appreciate why markets may not always ensure the 'best' allocation of resources within the transport sector

➤ understand the nature and features of an integrated transport policy

➤ be familiar with the Private Finance Initiative as one way in which private funding of transport projects can be encouraged

➤ be aware of the importance of cost–benefit analysis as a method of appraising capital projects in the transport sector

➤ be able to discuss the uses and limitations of the cost–benefit approach to transport decision making

➤ appreciate the need for a range of appraisal techniques

The importance of transport policy

Transport is important for businesses because both inputs and outputs need to be transported, and workers need to travel to work. Transport is important for consumers because they have a derived demand for transport in connection with their employment (travel to work), and also in relation to their consumption of leisure (travel to holiday destinations or for other leisure activities) and their consumption of goods and services, whereby the goods consumed need to be transported to the

consumer. From the point of view of firms operating in the economy, transport may be seen as an important input, and in many cases a significant item of costs. For firms competing internationally, an efficient transport system can be vital in maintaining competitiveness, by keeping down firms' costs relative to their foreign competitors. Equally, an inefficient transport system can be an obstacle to competing successfully in overseas markets.

Can the provision of the required transport services be left to the market? Would a good allocation of resources be achieved in the transport sector if the authorities allowed the free market to hold sway? Or is there a need for a transport policy by which the government can direct and guide the allocation of resources towards a better balance for consumers and businesses? Chapter 11 has highlighted the importance of externalities that may be connected to the transport sector, which may impose costs on society. This would prevent the achievement of allocative and productive efficiency, but it is not the only reason to believe that there is a role for government in shaping transport policy.

In this context, it is important to appreciate the different roles of the public and private sectors in the transport sector. The role of the public sector is partly in taking measures to combat market failure. There is also an important coordination role, which will be discussed in this chapter.

Chapter 10 explored the influence of market structure on the transport sector. It showed that there are several markets within the transport sector that would not be expected to operate according to the perfectly competitive ideal, but could incline towards monopoly, or at least towards imperfect competition. To some extent this was likely to be mitigated by the contestability of many transport markets. Where a market is contestable, the firm or firms within the market have limited power to influence the selling price of their product. Contestability in transport markets arises partly because of conditions within particular markets, but also because of the interconnections between modes. For example, a railway operating company faces competition from long-distance coaches and low-cost airlines on particular routes.

Market structure is not the only source of market failure. There are other aspects of the transport sector which might suggest that some form of state intervention — or at least state monitoring — would be desirable. Externalities are especially significant in the transport sector: for example, in relation to the environment and traffic congestion, as was shown in Chapter 11. To some extent, such problems can be tackled through taxation, regulation and measures such as road pricing.

However, there is also reason to argue that transport is sufficiently important to the economy for the government to take a long view of the market. Indeed, one reason for this is that the market for transport is not really a single market, but a series of interconnected markets. It then becomes important to have a coordinated view, rather than allowing markets for rail, air, road and water transport to operate independently. This may be especially important because different modes of transport have differing effects in the long run: for example, in terms of their impact on the environment. Thus there may be reasons for the government to intervene to influence the future balance of the transport system.

Transport involves the movement of people and goods from one place to another, and is a vital part of a modern economy

Many transport investment projects have long gestation lags. In other words, the decision to build a new road, Channel Tunnel or airport takes a long time to bear fruit. It may be many years after the original decision to proceed before such schemes come into operation and generate benefits for users. Such long-term planning is best undertaken by the government, which may be able to afford to take a longer-term view of investment decisions. Furthermore, the government may be in a better position to take appropriate account of externality effects in reaching such decisions.

A further complication is that, in many cases, aspects of transport infrastructure have some characteristics of public goods. Again, this suggests that some form of government intervention may be needed in order to ensure the appropriate provision of such infrastructure.

Putting all of these arguments together, it would seem that there is a pressing need for a transport policy that is carefully integrated, so as to be able to take all of these various issues fully into account. More specifically, the DfT set out four key ways in which a transport policy needs to be integrated:

➤ integration within and between different forms of transport, so that each contributes its full potential and people can move easily between them;

➤ integration with the environment, so that the transport choices available support a better environment;

➤ integration with land-use planning, at national, regional and local level, so that transport and planning work together to support more sustainable travel choices and reduce the need for travel; and

➤ integration with policies for education, health and wealth creation, so that transport helps make a fairer, more inclusive society.
(www.dft.gov.uk/webtag/overview/integration.php)

part 3

Summary

➤ Transport involves the movement of people and goods from one place to another, and is a vital part of a modern economy.

➤ It is therefore important to ensure good allocation of resources in the transport sector.

➤ This requires an integrated approach to transport policy to ensure an appropriate balance of resources across the various transport modes.

➤ Transport policy is also important because of the need to take a long-term view of the provision of transportation services.

The objectives of transport policy

The provision of infrastructure is of central importance in the transport sector. The major modes of transport all require investment in infrastructure, whether it be roads, a rail network, or airport or port facilities. Such projects have long planning horizons in the case of new ventures, and typically also entail high maintenance costs. One key objective for transport policy is thus to have a coherent overview of what constitutes a desirable long-term pattern of transportation.

This aspect of an **integrated transport policy** requires coordination across the various modes of travel as a result of their interconnectedness. For example, consider someone who needs to travel from, say, London to Edinburgh. The options are to drive, to take a train or coach, or to fly. The choice of mode will depend upon a range of factors, such as the relative travel times, relative prices, preferences and convenience. Perceptions of the relative safety of

Key term

integrated transport policy: an approach to transport policy that recognises the need to co-ordinate policy across transport modes

different modes of travel may also be a concern. A choice of one particular mode will be based on considerations of opportunity cost relative to the next best alternative mode of transport. This has implications for the supply side, as decisions taken now about investment in different parts of the transport sector will affect future comparisons between the modes. For example, there needs to be some coordination between investment in roads and in railways. Investment in the carrying capacity and attractiveness of the railways may have implications for the road-building programme.

This issue was recognised in the government White Paper, *A New Deal for Transport: Better for Everyone*, issued in 1998. This was followed in July 2000 by the publication of a Ten-Year Plan for transport, which the government claimed was 'the beginning of a more strategic approach' to the transport sector. A further White Paper, *The Future of Transport*, was issued in July 2004. This document updated the Ten-Year Plan and set out a strategy for a coherent transport network for 2030, covering the following aspects:

> 'the **road** network providing a more reliable and freer-flowing service for both personal travel and freight, with people able to make informed choices about how and when they travel;

the **rail** network providing a fast, reliable and efficient service, particularly for interurban journeys and commuting into large urban areas;

bus services that are reliable, flexible, convenient and tailored to local needs;

making **walking** and **cycling** a real alternative for local trips; and

ports and **airports** providing improved international and domestic links'.

It should be noted that there may be interactions with other markets as well. Traditionally, the government has taken an active role in planning land use across the nation. The establishment of a 'green belt' of protected rural landscape may have indirect effects on the transportation system, as land-use planning affects the location of industrial activity and housing. This has an impact on transport because of the need for people to travel to work, and for business to transport freight — that is, inputs and outputs. Decisions on housing developments or the location of industrial estates thus need to be coordinated with decisions on the provision of transport infrastructure.

The design of transport policy must also keep in mind the importance of achieving an *efficient* system. This is important from the commercial point of view. If UK firms face higher transportation costs than firms operating elsewhere in Europe, this could potentially put them at a considerable disadvantage. In other words, the transport system can be seen as essential in enabling markets to operate, and in facilitating economic growth. Indeed, the development of a functional transport system may be seen as an essential ingredient of economic development: the lack of such a system has hindered progress in many less developed countries and in the transition economies. Of course, there are many other factors as well, but the importance of transportation should not be underplayed.

From an economics point of view, a key question is: why can't markets be relied upon to deliver a coherent vision of the future transport network? In other words, why is it necessary for the government to intervene?

Public goods

AS Economics, Chapter 7 discussed the problems entailed in ensuring the provision of **public goods** — that is, goods which are non-excludable and non-rivalrous. Street lighting was the example used. It is not possible to exclude one person from enjoying the benefits of street lighting in a road (it is non-excludable). Furthermore, one person's consumption of street lighting does not leave less lighting for the next passer-by (it is non-rivalrous). In the absence of state intervention, the market will fail to provide the socially desirable amount of street lighting because of the **free-rider problem**. No individual consumer has an incentive to pay for the good in this situation.

 Key term

public good: a good that is non-exclusive and non-rivalrous; consumers cannot be excluded from consuming the good, and consumption by one person does not affect the amount of the good available for others to consume

free-rider problem: when an individual cannot be excluded from consuming a good, and thus has no incentive to pay for its provision

In the transport sector, it can be argued that there are aspects of transport infrastructure that have partial characteristics of a public good. It is not impossible to charge road users for making use of a particular stretch of road, but it would be difficult (given present technology) to extend charging to all roads in the country. This suggests that some government involvement in the provision of infrastructure is essential. This does not necessarily mean that the government has to provide the roads, but it may need to enable the private sector to be adequately rewarded for that provision in some way. The objectives of transport policy should thus include taking steps to ensure the provision of appropriate infrastructure in the presence of the free-rider problem.

Meeting demand?

Another argument that has been put forward is that the government should intervene to ensure that the demands for transportation in the future can be met. The need for intervention here may arise if the government is better able to evaluate the strength and nature of future demand than private firms. The need to coordinate with other aspects of government policy might help to reinforce this argument.

Even more important is the question of whether the transport system should be solely designed to meet future demand, or whether the future demand for transport should itself be managed. For example, it may be that the government has some vision of the future transport system in the UK, and may need to plan carefully in order to move towards that vision. This may be seen as a **merit good** argument, in which the government has better information about what is desirable than the population at large.

Key term

merit good: a good that society believes brings unanticipated benefits to the individual consumer

An important aspect of this issue arises in the context of road transport. Forecasts of the future demand for car journeys suggest a steady increase in the demand for road transport. One response to this might be to embark on a road-building programme in order to ensure that the increase in demand can be accommodated. But is this the best way forward?

This is a complex area. For one thing, there is some evidence that increasing the quantity of road space available does not simply help to accommodate existing traffic, but may actually lead to an increase in the number of journeys undertaken. If this is the case, then the road-building programme could never catch up with actual demand.

Furthermore, if there are negative externalities involved in car journeys, then private motorists will always choose to undertake more journeys than is desirable for society as a whole. In Chapter 11, the possibility of using road pricing to influence the demand for journeys was examined. However, in the longer term, it is important to ensure that the programme for road construction and improvement is in line with the overall objectives of transport policy and with the plans for other modes of transport.

Exercise 12.1

Table 12.1 presents some data about the relative safety record of different modes of transport. Discuss the extent to which these data should influence transport policy.

	1981	2009
Car users	2,287	1,059
Pedestrians	1,874	500
Motorcycle users	1,131	472
Pedal cyclists	310	104
Other road users	224	73
Bus/coach users	20	14

Table 12.1 Reported fatalities by road user, 1981 and 2009

Note: data are for Great Britain

Source: Social Trends.

A European perspective

The European Commission has recognised the importance of developing a coordinated approach to transport policy within the EU, especially given the rapid rise in the demand for mobility of people and goods as globalisation has accelerated. A White Paper was issued in 2001 setting out the framework for a European transport policy. This was reviewed in 2006, with an enhanced policy aiming to achieve 'sustainable mobility for the continent'. This is a central aspect of policy in the context of the Single Market measures of 1992 and the enlargement of the EU in 2004.

The context for this discussion is that the European Commission has calculated that between 1995 and 2005, goods and passenger transport in the EU grew by 31.3% and 17.8% respectively. Figure 12.1 shows that this growth is expected to continue into the future. The enlargement of the EU in 2004 has added extra pressures, and a greater need for mobility of people and goods in the continent. With carbon dioxide emissions from road traffic growing by 30% between 1995 and 2005, the environmental aspect of transport policy cannot be ignored. The European Commission has also estimated that the transport industry accounts for about 7% of GDP in the EU and about 5% of employment.

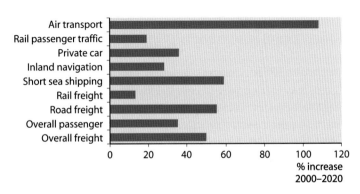

Figure 12.1 Forecast growth in transport activity in the EU25

Source: European Commission, *Keep Europe Moving: Sustainable mobility for our continent*, 2006.

Given that member states retain sovereignty over many areas of economic and social policy, there are limits to what can be achieved at a pan-European level. For example, the European Commission cannot enforce road pricing on individual member states. However, there are steps that can be taken at the European level that can influence the evolution of transport policy.

At the heart of the European Commission's approach is the perceived need to 'get prices right'. This means that transport users should face prices that reflect the real costs of their choices for society. In other words, some way should be found of ensuring that externalities are internalised in terms of the prices that consumers face. This is important in providing incentives for consumers to take good decisions. The Commission argues that economic instruments have a key role to play in bringing this about, through imposing taxes and charges, or implementing emission trading schemes. These policies were examined in Chapter 11.

Summary

➤ Transport policy aims to coordinate the planning of transport across the different modes: road, rail, bus, walking and cycling, water and air.

➤ Policy also needs to be coordinated with other aspects of economic policy, such as the location of housing and industrial developments.

➤ Transport infrastructure has some of the characteristics of a public good, so some state intervention is needed to ensure its provision.

➤ Policy cannot be purely reactive in trying to meet demand, but must also be proactive in managing the demand for transport services.

➤ Environmental sustainability must be an integral part of policy for transport.

Financing transport policy

If the government is to be active in influencing the future of the transport sector in the UK, especially if it is to be involved in the provision of transport infrastructure, the question arises as to how to raise the necessary finance — both for investment and for maintenance. Chapter 11 examined the possible use of taxation to finance transport projects, and to combat the impact of negative externalities. However, there have been some other initiatives in recent years to provide funding for transport projects, most importantly the Private Finance Initiative, launched in 1992.

The Private Finance Initiative (PFI)

PFI was launched in 1992 as a way of trying to increase the involvement of the private sector in the provision of public services. This established a partnership between the public and private sectors. The public sector specifies, perhaps in broad terms, the services that it requires, and then invites tenders from the private sector to design, build, finance and operate the scheme. In some cases, the project might be entirely freestanding: for example, the government may initiate a project such as a new bridge that is then taken up by a private firm, which will recover its costs entirely through user charges such as tolls. In other cases, the project may be a joint venture between the public and private sectors. The public sector could get involved with such a venture in order to secure wider social benefits, perhaps through reductions in traffic congestion that would not be reflected in market prices, and thus would not be fully taken into account by the private sector. In other cases, it may be that the private sector undertakes a project and then sells the services to the public sector.

Figure 12.2 shows the range of PFI deals that were signed during the first 10 years of the scheme: you can see that a sizeable proportion of these were in transport, involving road construction, street lighting, bridges and rail projects. The largest project in this period was the Channel Tunnel Rail Link (£4,178 million), signed in 2000. Subsequently, projects involving the London Underground totalling £10,695 million were signed in 2003.

The aim of PFI is to improve the financing of public sector projects. This is partly achieved by introducing a competitive element into the tendering process, but in addition it enables the risk of a project to be shared between the public and private sectors. This should enable efficiency gains to be made.

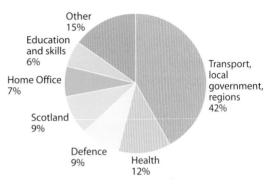

Figure 12.2 PFI signed deals as at 1 September 2001

However, PFI has been much debated – and much criticised. One effect of PFI is to reduce the pressures on public finances by enabling greater private sector involvement in funding. But it might be argued that this may in fact raise the cost of borrowing, if the public sector would have been able to borrow on more favourable terms than commercial firms. The introduction of a competitive element in the tendering process may be beneficial, but on the other hand, it could be argued that the private sector may have less incentive than the public sector to give due attention to health and safety issues. In other words, there may be a concern that private firms will be tempted to sacrifice safety or service standards in the quest for profit. Achieving the appropriate balance between efficiency and quality of service is an inevitable problem to be faced in whatever way transport is financed and provided, but it becomes a more critical issue to the extent that use of PFI switches the focus more towards efficiency and lower costs.

Appraisal of transport projects

Cost–benefit analysis

The importance of externalities in regard to environmental issues means that it is especially important to be aware of externalities when taking decisions that are likely to affect the environment. One area in which this has been especially contentious in recent years is road-building programmes. If decisions to build new roads, or to expand existing ones such as the M25, are taken only by reference to commercial considerations, there could be serious implications for resource allocation.

In taking such decisions, it is desirable to weigh up the costs and benefits of a scheme. If it turns out that the benefits exceed the costs, it might be thought appropriate to go ahead. However, in valuing the costs and the benefits, it is clearly important to include some estimate for the externalities involved in order that the decision can be based on all relevant factors. A further complication is that, with many such schemes, the costs and benefits will be spread out over a long period of time, and it is important to come to a reasonable balance between the interests of present and future generations.

It is therefore vital to have a framework within which the costs and benefits can be evaluated, whether or not they have a market value attached to them. *Social cost–benefit analysis* offers just such a framework. The Department for Transport (DfT) routinely applies cost–benefit analysis to major road schemes using a standard approach. This is based on computer software that has been in use since the 1970s: the COBA (**Co**st–**B**enefit **A**nalysis) programme. In evaluating transport projects, the DfT appraises on the basis of five key objectives: environment, safety, economy, accessibility and integration.

Suppose that a new section of trunk road is proposed. What are the steps that COBA goes through in order to reach an evaluation of the project? There are three key procedures to invoke. First, the expected construction cost needs to be measured. Second, the benefits to users must be evaluated. These costs and benefits should ideally incorporate all of the costs and benefits that will be associated with the scheme, including some that would not normally be given a monetary value. Third, it is important to be aware that the scheme is likely to provide a stream of costs and benefits over a period of time. In taking decisions in the present period, analysts need to be careful not to give too much weight to benefits (or costs) that will only accrue in the very long term. It would not be sensible to regard benefits that will appear in 30 years' time as highly as benefits that will flow after only 5 years. Future costs and benefits thus need to be converted into their 'present values' through a process of discounting future values.

Figure 12.3 shows the process adopted within the COBA system, reproduced from the DfT's *COBA Manual.* Notice that the first step is to identify user costs on the existing road network (A1 in the diagram), so that the benefits from the scheme can be evaluated as the reduction in user costs. In other words, first check the existing scenario, and then see how this will improve as a result of the new project. The costs of the project are then deducted to give an estimate of the net present value of the project. If this is positive, the scheme may be viewed favourably, although, of course, there may be other schemes under consideration and these might come out with a higher net present value. In this case, the process enables the DfT to set priorities among a range of projects, remembering that the opportunity cost of a project can be seen in terms of the net present value of the next best alternative. If funds are committed to a particular project, this may have to be at the expense of another scheme, given the limits of the overall budget.

In many ways, the difficult part of applying such a system comes in the way in which the user costs are evaluated. In order for the process to be carried out, it is vital that

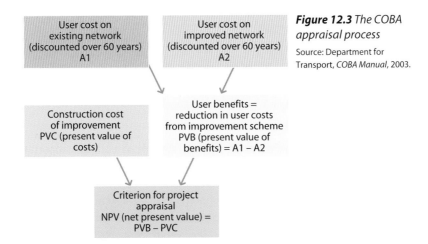

Figure 12.3 *The COBA appraisal process*

Source: Department for Transport, *COBA Manual*, 2003.

a monetary value is placed on the various user costs involved, both with the existing road network and under the new proposal. Under the COBA process, the user costs include changes in time, operating costs and the cost of accidents. In other words, the question is whether the new scheme will allow more speedy travel, cheaper travel and safer travel. The costs of the scheme are appraised in terms of the capital costs (including the preparation and supervision costs), and any changes in the capital cost of maintaining the proposed new network as compared to the existing one.

The need to assign monetary values is both the strength and the weakness of COBA. It is a strength because it enables external benefits and costs to be brought into consideration. It is a weakness because such valuations may be contentious, although the process is now so well established that at least some of the issues are now familiar to analysts. It might also be argued that, as long as similar methods are applied consistently across a range of projects, then at least the ranking procedure should be reliable.

The New Approach to Appraisal

Using cost–benefit analysis to evaluate the benefit of new road projects is just part of the appraisal of transport in the UK. The Integrated Transport White Paper 1998 led to the adoption of the New Approach to Appraisal (NATA). This was a framework intended to appraise a wide range of transport proposals and projects. As mentioned in Chapter 11, the Transport Ten Year Plan 2000 was launched after the 1998 White Paper, setting out a strategy designed to tackle congestion and pollution by improving all types of transport. Some important studies persuaded the Department for Transport to initiate some major changes in the appraisal mechanism in the late 2000s.

The Stern Review

The first of these studies was the Stern Review, an independent study of the effects of climate change commissioned by the chancellor of the exchequer. Sir Nicholas Stern was then the head of the Government Economic Service, and a former chief economist

at the World Bank. He brought techniques of economic analysis to bear on the issue of climate change, and highlighted the need to take urgent action to combat climate change – for example, by reducing emissions of greenhouse gases. It was noted in the Stern Review that more than 20% of greenhouse gas emissions from the use of energy in the UK in 2000 arise from the transport sector.

The Eddington Study

Sir Rod Eddington headed up a further study that highlighted both the importance of having an efficient and effective transport system and the need to remain aware of the environmental consequences of increased transportation. In other words, transport is essential for the economic prosperity of the economy, but it is also important to balance this against the environmental damage caused by the use of transportation. This argues that there is a need for an approach to transport policy that sees the transportation system as an integrated whole, and which takes account of the need to protect the environment.

Delivering a Sustainable Transport System, 2008

In response to the Stern Report and the Eddington Study, the Department for Transport produced a report in 2008 that set out five key goals for transport policy:

> ➤ to support national economic competitiveness and growth;

> ➤ to reduce transport's emissions of greenhouse gases in order to help in tackling climate change;

> ➤ to contribute to better safety, security and health;

> ➤ to promote greater equality of opportunity for all citizens;

> ➤ to improve quality of life for transport users and non-transport users, and to promote a healthy natural environment.

The key challenge in achieving these goals is seen to be resolving the potential tension between tackling climate change and achieving economic growth. The report set out a set of priorities until 2014. A result was that the NATA was refreshed and updated to incorporate these priorities, notably the climate change goal, which had not previously been included in the appraisal methodology.

Under the NATA, ministerial decision making was assisted by the production of an Appraisal Summary Table (AST), which was a way of drawing together the relevant pieces of evidence from assessing the impact of a proposal. The sub-categories explored under each of these headings are set out in Figure 12.4. This approach provides a focus for appraisal by identifying the issues that need to be considered. However, such items will not be fully taken into account until a way is found of giving them a monetary valuation. Some attempt is made to move towards a measurement by rating a project under each heading on a seven-point scale, from 'large negative' to 'large positive'.

In April 2011 the secretary of state for transport announced further reforms to the way in which appraisal of transport projects would be undertaken. There would no longer

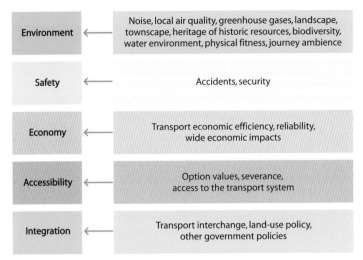

Figure 12.4 *The AST approach*

be a separate NATA process, but decisions would be taken on the basis of five business cases, designed to show whether schemes:

> 'are supported by a robust **case for change** that fits with wide public policy objectives – the "strategic case";

> demonstrate **value for money** – the "economic case";

> are **commercially viable** – the "commercial case";

> are **financially affordable** – the "financial case";

> are **achievable** – the "management case".'

(www.dft.gov.uk/news/statements/hammond-20110427)

In place of NATA, a collection of advice and guidance covering recommended techniques for modelling and appraisal was published – known as webTAG **(www.dft.gov.uk/webtag/).**

This succession of modifications to policies and procedures highlights the way in which the national economy has been changing, together with large-scale changes in technology. It also highlights the importance of economic analysis in underpinning the policies and the appraisal mechanisms. The imperative of dealing with climate change and environmental damage means that economists are seen to be as important as engineers and politicians by providing the tools needed to devise and implement a coherent and integrated transport policy.

Summary

> An important part of transport policy relates to the way that investment in and maintenance of transport projects are financed.

- The Private Finance Initiative was devised to provide greater encouragement of the private sector in the provision of public services; this has been used extensively in the transport sector.
- Cost–benefit analysis has been widely used as a framework for evaluating the net present value of transport projects.
- This entails evaluating the benefits and costs of a project, including some external benefits and costs.
- The Department for Transport routinely uses this method (using computer software COBA) for all road projects.
- The Department for Transport has refined its methodology for appraising transport projects over the years.
- The importance of factoring in the impact of transport on climate change has been increasingly recognised, and reflected in the approach to transport policy.

Exercise 12.2

Suppose there is a proposal to construct a new stretch of motorway close to where you live. Identify the costs and benefits of the scheme, including direct costs and benefits and not forgetting externalities. Discuss how you would seek to evaluate the proposal.

The global economy

Part 4

Chapter 13
Macroeconomic performance

This chapter examines the performance of the UK economy in more depth than was possible at AS level. Analysis of the multiple objectives of macroeconomic policy reveals some important sources of conflict, as policies designed to meet one objective can be seen to jeopardise the meeting of other targets. The multiplicity of objectives also means that there are multiple dimensions over which the performance of the economy has to be monitored and measured. Given the trade-offs that exist between some objectives, it is also important to prioritise them appropriately. All this must be set in the context of recent economic history, which provides the backdrop to analysing the performance of the UK economy.

Learning outcomes

After studying this chapter, you should:
➤ be familiar with the prime aims of macroeconomic policy
➤ be aware of key measures of economic performance
➤ be able to analyse and evaluate the performance of the UK economy in relation to the main policy objectives
➤ understand the existence and causes of the economic cycle
➤ be aware of the distinction between short-run and long-run economic growth and their causes
➤ be familiar with the concepts of the multiplier and accelerator and the interactions between them
➤ be able to appreciate the consequences of economic growth for inflation, employment, unemployment, the balance of payments and the government's fiscal position

Measuring performance

What is meant by the 'performance' of an economy? A simple response would be to say that performance is an indication of how well the economy is doing — but this only has meaning in relation to some notion of what represents 'good' and 'bad' performance. It is also crucial to know in what dimensions the economy's performance is important.

AS Economics, Chapter 13 set out a number of objectives of macroeconomic policy, and it seems sensible to regard these as defining the areas in which the economy's performance needs to be measured and monitored. After all, if policy is used to influence the economy in certain ways, this must be because that policy is intended to lead to desirable outcomes. According to this argument, the performance of an economy must be judged against the objectives that have been set. This is important to remember when comparing the performance of different countries that may have set out to achieve different objectives or set different priorities. Here is a brief reminder of the objectives discussed previously.

Price stability

The control of inflation has been the prime target of macroeconomic policy in the UK since the mid-1970s. Prices play a key role in an economy, acting as signals that guide the allocation of resources. When prices are unstable, firms may find it difficult to interpret these price signals, which may lead to a misallocation of resources. Furthermore, instability of prices creates difficulties for firms trying to forecast future expected demand for their products, which may discourage them from undertaking investment. This in turn means that the economy's capacity to produce may expand by less than it could otherwise have done — in other words, high or unstable inflation may dampen economic growth through its effect on investment. (*AS Economics, Chapter 13* identified some other costs of inflation, and you might wish to look back to remind yourself of them. However, the effects on resource allocation and investment are widely accepted to be the most important damaging effects of inflation.)

Full employment

A second key policy objective is full employment. Unemployment imposes costs on society and on the individuals who are unemployed. From society's point of view, the existence of substantial unemployment represents a waste of resources and indicates that the economy is working below full capacity.

Balance of payments

Under a flexible exchange rate system, the overall balance of payments will always be zero because the exchange rate adjusts to ensure that this is so. Nevertheless, the balance of payments remains an objective, not so much to ensure overall balance as to maintain an appropriate balance between the current account and the financial account. If the current account is in persistent deficit, this could cause problems in the long run, as the implication is that the country is selling off its assets in order to obtain goods for present consumption. Under a fixed exchange rate system, the need to maintain the exchange rate acts as a constraint upon economic growth, which tends to lead to an increase in imports, creating a current account deficit. This is what happened in the UK economy in the period after the Second World War, as is discussed in Chapter 15.

Economic growth

It is through long-run economic growth that the productive capacity of the economy is raised, and this in turn allows the living standards of the country's citizens to be progressively improved over time. In a sense, this is the most fundamental of the policy objectives. However, attaining other policy objectives may be a prerequisite for success in achieving growth.

Environmental considerations

It must be recognised that it is not only resources that contribute to living standards: conserving a good environment is also important. Sustainable growth and development means growth that does not prejudice the consumption possibilities of future generations, and this consideration may act as a constraint on the rate of economic growth.

Income redistribution

The final macroeconomic policy objective considered in *AS Economics, Chapter 14* concerned attempts to influence the distribution of income within a society. This may entail transfers of income between groups — that is, from the rich to the poor — in order to protect the vulnerable. Such transfers may take place through progressive taxation (whereby those on higher incomes pay a greater proportion of their income in tax) or through a system of social security benefits such as the Jobseeker's Allowance or Income Support.

Correcting market failure

At the *microeconomic* level there are policy measures designed to deal with various forms of market failure. Competition policy is one example of this; it is designed to prevent firms from abusing monopoly power, and to improve the allocation of resources. Although such policies operate at the microeconomic level, they have consequences for macroeconomic objectives such as economic growth.

Productivity

A further measure of the performance of the economy is productivity, which may be regarded as a measure of the efficiency with which factors of production are being utilised in the economy. This is important if the economy's performance is to be judged relative to that of other countries. For example, if the UK's trading competitors were all experiencing greater improvements in productivity, this would have potentially damaging effects on the competitiveness of UK goods and services in international markets.

Exercise 13.1

Based on your previous study of macroeconomic policy objectives in AS economics, discuss which of the above objectives you consider to be of most importance. Can you see reasons why it might not be possible to achieve all of the objectives simultaneously?

Measurement and analysis

Accepting these policy objectives as representing the criteria by which an economy should be judged, what indicators or measurements can be used to monitor performance? And what level of performance would be evidence of 'success'? These questions may be more straightforward for some of the policy objectives than for others, but in each case it is important to consider carefully how performance is to be monitored and judged.

Inflation

In the case of **inflation**, the government since 1997 has provided a clear target by which policy should be judged. The Bank of England's Monetary Policy Committee (MPC) is charged with the responsibility of ensuring that the government's inflation target of 2% per year is achieved. The way in which this is done is discussed in Chapter 14. The MPC's brief is to keep inflation within one percentage point (either way) of the target.

Figure 13.1 shows the extent to which this has been achieved. Until the end of 2003, the target was expressed in terms of the **retail price index** (RPIX), with the target being 2.5%. Since the beginning of 2004 the target has been defined relative to the **consumer price index** (CPI), with the target being 2%. The graph shows that the MPC was successful in keeping inflation within one percentage point of the target for most of the period shown. The only period in which inflation went substantially above the target was towards the end of the period shown on the graph. This was accompanied by a slowdown in economic activity in the economy, and it was for this reason that the MPC in mid-2008 decided to maintain the bank rate at 5%, rather than raising it in order to dampen inflation. Subsequently, as the economy headed towards recession, the Bank's forecasts of inflation suggested there was danger of it falling below its target, so bank rate was reduced dramatically — as can be seen on the figure. Indeed, in March 2009 bank rate reached 0.5%, which

> **Key term**
>
> **inflation:** a rise in the general price level
>
> **consumer price index:** a measure of the average level of prices in the UK; the government's inflation target is set in terms of the percentage rate of change of this index
>
> **retail price index:** an alternative measure of the general level of prices in the UK

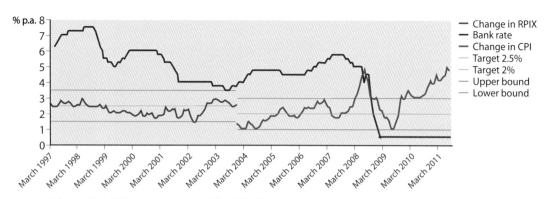

Figure 13.1 *UK interest rates and the UK inflation target, 1997–2011*
Sources: ONS, Bank of England.

was effectively as low as it could possibly go. The need to cope with recession and slow growth of the economy meant that bank rate was kept at this low level even as inflation began to accelerate well beyond its target level.

Why should the target be 2%? Why not 5%, or 0%? The fundamental rationale for having low inflation is that it can help to foster long-run sustainable economic growth. The argument is that when inflation is low and predictable, firms will be more confident in forming expectations about the future, so will be prepared to undertake the investment that is needed to expand the productive capacity of the economy and shift the aggregate supply curve to the right.

However, it is argued that a modest rate of inflation is preferable to zero inflation. This is because prices need to act as signals to firms and thus guide resource allocation. In other words, relative prices need to adjust if resources are to be used in the best way for society as a whole. It is thought that relative prices can adjust more easily when there is a little bit of inflation than if the overall price level is completely stable — that is, if the inflation target were to be zero.

The change of inflation target from RPI to CPI reflected concerns that it is important to measure inflation as accurately as possible to ensure that the indicator is appropriate, given what it is intended to represent. The CPI has some advantages in this respect (see *AS Economics, Chapter 9*). The difficulties of measuring with precision is another reason for setting a non-zero target and for allowing a range of acceptable values either side of that target. The difficulty of allowing for quality changes is one complication here. In other words, part of the observed price change (especially for products such as computers and mobile phones) represents improvements in the quality of products. This means that observed inflation is likely to overstate the actual (quality-adjusted) change in prices over time.

Figure 13.2 compares annual inflation in the UK with that in other selected countries. Notice that the time path of inflation in the UK has been similar to that experienced in Germany, and that Italy's inflation rate seems to have converged on these countries towards the end of the period shown, having started in the mid-1990s with inflation

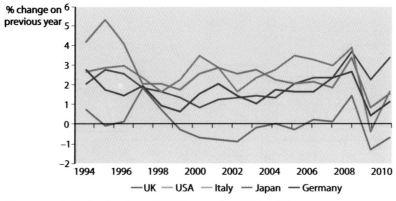

Figure 13.2 Inflation in selected OECD countries, 1994–2010

Source: OECD.

at a higher rate. Inflation in the USA has generally been somewhat higher than in the European countries shown, but Japan has followed a very different pattern, experiencing negative inflation (i.e. deflation) for several years in the period. During this time, the Japanese economy has been going through a period of recession, with real GDP per capita falling in some years – indeed, real GDP per capita fell by more than 2% in 1998 at the start of the period of deflation. All of these countries experienced a common fall in the inflation rate in 2009 during the recession, with Japan having deflation (falling prices) in 2009/10.

Unemployment

Figure 13.3 shows the numbers unemployed in the UK using the ILO definition. This is the accepted definition of unemployment for official purposes. As was explained in *AS Economics, Chapter 9*, the **ILO unemployment rate** identifies the number of people available for work, and seeking work, but without a job.

Key *term*

ILO unemployment rate: measure of the percentage of the workforce who are without jobs but are available for work, willing to work and looking for work

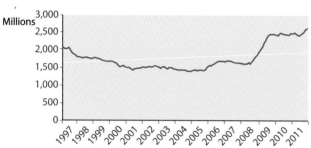

Figure 13.3
Unemployment in the UK,
1997–2011 (ILO definition)

Source: ONS.

Unemployment is regarded as an important policy target because the existence of high levels of unemployment implies that the country's resources are not being used efficiently. If the labour that is underutilised could be brought into productive activity, this would increase the real output being produced, and thus enhance average incomes. This is the equivalent of observing an economy that is operating within its production possibility curve (*PPC*) at point *A* on Figure 13.4. A reduction in unemployment would enable the economy to move to a point on the *PPC*, say, at *B*. Of course, unemployment that is involuntary may also be costly for those individuals who are unemployed but would prefer to be working.

In evaluating the level of unemployment in an economy, it is important to be aware that unemployment can never be zero. There will always be some people who are unable to find jobs, or are unemployed for a period between jobs, while searching for a job. It is not possible to put a precise number on this irreducible

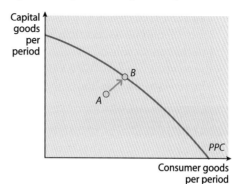

Figure 13.4 A reduction in
unemployment enables a move to the
production possibility curve

minimum unemployed, but it has been argued that the UK economy was close to this in the first few years of the twenty-first century, at least until the recession hit from 2008.

It should also be remembered that it may be desirable to have some unemployment present, as the process of job search is crucial in the evolution of an economy through time. At any particular moment, there will be some forms of economic activity that are in decline in an economy, and some which are expanding. This is how the economy adjusts to changing patterns of consumer demand, and changing patterns of international specialisation. Having said that, it is also desirable to have labour markets operating as efficiently and flexibly as possible, in order to minimise the time that people need to devote to job search or retraining. Chapter 14 examines some policies designed on the supply side of the economy to improve the flexibility with which the labour market can operate.

Unemployment in selected countries is shown in Figure 13.5 for the period since 1985. Notice that the UK began this period with the highest unemployment rate of this group of countries, but by the end its relative position had improved, being closer to the rates shown in the USA and Japan, and below those of Germany and Italy. It has been suggested that one reason that this pattern emerged was the relatively more flexible nature of the labour markets in the UK and the USA as compared with those in much of Europe.

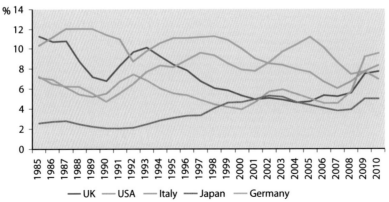

Figure 13.5
Unemployment in selected OECD countries, 1985–2010

Source: OECD.

At the heart of the discussion of unemployment is the notion that resources should be allocated as efficiently as possible to keep the economy as close to the full employment level of output as possible. Recognising that the economy operates within an international context, it is also important to strive for efficiency in order to maintain the competitiveness of UK goods and services relative to the country's trading partners. This leads to the question of the balance of payments.

Summary

➤ The control of inflation has been regarded as the prime target for macroeconomic policy in recent years, until the recession that began in 2008, when priorities began to shift.

➤ The target is set at 2% per annum change in the consumer price index (CPI).

➤ The Bank of England's Monetary Policy Committee has the responsibility of conducting monetary policy in such a way as to meet the target.

➤ The percentage change in the CPI is as good a measure of inflation as any available, but it still overestimates the true rate of inflation because of the difficulty in identifying quality changes.

➤ Another key objective of policy is to maintain low unemployment, so that the economy's resources are being fully utilised.

➤ Some unemployment will always be present to allow the structure of economic activity to change over time, which requires people to be able to engage in retraining and job search.

The balance of payments

AS Economics, Chapter 12 introduced the **balance of payments**, a set of accounts that monitors the transactions that take place between UK residents and the rest of the world. For an individual household it is important to monitor incomings and outgoings, as items purchased must be paid for in some way — either by using income or savings, or by borrowing. In a similar way, a country has to pay for goods, services or assets that are bought from other countries. The balance of payments accounts enable the analysis of such international transactions.

> **Key term**
>
> **balance of payments:** a set of accounts showing the transactions conducted between residents of a country and the rest of the world

Figure 13.6 shows the relative size of the main accounts since 1950. Notice that these data are as a percentage of nominal GDP to avoid problems caused by changing prices.

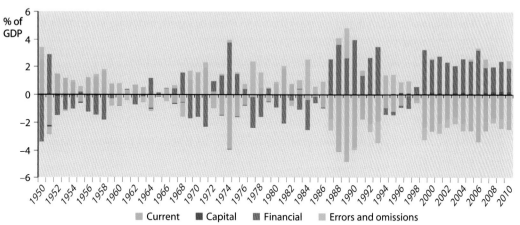

Figure 13.6 *The UK balance of payments, 1950–2010 (% of GDP)*
Source: ONS.

As the total balance of payments must always be zero, the surplus (positive) components above the line must always exactly match the deficit (negative) items below the line. However, both graphs indicate that the magnitudes of the three major accounts vary through time.

AS Economics, Chapter 12 (pages 145–50) discussed the key characteristics of the accounts, and you may find it helpful to refresh your memory of these.

The significance of the balance of payments is not in its overall position, as the overall balance must always be zero. Rather, the significance is seen in terms of the way in which the overall position is achieved. The balance of payments may be zero overall with balance being achieved on all of the component accounts, or it may be achieved with a current account deficit being matched by a surplus on the financial account. This has been typical of recent years in the UK.

Effectively, what is happening is that, in order to fund the current account deficit, the UK is selling assets to foreign investors and borrowing abroad. An important question is whether this practice is sustainable in the long run. Selling assets or borrowing abroad has future implications for the current account, as there will be outflows of investment income, and debt repayments in the future following today's financial surplus. It also has implications for interest rate policy. If the authorities hold interest rates high relative to the rest of the world, this will tend to attract inflows of investment, again with future implications for the current account. In this context, the interaction with the exchange rate is also important.

Summary

> The balance of payments is a set of accounts that contains details of the transactions that take place between the residents of an economy and the rest of the world.

> The accounts are divided into three sections: the current, financial and capital accounts.

> The current account identifies transactions in goods and services, together with some income payments and international transfers.

> The financial account measures transactions in financial assets, including investment flows and central government transactions in foreign reserves.

> The capital account, which is relatively small, contains capital transfers.

> The overall balance of payments must always be zero.

> The current account has been in persistent deficit since 1984, reflecting a deficit in trade in goods that is partly offset by a surplus in invisible trade.

> The financial account has been in strong surplus — as is required to balance the current account deficit.

Exercise 13.2

Discuss why the balance of payments needs to be considered in the formulation of macroeconomic policy.

The economic cycle

The notion of the **economic cycle** was introduced in *AS Economics, Chapter 9*. It is illustrated in Figure 13.7. The economic cycle describes the way in which GDP fluctuates

 Key *term*

economic cycle: a phenomenon whereby GDP fluctuates around its underlying trend, following a regular pattern

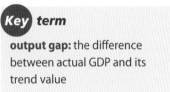
through time around an upward trend. At any point in time, GDP may be below or above its trend value, the difference being known as the **output gap**. This is defined as the actual level of output minus the potential level. If the economy is in recession, with actual GDP below potential GDP, then the gap is negative; if actual GDP is above the trend level, the gap is positive.

> **Key term**
>
> **output gap:** the difference between actual GDP and its trend value

Consider an economy at point *A* on Figure 13.7. At this stage in the cycle, the economy is entering a period of recession, in which GDP is falling. This continues until point *B*, the trough of the cycle, at which point GDP stops falling and begins to grow again. At point *C*, the economy is showing growth in actual GDP, but GDP is still below its trend value; only at point *D* does the economy hit the trend. In other words, between points *A* and *D*,

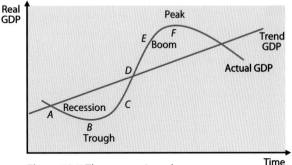

Figure 13.7 *The economic cycle*

the output gap is negative. Beyond point *D* the economy moves into a boom period (as at point *E*), where GDP grows more rapidly than its trend value, and the level of GDP is above its trend value; the output gap is positive. At point *F* the cycle reaches its peak and stops increasing; beyond this point actual GDP again begins to fall, and then the story repeats.

This process highlights an important distinction between growth in the short run, and growth in the long run. The term **long-run economic growth** is used to refer to the process by which there is an increase in the trend, or potential, rate of growth of GDP. One way of looking at this is that long-run economic growth occurs when there is an increase in long-run aggregate supply — an increase in the productive capacity of the economy. Indeed, this is the process by which GDP is able to follow an

> **Key term**
>
> **long-run economic growth:** an increase in the productive capacity of the economy
>
> **short-run economic growth:** an increase in GDP as the economy moves towards capacity output

upward trend over time as productive capacity increases. However, there are also short-run changes in the actual level of GDP; for example between points B and C on Figure 13.7, there will be an observed increase in real GDP. This is **short-run economic growth**, and is not to be confused with the changing capacity of the economy through time. This short-run economic growth can occur (for example) because unemployed factors of production are being drawn into use when the economy is recovering or in boom.

From a policy perspective, it is important to know at what stage the economy is located. When the output gap is negative, and the level of output is below trend, then it may be tempting for policy-makers to try to 'fill the gap' by stimulating aggregate demand. However, this would be dangerous when the output gap is positive, as the main effect would be on the price level. This will soon be explained more thoroughly.

Figure 13.8 shows the rate of change of (actual) real GDP each year since 1949. Also marked on the graph is the long-run average rate of growth, which is about 2.3% p.a. This shows that the rate of growth of actual real GDP has been relatively volatile over this period – sometimes showing substantial variation from one year to the next, the most extreme example being when the annual growth rate fell from +7.1% in 1973 to −1.4% in 1974. This graph suggests that the economic cycle is not very regular, and certainly the growth rate appears to become more stable towards the end of the period shown. One classic example of a cycle occurred from 1984 to 1993, as shown in Figure 13.9; here the output gap was positive from 1985 to 1988, then becoming negative as the economy went into recession.

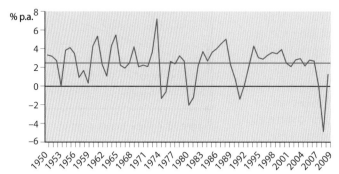

Figure 13.8 *Growth of real GDP, 1949–2010 (% change over previous year)*

Source: ONS.

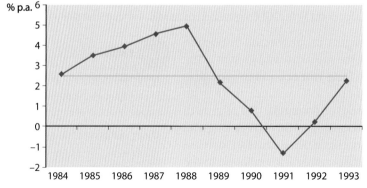

Figure 13.9 *A classic economic cycle*

Source: ONS.

In mid-2008, the chancellor of the exchequer took the unprecedented step of stating publicly that the UK was heading for its biggest recession since the Second World War. Figure 13.10 shows quarterly data for the period 2003 to 2008, showing the information that was available to the chancellor when he made this claim. He proved to be correct.

Chancellor of the Exchequer Alistair Darling warned of an impending recession

Figure 13.11 shows the growth rates of GDP per capita in selected countries from 1971 to 2009. Although the graph looks a little congested, it is useful because it shows that there are some periods when fluctuations occur simultaneously across countries. For example, look at what happened in 1974/75, when all countries shown were negatively affected by the oil price shock of 1973/74. Notice that all countries enjoyed a more stable period of growth between about 1984 and 1990. So there may be periods in which there are common cycles across countries. On the other hand, there are also exceptions to this – for example, Japan's negative growth in 1998 and 1999, which was not shared by the other countries in the graph. The recession of the late 2000s clearly affected all of these economies, sending growth strongly negative at the end of the period shown.

The oil price shock of 1973/74 negatively affected most countries

It is important to be aware that if countries do follow common patterns – at least in some periods – then this implies that domestic economic policy may not be the only influence on an economy's performance.

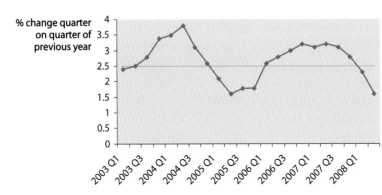

Figure 13.10
The UK economy heading for recession?

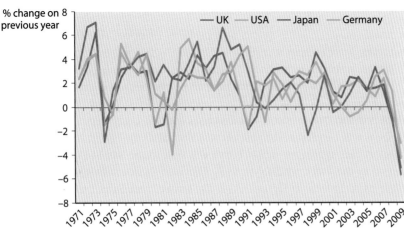

Figure 13.11
Growth of real GDP per capita in selected OECD countries, 1971–2009

Source: OECD.

Economic growth and the *AD/AS* model

The *AD/AS* model can be used to explain how economic growth takes place in an economy. The model was introduced during AS economics. It is now important to distinguish carefully between the short run and the long run, especially in relation to the aggregate supply curve.

Economic growth in the short run

Figure 13.12 illustrates short-run macroeconomic equilibrium. Suppose that the economy begins in equilibrium with **aggregate demand curve** AD_0 and the **short-run aggregate supply curve** at SAS_0. Recall from AS economics that the main components of aggregate demand are consumption, investment, government spending and net exports. The short-run aggregate supply curve shows how much output firms would be prepared to supply in the short run at any given overall price level. Macroeconomic equilibrium is achieved with real output given by Y_0 and with the overall price level at P_0.

If for some reason there is an increase in aggregate demand from AD_0 to AD_1, then the immediate response is a movement along the *SAS* curve, with real output increasing to Y_1 and the price level rising to P_1. What is happening here is that firms are responding to the increase in demand, expanding their production as prices rise.

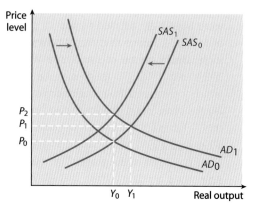

Figure 13.12 *Short-run macroeconomic equilibrium*

Key term

aggregate demand curve (AD): a curve showing the relationship between the level of aggregate demand in an economy and the overall price level; it shows planned expenditure at any given overall price level

short-run aggregate supply curve: a curve showing how much output firms are prepared to supply in the short run at any given overall price level

The macroeconomy may not settle at this new position. As prices rise, there will be further adjustments. For example, workers may bid for higher wages to compensate for the higher prices, and firms may charge higher prices for the components that they supply to other firms. Or it may be that firms have to pay workers at overtime rates in order to induce them to work longer hours — especially if the economy is close to its full employment position. These effects will feed back into the costs faced by firms. As this happens, firms will be prepared to supply less output at any given overall price level, and the short-run aggregate supply curve will shift to the left. In Figure 13.12, this is represented by the shift from SAS_0 to SAS_1. The overall price rises again, but real output now falls back. Indeed, in Figure 13.12, the level of real output returns to its original level at Y_0, but with a higher overall price level at P_2.

This suggests that an increase in aggregate demand may lead to higher real output in the short run, but that this may not be a permanent increase — which is why this is described as short-run economic growth.

The multiplier

AS Economics, Chapter 10 introduced the concept of the **multiplier**, which suggested that for any increase in autonomous spending, there would be a multiplied increase in equilibrium output. The idea of the multiplier is that, if there is an increase in (say) government expenditure, this provides income for workers, who will then spend that income and create further expenditure streams.

Notice that it is the act of spending that allows these effects to be perpetuated. If the workers who receive additional income do not spend some of that income, the effects are diluted. The amounts that are not spent are referred to as 'withdrawals'.

Key term

multiplier: the ratio of a change in equilibrium real income to the autonomous change that brought it about; it is calculated as 1 divided by the marginal propensity to withdraw

marginal propensity to withdraw: the sum of the marginal propensities to save, tax and import; it is the proportion of additional income that is withdrawn from the circular flow

There are three ways in which these withdrawals take place. First, it may be that households decide to save some of the extra income that they receive instead of spending it. The amount of additional income that is saved is known as the *marginal propensity to save* (*s*). Second, some of the extra income will be spent on imports, and the *marginal propensity to import* (*m*) represents the fraction of extra income spent on imported goods or services. Third, a proportion of the extra income (*t*) is taken back by the government as taxes on income. The overall size of these induced effects will depend upon the marginal propensity to withdraw. The **marginal propensity to withdraw** (*mpw*) is thus the sum of these three effects (*s* + *m* + *t*).

The size of the multiplier can then be calculated. For example, suppose that households save 5% of extra income (*s* = 0.05) and spend 10% of the extra income on imports (*m* = 0.1), and that 25% goes in tax (*t* = 0.25). The *mpw* is then 0.05 + 0.1 + 0.25 = 0.4, and the multiplier is 2.5. An increase in the savings rate to 15% would increase the *mpw* to 0.5 and reduce the multiplier to 2.

In terms of the *AD/AS* diagram, the existence of the multiplier means that if there is an increase in an item of autonomous expenditure (e.g. investment or government spending), the *AD* curve moves further to the right than it otherwise would have done, because of the multiplier effects.

Exercise 13.3

Calculate the multiplier if households save 20% of any additional income that they receive and spend 10% on imports. Assume that the marginal tax rate is 10%. Check how the multiplier changes if the marginal tax rate increases to 20%.

The accelerator

The idea of the multiplier is based on the induced effects of expenditure that spread the initial effects of an increase in spending. A similar notion is that of the **accelerator**. The notion of the accelerator arises from one of the driving forces behind firms' investment. Although some investment is needed to replace old equipment (known as depreciation), most investment is needed when firms wish to expand capacity. If there

> **Key** *term*
>
> **accelerator:** a theory by which the level of investment depends upon the change in real output

is an increase in demand for a firm's product (or if a firm *expects* there to be an increase in demand), it may need to expand capacity in order to meet the increased demand. This suggests that one of the determinants of the level of investment is a *change* in expected demand. Notice that it is the change in demand that is important, rather than the level, and it is this that leads to the notion of the accelerator.

Suppose that the economy is in recession and begins to recover. As the recovery begins, demand begins to increase, and firms have to undertake investment in order to expand capacity. However, as the economy approaches full capacity, the growth rate slows down — and hence investment falls, as it reacts to the change in output.

The multiplier and accelerator interact with each other. If there is an increase in output following an increase in aggregate demand, the accelerator induces an increase in investment. The increase in investment then has a multiplier effect that induces an additional increase in demand. In this way, the multiplier and accelerator reinforce each other. The downside to this is that the same thing happens when output slows as this leads to a fall in investment, which has negative multiplier effects. This interaction between the multiplier and the accelerator can result in cyclical fluctuations in the level of output.

Summary

> An increase in aggregate demand in the short run may lead to higher real output, but this may only be temporary.

> The multiplier reinforces the effects of an increase in aggregate demand.

> Short-run economic growth occurs at some points in the economic cycle when the economy is in recovery or boom.

> The accelerator effect reinforces the multiplier when investment by firms responds to a change in output.

> The interaction between the multiplier and the accelerator can give rise to fluctuations in equilibrium output.

Economic growth in the long run

It was argued above that economic growth in the short run may be short-lived because the adjustments to an increase in aggregate demand may offset the initial increase in real output. Indeed, it could be argued that there is a full capacity level of real output beyond which no increase in real output can be sustained. This full capacity level of output corresponds to the notion of full employment. In the short run, output may rise beyond this, but only if firms are able to employ workers on overtime, which is not likely to be sustainable in the long term as it adds to the firms' labour costs. This suggests that the **long-run aggregate supply curve** is different in character from the short-run version.

 term

long-run aggregate supply curve: a curve that shows the amount of real output that will be supplied in the economy in the long run at any given overall price level

Figure 13.13 illustrates the situation. As before, *AD* is the aggregate demand curve, with the chief components of aggregate demand again being consumption, investment, government spending and net exports. *AS* is the aggregate supply curve, which becomes vertical at the full capacity level of output. In other words, Y^* represents the maximum amount of output that the economy can produce in a period if all its resources are being fully utilised. This can be described as the full employment level of output. The intersection of *AD* and *AS* provides the equilibrium position for the economy, with P^* in Figure 13.13 being the equilibrium price level. Remember that the *AD* curve is very different in nature from the individual demand curve for a commodity. Here the relationship is between the *total* demand for goods and services and the *overall* price level.

It is important to be aware of a debate that developed over the shape of the aggregate supply curve. This is important because it has implications for the conduct and effectiveness of policy options, which will be discussed in Chapter 14.

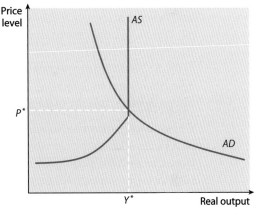

Figure 13.13 *Macroeconomic equilibrium revisited*

During the 1970s, an influential school of macroeconomists, which became known as the **Monetarist school**, argued that the economy would always converge on an equilibrium level of output that they referred to as the *natural rate of output*. They also argued that the adjustment to this natural rate would be rapid, perhaps almost instantaneous. Associated with this long-run equilibrium was a **natural rate of unemployment**. In this case, the long-run relationship between aggregate supply and the price level would be vertical, as shown in Figure 13.14. Here Y^* is the full employment level of aggregate

Key term

Monetarist school: group of economists who believed that the macroeconomy always adjusts rapidly to the full employment level of output; they also argued that monetary policy should be the prime instrument for stabilising the economy

natural rate of unemployment: equilibrium full employment level of unemployment

output — the natural rate of output. In this view of the world, a change in the overall price level does not affect aggregate output because the economy always readjusts rapidly back to full employment. Indeed, no change in aggregate demand can affect aggregate output, as it is only the price level that will adjust to restore equilibrium.

An opposing school of thought (often known as the **Keynesian school**) held that the macroeconomy was not sufficiently flexible to enable continuous full employment. They argued that the economy could settle at an equilibrium position below full employment, at least in the medium term. In particular, inflexibilities in labour markets would prevent adjustment. For example, if firms had pessimistic expectations about aggregate demand, and thus reduced their supply of output, this would lead to lower incomes because of workers being laid off. This would then mean that aggregate demand was indeed deficient, so firms' pessimism was self-fulfilling. Pessimistic expectations would also affect investment, and thus have an impact on the long-run productive capacity of the economy.

Keynesian arguments led to a belief that there would be a range of outputs over which aggregate supply would be upward sloping. Figure 13.15 illustrates such an aggregate supply curve, and will be familiar from *AS Economics, Chapter 11*. In this diagram, Y^* still represents full employment; however, when the economy is operating below this level of output, aggregate supply is somewhat sensitive to the price level, becoming steeper as full employment is approached.

The policy implications of the Monetarist *AS* curve are strong. If the economy always converges rapidly on the full employment level of output, no manipulation of aggregate demand can have any effect except on the price level. This is readily seen in Figure 13.16, where, regardless of the position of the aggregate demand curve, the level of real output remains at Y^*. If aggregate demand is low at AD_0, then the price level is also relatively low, at P_0. An increase in aggregate demand to AD_1 raises the price level to P_1 but leaves real output at Y^*. In such

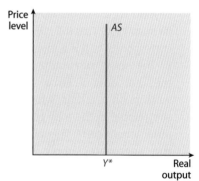

Figure 13.14 *Aggregate supply in the long run: the 'Monetarist' view*

> ### Key term
>
> **Keynesian school:** group of economists who believed that the macroeconomy could settle in an equilibrium that was below the full employment level

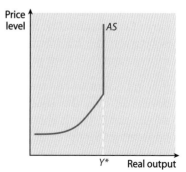

Figure 13.15 *Aggregate supply in the long run: the 'Keynesian' view*

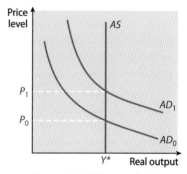

Figure 13.16 *Demand-side policy with a vertical AS curve*

a world, only supply-side policy (which affects the position of the aggregate supply curve) has any effect on real output.

So, economic growth in the long run is defined as an increase in the productive capacity of the economy, which would be reflected in a rightward shift of the long-run aggregate supply curve. It is the process by which the total resources available to inhabitants of a country expand as time goes by. The measurement of economic growth is normally based on changes in real GDP over time, but it is important to recall that GDP is subject to the fluctuations of the economic cycle. This means that to measure economic growth, the underlying trend growth of real GDP needs to be identified.

In some ways, economic growth may be seen as the most fundamental policy objective for an economy. It is economic growth that enables a country to improve the standard of living of its inhabitants, which is ultimately what most societies wish to achieve. However, care needs to be taken in this respect, as the standard of living of people in a country does not only depend upon the *quantity* of resources that are available. The standard of living also depends upon the *quality* of those resources, and on the way in which they are divided up among members of a society. For this purpose, the members of a society may need to include future generations as well as the present one, in the sense that economic growth that is achieved at the expense of the environment may leave future generations worse off. In other words, the unremitting pursuit of economic growth without regard to the costs may not be the best policy.

Nonetheless, economic growth is a central target of economic policy, as without it the well-being of a country's inhabitants is likely to stagnate. Indeed, a policy objective such as low inflation may be regarded as a target because achieving it is expected to encourage investment in order to enable a higher rate of economic growth. Thus other targets may be seen as subservient to economic growth.

The causes of economic growth

It is important to be aware that the causes of short- and long-run economic growth are quite different. In the short run, economic growth is observed in changes in actual real GDP. Such changes may arise from changes in aggregate demand, although such changes may be short-lived as the macroeconomy returns to equilibrium. Growth may also occur in the short run as a consequence of the economic cycle, by which the level of economic activity tends to fluctuate around its underlying trend. The interaction of the multiplier and accelerator can also induce cycles in economic activity, which may be manifest as short-run economic growth.

Long-run economic growth refers to the underlying trend increase in real potential GDP and is represented by a rightward shift in the long-run aggregate supply curve. Such a shift may be the result of an increase in the quantity of factors of production available in the economy, or an increase in the efficiency with which those factors of production are utilised.

The quantity of factors of production in an economy tends to change very slowly through time. The labour force grows relatively slowly in normal circumstances,

Migrant workers have an effect on the productive capacity of the economy

especially in a mature economy like the UK, where the rate of natural population increase is slow. Since the expansion of the EU in 2004, there has been a certain amount of in-migration of workers from the new EU member states — especially from eastern European countries such as Poland. This would be expected to have an effect on the productive capacity of the economy, by shifting the long-run aggregate supply curve to the right. Similarly, the quantity of capital services available changes relatively slowly through time, depending on the degree to which firms are willing to undertake investment. Remember that investment in future productive capacity can only be undertaken at the expense of current consumption.

The other way in which productive capacity can be increased is through improvements in the efficiency with which factors of production can be utilised. Another way of viewing this is to look for improvements in productivity. Productivity was discussed in Part 2 of the book (see Chapter 5), where some of the measurement issues were outlined. It was also noted that although productivity is often defined in terms of labour productivity (i.e. the efficiency with which labour is utilised), total factor productivity is also important. This measures the overall efficiency of all factors of production in the production process.

These determinants of the long-run rate of economic growth are the target for supply-side policies, which aim to influence the position of the long-run aggregate supply curve. These will be discussed in Chapter 14.

The consequences of economic growth

Economic growth is a prime objective of policy for an economy as it expands the resources available to the residents of a country and thus enables improvements in the standard of living. However, this does not mean that a country can pursue economic growth without having regard for the possible consequences, as the pursuit of economic growth may have other effects on the economy. This is because the macroeconomy is interconnected, so changes in one area can have knock-on effects elsewhere.

Inflation

One possible consequence of a single-minded pursuit of economic growth is that it could endanger macroeconomic stability. This is especially the case when the economy is close to its capacity level. Trying to boost economic growth by persistently stimulating aggregate demand in such a position will push up the overall price level, but may have no discernible effect on real output. An extreme example of this was shown in Figure 13.14, where the long-run aggregate supply curve was assumed to be vertical.

This argument does not apply if the economic growth stems from an expansion in the economy's productive capacity. A rightward shift of the long-run aggregate supply curve does not have consequences for inflation − indeed, with aggregate demand unchanged, a shift to the right of the *AS* curve results in a lower equilibrium overall price level, thus reducing inflationary pressure.

This clearly has implications for policy design. In the pursuit of economic growth, it is important to distinguish between demand-led and supply-led growth, and there needs to be an awareness of the position of the economy relative to the full employment or capacity level, and the current stage of the economic cycle.

Employment and unemployment

The consequences of economic growth for employment and unemployment are likely to be favourable. In the short run, economic growth can have the effect of drawing more workers into the labour force, raising employment and reducing unemployment. In the long run, economic growth raises real output, and thus real incomes, and may provide more security of employment.

The balance of payments

It is possible that economic growth will have consequences for the balance of payments. One the one hand, it is possible that an expansion in the productive capacity of the economy will enable the country to increase its exports, thus having a positive effect on the current account of the balance of payments. This could then fuel further growth. In part, this is what has been happening to China's economy, which has gone through a period of very rapid economic growth based in large measure on its ability to export goods to the rest of the world. In earlier decades, other countries in southeast Asia, such as Singapore, Taiwan and South Korea, went through a similar pattern of rapid economic growth based on an expansion of exports.

However, expanding exports is only part of the picture. An increase in the rate of economic growth could also result in an increase in imports, thus having a negative effect on the current account of the balance of payments. This could arise if firms rely heavily on imported materials or components for manufacturing activity, or if the increase in real incomes resulting from growth induces consumers to increase their expenditure on imported consumer goods. In the period following the Second World War, the British economy was subject to this phenomenon. Every time the economy began to experience economic growth, the current account of the balance of payments went into deficit. As the economy was operating under fixed exchange rates

at the time, the current account deficit could not be sustained and the growth had to be slowed. The result was a 'stop–go' cycle that hindered long-run growth.

The government's fiscal position

As will be explained in the next chapter, it is important for the government to avoid borrowing too much in order to fund its expenditures. The danger is that by borrowing, the government has the effect of 'crowding out' private sector activity, by making it more difficult for firms to obtain finance for investment. If the private sector is more efficient than the public sector, then this will damage the long-term productive capacity of the economy. Economic growth may help to prevent this from happening, as when growth takes place and real incomes rise the revenues that the government receives from taxation tend to increase and its expenditure on social security tends to fall, as unemployment will tend to be low. This then improves the government's financial position and reduces the need for public sector borrowing.

Economic policy objectives — an overview

You will realise from the discussion above that there are several targets for macroeconomic policy. However, we can put these into perspective by recognising that policy is aimed at a relatively small number of ultimate objectives, which we can summarise as

- ➤ economic stability
- ➤ economic growth
- ➤ international competitiveness

We could argue that the most important of these overarching objectives is economic growth. It is through economic growth that it becomes possible to improve the quality of life of a nation's citizens, as it is only through economic growth that the quantity of resources available to citizens can be expanded. This is not to say that the other two objectives are unimportant. Economic stability is important – but partly because it creates an environment within which economic growth can take place. For example, if we have price stability, then firms will have more confidence to invest in the future, thus stimulating economic growth. Similarly, maintaining or improving the international competitiveness of domestically produced goods also contributes to economic stability and provides a solid demand base to encourage firms to expand by selling in global markets – again helping to increase economic growth. In the chapters following, we will examine a range of different policy approaches, and you will find that some of these are likely to be more useful in achieving some of the objectives.

Exercise 13.4

Discuss the possible consequences of economic growth for the environment.

Summary

➤ In using the *AD/AS* model, it is useful to distinguish between Monetarist and Keynesian views about the shape of aggregate supply.

➤ Monetarist economists have argued that the economy always converges rapidly on equilibrium at the natural rate of output, implying that changes in aggregate demand have an impact only on prices, leaving real output unaffected. The aggregate supply curve in this world is vertical.

➤ The Keynesian view is that the economy may settle in an equilibrium that is below full employment, and that there is a range over which the aggregate supply curve slopes upwards.

➤ Economic growth is an increase in the productive capacity of an economy.

➤ It may be seen as the ultimate target of macroeconomic policy, as it allows an improvement in the well-being of a country's inhabitants.

➤ It is important to distinguish between the underlying trend growth rate and temporary changes in GDP due to the economic cycle.

➤ Economic growth has consequences for inflation, employment, unemployment, the balance of payments and the government's fiscal position.

Chapter 14
Monetary policy

The setting of objectives for macroeconomic policy implies that there are ways in which the authorities can seek to influence the course of the economy at the macroeconomic level. This chapter and the next explore the main policy instruments that the authorities can use in seeking to control the performance of the UK economy, and evaluates the extent to which such methods of control are likely to be effective. The main focus of discussion will be on the ways in which policy influences economic stability, growth and international competitiveness. Monetary policy has been the most prominent method of influencing the economy in recent years, but, in addition, the role of the exchange rate must be taken into account. Fiscal policy and supply-side policies will be investigated in the following chapter.

Learning outcomes

After studying this chapter, you should:
- be familiar with the prime instruments of monetary policy
- be aware of the functions and measures of money, and the importance of interest rates in the economy
- appreciate the importance of the impact of the exchange rate on the conduct of monetary policy
- be aware of the significance of international competitiveness and how to monitor it
- be able to understand the monetary transmission mechanism
- be familiar with the operation of monetary policy and its effectiveness in helping to manage the economy

Policy targets and instruments

At the macroeconomic level, the government has three key objectives. The most fundamental of these objectives is economic growth, as this allows improvements in the standard of living. However, in order to achieve economic growth, it is crucial to maintain economic stability, thus providing the economic environment within which economic growth can take place. Finally, it is also important to be aware of

international competitiveness. The government has three main types of policy instrument with which to attempt to meet these macroeconomic objectives.

Monetary policy entails the use of monetary variables such as money supply and interest rates to influence aggregate demand. It will be shown that under a fixed exchange rate system, monetary policy becomes wholly impotent, as it has to be devoted to maintaining the exchange rate. So, the effectiveness of monetary policy depends upon the policy environment in which it is used. In recent years, the prime use of monetary policy has been in seeking to create a stable macroeconomic environment.

The term '*fiscal policy*' covers a range of policy measures that affect government expenditures and revenues through the decisions made by the government on its expenditure, taxation and borrowing. Fiscal policy is used to influence the level and structure of aggregate demand in an economy. The effectiveness of fiscal policy also depends crucially on the whole policy environment in which it is utilised.

Supply-side policies comprise a range of measures intended to have a direct impact on aggregate supply — specifically, on the potential capacity output of the economy. These measures are often microeconomic in character and are designed to increase output and hence economic growth.

The underpinning of monetary policy

Monetary policy has become the prime instrument of government macroeconomic policy, with the interest rate acting as the key control variable. Monetary policy involves the manipulation of monetary variables in order to influence aggregate demand in the economy, with the intention of meeting the government's inflation target.

In order to understand how monetary policy can influence the level of aggregate demand, it is important to examine the characteristics of key monetary variables — the money supply, interest rates and the exchange rate.

Key term

monetary policy: decisions made by the government regarding monetary variables such as money supply and interest rates

money stock: the quantity of money that is in circulation in the economy

Money supply

The **money stock** is the quantity of money that is in circulation in the economy. In a modern economy, money performs four important functions. First, it is a *medium of exchange*. In other words, money is what is used when people undertake transactions — for example, when you buy a sandwich or a burger for lunch. Second, money is a *store of value*: people (or firms) may choose to hold money in order to undertake transactions in the future. If this were not the case, there would be no reason for people to accept money in exchange for goods or services. Money is also a *unit of account*: it is a way of setting prices so that the value of different goods and services can be compared. Finally, money is a *standard of deferred* *payment.* Firms signing contracts for future transactions need to be able to set prices for those transactions.

Firms and households choose to hold some money. They may do this in order to undertake transactions, or as a precaution against the possible need to undertake transactions at short notice. In other words, there is a *demand for money.* However, in choosing to hold money they incur an opportunity cost, in the sense that they forgo the possibility of earning interest by purchasing some form of financial asset.

This means that the interest rate can be regarded as the opportunity cost of holding money; put another way, it is the price of holding money. At high rates of interest, people can be expected to choose to hold less money, as the opportunity cost of holding money is high. *MD* in Figure 14.1 represents such a money demand curve. It is downward sloping.

The notes and coins in circulation in the UK are known as the 'monetary base'

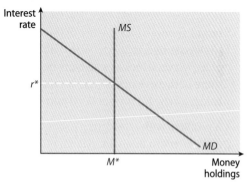

Figure 14.1 *The demand for money*

Suppose the government wants to set the money supply (*MS*) at *M** in Figure 14.1. This can be achieved in two ways. If the government controls the supply of money at *M**, equilibrium will be achieved only if the interest rate is allowed to adjust to *r**. An alternative way of reaching the same point is to set the interest rate at *r** and then allow the money supply to adjust to *M**. The government can do one or the other – but it cannot set money supply at *M** and hold the interest rate at any value other than *r** without causing disequilibrium. In other words, it is not possible to control both money supply and interest rates simultaneously and independently.

Measuring money stock

An important characteristic of money is **liquidity**. This refers to the ease with which an asset can be spent. Cash is the most liquid asset, as it can be used for transactions. However, if you are holding funds in a savings account whereby you must

 Key term

liquidity: the extent to which an asset can be converted to cash without the holder incurring a cost

either give notice of withdrawal or forfeit some return to withdraw it instantly, then such funds are regarded as being less liquid, as they cannot costlessly or instantly be used for transactions.

One traditional way of measuring the money stock was from the *monetary base*, which comprised all notes and coins in circulation. Together with the commercial banks' deposits at the Bank of England, this was known as **M0** or **narrow money**. This was intended to measure the amount of money held for transactions purposes. However, with the increased use of electronic means of payment, M0 has become less meaningful as a measure, and the Bank of England stopped issuing data for M0 in 2005.

However, there are many assets that are 'near-money', such as interest-bearing current account deposits at banks. These are highly liquid and can readily be converted into cash for transactions. **M4** or **broad money** is a measure of the money stock that includes M0 together with sterling wholesale and retail deposits with monetary financial institutions such as banks. In other words, it includes all bank deposits that can be used for transactions, even though some of these deposits may require a period of notice for withdrawal. However, M4 is held not only for transactions purposes, but also partly as a store of wealth.

> **Key** *term*
>
> **narrow money (M0):** notes and coins in circulation and as commercial banks' deposits at the Bank of England
>
> **broad money (M4):** M0 plus sterling wholesale and retail deposits with monetary financial institutions such as banks and building societies

A problem with attempting to control the money supply directly is that the complexity of the modern financial system makes it quite difficult to pin down a precise definition or measurement of money. For this and other reasons, the chosen instrument of monetary policy is the interest rate. By setting the interest rate, monetary policy affects aggregate demand.

It is also important to realise that the lending behaviour of the commercial banks can influence money supply, as by increasing their lending, banks can create credit. This makes it more difficult for the central bank to exert control over money supply. This could be achieved by forcing the banks to hold a proportion of their assets as cash or liquid assets, but this was abandoned in favour of controlling via the interest rate.

Interest rates

Although the previous section talked about 'the interest rate', this is a simplification. In the real-world economy, there are many different interest rates. For example, if you borrow from a bank, you will pay a higher interest rate than would be paid to you on your savings. Indeed, it is this difference between the rates for savers and borrowers that enables the banks to make a profit. This is shown in Figure 14.2, which shows interest rates set by the retail banks since 1995. You can see that the rates tend to move together through time, but that the rate charged on mortgage lending is consistently higher than the rates paid to savers on deposits. There is also a differential between these savings accounts, reflecting the fact that savers can get a higher return by forgoing the right to withdraw their funds without notice (hence the term 'time deposits').

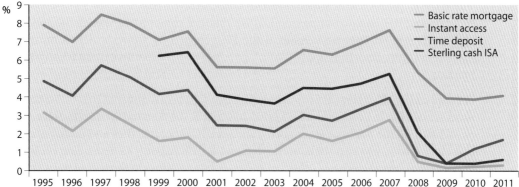

Figure 14.2 *Interest rates (retail banks)*

Note: data refer to December of each year.

Source: ONS.

Similarly, interest rates on financial assets differ depending on the nature of the asset. In part, these differences reflect different degrees of risk associated with the assets. A risky asset pays a higher interest rate than a relatively safe asset. A long-term asset tends to pay a higher interest rate than a short-term asset, although the differences have been quite small in the first few years of the twenty-first century.

The exchange rate

In considering the tools of monetary policy, it is also important to consider the **exchange rate** – that is, the rate at which one currency exchanges against another. This is because the exchange rate, the interest rate and the money supply are all intimately related. If UK interest rates are high relative to elsewhere in the world, they will attract overseas investors, increasing the demand for pounds. This will tend to lead to an appreciation in the exchange rate – which in turn will reduce the competitiveness of UK goods and services, reducing the foreign demand for UK exports and encouraging UK residents to reduce their demand for domestic goods and buy imports instead.

Key term

exchange rate: the price of one currency in terms of another

Indeed, under a fixed exchange rate regime, the monetary authorities are committed to maintaining the exchange rate at a particular level, so could not allow an appreciation to take place. In this situation, monetary policy is powerless to influence the real economy, as it must be devoted to maintaining the exchange rate. Under a floating exchange rate system, monetary policy is freed from this role, but even so it must be used in such a way that the current account deficit of the balance of payments does not become unsustainable in the long run. In other words, the use of interest rates to target inflation has implications for the magnitude of the current and financial accounts of the balance of payments.

The exchange rate and international competitiveness

In analysing the balance of payments, the relative competitiveness of UK goods and services is an important issue. If the UK persistently shows a deficit on the current account, does that imply that UK goods are uncompetitive in international markets?

The demand for UK exports in world markets depends upon a number of factors. In some ways, it is similar to the demand for a good. In general, the demand for a good depends on its price, on the prices of other goods, and on consumer incomes and preferences. In a similar way, you can think of the demand for UK exports as depending on the price of UK goods, the price of other countries' goods, incomes in the rest of the world and foreigners' preferences for UK goods over those produced elsewhere. However, in the case of international transactions the exchange rate is also relevant, as this determines the purchasing power of UK incomes in the rest of the world. Similarly, the demand for imports into the UK depends upon the relative prices of domestic and foreign goods, incomes in the UK, preferences for foreign and domestically produced goods and the exchange rate. These factors will all come together to determine the balance of demand for exports and imports.

The exchange rate plays a key role in influencing the levels of both imports and exports. Figure 14.3 shows the time path of the US$/£ exchange rate since 1971. It shows some fluctuations between 1971 and the late 1980s, around a declining trend. Since then the exchange rate seems to have remained fairly steady.

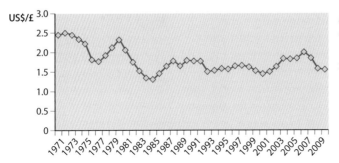

Figure 14.3 *The nominal exchange rate, US$/£, 1971–2010*

Source: ONS.

Nonetheless, there was a fall from a peak of $2.50 to the pound in 1972 to $1.50 some 30 years later. Other things being equal, this suggests an improvement in the competitiveness of UK products. In other words, Americans wanting to buy UK goods got more pounds for their dollars in 2002 than in 1972, and thus would have tended to find UK goods more attractive.

However, some care is needed because other things do not remain equal. In particular, remember that the competitiveness of UK goods in the US market depends not only on the exchange rate, but also on movements in the prices of goods over time, so this needs to be taken into account – which is why Figure 14.3 refers to the *nominal exchange rate*. In other words, if the prices of UK goods have risen more

The exchange rate influences the demand for imports and exports

rapidly than prices in the USA, this will have partly offset the downward movement in the exchange rate.

Figure 14.4 shows the nominal exchange rate again, but also the ratio of UK/US consumer prices (plotted using the right-hand scale). This reveals that between 1971 and 1977 UK prices rose much more steeply than those in the USA, and continued to rise relative to the USA until the 1990s. Thus, the early decline in the nominal exchange rate was offset by the movement in relative prices.

In order to assess the overall competitive-ness of UK goods compared with the USA, it is necessary to calculate the **real exchange rate**, which is defined as the nominal exchange rate multiplied by the ratio of relative prices.

 Key term

real exchange rate: the nominal exchange rate adjusted for differences in relative inflation rates between countries

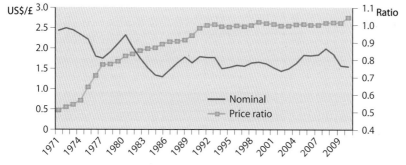

Figure 14.4 *The nominal exchange rate, US$/£, and the ratio of UK/US prices, 1971–2010*

The real exchange rate is shown in Figure 14.5. The real exchange rate also shows some fluctuations, especially between about 1977 and 1989. However, there does not seem to be any strong trend to the series, although the real rate was higher at the end of the period than at the beginning.

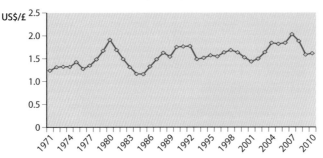

Figure 14.5 *The real exchange rate, US$/£, 1971–2010*

Source: calculated from figures shown in Figure 14.4

Notice that the series in Figure 14.5 relates only to competitiveness relative to the USA, as it is the real US$/£ exchange rate.

Exercise 14.1

Table 14.1 provides data for the €/£ exchange rate, together with the consumer price index for the euro area and for the UK. Use these data to calculate the real exchange rate for the period, and comment on the effect that any movement will have had on the competitiveness of UK goods and services relative to the euro area.

	Nominal exchange rate (€/£)	Consumer price index (2000 = 100)	
		UK	Euro area
2000	1.6422	100.0	100.0
2001	1.6087	101.8	102.4
2002	1.5909	103.5	104.7
2003	1.4456	106.5	106.9
2004	1.4739	109.7	109.2
2005	1.4629	112.8	111.6
2006	1.4670	116.4	114.0
2007	1.4619	121.3	116.4

Table 14.1 *Competitiveness of the UK compared to the euro area*

Source: IMF.

Summary

➤ Monetary policy entails the manipulation of monetary variables in order to influence aggregate demand in the economy.

➤ The prime instrument of monetary policy is the interest rate.

➤ People hold money in order to undertake transactions (among other reasons), and the interest rate can be regarded as the opportunity cost of holding money.

➤ There are several alternative definitions of money, depending upon how wide or narrow is the focus.

➤ There is not a single interest rate in the economy, but a variety of rates associated with the wide range of financial assets available.

➤ The monetary authorities can control either the money supply or interest rates, but not both independently.

➤ The exchange rate is also closely associated with money supply and the interest rate, and cannot be ignored in policy design.

➤ The real exchange rate is a measure of the international competitiveness of an economy's goods.

How does monetary policy work?

In evaluating the tools of monetary policy, it is important to understand the route by which a change in a monetary variable can have an effect on the real economy. In other words, how can a change in money supply, or the interest rate, affect the level of equilibrium output in the economy?

The monetary transmission mechanism

In drawing this analysis together, an important issue concerns the relationship between the rate of interest and the level of aggregate demand. This is critical for the conduct of monetary policy. Indeed, the interest rate has been seen as the prime instrument of monetary policy in recent years — and monetary policy is seen as the prime instrument of macroeconomic policy. By setting the interest rate, monetary policy is intended to affect aggregate demand through the so-called **monetary transmission mechanism**.

Key term

monetary transmission mechanism: the channel by which monetary policy affects aggregate demand

At a higher interest rate, firms undertake less investment expenditure because fewer projects are worthwhile. In addition, a higher interest rate may encourage higher saving, which also means that households undertake less consumption expenditure. This may then reinforce the impact on investment because if firms perceive consumption to be falling, this will affect their expectations about future demand, and further dampen their desire to undertake investment. Furthermore, if UK interest rates are high relative to elsewhere in the world, they will attract overseas investors, increasing the demand for pounds. This will tend to lead to an appreciation in the exchange rate, which in turn will reduce the competitiveness of UK goods and services, reducing the foreign demand for UK exports and encouraging UK residents to reduce their demand for domestic goods and buy imports instead. All these factors lower the level of aggregate demand, shifting the AD curve to the left.

This can be seen by looking at Figure 14.6. The initial equilibrium is with real output at Y_0, the price level at P_0 and the rate of interest at r_0. An increase in the rate of interest to

r_1 will need to be balanced by a decrease in money supply to maintain money market equilibrium. However, more significant is the effect on investment, which is shown in the middle panel of the figure. The increase in the rate of interest leads to a fall in investment from I_0 to I_1. This will cause the aggregate demand curve to move from AD_0 to AD_1, resulting in a lower overall price level P_1 and a lower real output level at Y_1. The lower level of real output arises because the AS curve was drawn with an upward-sloping segment.

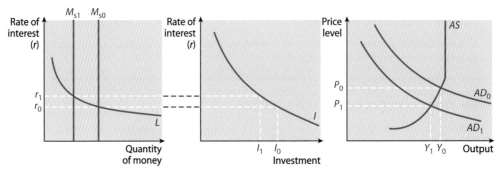

Figure 14.6 *The interest rate and aggregate demand*

Notice that this may not be the end of the story. If one of the effects of the higher interest rate is to discourage investment, this will also have long-term consequences. Investment allows the productive capacity of the economy to increase, leading to a rightward drift in the AS curve. With lower investment, this process will slow down, leaving the economy with lower productive capacity than it otherwise would have had.

The AD/AS graph is drawn in terms of the overall price level. However, in a dynamic context, such a policy stance may be needed in order to maintain control of inflation. A reduction in interest rates would, of course, have the reverse effect. However, notice that the interaction of the money supply, interest rates and the exchange rate makes policy design a complicated business.

In creating a stable macroeconomic environment, the ultimate aim of monetary policy is not simply to keep inflation low, but to improve the confidence of decision-makers, and thereby encourage firms to invest in order to generate an increase in production capacity. This will stimulate economic growth and create an opportunity to improve living standards.

Exercise 14.2

Outline the mechanism by which an increase in the rate of interest affects aggregate demand in an economy.

Monetary policy in practice

The monetary transmission mechanism explains the way in which a change in the interest rate affects aggregate demand in the economy. In summary, suppose there is a reduction in the interest rate. From firms' point of view, this lowers the cost of borrowing, and would be expected to encourage higher investment spending. Furthermore, consumers may also respond to a fall in the interest rate by increasing their expenditure, both because this lowers the cost of borrowing – so there may be an increase in the demand for consumer durable goods – and because households may perceive that saving now pays a lower return, so may decide to spend more. Thus a fall in the interest rate is expected to have an expansionary effect on aggregate demand. In terms of the *AD/AS* model, this has the effect of shifting the aggregate demand curve to the right. The effectiveness of this will depend upon the shape of the aggregate supply curve and the starting position of the aggregate demand curve.

An expansionary monetary policy intended to stimulate aggregate demand would be damaging if the economy were close to (or at) full employment, as the main impact would be on the overall price level rather than real output. This suggests that monetary policy should also not be used to stimulate aggregate demand. However, monetary policy can still play an important role in managing the economy. This arises through its influence on the price level and hence the rate of change of prices – that is, inflation.

As has been explained, monetary policy in the UK is the responsibility of the Bank of England. The Bank's Monetary Policy Committee (MPC) meets each month to decide whether or not the interest rate needs to be altered. The objective of this exercise is to ensure that the government's inflation target is met. If the rate of inflation threatens to accelerate beyond the target rate, the Bank of England can intervene by raising interest rates, thereby having a dampening effect on aggregate demand and reducing the inflationary pressure. In reaching its decisions, the MPC takes a long-term view, projecting inflation ahead over the next 2 years.

However, decisions to change the rate of interest are not taken solely in the light of expected inflation. In its deliberations about the interest rate, the MPC takes a wide variety of factors into account, including developments in:

- financial markets
- the international economy
- money and credit
- demand and output
- the labour market
- costs and prices (e.g. changes in oil prices)

A good example was in 2008, when the UK and other countries were struggling to cope with the so-called 'credit crunch'. At this time, inflation was accelerating, and had reached a rate that was more than one percentage point above the target. This

being so, it might have been expected that the Bank of England would raise interest rates in order to stem aggregate demand and bring inflation back into line with the target. However, this would have been damaging in other ways, pushing the economy further into recession. With house prices falling, an increase in interest rates could have damaged this sector also. It was also thought that there were other pressures affecting the world economy that would in any case mean that the rate of inflation was likely to slow down of its own accord. In the event, inflation accelerated way beyond its target range, but the MPC refrained from raising the bank rate because of fears that the recession would become even deeper, or that the economy would recover more slowly. This is a good example of how different policy targets may come into conflict, and of how it may be prudent not to stick to a rule just for its own sake.

It is also important to remember that the transmission mechanism has a third channel in addition to the effects of the change in interest rate on consumption and investment. This third channel arises through the exchange rate, so that monetary policy cannot be considered in isolation from exchange rate policy. The channels of the transmission mechanism are summarised in Figure 14.7.

Evaluation of monetary policy

For a decade after the responsibility for monetary policy was delegated to the Bank of England, monetary policy was seen to be highly effective in enabling the achievement of the inflation target. You can see this by looking back at Figure 13.1. Inflation stayed within the required one percentage point of its target, moving outside that range in only one month between May 1997 and April 2008. However, matters then took a turn for the worse with the onset of the financial crisis and the ensuing recession, and inflation accelerated beyond its limit before plummeting dramatically and then accelerating again.

The need to combat recession led to the bank rate being reduced to 0.5% in March 2009. Having fallen to this level, further reductions become ineffective, so the Bank

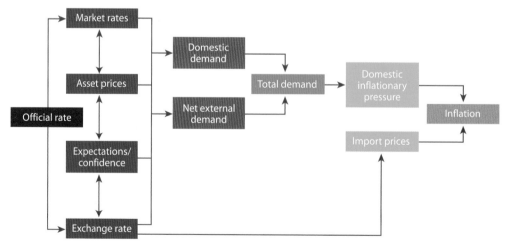

Figure 14.7 *The transmission of monetary policy*

announced that it would start to inject money directly into the economy, effectively switching the instrument of monetary policy away from the interest rate and towards the quantity of money. This would be achieved by a process known as *quantitative easing*, by which the Bank purchases assets such as government and corporate bonds, thus releasing additional money into the system through the banks and other financial institutions from which they buy the assets. The hope was that this would allow banks to increase their lending, and thus combat the threat of deflation – and perhaps help to speed recovery.

It is important to be aware that the UK was certainly not alone in facing this combination of circumstances. A number of countries had also enjoyed relative stability for several years, followed by a more turbulent period. This in itself suggests that the conduct of monetary policy cannot claim full responsibility for the period of calm, nor perhaps be entirely blamed for the subsequent problems. The process of globalisation that has been taking place means that the UK economy cannot be viewed in total isolation from events occurring elsewhere in the world, and macroeconomic policy is interconnected – through movements in the exchange rate and through trading links. This is illustrated by Figure 14.8, which shows monthly inflation (in % p.a.) from the beginning of 2000 for the world as a whole and for two country groupings. You can see how inflation in the world as a whole began to accelerate from mid-2007 onwards after a period of relative stability, only to plummet as the recession set in during 2008 and 2009. Latin America displays higher inflation – and more instability than the world as a whole – whereas the advanced economies experienced inflation rates below the world average throughout the period, but also began to see inflation rates creeping up towards the end of the period.

It is also important to realise that for monetary policy to be and remain effective, it must be viewed in combination with other policies being implemented at the same time. In other words, monetary policy needs to be supported and augmented by other

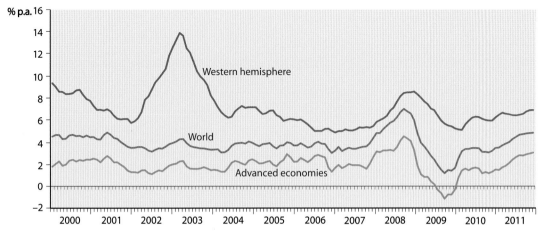

Figure 14.8 *World inflation, 2000–2011*

Source: IMF.

policy measures — in particular, fiscal policy and supply-side policies. These are the subject of the next chapter.

Summary

➤ Monetary policy is the use of financial variables, such as money supply or the rate of interest, to influence the performance of the economy.

➤ Money supply does not provide a reliable control mechanism, so the prime instrument of monetary policy is the interest rate.

➤ The transmission mechanism from the interest rate to aggregate demand works through investment and consumption and indirectly via the exchange rate.

➤ The Bank of England's Monetary Policy Committee has the responsibility for setting the interest rate at such a level as to achieve the government's inflation target, taking account of the general domestic and international economic environment.

➤ Monetary policy cannot focus solely on meeting the inflation target, but must also operate with an awareness of other developments in the macroeconomy.

➤ It is also important that monetary policy is coordinated with other policy measures being implemented that affect the macroeconomy.

Exercise 14.3

Visit the Bank of England website at www.bankofengland.co.uk and check the most recent decision of the MPC on bank rate. Use the most recent minutes of the MPC and the Inflation Report to see the sorts of factors that the MPC took into account in reaching its decision on bank rate.

Chapter 15
Fiscal and supply-side policies

Although monetary policy has been the most high-profile part of the UK's macroeconomic policy in recent years, there are other components that are just as important for the performance of the economy. Fiscal policy has always been an important part of the government's armoury of instruments, and the way that it carries out its expenditure and taxation policies has important impacts on performance. In addition, it has come to be widely recognised that sustainable economic growth can be facilitated by appropriate policies that are designed to affect the supply side of the economy. These policy tools and their effects are examined in this chapter.

Learning outcomes

After studying this chapter, you should:

➤ understand the alternative types of fiscal policy instrument, including the use of alternative tax instruments and government spending

➤ be able to analyse the impact of changing fiscal instruments on the distribution of income

➤ understand the consequences of a fiscal budget deficit or surplus

➤ appreciate the difference between direct and indirect taxation as means of raising revenue

➤ be able to evaluate the contribution of supply-side policies to the improvement of economic performance

Fiscal policy

You may recall from *AS Economics, Chapter 15* that **fiscal policy** covers a range of policy measures that affect government expenditures and revenues. As the government has discretion over the amount of expenditure that it undertakes and the amount of revenue that it chooses to raise from taxation, these can be manipulated in order to influence the course of the economy.

Key *term*

fiscal policy: decisions made by the government on its expenditure, taxation and borrowing

What is the role of fiscal policy in a modern economy? Traditionally fiscal policy was used to affect the level of aggregate demand in the economy. The overall balance between government receipts and outlays affects the position of the aggregate demand curve, which is reinforced by multiplier effects. When government outlays exceed government receipts, the result is a *fiscal deficit.* This occurs when the revenues raised through taxation are not sufficient to cover the government's various types of expenditure.

The overall size of the budget deficit may limit the government's actions in terms of fiscal policy. In addition, the overall pattern of revenue and expenditure has a strong effect on the overall balance of activity in the economy. A neutral government budget can be attained either with high expenditure and high revenues, or with relatively low expenditure and revenues. Such decisions affect the overall size of the public sector relative to the private sector. Over the years, different governments in the UK have taken different decisions on this issue – and different countries throughout the world have certainly adopted different approaches.

In part, such issues are determined through the ballot box. In the run-up to an election, each political party presents its overall plans for taxation and spending, and typically they adopt different positions as to the overall balance. It is then up to those voting to give a mandate to whichever party offers a package that most closely resembles their preferences.

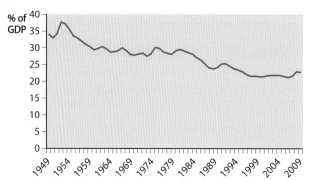

Figure 15.1 *Government final consumption, 1949–2010*

Source: ONS.

Figure 15.1 shows the time path of government consumption as a share of GDP from 1949 to 2010; it shows fluctuations around a downward trend, suggesting that the public sector has been gradually reducing its share of the economy. Notice that this does not give the full picture, as public sector investment is not taken into account in these data. There are one or two periods in the figure where the decline seems to have been especially rapid. In the early 1950s, this partly reflects the winding down of government activity after the rebuilding that followed the Second World War. The steep decline in the 1980s reflects the privatisation drive of that period, when the government was withdrawing from some parts of the economy.

Figure 15.2 provides an international perspective, showing the share of current and capital expenditure by governments in a range of countries. This reveals something of a contrast between, on the one hand, Switzerland, Australia, Japan and North

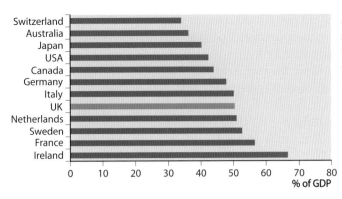

Figure 15.2 Total
government expenditure
as a percentage of GDP,
selected countries, 2009

Source: OECD.

America, and on the other hand, many European countries, where governments have been more active in the economy. In part this reflects the greater role that government plays in some countries in providing services such as education and healthcare, whereas in other countries the private sector takes a greater role, often through the insurance market.

Direct and indirect taxes

Fiscal policy, and taxation in particular, has not only been used to establish a balance between the public and private sectors of an economy. In addition, taxation remains an important weapon against some forms of market failure, and it also influences the distribution of income. In this context, the choice of using direct or indirect taxes is important.

Direct taxes are taxes levied on income of various kinds, such as personal income tax. Such taxes are designed to be progressive and so can be effective in redistributing income: for example, a higher income tax rate can be charged to those earning high incomes. In contrast, **indirect taxes** – taxes on expenditure, such as VAT and excise duties – tend to be regressive. As poorer households tend to spend a higher proportion of their income on items that are subject to excise duties, a greater share of their income is taken up by indirect taxes. Even VAT can be regressive if higher-income households save a greater proportion of their incomes.

When Margaret Thatcher came to power in 1979, one of her first actions was to introduce a switch away from direct taxation towards indirect taxes. VAT was increased and the rate of personal income tax was reduced. In support

Key *term*

direct tax: a tax levied directly on income

indirect tax: a tax levied on expenditure on goods or services

Margaret Thatcher introduced a switch away from direct taxation towards indirect taxes

of this move, it was pointed out that if an income tax scheme becomes too progressive, it can provide a disincentive towards effort. If people feel that a high proportion of their income is being taken in tax, their incentives to provide work effort are weak. Indeed, a switch from direct to indirect taxation is regarded as a sort of supply-side policy intended to influence the position of aggregate supply.

Sustainability of fiscal policy

Another important issue that came to the fore during the 1990s concerned the sustainability of fiscal policy. This is wrapped up with the notion that current taxpayers should have to fund only expenditure that benefits their own generation, and that the taxpayers of the future should make their own decisions, and not have to pay for past government expenditure that has been incurred for the benefit of earlier generations.

In this context, what is significant is the overall balance between receipts and outlays through time. If outlays were always larger than receipts, the spending programme could be sustained only through government borrowing, thereby shifting the burden of funding the deficit to future generations. This could also be a problem if it made it more difficult for the private sector to obtain funds for investment, or if it added to the national debt. The Labour government introduced a so-called **'Golden Rule' of fiscal policy**,

Key term

Golden Rule of fiscal policy: rule stating that, over the economic cycle, net government borrowing will be for investment only, and not for current spending

which stated that, on average over the economic cycle, the government should borrow only to invest and not to fund current expenditure. This was intended to help achieve equity between present and future generations. It should perhaps be noted that this was a self-imposed guideline, so there would be no penalty for breaking the rule other than political credibility. The Coalition Government that followed was less committed to the concept of the Golden Rule, and the onset of the financial crisis — and the need to bail out commercial banks in order to safeguard the financial system — rendered the Golden Rule impossible to follow.

Figure 15.3 shows total public sector receipts and outlays since 1984/85. Outlays here include investment, but you can see how the two series tend to move in opposite directions over the cycle.

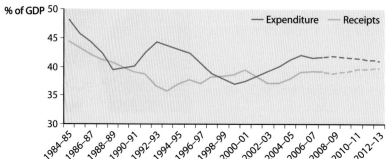

Figure 15.3 *UK public sector outlays and receipts*

Note: 2008–09 onwards are projected data.

Source: H.M. Treasury.

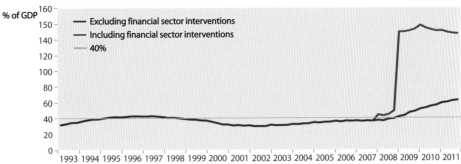

Figure 15.4 *Public sector net debt as a percentage of GDP, 1993–2011*

Source: ONS.

If receipts and outlays more or less balance over the economic cycle, the economy is not in a position whereby the current generation is forcing future generations to pay for its consumption. However, it is not practical to impose this rule at every part of the cycle, so the Golden Rule was intended to apply over the economic cycle as a whole. There was also a commitment to keep public sector net debt below 40% of GDP – again, on average over the economic cycle. Figure 15.4 shows data for this since 1993. The Golden Rule seemed secure until the onset of the credit crunch. However, the financial support offered to Northern Rock and other banks in the bailout of 2008 had a noticeable effect on public sector net debt, as is all too clear in the figure. Even without the financial sector interventions, net debt rose over the 40% mark in the last quarter of 2008 and continued to rise thereafter. This reflected other measures taken by the government to try to mitigate the effects of the recession. One example was the reduction in the rate of VAT from 17.5 to 15%. This is tantamount to a fiscal expansion, but when it was introduced, it was made clear that it was intended as a temporary boost for a specified period. This statement enabled the government to maintain that it was not breaching its long-term fiscal commitment. The rate of VAT returned to 17.5% in January 2010, and was increased to 20% in January 2011.

Summary

➤ Fiscal policy concerns the use of government expenditure and taxation to influence aggregate demand in the economy.

➤ The overall balance between private and public sectors varies through time and across countries.

➤ Direct taxes help to redistribute income between groups in society, but if too progressive they may dampen incentives to provide effort.

➤ Indirect taxes tend to be regressive.

➤ The Golden Rule of fiscal policy was that the government should aim to borrow only for investment, and not for current expenditure (averaged over the economic cycle).

➤ There was also a commitment to keep the national debt below 40% of GDP; this commitment did not survive the financial crisis and recession of the late 2000s.

Exercise 15.1

Discuss the extent to which the major British political parties adopt differing stances towards establishing a balance between the private and public sectors: in other words, the extent to which each is 'high tax/high public spending' or 'low tax/low public spending'. Analyse the economic arguments favouring each of the approaches.

Fiscal policy and the *AD/AS* model

It is important to understand how fiscal policy can be analysed using the *AD/AS* model. As already noted, the overall balance between government receipts and outlays affects the position of the aggregate demand curve, which is reinforced by multiplier effects. When government outlays exceed government receipts, the result is a *fiscal deficit*. This occurs when the revenues raised through taxation are not sufficient to cover the government's various types of expenditure. An increase in the fiscal deficit has the effect of shifting the aggregate demand curve to the right.

Figure 15.5 shows that shifting the aggregate demand curve in this way affects only the overall price level in the economy when the aggregate supply curve is vertical — and remember that the Monetarist school of thought argued that it would always be vertical. Hence a key issue for a government considering the use of fiscal policy is knowing whether there is spare capacity in the economy, because otherwise an expansion in aggregate demand from increased government spending will push up prices, but leave real output unchanged.

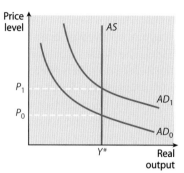

Figure 15.5 *Demand-side policy with a vertical AS curve*

Chapter 13 introduced the concept of the multiplier, which suggested that for any increase in autonomous spending, there would be a multiplied increase in equilibrium output. The idea of the multiplier is that, if there is an increase in (say) government expenditure, this provides income for workers, who will then spend that income and create further expenditure streams. The size of these induced effects will depend upon the marginal propensity to withdraw.

In terms of the *AD/AS* diagram, the existence of the multiplier means that if there is an increase in government expenditure, the *AD* curve moves further to the right than it otherwise would have done, because of the multiplier effects. However, this does not mean that equilibrium income will increase by the full multiplier amount. Looking more closely at what is happening, you can see that there are some forces at work that are acting to weaken the multiplier effect of an increase in government expenditure. One way in which this happens is through interest rates. If the government finances its deficit through borrowing, a side effect is to put upward pressure on interest rates, which then may cause private sector spending — by households on consumption and by firms on investment — to decline, as the cost of borrowing has been increased. This

process is known as the **crowding out** of private sector activity by the public sector. It limits the extent to which a government budget deficit can shift the aggregate demand curve, especially if the public sector activity is less productive than the private sector activity that it replaces.

Automatic and discretionary fiscal policies

It is important to distinguish between automatic and discretionary changes in government expenditure. Some items of government expenditure and receipts vary automatically with the economic cycle. They are known as **automatic stabilisers**. For example, if the economy enters a period of recession, government expenditure will rise because of the increased payments of unemployment and other social security benefits, and revenues will fall because fewer people are paying income tax, and because receipts from VAT are falling. This helps to offset the recession without any active intervention from the government.

Key *term*

crowding out: process by which an increase in government expenditure 'crowds out' private sector activity by raising the cost of borrowing

automatic stabilisers: process by which government expenditure and revenue vary with the economic cycle, thereby helping to stabilise the economy without any conscious intervention from government

More important, however, is the question of whether the government can or should make use of discretionary fiscal policy in a deliberate attempt to influence the course of the economy. As already mentioned, the key issue is whether or not the economy has spare capacity, because attempts to stimulate an economy that is already at full employment will merely push up the price level.

There are many examples of how excessive government spending can create problems for the economy. Such problems arose in a number of Latin American economies during the 1980s. In Brazil, a range of policies was brought to bear in an attempt to reduce inflation – including direct controls on prices. However, with no serious attempt to control the fiscal deficit, inflation continually got out of control – reaching almost 3,000% in 1990. Only when the deficit was reduced did it become possible to bring inflation to a more reasonable level. More recently, the collapse of the economy of Zimbabwe was accompanied by inflation at such a high level that the printing presses could not keep up with the need for banknotes.

The conduct of fiscal policy

Having discussed the policy environment, the next step is to see how different types of policy are conducted, and how the effectiveness of policy is determined by the economic models that have been introduced, and by the assumptions made. We will begin with fiscal policy.

Fiscal policy is the manipulation of the government's taxation and expenditure in order to influence the economy. For a period after the Second World War the prime aim of economic policy was to maintain full employment, and the main way of trying to achieve this was through an active fiscal policy. It was thought that by manipulating aggregate demand through changes in the government's fiscal balance, the economy could be stabilised close to full employment.

Figure 15.6 shows how this is intended to work. The figure shows an economy with *AS* being the aggregate supply curve, becoming vertical at the full employment level of output Y^*. Suppose that the economy is initially operating with the aggregate demand curve AD_0, such that short-run equilibrium is with real output at Y_0 and an overall price level at P_0. The intention of fiscal policy is to raise the real output level in order to take the economy closer to full employment. An increase in government spending would shift the *AD* curve to AD_1, and real output would increase to Y_1 in the new equilibrium. The overall price level would also rise, to P_1.

The active use of fiscal policy to influence the economy in this way went out of fashion under the influence of the Monetarist school of macroeconomists. They argued that the aggregate supply curve is vertical, such that the economy will return of its own accord to full employment relatively quickly. If this is the case, then active fiscal policy is damaging to the economy. Figure 15.7 shows an expansionary fiscal policy under the assumption of a vertical aggregate supply curve. The increase in government spending again has the effect of shifting the aggregate demand curve to the right, from AD_0 to AD_1, but now the impact is *only* on the overall price level, which increases from P_0 to P_1.

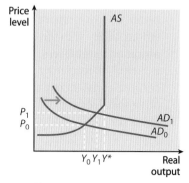

Figure 15.6 *An expansionary fiscal policy*

Therefore, according to Monetarist economists, if the government continues trying to simulate the economy by increasing spending, the result will be that the price level will keep rising, but that real output will remain unchanged. Some countries in Latin America acted in this way during the 1980s, and the result was hyperinflation. Eventually, the continuing inflation acts to discourage investment, and causes the economy to have a lower productive capacity than it otherwise could have reached.

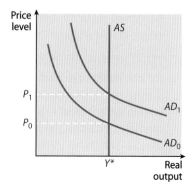

Figure 15.7 *Fiscal policy with a vertical AS curve*

Balance between the public and private sectors

Both economic analysis and the UK experience support the view that fiscal policy should not be used as an active stabilisation device. However, this does not mean that there is no role for fiscal policy in a modern economy. Earlier, it was pointed out that decisions about the size of government expenditure and revenue influence the overall balance between the public and private sectors. The balance that is achieved can have an important influence on the overall level of economic activity, and upon economic growth, so the importance of designing an appropriate fiscal policy should not be underestimated. An important theme that runs through much economic analysis is that governments may be justified in intervening in the economy in order to correct market failure. Some of this intervention requires the use of fiscal policy: for example, taxes to correct for the effects of externalities, or expenditure to ensure the provision of public goods. In other words, fiscal policy can be an instrument that operates at the microeconomic level, as well as having macroeconomic implications.

Take infrastructure as an example. Infrastructure covers a range of goods that are crucial for the efficient operation of a market economy. Businesses need good transport links and good communication facilities. Households need good healthcare, education and sanitation facilities, not only in

Different governments have taken different approaches regarding which industries should remain part of the public sector

order to enjoy a good standard of life, but also to be productive members of the labour force. Both public goods and externality arguments come into play in the provision of infrastructure, so there needs to be appropriate government intervention to ensure that such goods are adequately provided. The consequence of failing to do this will be to lower the productive capacity of the economy below what would otherwise have been possible. In other words, the aggregate supply curve will be further to the left than it need be.

On the other hand, too much government intervention may also be damaging. One of the most compelling arguments in favour of privatisation was that when the managers of public enterprises are insufficiently accountable for their actions, X-inefficiency becomes a major issue, so public sector activity tends to be less efficient than private sector enterprise. On this argument, too large a public sector may have the effect of lowering aggregate productive capacity below its potential level.

These arguments suggest that an important role for fiscal policy is in affecting the supply side of the economy, ensuring that markets operate effectively to make the best possible use of the economy's resources. Some further aspects of this will be discussed in the context of supply-side policies later in the chapter.

Income distribution

The other key role for fiscal policy is in affecting the distribution of income within society. Taxes and transfers can have a large effect on income distribution. This in turn may have effects on the economy by affecting the incentives that people face in choosing their labour supply.

Benefits

There are two forms of benefit that households can receive to help equalise the income distribution. First, there are various types of *cash benefit*, such as income support, child benefit, incapacity benefit and working families' tax credit. These are designed

part 4

to protect families whose income in certain circumstances would otherwise be very low. Second, there are *benefits in kind*, such as health and education. These accrue to individual households depending on the number of members of the household and their age and gender.

Taxation

Direct taxes (taxes on incomes) tend to be progressive. In other words, higher income groups pay tax at a higher rate. In 2002/03 the top quintile paid 24% of its gross income in tax, compared with only 9% paid in the bottom quintile.

In the UK, the main direct taxes are income tax, corporation tax (paid by firms on profits), capital gains tax (paid by individuals who sell assets at a profit), inheritance tax and petroleum revenue tax (paid by firms operating in the North Sea). There is also the council tax, collected by local authorities. National Insurance contributions are another form of direct taxation.

With a tax such as income tax, its progressive nature is reflected in the way the tax rate increases as an individual moves into a higher income range. In other words, the **marginal tax rate** increases as income increases. The **progressive** nature of the tax ensures that it does indeed help to reduce inequality in income distribution – although its effects are less than the cash benefits discussed earlier.

Table 15.1 shows average tax rates for taxpayers in different income bands in 2007/08. Notice that the table shows *average* rather than *marginal* tax rates. When average rates are rising, marginal tax rates are higher than the average. Exercise 15.2 illustrates this.

 Key term

marginal tax rate: tax on additional income, defined as the change in tax payments due divided by the change in taxable income

progressive tax: a tax in which the marginal tax rate rises with income, i.e. a tax bearing most heavily on the relatively well-off members of society

Income band	Number of taxpayers (m)	Average rate of tax payable (%)	Average amount of tax payable (£)
£5,225–£7,499	2.5	1.7	107
£7,500–£9,999	3.6	4.2	365
£10,000–£14,999	6.4	8.8	1,100
£15,000–£19,999	4.9	12.4	2,150
£20,000–£29,999	6.7	14.9	3,660
£30,000–£49,999	5.2	17.1	6,460
£50,000–£99,999	1.75	24.5	16,200
£100,000–£199,999	0.4	30.8	41,200
£200,000–£499,999	0.1	34.0	98,200
All incomes	31.6	18.1	4,630

Table 15.1 *Income tax payable in the UK by annual income 2007/08*
Source: *Social Trends*, no. 38.

OCR A2 Economics

Exercise 15.2

The table shows the amount of tax paid by an individual as income increases. Calculate the average and marginal tax rates at each of the income levels. (*Remember the definition of the marginal tax rate provided above.*)

Income	Tax paid
£1,000	£100
£2,000	£300
£3,000	£600
£4,000	£1,000

The effect of indirect taxes, on the other hand, can sometimes be **regressive**: in other words, indirect taxes may impinge more heavily on lower-income households. Indirect taxes are taxes that are paid on items of expenditure, rather than on income.

Examples of indirect taxes are value added tax (VAT), which is charged on most goods and services sold in the UK, tobacco taxes, excise duties on alcohol and oil duties. These specific taxes are levied per unit sold. *AS Economics, Chapter 8* analysed how the incidence of a tax is related to the price elasticity of demand of a good or service. It explained how, where demand is price-inelastic, producers are able to pass much of an increase in the tax rate on to consumers, whereas if demand is price-elastic, producers have to absorb most of the increase as part of their costs.

 term

regressive tax: a tax bearing more heavily on the relatively poorer members of society

Why are some of these taxes regressive? Take the tobacco tax. In the first place, the number of smokers is higher among lower-income groups than among the relatively rich — research has shown that only about 10% of people in professional groups now smoke compared with nearly 40% of those in unskilled manual groups. Second, expenditure on tobacco tends to take a lower proportion of income of the rich compared with that of the poor, even for those in the former group who do smoke. Thus, the tobacco tax falls more heavily on lower-income groups than on the better-off.

As pointed out earlier, achieving a balance of taxation between direct and indirect taxes is an important aspect of the government's redistributive policy. A switch in the balance from direct to indirect taxes will tend to increase inequality in a society. The incentive effects must also be kept in mind. High marginal tax rates on income can have a disincentive effect; if people know that a large proportion of any additional work they undertake will be taxed away, they may be discouraged from providing more work. In other words, cutting income tax can encourage work effort by reducing marginal tax rates. This is yet another reminder of the need for a balanced policy — one that recognises that, while some income redistribution is needed to protect the vulnerable, disincentive effects may arise if the better-off are over-taxed.

Exercise 15.3

Using appropriate economic analysis, discuss the various policy measures available to a government wishing to ensure an equitable distribution of income without damaging incentives to work.

Summary

➤ Fiscal policy entails changes in taxation and in the government's expenditure to influence the level or pattern of aggregate demand.

➤ Fiscal policy has gone out of fashion as a short-run stabilisation device, and now operates under the Golden Rule, which aims to ensure fiscal responsibility and equity between generations.

➤ Fiscal policy retains a key role in ensuring an appropriate balance between private and public sectors, and ensuring the provision of public goods and tackling externality effects.

➤ It also plays a key role in influencing the distribution of income between groups within society.

➤ In doing this, an appropriate balance needs to be found between achieving a desired level of equity between individuals, and providing incentives to work.

Supply-side policies

Supply-side policies are directed at influencing the position of the aggregate supply curve. In Figure 15.8, Y^* represents full employment output before the policy, with the equilibrium overall price level at P_0. Supply-side policies, which lead to an increase in the economy's productive capacity, shift equilibrium output to Y^{**} and the overall price level to P_1.

Notice that the effect on real output is achieved from supply-side policies whether the equilibrium is in the vertical segment of the Keynesian AS curve (or with a Monetarist AS curve), as shown in Figure 15.8, or in the upward-sloping segment of the Keynesian AS curve, as in Figure 15.9. Here the shift in aggregate supply raises equilibrium real output from Y_0 to Y_1.

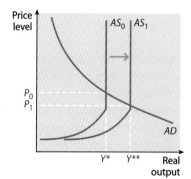

Figure 15.8 *A shift in aggregate supply (with a Monetarist effect)*

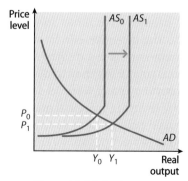

Figure 15.9 *A shift in aggregate supply (with a Keynesian effect)*

Supply-side policies include encouraging education and training, improving the flexibility with which markets operate and promoting competition. These policies were first introduced in *AS Economics, Chapter 15*.

Notice that it is quite difficult to quantify the effects of these supply-side policies. In the case of education and training, the idea is that by increasing education and training, the human capital of the labour force is increased, thus resulting in improvements in productivity, which enables an increase in the overall productive capacity of the economy — in other words, this will lead to a rightward shift of the aggregate supply curve. However, some of the effects of increased spending become evident only after very long time lags.

In the case of competition policy, again, it is not easy to identify the effects on productive capacity, although it is argued that the use of competition policy will provide incentives for firms to be more productively efficient, and will reduce the loss of allocative inefficiency through the abuse of market power.

It is particularly difficult to isolate the impact of these policies when so much else in the economy is changing through time. Nonetheless, these policies do have the effect of stimulating economic growth without inflationary pressure.

Another example that is important to examine is the effect of changing the rate of income tax. When people face high marginal rates of income tax, there is a disincentive to offer additional labour hours, or even to participate in the labour force at all. A reduction in income tax rates would therefore provide an incentive for people to work more hours or to participate in the labour force. This would then lead to higher employment, and a higher potential capacity output for the economy as a whole.

Such high marginal tax rates are normally found at the high end of the income distribution, but there may also be disincentive effects to consider at low incomes. These effects may arise where unemployment benefits are set at such a level that individuals would be little better off if they accepted a low-paid job — a situation sometimes known as the 'unemployment trap'. This effect may be reinforced if the search costs for jobs are relatively high — for example, if the jobs available are not in areas where unemployment is high. There may then be people who do not find it worth their while undertaking a costly search for jobs, especially if the wage they could command would be only marginally better than the benefits that they can receive.

In this situation, a reduction in the rate of unemployment benefits or social security benefits could have the effect of increasing people's willingness to accept jobs. This would reduce unemployment and again lead to an expansion of the economy's potential productive capacity. However, there is a need to keep an appropriate balance between providing incentives to work and protecting the vulnerable.

Supply-side policies may also have an effect on the balance of payments current account. Policies that affect trade and competitiveness fall into this category: for example, supply-side policies to improve the flexibility of the labour market could be seen to improve the international competitiveness of UK firms, and thus to improve

the current account deficit. In addition, it might be argued that steps taken to increase the productive capacity of the economy would allow an increase in exports that would (ceteris paribus) reduce the current account deficit.

Exercise 15.4

For each of the following, analyse the effect on the productive capacity of the economy, explaining how this happens.

a The government introduces subsidies for firms to train unskilled workers.

b Immigrant workers are encouraged to return to their home countries.

c A monopoly firm is forced to reduce barriers to the entry of new firms into its market.

d There is a reduction in the highest rate of income tax.

e There is an increase in the threshold of income below which no income tax is payable.

f There is a decrease in the rate of social security payments for the unemployed.

Summary

➤ Supply-side policies are directed at influencing the position of the aggregate supply curve by increasing the potential productive capacity of the economy.

➤ Such policies include policies to affect the flexibility of labour markets, including education and training.

➤ Policies that promote competition may also lead to efficiency improvements.

➤ Changes in income tax rates, or in social security benefits, can also have an effect on potential capacity by affecting incentives to work.

➤ Improvements in efficiency may have spillover effects on the balance of payments if they improve the international competitiveness of UK goods in world markets.

Institutions and economic policy

The environment within which policy is set and the institutions that are responsible for putting policy into practice also contribute to the operation and effectiveness of macroeconomic policy, whether it be monetary, fiscal or supply-side policies.

In a democratic society, the process begins with the electoral system. For example, in the UK each of the political parties puts together a manifesto that sets out its intentions regarding the way it will govern — including its attitudes towards and intentions for economic policy. The party that is voted into power then has a mandate to carry out those policies on which it was elected. This can be seen as an example of the principal–agent scenario introduced in Chapter 1. In this case, the government acts as the agent of the electorate (the principal). As with other instances of the principal–agent situation, there may sometimes be problems where a government does not perceive itself to be fully accountable to the electorate.

The government has the responsibility of ensuring that the policies desired by the electorate are put into effect. Part of this responsibility lies in ensuring that markets are free to operate effectively. In particular, this entails ensuring there are secure property rights, without which a market system cannot work. The issues of accountability and security of property rights are taken for granted in countries like the UK, but constitute major problems in some countries elsewhere in the world.

In the UK, the government takes decisions on how the economy should operate, but delegates day-to-day decisions to some key institutions. In the case of fiscal policy, the chancellor of the exchequer is responsible for drawing up the annual budget. This sets the parameters for fiscal policy in terms of taxation and government expenditure. The chancellor is assisted in this by the Treasury, which is the UK's economics and finance ministry, and has responsibility for 'formulating and implementing the government's economic and financial policy' (**www.hm-treasury. gov.uk**). As explained in Chapter 13, responsibility for monetary policy is delegated to the Monetary Policy Committee of the Bank of England.

The Treasury building, Whitehall, London

In the opening years of the twenty-first century, the UK economy operates in a global environment, and there are other institutions set up to oversee aspects of that global economy.

At the end of the Second World War a conference was held at Bretton Woods in the USA to agree on a set of rules under which international trade would be conducted. This conference established an exchange rate system under which countries agreed to set the price of their currencies relative to the US dollar. In addition, the conference set up three institutions to oversee matters. The *International Monetary Fund* (IMF) would provide assistance (and advice) to countries experiencing balance of payments difficulties, and the World Bank would provide assistance (and advice) on long-term development issues. However, it was also recognised that the conduct of trade would need some oversight. Initially, this role was fulfilled by the *General Agreement on Tariffs and Trade* (GATT), under the auspices of which there was a sequence of 'rounds' of reductions in tariffs, together with a significant reduction in quotas and voluntary export restraints. The last of these was the Uruguay Round, which covered the period 1986–94 and led to the formation of the *World Trade Organization* (WTO), which replaced the GATT in 1995.

While continuing to pursue reductions in barriers to trade, the WTO has also taken on the role of providing a framework for the settlement of trade disputes. You will appreciate that, with all the moves towards regional integration and protectionism, such a role is very important. Indeed, the WTO reports that around 300 cases for settlement of disputes were brought to the WTO in its first 8 years – about the same number that were dealt with over the entire life of the GATT from 1947 to 1994.

part **4**

Summary

➤ Proposals for economic policy constitute an important part of the political parties' manifestos prepared in the run-up to elections.

➤ This provides an opportunity for the electorate to express preferences on the role of government during its term in office.

➤ The UK government delegates day-to-day responsibility for economic policy to the Treasury (for fiscal policy) and to the Bank of England (for monetary and exchange rate policy).

➤ The international environment for economic policy is overseen by the World Bank, the International Monetary Fund and the World Trade Organization.

Policy in an international context

In practice, then, the design of domestic economic policy has to be undertaken with due regard for the international environment within which the UK economy operates. This is because the UK is an open economy. It depends upon international trade, and thus needs to interact with other economies.

Part of the interaction comes through financial markets and the balance of payments. If interest rates within Europe or the USA change relative to those in the UK, this will have an effect on the UK economy through the flows of financial capital that will be initiated by the change, with investors looking to move their funds in order to obtain the highest return.

Interaction also comes through trade agreements and the operations of the World Trade Organization. The WTO administers the international trading environment, and has a brief to encourage countries to reduce tariffs and to open their markets more freely to trade. This may also affect the way that the UK frames its domestic policy. For instance, the UK would not be free to raise tariffs to try to protect its domestic manufacturing industry – although economic arguments would suggest that this is not a sensible policy in any case, as will be discussed in Chapter 16.

Another important issue concerns the UK's relations with the rest of Europe. Although the UK chose not to join the single currency area when it was established, it remains part of Europe, and an increasing share of UK trade is with other European countries. As part of the European single market, the UK needs to adopt policies that are consistent with its EU membership.

Conflicts between policy objectives

Having reviewed the main macroeconomic policy objectives and instruments, it should be clear that the designing of economic policy is likely to be something of a juggling act. This is especially so because there may be conflict and trade-offs between some of the targets of policy. For example, there may be a conflict between economic growth and the environment, so that the pursuit of economic growth may need to be tempered by concern for the environment. Policy must therefore be designed bearing in mind that there may be a trade-off between these two objectives – at some point,

it could be that more economic growth is possible only by sacrificing environmental objectives, or that protecting the environment can only be achieved at the cost of a slower rate of economic growth.

Unemployment and inflation

This notion of trade-off between conflicting objectives applies in other areas too. One important trade-off was discovered by the Australian economist Bill Phillips. In 1958 Phillips claimed that he had found an 'empirical regularity' that had existed for almost a century and that traced out a relationship between the rate of unemployment, and the rate of change of money wages. This was rapidly generalised into a relationship between unemployment and inflation (by arguing that firms pass on increased wages in the form of higher prices).

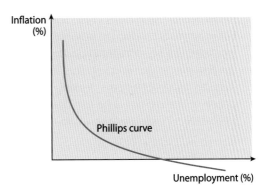

Figure 15.10 The Phillips curve

Figure 15.10 shows what became known as the **Phillips curve**. Although Phillips began with data, he also came up with an explanation of why such a relationship should exist. At the heart of his argument was the idea that when the demand for labour is high, firms will be prepared to bid up wages in order to attract labour. To the extent that higher wages are then passed on in the form of higher prices, this would imply a relationship between unemployment and inflation: when unemployment is low, inflation will tend to be higher, and vice versa.

> **Key** *term*
>
> **Phillips curve:** an empirical relationship suggesting that there is a trade-off between unemployment and inflation

From a policy perspective, this suggests a trade-off between unemployment and inflation objectives. If the Phillips curve relationship holds, attempts to reduce the rate of unemployment are likely to raise inflation. On the other hand, a reduction in inflation is likely to result in higher unemployment. This suggests

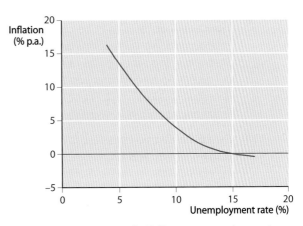

Figure 15.11 The Phillips curve unemployment/inflation trade-off

that it might be difficult to maintain full employment and low inflation at the same time. For example, Figure 15.11 shows a Phillips curve that is drawn such that to achieve an unemployment rate of 5%, inflation would need to rise to almost 15% per annum; this

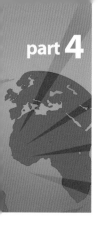
would not be acceptable these days, when people have become accustomed to much lower inflation rates. Furthermore, to bring inflation down to zero would require an unemployment rate of 15%. Having said that, as recently as 1990 the UK economy was experiencing inflation of nearly 10% and unemployment of 7%, which is not far from this example.

Nonetheless, the Phillips curve trade-off offers a tempting prospect to policy-makers. For example, if an election is imminent, it should be possible to reduce unemployment by allowing a bit more inflation, thereby creating a feel-good factor. After the election, the process can be reversed. This suggests that there could be a political business cycle induced by governments seeking re-election. In other words, the conflict between policy objectives could be exploited by politicians who see that in the short run an electorate is concerned more about unemployment than inflation.

The 1970s provided something of a setback to this theory, when suddenly the UK economy started to experience both high unemployment and high inflation simultaneously, suggesting that the Phillips curve had disappeared. This combination of stagnation and inflation became known as **stagflation**. One possibility that was put forward was that the Phillips curve had not in fact disappeared, but had moved. Suppose that wage bargaining takes place on the basis of *expectations* about future rises in retail prices. As inflation becomes embedded in an economy, and people come to expect it to continue, those expectations will be built into wage negotiations. Another way of viewing this is that expectations about price inflation will influence the *position* of the Phillips curve.

 Key term

stagflation: a situation describing an economy in which both unemployment and inflation are high at the same time

Economic growth and sustainability

It is clear that there may be conflict between achieving economic growth and the environment. Nowhere is this better seen than in the case of China in the early part of the twenty-first century. China's persistently rapid growth has had consequences for the quality of the environment. Figure 15.12 shows one aspect of this — the emissions of carbon dioxide, which is one of the key so-called greenhouse gases that contribute to the process of global warming.

The acceleration of emissions in China in the early years of the century is very apparent in the diagram, and China overtook the USA to become the largest emitter of CO_2 in the early 2000s.

The link between economic growth and environmental degradation is a clear one. In the case of China, there are several aspects to notice. During the process of industrialisation, it is crucial to ensure that energy supplies keep pace with the demand, as factories cannot operate effectively without reliable electricity and other energy sources. China has become the world's second biggest oil importer (behind the USA), and is the world's

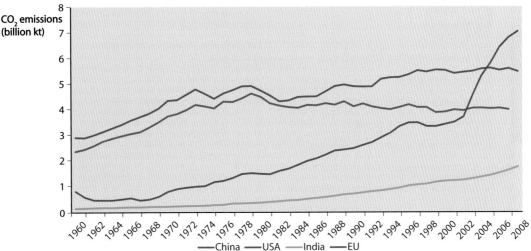

Figure 15.12 Carbon dioxide emissions in selected countries, 1960–2008

largest producer of coal, which accounts for some 80% of its total energy use – and is not the cleanest of energy technologies. It is also possible that inadequate regulation can add to environmental degradation, such as an explosion at a chemical plant that caused pollution in the Songhua River, which not only affected the city of Harbin, but also affected part of Russia, which was downstream from the incident.

For economic growth to be sustainable, these environmental effects must be taken into account, or there is a real danger that the improved standard of living that flows from the growth process will be obtained only at the expense of the quality of life of future generations. This may require growth to be slowed in the short run in order to devote resources to the development of renewable and cleaner energy sources. However, it is difficult to impose this on newly emerging societies in which there is widespread poverty, especially when the richer nations of the world continue to enjoy high standards of living while causing pollution of their own.

Economic growth and the current account of the balance of payments

In some circumstances, conflict can also arise between achieving economic growth, and attaining equilibrium on the current account of the balance of payments. An increase in economic growth resulting in higher real incomes could lead to an increase in imports of goods and services, if UK residents spent a high proportion of their additional income abroad. This was seen as a major problem during the fixed exchange rate era of the 1950s and 1960s, when any deficit on the current account had to be met by running down foreign exchange reserves. This led to a 'stop–go' cycle of macroeconomic policy, where every time growth began to accelerate the current account went into deficit, and policy then had to be adjusted to slow down the growth rate to deal with the deficit.

Exercise 15.5

Given the following list of policy objectives, discuss the possible conflicts that may arise between them, and discuss how these might be resolved:

a low inflation

b low unemployment

c high economic growth

d a low deficit on the current account of the balance of payments

e maintenance of a high environmental quality

f equity in the distribution of income

The policy environment — a summary

In the early years of the twentieth century, it seemed that the policy environment had become relatively stable. Accepting that the ultimate policy objective is to ensure a good standard of living for the UK population, the prime aim of policy must be to achieve economic growth — and to achieve it in a sustainable manner.

Macroeconomic stability is seen as a key prerequisite for economic growth to take place because firms need a stable environment if they are to feel confident about the future, and thus undertake investment. Monetary policy is therefore dedicated to achieving low inflation in line with the government's target. Fiscal policy needs to support monetary policy by maintaining a stable pattern over time, while at the same time dealing with key areas of market failure and producing an acceptable distribution of income between groups within society. Supply-side policies can then be implemented in order to ensure that markets operate effectively and that efficiency gains can be made. At the same time, the UK must operate within an international environment, observing the rules set down for international trade and providing some stability of the exchange rate.

Exercise 15.6

Discuss why it is so important to view the UK in an international context.

Summary

➤ The international economic environment is a strong influence on the design of economic policy, given that the UK is an open economy.

➤ The UK interacts with other countries through its network of international trade, and through the operation of financial markets.

➤ In particular, the role of the UK within the European Union is an important part of policy design.

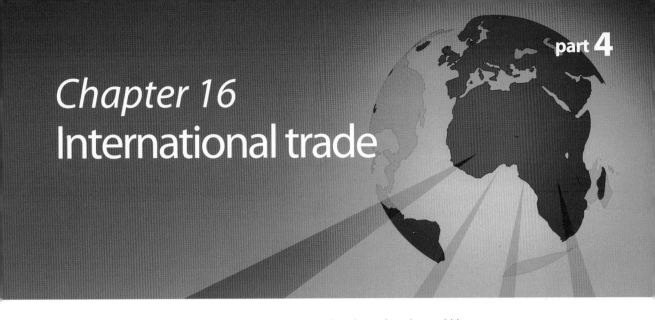

Chapter 16
International trade

Countries around the world engage in international trade, and as the world becomes more closely integrated this global trade becomes more important. The economic arguments that suggest that countries can gain from trade have been well known for many years and help to explain the pattern of trade that has emerged over time. Trade patterns depend upon a range of factors and are influenced by changing patterns of relative prices which, together with foreign exchange rates, determine the international competitiveness of countries. In some circumstances, it becomes important to be able to introduce policies to maintain balance in the balance of payments; some countries have also tried to establish protectionist policies that inhibit trade in certain commodities.

Learning outcomes

After studying this chapter, you should:

➤ understand the distinction between absolute and comparative advantage

➤ be able to analyse the effects of international trade

➤ be familiar with the pattern of global trade

➤ be aware of the significance of the terms of trade

➤ understand the way in which exchange rates are determined in different systems

➤ be able to explain the causes and consequences of exchange rate fluctuations

➤ be familiar with the causes of imbalances in the balance of payments and policies to correct them

➤ be able to evaluate the case for and against protectionism

The importance of international trade

The central importance of international trade for growth and development has been recognised since the days of Adam Smith and David Ricardo. For example, during the Industrial Revolution a key factor was that Britain could bring in raw materials from its colonies for use in manufacturing activity. Today, consumers in the UK are able to

buy and consume many goods that simply could not be produced within the domestic economy. From the point of view of economic analysis, Ricardo showed that countries could gain from trade through a process of *specialisation.*

Absolute and comparative advantage

The notion of specialisation was introduced in *AS Economics, Chapter 1*, where you were introduced to Colin and Debbie, who produced pots and bracelets with varying levels of effectiveness. Colin and Debbie's relative skill levels in producing these two goods can now be extended. Table 16.1 reminds you of Colin and Debbie's production possibilities.

Colin		Debbie	
Pots	Bracelets	Pots	Bracelets
12	0	18	0
9	3	12	12
6	6	6	24
3	9	3	30
0	12	0	36

Table 16.1
Colin and Debbie's production

You may remember that Debbie was much better at both activities than Colin. If they each devote all their time to producing pots, Colin produces only 12 to Debbie's 18. If they each produce only bracelets, Colin produces 12 and Debbie, 36.

This illustrates **absolute advantage**. Debbie is simply better than Colin at both activities. Another way of looking at this is that, in order to produce a given quantity of a good, Debbie needs less labour time than Colin.

There is another significant feature of this table. Although Debbie is better at producing both goods, the difference is

 Key term

absolute advantage: the ability to produce a good more efficiently (e.g. with less labour)

comparative advantage: the ability to produce a good *relatively* more efficiently (i.e. at lower opportunity cost)

much more marked in the case of bracelet production than for pot production. So Debbie is relatively more proficient in bracelet production: in other words, she has a **comparative advantage** in making bracelets. This is reflected in differences in opportunity cost. If Debbie switches from producing pots to producing bracelets, she gives up 6 pots for every 12 additional bracelets that she makes. The opportunity cost of an additional bracelet is thus $6/12 = 0.5$ pots. For Colin, there is a one-to-one trade-off between the two, so his opportunity cost of a bracelet is 1 pot.

More interesting is what happens if the same calculation is made for Colin and pot making. Although Debbie is absolutely better at making pots, if Colin increases his production of pots, his opportunity cost in terms of bracelets is still 1. But for Debbie the opportunity cost of making pots in terms of bracelets is $12/6 = 2$, so Colin has the lower opportunity cost. Although Debbie has an *absolute* advantage in pot making, Colin has a *comparative* advantage. It was this difference in comparative advantage that gave rise to the gains from specialisation that were set out in *AS Economics, Chapter 1*.

The **law of comparative advantage** states that overall output can be increased if all individuals specialise in producing the goods in which they have a comparative advantage.

Gains from international trade

This same principle can be applied in the context of international trade. Suppose there are two countries — call them Overthere and Elsewhere. Each country can produce combinations of agricultural goods and manufactures. However, Overthere has a comparative advantage in producing manufactured goods, and Elsewhere has comparative advantage in agricultural goods. Their respective *PPC*s are shown in Figure 16.1.

Key term

law of comparative advantage: a theory arguing that there may be gains from trade arising when countries (or individuals) specialise in the production of goods or services in which they have a comparative advantage

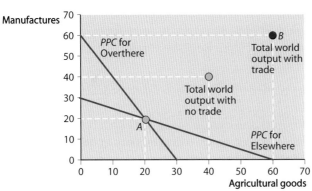

Figure 16.1
PPCs for Overthere and Elsewhere

You can see the pattern of comparative advantage reflected in the different slopes of the countries' *PPC*s. If the countries each produce some of each of the goods, one possibility (chosen for simplicity) is that they produce at point *A*, which is the intersection of the two *PPC*s. At this point each country produces 20 units of manufactures and 20 units of agricultural goods. Total world output is thus 40 units of manufactures and 40 units of agricultural goods — this point is marked on the figure.

However, suppose each country were to specialise in the product in which it has a comparative advantage. Overthere could produce 60 units of manufactured products, and Elsewhere could produce 60 units of agricultural goods. This would produce total world output at point *B*. Trade could take place such that each country had 30 units of each good, leaving them both unequivocally better off: they would each have more of both commodities. The figure shows that total world output of each type of good has increased by 20 units.

In this example, each of the countries has a comparative advantage in one of the goods. In the case of Debbie and Colin, Debbie had an *absolute* advantage in both goods, but Colin had a comparative advantage in making pots. Consider Figure 16.2, which again features Overthere and Elsewhere. This time, it can be seen that Overthere has an absolute advantage in the production of both manufactures and agricultural goods, but Elsewhere has a comparative advantage in agricultural goods.

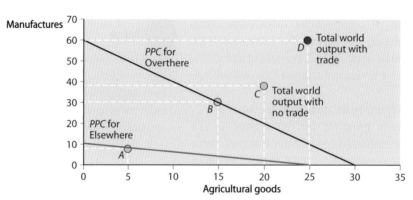

Figure 16.2 *PPCs for Overthere and Elsewhere revisited*

Suppose that without trade, Elsewhere produces at point *A* and Overthere at point *B*. The combined world output is at point *C*. If both countries were to specialise, with Elsewhere producing 25 units of agricultural goods, and Overthere producing 60 units of manufactures, then total world output would be at point *D*, with more of both goods being produced.

It can be seen that in this situation trade may be mutually beneficial. Notice that these particular results of trading have assumed that the countries exchange the goods on a one-to-one basis. Although this exchange rate makes both better off, it is not the only possibility. It is possible that exchange will take place at different prices for the goods, and clearly, the prices at which exchange takes place will determine which of the countries gains most from the trade that occurs.

In the above examples, specialisation and trade are seen to lead to higher overall production of goods. Although the examples have related to goods, you should be equally aware that services too may be a source of specialisation and trade. This is potentially important for an economy like that of the UK, where there is a comparative advantage in the provision of financial services.

Who gains from international trade?

Specialisation can result in an overall increase in total production. However, one of the fundamental questions of economics in *AS Economics*, Chapter 1 was 'for whom?' So far nothing has been said about which of the countries will gain from trade. It is possible that exchange can take place between countries in such a way that both countries are better off. But whether this will actually happen in practice depends on the prices at which exchange takes place.

This Second World War poster called on people in Britain to keep allotments as declining food imports became a serious issue

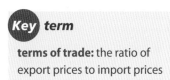

In particular, specialisation may bring dangers and risks, as well as benefits. One obvious way in which this may be relevant is that, by specialising, a country allows some sectors to run down. For example, suppose a country came to rely on imported food, and allowed its agricultural sector to waste away. If the country then became involved in a war, or for some other reason was unable to import its food, there would clearly be serious consequences if it could no longer grow its own foodstuffs. For this reason, many countries have in place measures designed to protect their agricultural sectors — or other sectors that are seen to be strategic in nature.

Over-reliance on some commodities may also be risky. For example, the development of artificial substitutes for rubber had an enormous impact on the demand for natural rubber; this was reflected in falls in its price and caused difficulties for countries that had specialised in producing rubber.

The terms of trade

One of the factors that determines who gains from international trade is the **terms of trade**, defined simply as the ratio of export prices to import prices.

> **Key term**
>
> **terms of trade:** the ratio of export prices to import prices

Suppose that both export and import prices are rising through time, but import prices are rising more rapidly than export prices. This means that the ratio of export to import prices will fall — which in turn means that a country must export a greater volume of its goods in order to acquire the same volume of imports. In other words, a fall in the terms of trade makes a country worse off.

In recent years, concerns have been raised about the effect of changes in the terms of trade for less developed countries (LDCs). One problem faced by LDCs that export primary products is that they are each too small as individual exporters to be able to influence the world price of their products. They must accept the prices that are set in world commodity markets.

Short-run volatility

In the case of agricultural goods, demand tends to be relatively stable over time, but supply can be volatile, varying with weather and climatic conditions from season to season. Figure 16.3 shows a typical market in two periods. In period 1 the global harvest of this commodity is poor, with supply given by S_1: equilibrium is achieved with price at P_1 and quantity traded at Q_1. In period 2 the global harvest is high at S_2, so that prices plummet to P_2 and quantity traded rises to Q_2.

Notice that in this case the movement of prices is relatively strong compared with the variation in quantity. This reflects the price elasticity of demand, which is expected to be relatively inelastic for many primary products. From the consumers' point of view,

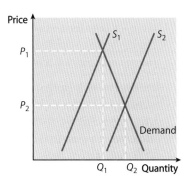

Figure 16.3 *Volatility in supply*

the demand for foodstuffs and other agricultural goods will tend to be inelastic, as demand will not be expected to respond strongly to changes in prices.

For many minerals and raw materials, however, the picture is different. For such commodities, supply tends to be stable over time, but demand fluctuates with the economic cycle in developed countries, which are the importers of raw materials. Figure 16.4 illustrates this. At the trough of the economic cycle, demand is low, at D_1, and so the equilibrium price will also be low, at P_1. At the peak of the cycle, demand is more buoyant, at D_2, and price is relatively high, at P_2.

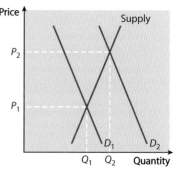

Figure 16.4 *Volatility in demand*

From an individual country's point of view, the result is the same: the country faces volatility in the prices of its exports. From this perspective it does not matter whether the instability arises from the supply side of the market or from the demand side. The problem is that prices can rise and fall quite independently of conditions within the domestic economy.

Instability of prices also means instability of export revenues, so if the country is relying on export earnings to fund its development path, to import capital equipment or to meet its debt repayments, such volatility in earnings can constitute a severe problem, e.g. if export earnings fall such that a country is unable to meet its commitments to repaying debt.

Long-run deterioration

The nature of the demand for primary products may be expected to influence the long-run path of relative prices. In particular, the income elasticity of demand is an important consideration. As real incomes rise in the developed countries, the demand for agricultural goods can be expected to rise relatively slowly. Ernst Engel pointed out that at relatively high income levels, the proportion of expenditure devoted to foodstuffs tends to fall and the demand for luxury goods rises. This suggests that the demand for agricultural goods shifts relatively slowly through time.

In the case of raw materials, there have been advances in the development of artificial substitutes for many commodities used in manufacturing. Furthermore, technology has changed over time, improving the efficiency with which inputs can be converted into outputs. This has weakened the demand for raw materials produced by LDCs.

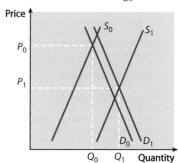

Figure 16.5 *Long-term movements of demand and supply*

Furthermore, if some LDCs are successful in boosting output of these goods, there will be an increase in supply over time. Figure 16.5 shows the result of such an increase. Suppose that the market begins with demand at D_0 and supply at S_0. Market equilibrium results in a price of P_0 and quantity of Q_0. As time goes by, demand moves to the right a little to D_1, and supply shifts to S_1. The result is a fall in the price of the commodity to P_1.

It is thus clear that, not only may LDCs experience short-run volatility in prices, but the terms of trade may also deteriorate in the long run.

In the light of these twin problems, it is perhaps no surprise that many LDCs see themselves as trapped by their pattern of comparative advantage, rather than being in a position to exploit it. They are therefore reluctant to continue in such a state of dependency on primary products, but the process of diversification into a wide range of products has been difficult to achieve.

A potential change in this pattern was seen in 2007 and 2008, with food prices rising rapidly. This included the prices of some staple commodities such as maize and rice. The net effect of this on LDCs was not clear. Countries in a position to export these commodities would benefit from the rise in prices — that is, an increase in their terms of trade. However, there are many LDCs that need to import these staple commodities and for them the terms of trade deteriorated. These trends were interrupted by the onset of recession in many developed countries in 2008.

The pattern of global trade

The pattern of world trade between the regions of the world was introduced in *AS Economics, Chapter 16*. One feature that emerged from that discussion was that the degree to which regions participate in world trade varies substantially. For example, Europe accounts for more than 30% of all trade that takes place between nations, whereas sub-Saharan Africa accounts for well below 1%.

The degree to which a country or region engages in trade depends upon several factors. One important influence is the extent to which a country has the resources needed to trade — in other words, whether it can produce the sorts of goods that other countries wish to buy. However, it also depends upon the policy stance adopted by a country. Some countries have been very open to international trade. For example, a number of countries in southeast Asia built success in economic growth on the basis of promoting exports. In contrast, there are countries such as India that in the past have been less eager to trade, and have introduced policies that have hindered their engagement with trade.

Two Swedish economists, Eli Heckscher and Bertil Ohlin, argued that a country's comparative advantage would depend crucially on its relative endowments of factors of production. They argued that the optimal techniques for producing different commodities varied. Some commodities are most efficiently produced using labour-intensive techniques, whereas others could be more efficiently produced using relatively capital-intensive methods. This then suggests that if a country has abundant labour but scarce capital, then its natural comparative advantage would lie in the production of goods that require little capital but lots of labour. In contrast, a country with access to capital but facing a labour shortage would tend to have a comparative advantage in capital-intensive goods or services.

Under these arguments, it would seem to make sense for LDCs to specialise in labour- or land-intensive activities such as agriculture or other primary production. Countries like the UK or the USA could then specialise in more capital-intensive activities such

as manufacturing activity or financial services. By and large, this describes the way in which the pattern of world trade developed. However, the pattern is not static and there have been changes over time. For example, countries in southeast Asia, such as Hong Kong, Singapore and Taiwan, encouraged the structure of their economies to change over time, switching away from labour-intensive activities as the access to capital goods improved over time. Their success then induced changes in the structure of activity in more developed countries as the availability of imported manufactured goods allowed the expansion of service sector activity. In more recent years, China's economy has been undergoing even further structural change, with the rapid expansion of the manufacturing sector, supported by an exchange rate policy that made its exports highly competitive in global markets. Figure 16.6 shows how this change has occurred – notice how the primary sector has steadily declined in terms of its relative contribution to GDP, whereas industry has expanded.

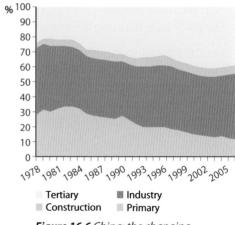

Figure 16.6 *China: the changing composition of GDP, 1978–2007*

Source: National Bureau of Statistics of China.

Whether it is good for countries to rely on this pattern of natural comparative advantage is a different matter – for example, in the light of the changing patterns of relative prices reflected in the evolution of the terms of trade over time. This may suggest that there is potential for countries to seek to alter the pattern of their comparative advantage by diversifying their economies and developing new specialisms in the face of changing patterns of global consumer demand. This is not an easy path for an economy to travel, and it may be tempting to turn instead to a more inward-looking protectionist strategy. These policy options will be examined later in the chapter.

Summary

➤ Specialisation opens up the possibility of trade.

➤ The theory of comparative advantage shows that even if one country has an absolute advantage in the production of goods and services, trade may still increase total output if each country specialises in the production of goods and services in which it has a comparative advantage.

➤ Who gains from specialisation and trade depends crucially on the prices at which exchange takes place.

➤ The terms of trade are measured as the ratio of export prices to import prices.

➤ When the terms of trade deteriorate for a country, it needs to export a greater volume of goods to be able to maintain the same volume of imports.

➤ The terms of trade have tended to be volatile in the short run, and to deteriorate over the longer term for countries that rely heavily on non-fuel primary production.

➤ The pattern of comparative advantage that characterises a country may depend upon the relative endowments of the factors of production.

➤ There is a choice to be made between seeking to exploit this natural comparative advantage, or diversifying the economy in an attempt to develop new specialisms.

Exercise 16.1

Discuss where you think the UK's natural comparative advantage lies. How would you expect this pattern to differ from that which would apply to countries such as France, India, China, Brazil or a country in sub-Saharan Africa?

The balance of payments

For an economy that is open to international trade, it is important to be able to monitor the transactions that take place. The balance of payments accounts enable this by itemising all the transactions in goods, services and financial assets that take place between one country and the rest of the world. The exchange rate is also critical in this respect, as it has a strong influence on the relative competitiveness of domestic goods in international markets, and on which countries gain from specialisation and international trade. The way in which the exchange rate is determined thus plays a crucial role in modelling the macroeconomy and in policy design and effectiveness.

The foreign exchange market

The foreign exchange market involves demand and supply, just like any normal market. A foreign exchange transaction is needed whenever trade takes place. If, as a UK resident, you buy goods from abroad, you need to purchase foreign exchange — say, euros — and you will have to supply pounds in order to buy euros. Similarly, if a French tourist in the UK buys UK goods or services, the transaction needs to be carried out in pounds, so there is a demand for pounds.

This market is shown in Figure 16.7. The demand curve is downward sloping because when the €/£ rate is low, UK goods, services and assets are relatively cheap in terms of euros, so demand is relatively high. On the other hand, when the €/£ rate is relatively high, people in the Eurozone receive fewer euros for their pounds, so the demand will be relatively low.

The supply curve of pounds is upward sloping. When the €/£ rate is relatively high, the supply of pounds will be relatively strong, as UK residents will get plenty of euros for their pounds and thus will demand goods, services and assets from the Eurozone, supplying pounds in order to buy the foreign exchange needed for the transactions. When the €/£ rate is low, Eurozone goods, services and

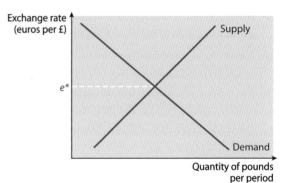

Figure 16.7 *The market for pounds*

assets will be relatively expensive for UK residents, so fewer pounds will be supplied.

The market is in equilibrium at e^*, where the demand for pounds is just matched by the supply of pounds. This position has a direct connection with the balance of payments. If the demand for pounds exactly matches the supply of pounds, this implies that there is a balance between the demand from Eurozone residents for UK goods, services and assets, and the demand by UK residents for Eurozone goods, services and assets. In other words, the balance of payments is in overall balance. The key question for consideration is how the market reaches e^* — in particular, do the authorities allow the exchange rate to find its own way to e^*, or do they intervene to ensure that it gets there?

Summary

> The foreign exchange market can be seen as operating according to the laws of demand and supply.

> The demand for pounds arises when non-residents want to buy UK goods, services or assets.

> The supply of pounds arises when UK residents wish to buy foreign goods, services or assets.

> When the exchange rate is at its equilibrium level, this automatically ensures that the overall balance of payments is zero.

A fixed exchange rate system

In the Bretton Woods conference at the end of the Second World War, it was agreed to establish a fixed exchange rate system, under which countries would commit to maintaining the price of their currencies in terms of the US dollar. This system remained in place until the early 1970s. For example, from 1950 until 1967 the sterling exchange rate was set at $2.80, and the British government was committed to making sure that it stayed at this rate. This system became known as the

 Key *term*

fixed exchange rate system: a system in which the government of a country agrees to fix the value of its currency in terms of that of another country

chapter *16*

dollar standard. Occasional changes in exchange rates were permitted after consultation if a currency was seen to be substantially out of line — as happened for the UK in 1967.

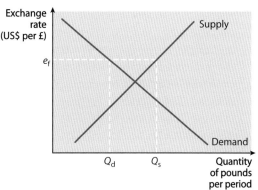

Figure 16.8 *Maintaining a fixed exchange rate*

Figure 16.8 illustrates how this works. Suppose the authorities announce that the exchange rate will be set at e_f. Given that this level is set independently by the government, it cannot be guaranteed to correspond to the market equilibrium, and in Figure 16.8 it is set above the equilibrium level. At this exchange rate, the supply of pounds exceeds the demand for pounds. This can be interpreted in terms of the overall balance of payments. If there is an excess supply of pounds, the implication is that UK residents are trying to buy more US goods, services and assets than Americans are trying to buy British: in other words, there is an overall deficit on the balance of payments.

In a free market, you would expect the exchange rate to adjust until the demand and supply of pounds came back into equilibrium. However, with the authorities committed to maintaining the exchange rate at e_f, such an adjustment cannot take place. As the UK owes the USA for the excess goods, services and assets that its residents have purchased, the authorities then have to sell **foreign exchange reserves** in order to make the books balance.

Key *term*

foreign exchange reserves: stocks of foreign currency and gold owned by the central bank of a country to enable it to meet any mismatch between the demand and supply of the country's currency

In terms of Figure 16.8, Q_d represents the demand for pounds at e_f and Q_s represents the supply. The difference represents the amount of foreign exchange reserves that the authorities have to sell to preserve the balance of payments. Such transactions used to be known as 'official financing', and are now incorporated into the financial account of the balance of payments.

Notice that the *position* of the demand and supply curves depends on factors other than the exchange rate that can affect the demand for UK and US goods, services and assets in the respective countries. It is likely that through time these will shift in position. For example, if the preference of Americans for UK goods changes through time, this will affect the demand for pounds.

Consider Figure 16.9. For simplicity, suppose that the supply curve remains fixed, but demand shifts through time. Let e_f be the value of the exchange rate that the UK monetary authorities have undertaken to maintain. If the demand for pounds is at D_1, the chosen exchange rate corresponds to the market equilibrium, and no action by the authorities is needed. If demand is at D_0, then with the exchange rate at e_f there

is an excess supply of pounds (as was the case in Figure 16.8). The monetary authorities in the UK need to buy up the excess supply by selling foreign exchange reserves. Conversely, if the demand for pounds is strong, say because Americans have developed a preference for Scotch whisky, then demand could be at D_2. There is now excess demand for pounds, and the UK monetary authorities supply additional pounds in return for US dollars. Foreign exchange reserves thus accumulate.

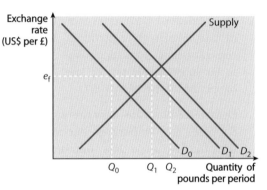

Figure 16.9 *Maintaining a fixed exchange rate in the face of changing demand for pounds*

In the long term, the system will operate successfully for the country as long as the chosen exchange rate is close to the average equilibrium value over time, so that the central bank is neither running down its foreign exchange reserves nor accumulating them.

A country that tries to hold its currency away from equilibrium indefinitely will find this problematic in the long run. For example, in the first few years of the twenty-first century, China and some other Asian economies were pegging their currencies against the US dollar at such a low level that they were accumulating reserves. In the case of China, it was accumulating substantial amounts of US government stock. The low exchange rate had the effect of keeping the exports of these countries highly competitive in world markets. However, such a strategy relies on being able to continue to expand domestic production to meet the high demand; otherwise inflationary pressure will begin to build.

During the period of the dollar standard, the pound was probably set at too high a level, which meant that UK exports were relatively uncompetitive, and in 1967 the UK government announced a **devaluation** of the pound from $2.80 to $2.40.

During the period of the dollar standard, the UK economy went through what became known as a 'stop–go' cycle of growth. When the government tried to stimulate economic growth, the effect was to suck in imports, as the marginal propensity to import was high. The effect of this was to generate a deficit on the current account of the balance of payments, which then needed to be financed by selling foreign exchange reserves.

Key term

devaluation: a process whereby a country in a fixed exchange rate system reduces the price of its currency relative to an agreed rate in terms of a foreign currency

revaluation: a process whereby a country in a fixed exchange rate system raises the price of the domestic currency in terms of a foreign currency

This process has two effects. First of all, in selling foreign exchange reserves, domestic money supply increases, which then puts upward pressure on prices, threatening inflation. In addition, the Bank of England has finite foreign exchange reserves, and cannot allow them to be run down indefinitely. This meant that the government had to rein in the economy, thereby slowing the rate of growth again; hence the label 'stop–go'.

An important point emerges from this discussion. The fact that intervention to maintain the exchange rate affects domestic money supply means that, under a fixed exchange rate regime, the monetary authorities are unable to pursue an independent monetary policy. In other words, money supply and the exchange rate cannot be controlled independently of one another. Effectively, the money supply has to be targeted to maintain the value of the currency. Governments may be tempted to use tariffs or non-tariff barriers to reduce a current account deficit, but this has been shown to be distortionary.

The effects of devaluation

During the stop–go period there were many debates about whether there should be a devaluation. The effect of devaluation is to improve competitiveness. At a lower value of the pound, you would expect an increase in the demand for exports and a fall in the demand for imports, ceteris paribus.

However, this does not necessarily mean that there will be an improvement in the current account. One reason for this concerns the elasticity of supply of exports and import substitutes. If domestic producers do not have spare capacity, or if there are time lags before production for export can be increased, then exports will not expand quickly in the short run, and so the impact of this action on exports will be limited. Similar arguments apply to producers of goods that are potential substitutes for imported products, which reinforces the sluggishness of adjustment. In the short run, therefore, it may be that the current account will worsen rather than improve, in spite of the change in the competitiveness of domestic firms.

This is known as the *J-curve effect*, and is shown in Figure 16.10. Time is measured on the horizontal axis, and the current account is initially in deficit. A devaluation at time *A* initially pushes the current account further into deficit because of the inelasticity of domestic supply. Only after time *B*, when domestic firms have had time to expand their output to meet the demand for exports, does the current account move into surplus.

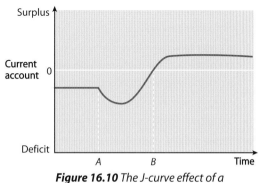

Figure 16.10 The J-curve effect of a devaluation

A second consideration relates to the elasticity of demand for exports and imports. Again, if competitiveness improves but demand does not respond strongly, there may

In order to finance the Vietnam War, the USA had to increase the supply of dollars

be a negative impact on the current account. If the demand for exports is price-inelastic, a fall in price will lead to a fall in revenue. Indeed, the *Marshall–Lerner condition* states that a devaluation will have a positive effect on the current account only if the sum of the elasticities of demand for exports and imports is negative and numerically greater than 1.

The Bretton Woods dollar standard broke down in the early 1970s. Part of the reason for this was that such a system depends critically on the stability of the base currency (i.e. the US dollar). During the 1960s the US need to finance the Vietnam War meant that the supply of dollars began to expand, one result of which was accelerating inflation in the countries that were fixing their currency in terms of the US dollar. It then became increasingly difficult to sustain exchange rates at fixed levels. The UK withdrew from the dollar standard in June 1972. Following this, the pound fell steadily for the next 5 years or so.

Summary

> After the Bretton Woods conference at the end of the Second World War, the dollar standard was established, under which countries agreed to maintain the value of their currencies in terms of US dollars.

> In order to achieve this, the monetary authorities engaged in foreign currency transactions to ensure that the exchange rate was maintained at the agreed level, accumulating foreign exchange reserves to accommodate a balance of payments surplus and running down the reserves to fund a deficit.

> Occasional realignments were permitted, such as the devaluation of sterling in 1967.

> Under a fixed exchange rate system, monetary policy can only be used to achieve the exchange rate target.

> A devaluation has the effect of improving international competitiveness, but the effect on the current account depends upon the elasticity of demand for exports and imports.

> The current account may deteriorate in the short run if the supply response is sluggish.

> The Bretton Woods system broke down in the early 1970s.

Exercise 16.2

A firm wants to purchase a machine tool which is obtainable in the UK for a price of £125,000, or from a US supplier for $300,000. Suppose that the exchange rate is fixed at £1 = $3.

a What is the sterling price of the machine tool if the firm chooses to buy in the USA?

b From which supplier would the firm be likely to purchase?

c Suppose that between ordering the machine tool and its delivery the UK government announces a devaluation of sterling, so that when the time comes for the firm to pay up the exchange rate is £1 = $2. What is the sterling price of the machine tool bought from the USA?

d Comment on how the competitiveness of UK goods has been affected.

e Discuss the effects that the devaluation is likely to have on the economy as a whole. (Use the *AD/AS* model to help you to analyse these changes.)

Floating exchange rates

Under a **floating exchange rate system**, the value of the currency is allowed to find its own way to equilibrium. This means that the overall balance of payments is automatically assured, and the monetary authorities do not need to intervene to make sure it happens. In practice, however, governments have tended to be wary of leaving the exchange rate entirely to market forces, and there have been occasional periods in which intervention has been used to affect the market rate.

An example of this was the **Exchange Rate Mechanism (ERM)**, which was set up by a group of European countries in 1979 with the objective of keeping member countries' currencies relatively stable against each other. This was part of the European Monetary System (EMS). Each member nation agreed to keep its currency within 2.25% of a weighted average of the members' currencies (known as the European Currency Unit, or ECU). This was an *adjustable peg* system. Eleven realignments were permitted between 1979 and 1987.

Key term

floating exchange rate system: a system in which the exchange rate is permitted to find its own level in the market

Exchange Rate Mechanism (ERM): a system which was set up by a group of European countries in 1979 with the objective of keeping member countries' currencies relatively stable against each other

The UK opted not to join the ERM when it was first set up, but started shadowing the Deutschmark in the mid-1980s, aiming to keep the rate at around DM3 to the pound, as you can see in Figure 16.11. The UK finally decided to become a full member of the ERM in September 1990, agreeing to operate within a 6% band. However, the rate at which sterling had been set against the Deutschmark was relatively high, and the situation was worsened by the effects of German reunification, which led to substantial capital flows into Germany, reinforcing the overvaluation of sterling. Once it became

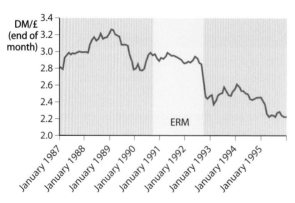

Figure 16.11 *The nominal DM/£ exchange rate, 1987–95*

Source: Bank of England.

apparent that sterling was overvalued, speculative attacks began, and the Bank of England's foreign exchange reserves were depleted; in 1992 the pound left the ERM. You can see in Figure 16.11 that the value of the pound fell rapidly after exit.

What determines exchange rates?

If the foreign exchange market is left free to find its own way to equilibrium, it becomes important to consider what factors will influence the level of the exchange rate. In particular, will the exchange rate resulting from market equilibrium be consistent with the government's domestic policy objectives?

Exchange rate equilibrium also implies a zero overall balance of payments. If the exchange rate always adjusts to the level that ensures this, it might be argued that the long-run state of the economy is one in which the competitiveness of domestic firms remains constant over time. In other words, you would expect the exchange rate to adjust through time to offset any differences in inflation rates between countries. The **purchasing power parity theory of exchange rates** argues that this is exactly what should be expected in the long run. If you look back at Figure 14.5 on p. 250, you will see that, aside from some fluctuations, the real exchange rate has remained fairly constant through time and shows no underlying trend. This is what would be expected if the nominal exchange rate was adjusting to offset changes in relative prices between countries.

However, in the short run the exchange rate may diverge from its long-run equilibrium. An important influence on the exchange rate in the short run is speculation. So far, the discussion of the exchange rate has stressed mainly the current account of the balance of payments. However, the financial account is also significant, especially since regulation of the movement of financial capital was removed. Some of these capital movements are associated with direct

 Key term

purchasing power parity theory of exchange rates: theory stating that, in the long run, exchange rates (in a floating rate system) are determined by relative inflation rates in different countries

investment. However, sometimes there are also substantial movements of what has come to be known as **hot money**: that is, stocks of funds that are moved around the globe from country to country in search of the best return. The size of the stocks of hot

Large movements of stock in the foreign exchange market can influence the exchange rate in the short term

money is enormous, and can significantly affect exchange rates in the short run. The precise amount of such funds is not known with any precision, but some have claimed that the daily foreign exchange market turnover can reach up to $1.5 trillion.

 term

hot money: stocks of funds that are moved around the globe from country to country in search of the best return

Such movements can influence the exchange rate in the short run. The returns to be gained from such capital flows depend on the relative interest rate in the country targeted, and on the expected exchange rate in the future, which in turn may depend on expectations about inflation.

Suppose you are an investor holding assets denominated in US dollars, and the UK interest rate is 2% higher than that in the USA. You may be tempted to shift the funds into the UK in order to take advantage of the higher interest rate. However, if you believe that the exchange rate is above its long-run equilibrium, and therefore is likely to fall, this will affect your expected return on holding a UK asset. Indeed, if investors holding UK assets expect the exchange rate to fall, they are likely to shift their funds out of the country as soon as possible, which may then have the effect of pushing down the exchange rate. In other words, this may be a self-fulfilling prophecy. However, speculators may also react to news in an unpredictable way, so not all speculative capital movements act to influence the exchange rate towards its long-run equilibrium value.

Speculation was a key contributing factor in the unfolding of the Asian financial crisis of 1997. Substantial flows of capital had moved into Thailand in search of high returns, and speculators came to believe that the Thai currency (the baht) was overvalued.

Outward capital flows put pressure on the exchange rate, and although the Thai central bank tried to resist, it eventually ran down its reserves to the point where it had to devalue. This then sparked off capital flows from other countries in the region, including South Korea.

Summary

➤ Under a floating exchange rate system, the value of a currency is allowed to find its own way to equilibrium without government intervention.

➤ This means that an overall balance of payments of zero is automatically achieved.

➤ The purchasing power parity theory argues that the exchange rate will adjust in the long run to maintain international competitiveness, by offsetting differences in inflation rates between countries.

➤ In the short run, the exchange rate may diverge from this long-run level, particularly because of speculation.

➤ The exchange rate is thus influenced by relative interest rates and expected inflation, as well as by news about the economic environment.

Exchange rate policy: fixed or floating?

Having examined the operation of both fixed and floating exchange rate systems, the next question is to analyse whether one is to be preferred over the other. In evaluating this question, there are many factors to be taken into account; this section will consider three of them. First, it is important to examine the extent to which the respective systems can accommodate and adjust to external shocks that push the economy out of equilibrium. Second, it is important to consider the stability of each of the systems. Finally, there is the question of which system best encourages governments to adopt sound macroeconomic policies.

Adjustment to shocks

Every economy has to cope with external shocks that occur for reasons outside the control of the country. A key question in evaluating exchange rate systems is whether there is an effective mechanism that allows the economy to return to equilibrium after an external shock.

Under a *floating exchange rate* system, much of the burden of adjustment is taken up by changes in the exchange rate. For example, if an economy finds itself experiencing faster inflation than other countries, perhaps because those other countries have introduced policies to reduce inflation, then the exchange rate will adjust automatically to restore competitiveness.

However, if the country is operating a *fixed exchange rate* system, the authorities are committed to maintaining the exchange rate, and this has to take precedence. Thus, the only way to restore competitiveness is by deflating the economy in order to bring inflation into line with other countries. This is likely to bring with it a transitional cost

in terms of higher unemployment and slower economic growth. In other words, the burden of adjustment is on the real economy, rather than on allowing the exchange rate to adjust.

The Bretton Woods system operated for more than 20 years in a period in which many economies enjoyed steady economic growth. However, in the UK the system brought about a stop–go cycle, in which the need to maintain the exchange rate hampered economic growth because of the tendency for growth to lead to an increase in imports and thus to a current account deficit. The increasing differences between inflation rates in different countries led to the final collapse of the system, suggesting that it was unable to cope with such variation.

Furthermore, a flexible exchange rate system allows the authorities to utilise monetary policy in order to stabilise the economy — remember that under a fixed exchange rate system, monetary policy has to be devoted to the exchange rate target.

Stability

When it comes to stability, a fixed exchange rate system has much to commend it. After all, if firms know that the government is committed to maintaining the exchange rate at a given level, they can agree future contracts with some confidence. Under a floating exchange rate system, trading takes place in an environment in which the future exchange rate has to be predicted. If the exchange rate moves adversely, firms then face potential losses from trading. This foreign exchange risk is reduced under a fixed rate regime.

In a climate where speculative activity creates volatility in exchange rates, international trade may be discouraged because of the exchange rate risk. The effects of such volatility can be mitigated to some extent by the existence of **futures markets**. In such a market, it is possible to buy foreign exchange at a fixed price for delivery at a specified future date.

 Key *term*

futures market: a market in which it is possible to buy a commodity at a fixed price for delivery at a specified future date; such a market exists for foreign exchange

For example, suppose a firm is negotiating a deal to buy component parts for a manufacturing process that will be delivered in 3 months' time. The firm can buy the foreign exchange needed to close the deal in the futures market, and then knows that the contract will be viable, having negotiated a price for the components based on the known exchange rate, rather than on the unpredictable rate that will apply at that future date. The firm might, of course, have to pay a price for the foreign currency that is above the current (*spot*) exchange rate, but as the future rate has been built into the terms of the contract, that will not affect the viability of the deal. The process by which a firm avoids losses by buying forward is known as *hedging*.

However, even with the use of hedging to reduce the risk, it is costly to engage in international trade when exchange rates are potentially volatile, so world trade is unlikely to be encouraged under such a system. Of course, it might be argued that the

risk to firms is still present under a fixed exchange rate system, since a government may choose to realign its currency, with even greater costs to firms that are tied into contracts. However, such realignments were rare under Bretton Woods and were more predictable than the volatility that can occur on a day-to-day basis in today's foreign exchange market.

Macroeconomic policy

Critics of the flexible exchange rate system argue that it is too flexible for its own good. If governments know that the exchange rate will always adjust to maintain international competitiveness, they may have no incentive to behave responsibly in designing macroeconomic policy. Thus, they may be tempted to adopt an inflationary domestic policy, secure in the knowledge that the exchange rate will bear the burden of adjustment. In other words, a flexible exchange rate system does not impose financial discipline on individual countries.

An example of this was seen in the UK in the early 1970s when the UK first moved to a floating exchange rate regime. Money supply was allowed to expand rapidly, and inflation increased to almost 25%, aided by the oil price shock. Other examples are evident in Latin America, where hyperinflation affected many countries during the 1980s and early 1990s. For the country itself, such policies are costly in the long run, as reducing inflation under flexible exchange rates is costly. If interest rates are increased in order to reduce domestic aggregate demand and thus reduce inflationary pressure, the high return on domestic assets encourages an inflow of hot money, thereby putting upward pressure on the exchange rate. This reduces the international competitiveness of domestic goods and services, and deepens the recession.

There may also be spillover effects on other countries. Suppose that two countries have been experiencing rapid inflation, and one of them decides to tackle the problem. It raises interest rates to dampen domestic aggregate demand, which leads to an **appreciation** of its currency. For the other country, the effect is a **depreciation** of the currency. (If one currency appreciates, the other must depreciate.) The other country thus finds that its competitive position has improved, and it faces inflationary pressure in the short run. It may then also choose to tackle inflation, which in turn will affect the other country. These spillover effects could be minimised if the countries were to harmonise their policy action.

Key terms

appreciation: a rise in the exchange rate within a floating exchange rate system

depreciation: a fall in the exchange rate within a floating exchange rate system

The exchange rate and macroeconomic policy

The discussion above has shown that the relationship between the exchange rate and macroeconomic policy is an important one. Under a fixed exchange rate system, the need to maintain the value of the currency is a constraint on macroeconomic policy, and forces adjustment to disequilibrium through the real economy. On the other hand, it does have the benefit of imposing financial discipline on governments.

Under floating exchange rates, the relationship with policy is less obvious. With a flexible exchange rate, the authorities can use monetary policy to stabilise the economy, knowing that there will be overall balance on the balance of payments. Nonetheless, the government needs to monitor the structure of the balance of payments. When interest rates are set at a relatively high level compared with other countries, the financial account will tend to be in surplus because of capital inflows, with a corresponding deficit on the current account. This may not be sustainable in the long run.

Summary

➤ There are strengths and weaknesses with both fixed and floating exchange rate systems. A floating exchange rate system is more robust in enabling economies to adjust following external shocks, but it can lead to volatility and thus discourage international trade. A fixed rate system has the added advantage of imposing financial discipline on governments, and may allow policy harmonisation.

➤ The move towards a fixed exchange rate system within the European Union is partly in recognition that international trade is encouraged by stability in trading arrangements. This development is discussed in the next chapter.

➤ Under a floating exchange rate system, much of the burden of adjustment to external shocks is borne by changes in the exchange rate. Under a fixed exchange rate system, adjustment is more likely to take place through variations in the level of economic activity.

Exercise 16.3

Critically evaluate the following statements, and discuss whether you regard fixed or floating exchange rates as the better system.
a A flexible exchange rate regime is better able to cope with external shocks.
b A fixed exchange rate system provides a more stable trading environment and minimises risk.
c Floating exchange rates enable individual countries to follow independent policies.
d A fixed exchange rate system may encourage governments to adopt distortionary policies such as tariffs and non-tariff barriers in order to control imports.

Managing the balance of payments

It was argued earlier that, although in the short run it may be possible to balance a deficit on the current account of the balance of payments by a surplus on the financial account, in the long run this might not be sustainable. The main reason for this is that there may be a limit on foreign exchange reserves and on the extent to which it is desirable to fund the current account by borrowing or by selling UK assets.

The question then is how the government could manage the balance of payments: in other words, how is it possible to alter the structure of transactions by reducing the size of the current account deficit? There are two basic routes that could be followed

if the government decided that it needed to do so: demand management policies and exchange rate adjustments. A third possibility would be to try to use protectionist policies, which will be discussed later in the chapter.

Demand management

One reason for a current account deficit is that, as real incomes rise in the economy, there is a tendency for UK residents to buy more imported goods or services, because the income elasticity of demand for imports tends to be relatively high. One possibility, therefore, would be to control the level of aggregate demand in order to limit the demand for imports: for example, the government could raise taxes, or reduce government expenditure. Whether the government wants to do this might depend upon whether such a policy would damage other aspects of the economy. For example, a reduction in aggregate demand might cause an increase in unemployment, and if the government gave a higher priority to achieving full employment, it might prefer to live with the current account deficit. It is also possible that long-run economic growth could be inhibited.

The alternative would be to introduce a policy that was targeted more towards reducing the demand for imports. For example, the use of tariffs or quotas would raise the price of imports, and so reduce demand for them, and at the same time would encourage domestic producers to increase their production. However, within the context of the EU it is not realistic to imagine that the UK could set its own independent tariff rates, even if it wanted to do so. In any case, as has already been explained, the use of tariffs entails a misallocation of resources in society, and a deadweight loss.

Exchange rate adjustment

The competitiveness of UK exports and of domestic goods and services relative to imports both depend crucially on the exchange rate: in particular, the exchange rate influences the size of the current account deficit. Under current policy procedures, the prime target of monetary policy is to keep inflation at a low level. This is achieved by the Bank of England setting interest rates at the level needed to hit the inflation target. However, if the interest rate required for this purpose is high relative to elsewhere in the world, there will tend to be flows of financial capital into the UK. In turn, this suggests that the equilibrium for the exchange rate will be relatively high, which limits the competitiveness of UK goods and services, and results in a balance of payments that is achieved through a current account deficit and a financial account surplus.

The high income elasticity of demand for imported goods has led to a deficit on the UK current account

In this way, the government may be restricted in the extent to which it can manipulate the exchange rate to reduce the current account deficit, unless it is prepared to give a higher priority to this than to other targets of macroeconomic policy. This helps to explain why supply-side policies, as described in the next section, have been at the forefront in ensuring the competitiveness of UK firms in international markets.

Summary

➤ Trade and competitiveness are affected by government policy, both directly and indirectly.

➤ Demand management could be used to reduce a deficit on the current account of the balance of payments, but governments might be reluctant to use this approach if it damages targets for full employment or economic growth.

➤ In principle, exchange rate adjustments could be used to influence the balance of payments, but careful attention needs to be paid to the effects on other targets of macroeconomic policy.

Protectionism

It is clear that the international context is important in seeking to manage an economy, with the need to maintain stability and encourage economic growth. This may be seen as challenging for some countries in the context of an increasingly integrated global economy, where national governments may feel that they are no longer in control of their own destiny. It may also be that some governments seeking to encourage diversification in their economies may see a need to provide protection for their newly developing sectors for a period while they learn the business and become competitive. For these and other reasons, many governments have looked for ways in which they can provide protection for domestic economic activities.

When recession threatened in 2008, there was strong lobbying from pressure groups in the USA and elsewhere in favour of introducing protectionist measures. Indeed, in the lead-up to the G20 Summit in April 2009, the World Bank reported that the 17 members of that group had taken a total of 47 trade-restricting steps in the previous months. However, the drive towards globalisation had created a more integrated global economy, in which many firms relied on a global supply chain. With the production process fragmented between different parts of the world, the dangers of protectionism become more severe, and the possibilities of rapid contagion from a crisis become acute.

The arguments in favour of allowing engagement with trade suggest that there are potential gains from trade, and moves towards protectionism may be seen to entail sacrifice of those gains.

Tariffs

A policy instrument commonly used in the past to give protection to domestic producers is a **tariff**. Tariff rates in the developed countries have been considerably reduced in the period since the Second World War, but nonetheless are still in place.

 Key *term*

tariff: a tax imposed on imported goods

Figure 16.12 shows how a tariff is expected to operate. D represents the domestic demand for a commodity, and S_{dom} shows how much domestic producers are prepared to supply at any given price. The price at which the good can be imported from world markets is given by P_w. If dealing with a global market, it is reasonable to assume that the supply at the world price is perfectly elastic. So, in the absence of a tariff, domestic demand is given by D_0, of which S_0 is supplied within the domestic economy and the remainder $(D_0 - S_0)$ is imported. If the government wishes to protect this industry within the domestic economy, it needs to find a way of restricting imports and encouraging home producers to expand their capacity.

When a tariff is imposed, the domestic price rises to $P_w + T$, where T is the amount of the tariff. This has two key effects. One is to reduce the demand for the good from D_0 to D_1; the second is to encourage domestic producers to expand their output of this good from S_0 to S_1. As a consequence, imports fall substantially $(D_1 - S_1)$. On the face of it, the policy has achieved its objective. Furthermore, the government has been able to raise some tax revenue (given by the green rectangle).

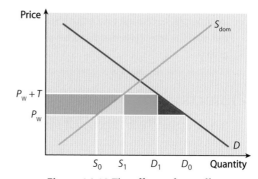

Figure 16.12 The effects of a tariff

However, not all the effects of the tariff are favourable for the economy. Consumers are certainly worse off, as they have to pay a higher price for the good; they therefore consume less, and there is a loss of consumer surplus. Some of what was formerly consumer surplus has been redistributed to others in society. The government has gained the tariff revenue, as mentioned. In addition, producers gain some additional producer surplus, shown by the dark-blue area. There is also a deadweight loss to society, represented by the red and pale-blue triangles. In other words, society is worse off overall as a result of the imposition of the tariff.

Effectively, the government is subsidising inefficient local producers, and forcing domestic consumers to pay a price that is above that of similar goods imported from abroad.

Some would try to defend this policy on the grounds that it allows the country to protect an industry, thus saving jobs that would otherwise be lost. However, this goes against the theory of comparative advantage, and forces society to incur the deadweight loss. In the longer term it may delay structural change. For an economy to develop new specialisations and new sources of comparative advantage, there needs to be a transitional process in which old industries contract and new ones emerge. Although this process may be painful, it is necessary in the long run if the economy is to remain competitive. Furthermore, the protection that firms enjoy that allows them to reap economic rents from the tariff may foster complacency and an inward-looking attitude. This is likely to lead to X-inefficiency, and an inability to compete in the global market.

Even worse is the situation that develops where nations respond to tariffs raised by competitors by putting up tariffs of their own. This has the effect of further reducing the trade between countries, and everyone ends up worse off, as the gains from trade are sacrificed.

Quotas and non-tariff barriers

An alternative policy that a country may adopt is to limit the imports of a commodity to a given volume. For example, a country may come to an agreement with another country that only a certain quantity of imports will be accepted by the importing country. Such arrangements are sometimes known as **voluntary export restraints (VERs)**.

Figure 16.13 illustrates the effects of a quota. D represents the domestic demand for this commodity, and S_{dom} is the quantity that domestic producers are prepared to supply at any given price. Suppose that, without any agreement, producers from country A would be prepared to supply any amount of the product at a price P_a. If the product is sold at this price, D_0 represents domestic demand, of which S_0 is supplied by domestic producers and the remainder $(D_0 - S_0)$ is imported from country A.

By imposing a quota, total supply is now given by S_{total}, which is domestic supply plus the quota of imports allowed into the economy from country A. The market equilibrium price rises to P_1 and demand falls to D_1, of which S_1 is supplied by domestic producers and the remainder is the agreed quota of imports.

> **Key term**
>
> **voluntary export restraint:** an agreement by a country to limit its exports to another country to a given quantity (quota)
>
> **non-tariff barrier:** an obstacle to free trade other than a tariff (e.g. quality standards imposed on imported products)
>
> **World Trade Organization (WTO):** multilateral body responsible for overseeing the conduct of international trade

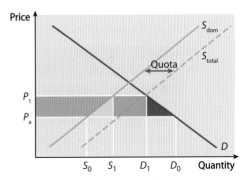

Figure 16.13 The effects of a quota

Figure 16.13 shows who gains and who loses by this policy. Domestic producers gain by being able to sell at the higher price, so (as in the case of the tariff) they receive additional surplus given by the dark-blue area. Furthermore, the producers exporting from country A also gain, receiving the green rectangle (which, in the case of the tariff, was tax revenue received by the government). As in the case of the tariff, the two triangles (red and pale blue) represent the loss of welfare suffered by the importing country.

Such an arrangement effectively subsidises the foreign producers by allowing them to charge a higher price than they would have been prepared to accept. Furthermore, although domestic producers are encouraged to produce more, the protection offered to them is likely to lead to X-inefficiency and weak attitudes towards competition.

There are a number of examples of such agreements, especially in the textile industry. For example, for a long time the USA and China had long-standing agreements on quotas for a range of textile products. Ninety-one such quotas expired at the end of 2004 as part of China's accession to the World Trade Organization. As you might expect, this led to extensive lobbying by producers in the USA, especially during the run-up to the 2004 presidential election. Trade unions in the USA supported the producers, arguing that 350,000 jobs had been lost since the expiry of earlier quota agreements in 2002. In the case of three of these earlier agreements, some restraint had been reinstated for bras, dressing gowns and knitted fabrics. Producers in other countries, such as Sri Lanka, Bangladesh, Nepal, Indonesia, Morocco, Tunisia and Turkey, were lobbying for the quotas to remain, regarding China as a major potential competitor. However, for the USA at least, it can be argued that the removal of the quotas would allow domestic consumers to benefit from lower prices, and would allow US textile workers to be released for employment in higher-productivity sectors, where the USA maintains a competitive advantage.

Similar problems arose in connection with the dismantling of quotas for Chinese textile products being imported into Europe. This led to problems in 2005 when warehouses full of fashion products were prohibited from entry into the EU following a late agreement to delay the dismantling of the quotas.

There are other ways in which trade can be hampered, one example being the use of what are known as **non-tariff barriers (NTBs)**. These often comprise rules and regulations that control the standard of products that can be sold in a country. It is difficult to quantify the importance of such measures, but the frequency with which disputes arise at the **World Trade Organization (WTO)** suggests that they have had significant effects on trade.

Exercise 16.4

Evaluate the case for and against protectionism. You may find it helpful to review some of the trade disputes that have been raised recently at the World Trade Organization (WTO), which has a role as international arbitrator for complaints about the conduct of international trade. You will find information about these at the WTO website (www.wto.org).

Summary

➤ There has often been a tendency for governments to intervene to inhibit trade by the use of protectionist measures.

➤ Such measures include tariffs, quotas and the imposition of regulations.

➤ The use of such measures entails the sacrifice of potential gains from trade, but there may be circumstances in which countries may feel justified in using them.

➤ The validity of these arguments is open to debate.

Chapter 17
Economic integration

The economic landscape of Europe since the Second World War has been shaped by the move towards ever-closer economic integration. The UK has been part of this, although at times a seemingly reluctant participant. The economic arguments in favour of closer economic integration are partly based on notions of comparative advantage and the potential gains of allowing freer trade. However, there are other pertinent issues to be taken into consideration in evaluating the costs and benefits of closer integration. Such integration also has political ramifications that can affect an individual country's attitude towards its potential partners. Two major steps towards economic integration have taken place in the period since 1990. On 1 January 1993, the Single European Market (SEM) came into operation. Then, on 1 January 2002, 12 European countries adopted the euro as their common currency. The expansion of the SEM in 2004 to incorporate ten new members was a further significant development; two further countries joined in 2007. This chapter highlights these developments and assesses their impact on the economic performance of the UK, referring to relevant areas of economic analysis that help in analysing the costs and benefits of closer economic integration.

Learning outcomes

After studying this chapter, you should:
- ➤ be aware of the different forms that economic integration may take: free trade areas, customs unions, common markets and economic and monetary union
- ➤ know the features of these alternative forms of integration and understand the distinction between them
- ➤ be able to explain why integration does not always operate as economic analysis suggests
- ➤ be familiar with the chronology of moves towards closer European integration
- ➤ appreciate the position of Europe in the global economy
- ➤ understand the significance of the SEM
- ➤ evaluate the costs and benefits of membership of a single currency area
- ➤ be aware of the role and effectiveness of monetary and fiscal policy within a single currency area
- ➤ be able to evaluate the arguments for and against the UK joining the Eurozone

Economic integration

Economies are becoming more interdependent over time. One aspect of this process deserves close attention, namely the growing formal integration of economies in regional groupings. This has been a gradual process, but it has accelerated as the technology of transport and communications has been transformed and as markets have been deregulated — especially financial markets; a process which has allowed the increased free movement of financial capital between countries.

There are many examples of such regional trade agreements. The European Union is perhaps one of the most prominent — and one of the furthest advanced — but there are also examples in the Americas (NAFTA, MERCOSUR), Asia (ASEAN, APEC), Africa (COMESA) and elsewhere. These agreements are at varying stages in the integration process. In addition, there has been a proliferation of regional trade agreements, and the World Trade Organization has estimated that there are some 400 agreements that are scheduled to be implemented by 2010. This may partly reflect the slow progress made in the latest round of trade negotiations — the Doha Development Agenda. There has been much debate as to whether these agreements are stepping stones to further global cooperation, or whether they may turn out to be obstacles to that process.

The process of regional trade integration entails four successive stages, under which countries link their economies more closely together. The stages are as follows:

➤ Free trade area
➤ Customs union
➤ Common market
➤ Economic and monetary union

These successive stages reflect different degrees of closeness. The underlying motivation for integration is to allow trading partners to take advantage of the potential gains from international trade, as illustrated by the law of comparative advantage. By reducing the barriers to trade, this specialisation can be encouraged, and there should be potential gains from the process. In practice, there may be other economic and political forces at work that affect the nature of the gains, and the extent to which integration will be possible — and beneficial.

Free trade areas

The first level of integration is the formation of a so-called **free trade area**. Before the UK joined the European Community in 1973, it was part of the European Free Trade Area (EFTA), together with other countries in Europe that had not joined the Community. The original countries were Austria, Denmark, Norway, Portugal, Sweden, Switzerland and the UK. Finland, Iceland and Liechtenstein joined later, but some EFTA members left in order to join the EU, leaving just Iceland, Liechtenstein, Norway and Switzerland as members of EFTA in the first years of the twenty-first century.

The notion of a free trade area is that countries within the area agree to remove internal tariff and quota restrictions on trade between them, while still allowing member countries to impose their own pattern of tariffs and quotas on non-members. The lack of a common external tariff wall may cause problems within the member countries. If one country has lower tariffs than the rest, the natural tendency will be for imports into the area to be channelled through that country, with goods then being resold to other member countries. This may distort the pattern of trade and cause unnecessary transaction costs associated with trading activity. It is worth noting that free trade areas are normally concerned with enabling free trade in goods and do not cover the movement of labour.

In spite of these problems, a free trade area does allow member countries to increase their degree of specialisation, and may bring gains. EFTA is not the only example of such an arrangement.

> **Key term**
>
> **free trade area:** a group of countries that agree to remove tariffs, quotas and other restrictions on trade between the member countries, but have no agreement on a common barrier against non-members

EFTA ministerial meeting in Lugarno, Switzerland, 2008

In Southeast Asia, the Association of South-East Asian Nations (ASEAN) began to create a free trade area in 1993. This involved six nations (Brunei, Indonesia, Malaysia, the Philippines, Singapore and Thailand). The group was later expanded to include Cambodia, Laos, Myanmar and Vietnam. Progress towards eliminating tariffs in this group has been relatively slow, but intense competition from the rapidly growing Chinese economy provides a strong motivation for accelerating the process.

Another major trading group operating a free trade area is the North American Free Trade Association (NAFTA), which covers the USA, Canada and Mexico. The agreement was signed in 1992 and launched in 1994, and has led to an expansion of trade between those countries. Unlike in Europe, there is as yet no stated intention that NAFTA should evolve into anything more than a free trade area.

Exercise 17.1

Figure 16.12 showed the effects of a tariff.

If a country decides to *remove* the tariff, identify the effects on:

a consumers of the good

b producers of the good

c the government

Customs unions

A **customs union** is one notch up from a free trade area, in the sense that in addition to eliminating tariffs and quotas between the member nations, a common external tariff wall is set up against non-member nations. Again, the prime reason for establishing a customs union is to encourage trade between the member nations.

customs union: a group of countries that agree to remove restrictions on trade between the member countries, and set a common set of restrictions (including tariffs) against non-member states

trade creation: the replacement of more expensive domestic production or imports with cheaper output from a partner within the trading bloc

Such increased trade is beneficial when there is **trade creation**. This is where the formation of the customs union allows countries to specialise more, and thus to exploit their comparative advantage. The larger market for the goods means that more economies of scale may be available, and the lower prices that result generate additional trade between the member nations. These lower prices arise partly from the exploitation of comparative advantage, but also from the removal of tariffs between the member nations.

Figure 17.1 illustrates the effects of trade creation. It shows the demand and supply of a good in a certain country that joins a customs union. Before joining the union, the price of the good is T, which includes a tariff element. Domestic demand is D_0, of which S_0 comes from domestic producers, and the remainder is imported. When the country joins the customs union, the tariff is removed and the domestic price falls to P. Consumers benefit from additional consumer surplus, given by the area $PTBG$.

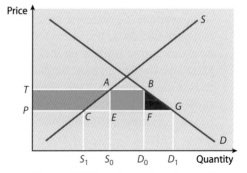

Figure 17.1 The effects of trade creation

However, notice that not all of this is pure gain to the country. The area $PTAC$ was formerly part of producer surplus, so there has been a redistribution from domestic firms to consumers. $ABFE$ was formerly tariff revenue collected by the government, so this represents effectively a redistribution from government to consumers. The area ACE is a net gain for the country, as this represents resources that were previously used up in the production of the good, but which can now be used for other purposes. The area BFG also represents a welfare gain to the country.

However, it is also important to be aware that becoming a member of a customs union may alter the pattern of trading relationships. A country that is part of a customs union will be more inclined to trade with other members of the union because of the agreement between them, and because of the absence of internal tariffs. However, given the common external tariff, it is quite possible that members of the union are not the most efficient producers on the global stage. So there may be a situation of **trade diversion**. This occurs where a member country of a customs union imports goods from other members *instead* of from more efficient producers elsewhere in the world. This may mean that there is no net increase in trade, but simply a diversion from an external source to a new source within the union. In this situation, there are not necessarily the same gains from trade to be made.

Key *term*

trade diversion:
the replacement of cheaper imported goods by goods from a less efficient trading partner within a bloc

Figure 17.2 helps to show the effects of trade diversion. Here, D represents the demand curve for a commodity that is initially imported from a country outside the customs union. It is assumed that the supply of the good from the non-member is perfectly elastic, as shown by S_n. However, the importing country imposes a tariff of the amount T, so the quantity imported is given by Q_n, and the price charged is $P_n + T$.

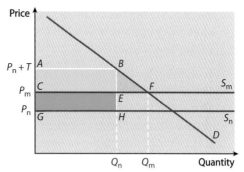

Figure 17.2 *The effects of trade diversion*

After the importing country joins the customs union, the tariff is removed, but the good is now imported from a less efficient producer within the union. The supply from this member country is assumed to be elastic at S_m, so the new price is P_m and the quantity is Q_m.

In examining the welfare effects, there are two issues to consider. First, notice that consumer surplus has increased by the area *ABFC*. However, this is not pure gain to the economy because, in the original position, the government was collecting tariff revenue of the amount *ABHG*. In other words, the increase in consumer surplus comes partly as a pure gain (the triangle *BFE*), but partly at the expense of the government (*ABEC*). This is not all, because the area *CEHG* was also formerly part of tariff revenue, but now is a payment by domestic consumers to producers in the other (member) country. This means that whether the country is better or worse off depends upon the relative size of the areas *BFE* (which is a gain) and *CEHG* (which is a loss).

There are some further disadvantages of customs unions. Certainly, the transactions costs involved in administering the union cannot be ignored, and where there are traditional rivalries between nations there may be political sensitivities to overcome. This may impede the free working of the union, especially if some member nations are more committed to the union than others, or if some countries have close ties with non-member states.

It is also possible that a geographical concentration of economic activity will emerge over time within the union. This may result where firms want to locate near the centre of the area in order to minimise transportation costs. Alternatively, it may be that all firms will want to locate near the richest part of the market. Over time, this could mean that firms tend to concentrate in certain geographical areas, while the countries that are more remote, or which have smaller populations or lower average incomes, become peripheral to the centre of activity. In other words, over time, there may be growing inequality between regions within the union.

These disadvantages must be balanced against the benefits. For example, it may be that it is the smaller countries in the union that have the most to gain from tapping economies of scale that would not be accessible to them if they were confined to selling only within their domestic markets.

In addition to these internal economies of scale, there may be external economies of scale that emerge over time as the transport and communications infrastructure within the union improves. Furthermore, opening up domestic markets to more intense competition may induce efficiency gains, as firms will only be able to survive in the face of international competition by adopting best practice techniques and technologies. Indeed, another advantage of a customs union is that technology may be disseminated amongst firms operating within the union.

Common markets

It may be that the countries within a customs union wish to move to the next stage of integration, by extending the degree of cooperation between the member nations. A **common market** adds to the features of a customs union by harmonising some aspects of the economic environment between them. In a pure common market, this would entail adopting common tax rates across the member states, and a common framework for the laws and regulations that provide the environment for production, employment and trade. A common market would also allow for the

 Key *term*

common market: a set of trading arrangements in which a group of countries remove barriers to trade among them, adopt a common set of barriers against external trade, establish common tax rates and laws regulating economic activity, allow free movement of factors of production between members and have common public sector procurement policies

free movement of factors of production between the member nations, especially in terms of labour and capital (land is less mobile by its nature!). Given the importance of the public sector in a modern economy, a common market would also set common procurement policies across member governments, so that individual governments did not favour their own domestic firms when purchasing goods and services. The Single European Market (discussed below) has encompassed most of

these features, although tax rates have not been harmonised across the countries that are included.

Economic and monetary union

Moving beyond a common market, there is the prospect of full **economic and monetary union**. This entails taking the additional step of adopting fixed exchange rates between the member states. This in turn requires member states to follow a common monetary policy, and it is also seen as desirable to harmonise other aspects of macroeconomic policy across the union.

 term

economic and monetary union: a set of trading arrangements the same as for a common market, but in addition having fixed exchange rates between the member countries and a common monetary policy

The adoption of fixed exchange rates is a contentious aspect of proposals for economic and monetary union. With fixed exchange rates, governments are no longer able to use monetary policy for internal domestic purposes. This is because monetary variables become subservient to the need to maintain the exchange rate, and it is not possible to set independent targets for the rate of interest or money supply if the government has to maintain the value of the currency on the foreign exchange market. This is all very well if all countries in the union are following a similar economic cycle, but if one country becomes poorly synchronised with the others, there may be major problems.

For example, it could be that the union as a whole is enjoying a boom, and setting interest rates accordingly. For an individual member country suffering a recession, this could mean deepening and prolonging the recession, as it would not be possible to relax interest rates in order to allow aggregate demand to recover.

A successful economic and monetary union therefore requires careful policy coordination across the member nations. Notice that economic and monetary union involves fixed exchange rates between the member countries, but does not necessarily entail the adoption of a common currency, although this may follow at some stage.

Structural change

A feature that all of these forms of integration have in common is that they involve the removal of barriers to trade amongst member countries. It is important to be aware that this will not be perceived as a good thing by all the parties involved. In order to benefit from increased specialisation and trade, countries need to allow the pattern of their production to change. The benefits to the expanding sectors are apparent, but it is also the case that industries that formerly enjoyed protection from competition will become exposed to competition, and will need to decline in order to allow resources to be transferred into the expanding sectors. This can be a painful process for firms that need to close down, or move into new markets,

and for workers who may need to undergo retraining before they are ready for employment in the newly expanding parts of the economy.

An especially contentious area of debate in the UK concerns the structural change that has taken place in recent decades, in which manufacturing activity has declined and financial services have expanded. This seems to reflect the changing pattern of the UK's comparative advantage, in which banking, finance and insurance have become a major strength of the economy, whereas the manufacturing sector has found it more difficult to compete with the host of new entrants into this market from elsewhere in the world.

Exercise 17.2

Find out how the structure of employment in the UK has changed in the last 15–20 years. Discuss whether the process of deindustrialisation that has taken place will benefit the economy in the long run.

Summary

➤ Economic integration can take a variety of forms, of differing degrees of closeness.

➤ A free trade area is where a group of countries agree to remove restrictions on trade between them, but without having a common external tariff.

➤ A customs union is a free trade area with an agreed common set of restrictions on trade with non-members.

➤ A customs union can entail trade creation, in which member countries benefit from increased trade and specialisation.

➤ However, there may also be trade diversion, in which countries divert their trading activity from external trade partners to countries within the union.

➤ Trade diversion does not always bring gains, as the producers within the union are not necessarily more efficient than external producers.

➤ A common market is a customs union in which the member countries also agree to harmonise their policies in a number of key respects.

➤ Economic and monetary union entails fixed exchange rates between member countries, but not necessarily agreement to adopt a common currency.

The European Union

The European Union is one of the most prominent examples of regional trade integration, and has progressed further than most in evolving towards economic and monetary integration. Figure 17.3 shows the population size of EU member countries in 2010, and the dates at which they joined.

Bulgaria and Romania were judged not to be ready to join in 2004, but joined in 2007; negotiations with Turkey began in 2005, but quickly ran into problems. If Turkey were to join, this would add a massive 76 million citizens to the EU.

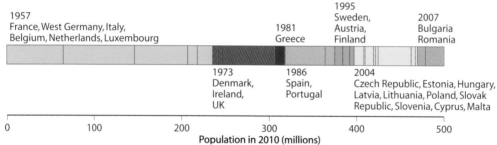

1957
France, West Germany, Italy,
Belgium, Netherlands, Luxembourg

1981
Greece

1995
Sweden,
Austria,
Finland

2007
Bulgaria
Romania

1973
Denmark,
Ireland,
UK

1986
Spain,
Portugal

2004
Czech Republic, Estonia, Hungary,
Latvia, Lithuania, Poland, Slovak
Republic, Slovenia, Cyprus, Malta

0   100   200   300   400   500

Population in 2010 (millions)

Figure 17.3 *Population of selected countries, 2010*

Source: data from the *World Development Report*, 2012.

Notice that the 15 pre-2004 member countries of the EU (the 'EU15') already contained more people than the USA; the combined population of the EU27 member states in 2010 was 501 million, compared with 310 million in the USA.

The Single European Market (SEM)

From the moment of formation of the European Economic Community (EEC) in 1957, the member countries began working towards the creation of a single market in which there would be free movement of goods, services, people and capital. In other words, the idea was to create a *common market* in which there would be no barriers to trade. The EEC was a *customs union* in which internal tariffs and non-tariff barriers were to be removed and a common tariff was to be set against the rest of the world.

A package of measures that came into effect in January 1993 might be seen as the final stages in the evolution of the SEM. The key measures were the removal (or reduction) of border controls and the winding down of non-tariff barriers to trade within the EU. In this way, physical, technical and fiscal barriers were removed. It has also become increasingly easy for people to move around within the EU, with passport and customs checks being abolished at most internal borders. Associated with these measures were a number of expected benefits.

Transaction costs

Tariff barriers between EU countries were abolished under the Treaty of Rome, but a range of non-tariff barriers had built up over the years as countries sought to protect domestic employment. It was expected that the removal of these obstacles to trade, combined with the removal of border controls, would reduce the costs of trade within the EU. However, it is difficult to gauge the significance of these transaction cost savings, as it is not easy to quantify them.

The member countries of the EU have been working towards establishing a common market with no barriers to trade

© EUROPEAN COMMUNITIES

Economies of scale

As trade increases, firms will find that they are operating in a larger market. This should allow them to exploit more fully the economies of large-scale production. From society's point of view, this should lead to a more efficient use of resources, as long as the resulting trade creation effects are stronger than any trade diversion that may take place.

It seems that the nature of technological change in recent years has favoured the growth of large-scale enterprises. Improved transport and communications have contributed to this process. The SEM has enabled firms in Europe to take advantage of these developments.

Intensified competition

Firms will find that they are facing more intense competition within that larger market from firms in other parts of the EU. This then brings up the same arguments that are used to justify privatisation — that intensified competition will cause firms or their managers to seek more efficient production techniques, perhaps through the elimination of X-inefficiencies. This again is beneficial for society as a whole.

From the perspective of individual countries, there has been a divergence of views concerning the large firms that have been created through mergers and acquisitions. In some countries, large firms have been seen as 'national champions'. These have been protected (or even subsidised) by domestic governments, based on the argument that they will then be better prepared to compete in the broader European market. Elsewhere, governments have taken the view that the only way to ensure that domestic firms are lean enough to be competitive in overseas markets is to face intense competition at home, as an inducement to efficiency.

Who gains most from the SEM?

As trade within Europe becomes freer, two groups of countries stand to gain the most. First, the pattern of comparative advantage between countries will be important. Many EU countries are advanced industrial nations, where labour is expensive relative to capital. These countries tend to specialise in manufacturing or capital-intensive service activities, and already have fairly similar structures. It is thus possible that the relatively labour-abundant countries of southern Europe may gain more from closer integration and an expansion of trade. This is because they have a pattern of comparative advantage that is significantly different from existing members. This diversity was reinforced by the new entrants who joined in May 2004.

Second, if the main effect of integration is to remove barriers to trade, the countries with the most to gain may be those that begin with relatively high barriers.

Figure 17.4 shows growth rates in the countries in 2001–02, just before the enlargement of 2004. This shows that the joining members were, on the whole, enjoying more rapid economic growth than the EU15 countries. The enlargement thus may have the effect of introducing new *dynamic economies*, and this may have spillover effects for the other member nations.

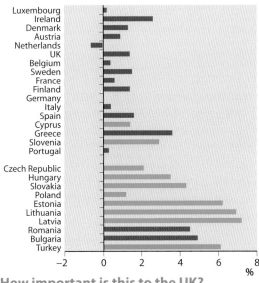

Figure 17.4 *Growth of GDP per capita, EU28, 2001–02*

Note: no data available for Malta.

Source: *World Development Report*, 2003.

How important is this to the UK?

An important piece of background information is that, over the years, UK trade has become increasingly focused on Europe. This means that the UK depends heavily on trade with other countries in the EU, so successful economic performance cannot be seen in isolation from events in the broader market.

Summary

➤ The Single Market package came into effect at the beginning of 1993, freeing up trade between participating countries and winding down non-tariff barriers.

➤ This was expected to encourage trade by lowering transaction costs, enabling firms to reap economies of scale, and enhancing efficiency by stimulating competition between European firms.

Exercise 17.3

Explain why it might be the relatively labour-intensive countries of southern Europe — and the countries of eastern Europe and the Baltic that joined in 2004 and 2007 — that stand to gain most from the SEM.

The single currency area

The establishment of the SEM was seen by some as an end in itself, but others regarded it as a step towards full monetary integration, in which all member states would adopt a single currency, thereby reducing the transaction costs of international trade even more. However, full monetary union and the adoption of a common currency is about much more than transaction costs and has raised considerable debate, not least because of the political dimension. Critics of closer integration are concerned about

the loss of sovereignty by individual countries. This concern is partly an economic one, focusing on the loss of separate currencies and (perhaps more significantly) the loss of control over national economic policy.

The European Monetary System

The foundations for monetary union began to be laid down in 1979, with the launch of the European Monetary System (EMS). One aspect of the EMS was the Exchange Rate Mechanism (ERM), which can be seen as a precursor of the single currency. Those countries that chose to opt into the ERM agreed to maintain their exchange rates within a band of plus or minus 2.25% against the average of their currencies — known as the European Currency Unit (ECU). The UK remained outside the ERM except for a brief flirtation between September 1990 and September 1992. During this period, the UK was operating within a slightly wider (6%) band.

During the period of the EMS/ERM, it was recognised that occasional realignment of currencies might be needed, and in fact there were 11 realignments between 1979 and 1987. However, the conditions under which such realignments were permitted were gradually tightened, so that they became less frequent as time went by.

Another key feature of the EMS period was the removal of capital controls. During the early part of this period, most of the member nations restricted the movement of financial capital across borders. This gave them some scope for using monetary policy independently of other countries. However, it was agreed that such capital controls would be phased out.

The Delors Plan, issued in 1989, set out proposals for creating European economic and monetary union (EMU), together with plans for a single currency and a European central bank. It was crucial to establish a European central bank because, with a single currency, a central bank is needed to administer monetary policy throughout the EU.

Treaty of Maastricht

The next major step was the Maastricht Treaty, which created the European Union (EU). This treaty encompassed not only economic issues, such as the introduction of the single currency, but also aspects of social policy, steps towards creating a common foreign, security and defence policy, and the development of a notion of European 'citizenship'.

It was considered that, if a single currency was to be established, the participating nations would need to have converged in their economic characteristics. If the countries were too diverse in their economic conditions, the transition to a single currency would be costly. For example, if they had very different inflation rates, interest rates or levels of outstanding government debt, the tensions of union might be too great to sustain. Strong countries would be dragged down, and weak countries would be unable to cope. The Maastricht Treaty therefore set out the *convergence criteria* by which countries would be eligible to join the single currency area. These criteria covered aspects of both monetary and fiscal policy.

The signing of the Maastricht Treaty

Monetary policy

This is obviously important, as monetary union entails the centralisation of monetary policy within the EU. If there is to be a single currency and a single central bank to control interest rates or money supply, the monetary conditions of the economies concerned need to be reasonably close before union takes place. It was thus important to evaluate whether countries were sufficiently close to be able to join with minimal tension.

Inflation

Could countries with widely different inflation rates successfully join in a monetary union? One view is that it would be unreasonable to expect a country with 10% or 20% inflation to join a monetary union along with a country experiencing inflation at just 1%. An alternative view is that it is equally unreasonable to expect a country to cure its inflation before joining a union when one of the alleged benefits of joining is that it will cure inflation by enforcing financial discipline and removing discretion over monetary policy from individual states. However, the first criterion specified by the treaty was that countries joining the union should be experiencing low and similar inflation rates – defined as inflation no more than 1.5% above the average of the three countries in the EMS with the lowest rate.

Interest and exchange rates

Given that financial capital tends to follow high interest rates, it is argued that diversity of interest rates before union may be undesirable, as this would imply instability of capital movements. Similarly, it has been argued that a period of exchange rate stability before union would be some indication that countries have been following mutually consistent policies, and would indicate that union is plausible.

The criteria set out in the treaty required that long-term interest rates be no more than 2% above the average of the three EMS countries with the lowest rate, and that each joining country should have been in the narrow band of the ERM for a period of 2 years without the need for realignment.

Fiscal policy

Should there also be conformity in fiscal stance between countries? Would there be severe problems if countries embarked upon union and policy coordination in conditions in which unemployment rates differed markedly? These are separate but related questions. If unemployment is high, this will be connected (via social security payments) with the fiscal stance adopted by the government — as judged in terms of the government budget deficit.

The reason why unemployment rates are relevant is that there may need to be fiscal transfers between member states in order to reduce the differentials. This will clearly be politically significant in the context of a monetary union, and is an issue that will affect the long-term viability of the union. However, although unemployment rates are potentially important for this reason, the convergence criteria did not refer to unemployment directly. Instead, the criteria included a reference to fiscal policy. In practice, the divergence in unemployment rates was substantial.

Two areas are critical in judging the distance between countries in terms of fiscal policy. First, there is the question of the short-term fiscal stance, which can be measured by the budget deficit. Second, it is important to consider some indication of a longer-term commitment to stability in fiscal policy, in terms of achieving sustainable levels of outstanding government debt. Thus, the treaty required that the budget deficit be no larger than 3% of GDP, and that the national debt be no more than 60% of GDP.

Economic and monetary union

The final stage of the transition towards the single currency was European Economic and Monetary Union (EMU). Under EMU, exchange rates between participating countries were permanently locked together: in other words, no further realignments were allowed. Furthermore, the financial markets of the countries were integrated, with the European Central Bank setting a common interest rate across the union. This was achieved in 1999.

Formation of the euro area

In the event, 11 countries were judged to have met the Maastricht criteria (Belgium, Germany, Spain, France, Ireland, Italy, Luxembourg, the Netherlands, Austria, Portugal and Finland). Together with Greece, these countries formed the single currency area, which came into operation on 1 January 2002. Slovenia joined the Eurozone in 2007, followed by Cyprus and Malta in 2008, Slovakia in 2009 and Estonia in 2011.

Figure 17.5 shows how interest rates in some of the Eurozone countries moved from 1977 (2 years before the formation of the EMS) until the first year of the euro. The graph shows interest rates in each country as an index, with the average of the original Eurozone countries at 100. You can see that, although there is some evidence that some of the countries were converging in the run-up to monetary union, there seems to have been little historical tendency for interest rates to move together. This is especially the case for Italy, which at times seemed to have followed opposite paths to the others. Germany showed consistently lower interest rates than most other

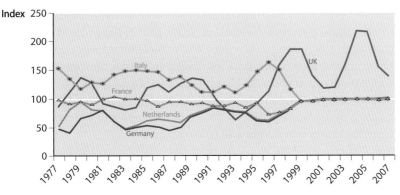

Figure 17.5 *Interest rates in Europe, 1977–2007 (EU12 = 100)*

Source: European Commission.

countries. From 1999, however, convergence was forced under EMU, which meant an especially rapid adjustment for Italy. The graph also reveals how a different time path of interest rates was followed by the UK.

Costs and benefits of a single currency

Some of the arguments for and against a single currency area such as the Eurozone are similar to those used in evaluating a fixed exchange rate system against a flexible one. This is because a common currency is effectively creating an area in which exchange rates between member nations are fixed for ever, even if that common currency varies relative to the rest of the world. The question of whether such an arrangement is beneficial overall for the member states rests on an evaluation of the benefits and costs of joining together. An *optimal currency area* occurs when a group of countries are better off with a single currency.

Benefits

The main benefits of a single currency area come in the form of a *monetary efficiency gain*, which has the effect of encouraging more trade between member countries. The hope is that this will bring further gains from exploiting comparative advantage between countries and enabling firms to reap the benefits of economies of scale.

The efficiency gain comes from two main sources. First, there are gains from reducing *transaction costs*, if there is no longer the need to convert from one currency into another. Second, there are gains from the *reduction in uncertainty*, in the sense that there is no longer a need to forecast future movements in exchange rates – at least between participating countries. This is similar to the gains from a fixed exchange rate system, but it goes further, as there is no longer a risk of occasional devaluation or revaluation of currencies.

The extent to which these gains are significant will depend upon the degree of integration between the participating nations. If most of the trade that takes place is between the participants, the gains will clearly be much more significant than if member nations are also trading extensively with countries outside the single currency area.

Costs

The costs come in the conduct and effectiveness of policy. Within the single currency area, individual countries can no longer have recourse to monetary policy in order to stabilise the macro economy. As with the fixed exchange rate system, one key question then is how well individual economies are able to adjust to external shocks. Thus, it is important for each economy to have flexibility. In addition, individual countries have to be aware that, once in the single currency area, it is impossible to use monetary policy to smooth out fluctuations in output and employment.

In this context, it is very important that the economic cycles of participating economies are well synchronised. If one economy is out of phase with the rest, it may find itself facing an inappropriate policy situation. For example, suppose that most of the countries within the Eurozone are in the boom phase of the economic cycle, and are wanting to raise the interest rate in order to control aggregate demand: if one country within the zone is in recession, then the last thing it will want is rising interest rates, as this will deepen the recession and delay recovery. These arguments came to the fore during the recession of the late 2000s.

National currencies were replaced in the Eurozone from January 1999 by the euro

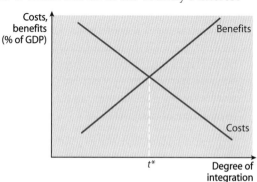

Evaluation

Paul Krugman has suggested a helpful way of using cost–benefit analysis to evaluate these aspects of a single currency area. He argues that both the costs and the benefits from a single currency area will vary with the degree to which member countries are integrated. Thus the benefits from joining such a currency area would rise as the closeness of integration increased, whereas the costs would fall.

Figure 17.6 illustrates the balance between costs and benefits. For countries that are not very closely integrated (that is, if 'integration' is less than t^*), the costs from joining the union exceed the benefits, so it would not be in the country's interest to join. However, as the degree of integration increases, so the benefits increase, and the costs decrease, so for any country beyond t^*, the benefits exceed the costs, and it is thus worth joining.

For an individual country considering whether or not to join the euro area, a first step is to reach a judgement on whether the country is to the left or to the right of t^*. There may be other issues to consider in addition to the

Figure 17.6 *Costs and benefits of a single currency area*

costs and benefits, but unless the country has at least reached t^*, it could be argued that entry into the union should not be considered.

One way of viewing the situation is that the costs are mainly macroeconomic, but the benefits are microeconomic. This complicates the evaluation process. Some research published in 2006 argued that most of the boost to trade within the euro area occurred during the initial period, and would not continue to build up over time. It was also suggested that the EU countries that decided not to join the euro (Britain, Sweden and Denmark) gained almost as much as the countries that had joined. Nonetheless, it is important to view the euro area from the perspective of possible UK entry.

Exercise 17.4

Use an *AD/AS* diagram to analyse the problems that could arise if a country that is part of a single currency area enters a period of recession at a time when other countries in the union are in a boom.

The UK and the euro

The UK government's policy stance on membership of the euro was set out by the chancellor of the exchequer in October 1997 after only a few months of the new Labour government. This stance was essentially that, while in principle the government was in favour of UK membership, it would be prepared to enter only at a time when the economic conditions were right. Table 17.1 sets out the five economic tests that the chancellor specified as his conditions for deciding whether a case can be made for entry. You will see that these go beyond looking at the simple cost–benefit analysis, although clearly some of the criteria do relate to the closeness of integration, especially in terms of convergence.

	Test	Explanation
1	Convergence	Are economic cycles and economic structures compatible, so that UK citizens and others could live comfortably with euro interest rates on a permanent basis?
2	Flexibility	If problems emerge, is there sufficient flexibility to deal with them?
3	Investment	Would joining EMU create better conditions for firms making long-term decisions to invest in the UK?
4	Financial services	What impact would entry into EMU have on the competitive position of the UK's financial services industry, particularly the City's wholesale markets?
5	Employment	Will joining EMU promote higher growth, stability and a lasting increase in jobs?

Table 17.1 *The chancellor's five tests*
Source: H. M. Treasury.

Convergence
Sustainable convergence is seen to be crucial if the UK is to be successful within the euro area. What sort of evidence should be looked for in order to judge whether the UK's economic cycle is converging on Europe? The chancellor could look at fluctuations in GDP, to see whether the phase of GDP growth in the UK is in tune with the rest of

Europe. However, if the concern is with interest rates because of their importance with respect to policy, it may make sense to look at interest rates directly.

Figure 17.5 showed that UK interest rates followed quite a different path to those of countries in the Eurozone. Figure 17.7 shows the growth rates of GDP for France, Germany, the UK and the USA. Although there is perhaps more similarity evident towards the end of this period, there are certainly times when growth rates have diverged significantly, which would have created problems in the context of EMU. For example, look at Germany in the early 1990s.

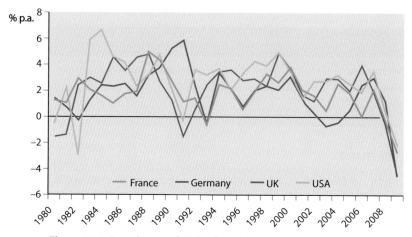

Figure 17.7 *Growth rates of GDP, selected countries, 1980–2009*

Another aspect of this issue that makes the convergence test especially important for the UK is the nature of the housing market. A larger proportion of home owners in the UK hold mortgages on a variable interest rate basis than their counterparts elsewhere in Europe, where fixed-rate mortgages are more common. This makes interest rates a particularly sensitive issue.

It is also argued that, in any approach to entry, the exchange rate is critical. The brief experience of the UK trying to tie its currency to the Exchange Rate Mechanism in the early 1990s illustrates the dangers of joining with the exchange rate at too high a level, and this is a mistake that the Treasury does not want to repeat.

Flexibility

The convergence test is concerned with whether the UK's economic cycle is sufficiently synchronised with the Eurozone. The flexibility test is about what would happen if this were not the case, or if the UK fell out of line. In other words, if the UK were to be out of phase, would the economy be sufficiently flexible to be able to get back into line in the absence of an independent monetary policy? It is about resilience.

It is quite difficult to measure flexibility in this sense, and there is no simple indicator that gives a ready judgement about whether an economy is sufficiently flexible to deal with situations that may or may not occur.

The key issues here concern the flexibility of markets, and the extent to which fiscal policy can be activated in order to help stabilise the economy, should that be deemed necessary. One danger is that inflation could become more variable if the UK joins the euro, as happened to Ireland. This is because at present the exchange rate is able to fluctuate in order to accommodate differences between national economies.

In the Treasury's assessment of the tests published in June 2003, the flexibility test was said to have been failed. Although the UK labour market was found to be relatively flexible, the Treasury identified a number of areas needing improvement. In particular, it argued that regional pay differentials were insufficient to reflect differences between the regions in the demand and supply of labour, and that there was a significant skills gap between the UK and the Eurozone members. It was also difficult to judge whether the UK tax system could be sufficiently flexible to allow rapid stabilisation. In these circumstances, it is hard to say whether or not any convergence would be sustainable.

Investment

The issue for investment revolves around the incentives for firms to invest in the UK. There are two aspects to this. First, there is the question of UK-based firms, and whether they would find membership of the Eurozone conducive to investment. Second, there is the question of overseas firms, and the conditions under which they would be prepared to invest in the UK.

The question of whether firms would be prepared to invest more if the UK were part of the Eurozone depends in part on the success of the economy in meeting the convergence and flexibility tests. If firms have high expectations about the future, they will be more prepared to invest, so if they see the UK as thriving within the euro area, this will be beneficial.

An additional consideration concerns the reduction in foreign exchange risk within the single currency area. This might encourage investment by reducing the risk premium required by firms considering investment.

Inward foreign direct investment (FDI) may depend on a number of factors. In particular, there may be US or Japanese firms looking to gain a foothold in Europe – will they choose the UK? Figure 17.8 shows annual FDI into the UK between 1965 and 2010,

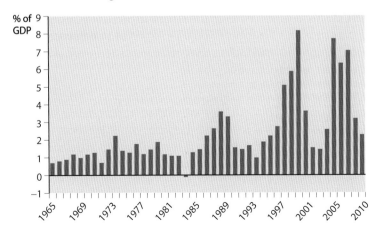

Figure 17.8 *Inward foreign direct investment in the UK, 1965–2010*

Source: ONS.

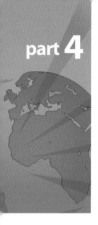

expressed as a percentage of GDP. A striking feature of the graph is the way that FDI appeared to boom towards the end of the 1990s, only to fall back quite dramatically in 2001–03. It is important to be a little careful in interpreting this pattern. It might be tempting to argue that the launching of the euro area at the beginning of 2002 may have contributed to the fall, with the UK becoming less attractive as a destination for FDI because of its decision not to join the euro. However, it is equally likely that the fall reflected the global reduction in flows of FDI following the 9/11 terrorist attacks in the USA. The graph shows that there was a recovery of inward FDI to the UK after 2004, only to fall again as the financial recession hit the global economy. The fact that there are often multiple factors influencing economic decisions is a common problem in economics.

Financial services

The fourth test concerns financial services. In the June 2003 Treasury analysis, this was the only test that the UK economy was judged to have passed. The financial services sector was singled out for a special mention because of its importance in the structure of the UK economy. The UK is seen to have a significant comparative advantage in wholesale financial services, and it was accepted that the City is the pre-eminent financial centre in Europe. There was thus a concern that becoming part of the single currency area would damage the competitiveness of this sector.

The evidence here seems to suggest that the UK financial sector benefits from EMU even with the UK being outside the euro area, but that it would gain even more if the UK were to join. Financial services have become a significant item in the balance of payments, with a positive balance of more than £12 billion in 2004. This is a substantial share of the overall surplus in trade in services, which was about £14.6 billion. If the UK were a full member of the single currency area, it is likely that this balance would be even more positive.

Growth, stability and employment

The final test relates to whether becoming part of the Eurozone would promote higher growth, stability and a lasting increase in jobs in the UK. This might be interpreted as an overall assessment of the potential success of the single currency in the long run. However, this test cannot be divorced from the others. In particular, sustainable convergence (i.e. convergence plus flexibility) would be expected to influence firms' expectations about the future and could affect their willingness to invest, which in turn would contribute to the rate of economic growth.

Figure 17.9 provides some context, showing rates of unemployment in 2001 and 2010 in a range of European countries. The countries are ranked in descending order of their unemployment rates in 2010. The relativities between countries seem to have altered quite a lot over this period, with the increase in unemployment in Ireland being especially evident. Italy and Germany are the only countries where unemployment was lower in 2010 than it had been in 2001.

OCR A2 Economics

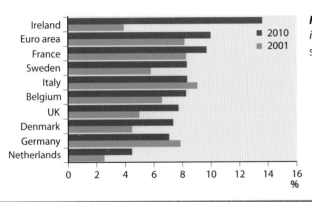

Figure 17.9 Unemployment in Europe, 1991 and 2010

Source: European Commission.

Exercise 17.5

Identify the costs and benefits that would be associated with the UK's entry into the euro single currency group of countries, and discuss whether you believe that the UK should join when the time is right.

Other regional trade agreements

There are many other examples of regional trade agreements that have been negotiated around the world, some of which are now well established. These have influenced the pattern of global trade, although it has been argued that the strengthening of regional groupings of countries may inhibit the development of freer global trade – especially, of course, where these agreements involved setting common tariffs against countries outside the blocs.

The North American Free Trade Agreement (NAFTA)

NAFTA is a trilateral agreement between the USA, Canada and Mexico that was launched on 1 January 1994, with the aim of removing tariff barriers between the countries. These provisions were fully implemented on 1 January 2008. Although NAFTA is primarily about trade in goods and services between the three countries, there are also side agreements dealing with environmental and labour issues.

The US Department of Agriculture claims that NAFTA is 'one of the most successful trade agreements in history', having stimulated 'significant increases in agricultural trade and investment' between the three member countries (**www.fas.usda.gov/info/factsheets/NAFTA.asp**).

Whether all partners have gained equally remains an open question. There is a strong protectionist lobby in the USA that has argued that jobs have been lost as a result of the agreement. Some commentators in Mexico have argued that NAFTA has damaged Mexico's agricultural sector as it has faced subsidised imports from the USA. Labour issues have also been highly contentious, and the proposal from the USA to erect new fences to stem the flow of migrants from Mexico into the USA has roused substantial debate.

It is important to treat these arguments with great care, as there are sensitive political issues that can sometimes override economic analysis. The law of comparative advantage suggests that there are potential gains from engaging in trade, but the process of liberalising trade entails short-run costs. These may be expected to be transitional, especially for economic activities that are forced into decline in the face of expanding imports from partner countries. The existence of these costs should not prevent trade liberalisation if the long-term gains are sufficient to overcome them eventually. There must be a balancing of the costs against the benefits.

The signing of the North American Free Trade Agreement in 1992

The Association of Southeast Asian Nations (ASEAN)

ASEAN was established in 1967 as an agreement between Indonesia, Malaysia, the Philippines, Singapore and Thailand. These nations were later joined by Brunei Darussalam (1984), Vietnam (1995), Lao PDR and Myanmar (Burma) in 1997 and Cambodia in 1999. By 2006, ASEAN nations included 560 million people. The original aim of the association was partly economic (to promote economic growth, social progress and cultural development), but also to promote regional peace and stability.

These original aims were bolstered in 1992 by the launch of AFTA (the ASEAN Free Trade Area), which set out to eliminate tariff and non-tariff barriers among the member nations. A longer-term aim is to move towards an East Asian Free Trade Area that would also include China, Japan and the Republic of Korea. Negotiations towards this have begun — indeed regular summit meetings of ASEAN+3 have been taking place since the mid-1990s. Another objective of ASEAN is to move towards closer economic integration, and 2007 saw the signing of a declaration announcing moves towards establishing the ASEAN Economic Community (AEC).

Exercise 17.6

Discuss the costs and benefits that need to be taken into account in evaluating the effects of a regional trade agreement.

Summary

➤ The first step towards monetary union was the launch of the European Monetary System (EMS) in 1979.

➤ An important part of this was the Exchange Rate Mechanism (ERM), under which participating countries (which did not include the UK) agreed to keep their currencies within a narrow band (2.25%) against the average of their currencies.

➤ The Maastricht Treaty created the European Union (EU), and set out the route towards closer integration.

➤ The treaty also set out the convergence criteria, to be used to judge which countries were ready to join in monetary union. These criteria covered financial and fiscal aspects.

➤ Twelve countries adopted the euro as their common currency in January 2002.

➤ The main benefits of a common currency area are that it encourages trade by reducing transaction costs and reducing foreign exchange risk.

➤ However, the downside is that individual countries have less autonomy in controlling their macroeconomies. Adjusting to external shocks and smoothing short-term fluctuations in output and employment become more difficult with a common monetary policy that may not always be set in ways that are appropriate for all participating countries.

➤ From the UK's point of view, the government stated in 1997 that it intended to join the euro area, but only when the economy had passed five economic tests set by the chancellor: on convergence, flexibility, investment, financial services and employment.

➤ There are many other examples of regional trade agreements that have reached various stages of integration, such as NAFTA and ASEAN.

Chapter 18
Development and the less developed countries

One of the gravest economic challenges facing the world today is the global inequity in the distribution of resources. Worldwide, it is estimated that at the beginning of the twenty-first century more than a billion people were living in what the United Nations regards as absolute poverty. Furthermore, there were 114 million primary-age children who were not enrolled for school, more than a billion people without access to safe water, and 2.4 billion without access to sanitation. Progress since then has been slow. This chapter considers how to come to terms with such facts, and applies economic analysis in an attempt to understand what has gone wrong. Countries in different parts of the world have followed different paths to development — with varying degrees of success. Differences partly reflect the different characteristics of each country. Less developed countries (LDCs) do seem to share some characteristics, but each country also faces its own configuration of problems and opportunities. This chapter explores some of the common characteristics that LDCs display, but also examines some of the key differences between them.

Learning outcomes

After studying this chapter, you should:

➤ understand what is meant by economic and human development

➤ be familiar with the most important economic and social indicators that can help to evaluate the standard of living in different societies

➤ recognise the strengths and limitations of such indicators in providing a profile of a country's stage of development

➤ be aware of the importance of political and cultural factors in influencing a country's path of development

➤ be familiar with the common characteristics of less developed countries

➤ be aware of the diversity of experience of less developed countries

➤ be aware of significant differences between regions of the world in terms of their level and pace of development

➤ understand the importance of the structure of economic activity in an economy

➤ be familiar with the relative importance of different forms of economic activity in the process of development

Defining development

The first step is to define what is meant by 'development'. You might think that it is about economic growth — if a society can expand its productive capacity, surely that is development? But development means much more than this. Economic growth may well be a necessary ingredient, since development cannot take place without an expansion of the resources available in a society; however, it is not a *sufficient* ingredient, because those additional resources must be used wisely, and the growth that results must be the 'right' sort of growth.

Wrapped up with development are issues concerning the alleviation of poverty — no country can be considered 'developed' if a substantial portion of its population is living in absolute poverty. Development also requires structural change, and possibly changes in institutions and, in some cases, cultural and political attitudes.

Key terms

Millennium Development Goals (MDGs): targets set for each less developed country, reflecting a range of development objectives to be monitored each year to evaluate progress

development: a process by which real per capita incomes are increased and the inhabitants of a country are able to benefit from improved living conditions: that is, lower poverty and enhanced standards of education, health, nutrition and other essentials of life

In recognition of the multifaceted nature of development, the United Nations Millennium Summit in 2000 agreed a set of **Millennium Development Goals (MDGs)** that encapsulated their views of the main priorities for development. These were:

➤ eradicate poverty and hunger;
➤ achieve universal primary education;
➤ promote gender equality and empower women;
➤ reduce child mortality;
➤ improve maternal health;
➤ combat HIV/AIDS, malaria and other diseases;
➤ ensure environmental sustainability;
➤ develop a global partnership for development.

These eight goals represent key facets of **development** that need to be addressed. They constitute an enormous challenge for the period up to 2015, especially as progress in the early years has been slow and uneven. In thinking about these goals, you can begin to understand the various dimensions of development, and realise that it is about much more than economic growth — although growth may be seen as a prerequisite for the achievement of the goals. At the same time, failure to achieve these goals will retard economic growth.

The first of the UN's Millennium Development Goals is to eradicate extreme poverty and hunger

To summarise, development is about more than just economic growth. Achieving higher real income per capita is a necessary part of development, but it is not all there is to it. A country will not be recognised as achieving development unless it is also able to alleviate poverty, improve education levels and health standards, and provide an enhanced physical and cultural environment. Furthermore, such improvements must reach all inhabitants of the country, and not be confined to certain groups within society. In other words, economic growth may be *necessary* for development to take place, but it is not *sufficient*. Expanding the resources available within a society is the first step, but those resources also need to be used well.

Summary

➤ Economic growth is one aspect of economic development, in that it provides an increase in the resources available to members of society in less developed countries.

➤ However, in addition, development requires that the resources made available through economic growth are used appropriately to meet development objectives.

➤ The Millennium Development Goals were set by the Millennium Summit of the United Nations in September 2000.

➤ These eight goals comprise a set of targets for each less developed country, to be achieved by 2015.

Exercise 18.1

Visit the Millennium Development Goals website at **www.beta.undp.org/content/ undp/en/home/mdgoverview.html**. Discuss which of the goals you see to be of most importance for development and explore the extent to which progress is being made towards the goals in two or three countries of your choice.

Which are the less developed countries?

In its *Human Development Report 2005*, the UNDP identified 137 countries or areas as 'developing'. In addition, there were 27 'transition' economies in Central and Eastern Europe and the Commonwealth of Independent States (CIS). However, the range of countries that fall under this definition of developing countries is very wide, including countries such as Singapore and South Korea, which were also classified as being in the 'high-income' bracket. In the discussion that follows, this wide range of countries will be referred to as *less developed countries* (*LDCs*), and the discussion will be illustrated by examples from a selection of countries from different regions of the world.

In broad terms, the countries regarded as LDCs are concentrated in four major regions: sub-Saharan Africa, Latin America, South Asia and Southeast Asia. This excludes some countries in the 'less developed' range, but relatively few. For some

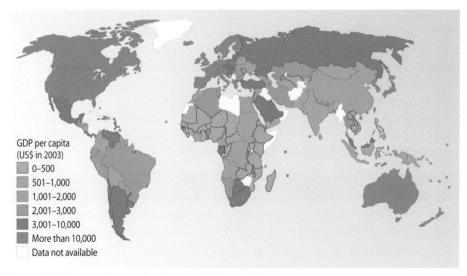

Figure 18.1 *Average income levels around the world*

purposes it may be necessary to treat China separately, rather than including it as part of Southeast Asia, partly because of its sheer size, and partly because it has followed a rather different development path. Figure 18.1 shows average income levels in countries around the world.

It is very important when discussing economic development to remember that there is wide diversity among the countries that are classified as LDCs, and although it is tempting to generalise, you need to be a little wary of doing so. Different countries have different characteristics, and face different configurations of problems and opportunities. Therefore, a policy that works for one country might fail totally in a different part of the world.

Indicators of development

GNI per capita

The first step is to be able to measure 'development'. One possible measure is GNI per capita — the average level of income per person in the population. GNI does have some advantages as a measure. First, it is relatively straightforward and thus is widely understood. Second, it is a well-established indicator and one that is available for almost every country in the world, so it can be used to compare income levels across countries. For this purpose, it naturally helps to adjust for population size by calculating GNI per person (GNI *per capita*, as it is known). This then provides a measure of average income per head.

Figure 18.2 provides data on GNI per capita for a selection of countries from each of the four major groupings. These countries will be used as examples throughout this discussion: they are colour-coded by region. Because of the diversity of countries in each of the regions, such a selection must be treated with a little caution. Singapore, South Korea and China have been chosen to represent East Asia and the Pacific, in

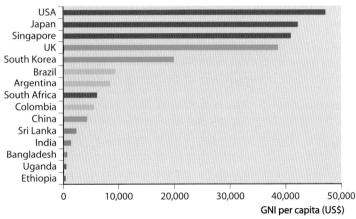

Figure 18.2 *GNI per capita, selected countries, 2010 (US$)*

Source: *World Development Report*, 2012.

order to highlight three of the countries that have achieved rapid economic growth over a sustained period.

The extreme differences that exist around the globe are immediately apparent from the data. GNI per capita in Ethiopia is just $380, whereas in the USA the figure is $47,140. (Luxembourg heads this particular league table, with average income of $79,510 in 2010.)

In trying to interpret these data, a number of issues need to be borne in mind, as the comparison is not as straightforward as it looks.

Exchange rate problems

The data presented in Figure 18.2 are expressed in terms of US dollars. This allows economists to compare average incomes using a common unit of measurement. At the same time, however, it may create some problems.

It is important to compare average income levels in order to evaluate the standard of living, and compare standards across countries. In other words, the aim is to assess people's command over resources in different societies, and to be able to compare the purchasing power of income in different countries.

GNI is calculated initially in terms of local currencies, and subsequently converted into US dollars using official exchange rates. Will this provide information about the relative local purchasing power of incomes? Not necessarily.

One reason for this is that official exchange rates are sometimes affected by government intervention. Indeed, in many of the less developed countries, exchange rates are pegged to an international currency — usually the US dollar. In these circumstances, exchange rates are more likely to reflect the government's policy and actions than the relative purchasing power of incomes in the country under scrutiny. For example, a government may choose to maintain an overvalued currency in order to try to maximise the earnings from its exports. In the case of China, the government has been tempted into the opposite situation, maintaining an undervalued currency in order to maximise export volume.

Where exchange rates are free to find their own equilibrium level, they are likely to be influenced strongly by the price of internationally traded goods, which is likely to be a very different combination of goods than that typically consumed by residents in these countries. Again, it can be argued that official exchange rates may not be a good reflection of the relative purchasing power of incomes across countries.

The United Nations International Comparison Project has been working on this problem for many years. It now produces an alternative set of international estimates of GNI based on *purchasing power parity* (PPP) exchange rates, which are designed to reflect the relative purchasing power of incomes in different societies more accurately. Figure 18.3 shows estimates for the same set of countries that were given in Figure 18.2.

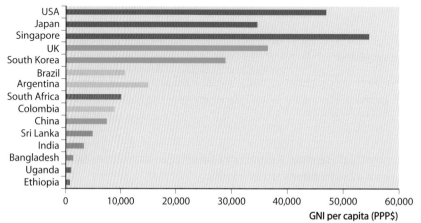

Figure 18.3 *GNI per capita, selected countries, 2010 (PPP$)*

Source: *World Development Report*, 2012.

Comparing the two graphs, you will notice that the gap between the low-income and high-income countries seems a bit less marked when PPP dollars (PPP$) are used as the unit of measurement. In other words, the US dollar estimates exaggerate the gap in living standards between rich and poor countries. This is a general feature of these measurements — that measurements in US dollars tend to understate real incomes for low-income countries and overstate them for high-income countries compared with PPP$ data. Put another way, people in the lower-income countries have a stronger command over goods and services than is suggested by US-dollar comparisons of GNI per capita. You will also see that in some cases, using PPP$ alters the rankings of the countries — for example, compare Singapore with Japan or the UK in the two figures.

Figure 18.4 shows the relative size of GNI per capita in PPP$ for the regional groupings of countries around the world in 2011. The gap in income levels between the LDCs and the 'very high human development' countries shows very clearly in the graph; equally, the gap between the countries of sub-Saharan Africa and South Asia, on the one hand, and those in East Asia and Latin America, on the other, is apparent. The graph also puts into context the position of the transition economies

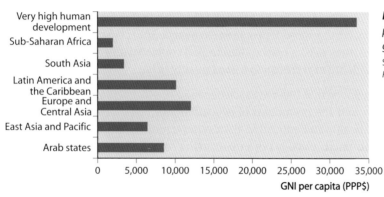

Figure 18.4 *GDP per capita, regional groupings, 2011 (PPP$)*

Source: *Human Development Report*, 2011.

of Central and Eastern Europe and the CIS, and the Arab states. The Arab states are rather different in character because their oil resources have enabled them to increase their average income levels.

The informal sector and the accuracy of data

Even when measured in PPP$, GDP has limitations as a measure of living standards. One limitation that is especially important when considering low-income countries is that in many LDCs there is considerable *informal economic activity*, which may not be captured by a measure like GDP, based on monetary transactions. Such activity includes subsistence agriculture, which remains important in many countries, especially in sub-Saharan Africa. In other words, GDP may not capture production that is directly used for consumption. Remember that GDP is measured by adding up the total transactions that take place in an economy. In the case of barter or production for consumption, there are no transactions to be measured, so they will not be captured in GDP.

Income distribution

Another important limitation of GDP per capita as a measure of living standards is that it is an *average* measure, and so does not reveal information about how income is distributed among groups in society.

In Brazil, the poorest 10% of households received less than 1% of total income in 1996, whereas the richest 10% received nearly half. In Belarus, on the other hand, the poorest 10% received 5% of income and the richest 10% received 20%. These are extreme examples of the degree of inequality in the distribution of income within countries.

Social indicators

A further question that arises is whether GDP can be regarded as a reasonable indicator of a country's *standard of living*. GDP provides an indicator of the total resources available within an economy in a given period, calculated from data about total output, total incomes or total expenditure. This focus on summing the transactions that take place in an economy over a period can be seen as a rather narrow view of what constitutes a country's standard of living. After all, it may be argued that the quality of people's lives depends on more things than simply the material resources that are available.

For one thing, people need to have knowledge if they are to make good use of the resources that are available. Two societies with similar income levels may nonetheless

provide very different quality of life for their inhabitants, depending on the education levels of the population. Furthermore, if people are to benefit from consuming or using the available resources, they need a reasonable lifespan coupled with good health. So, good standards of health are also crucial to a good quality of life.

It is important to remember that different societies tend to set different priorities for the pursuit of growth and the promotion of education and health. Some countries have higher levels of health and education than other countries with similar levels of GDP per capita. This needs to be taken into account when judging relative living standards by comparing GDP per capita. For a given level of real GDP per capita, there may be substantial differences in living standards between a country that places a high priority on providing education and healthcare, and one that devotes resources to military expenditure. In the longer term, there may also be significant differences between a society that spends its resources on present consumption, and one that engages in investment in order to increase consumption in the future.

A reasonable environment in which to live may be seen as another important factor in one's quality of life. There are some environmental issues that can distort the GDP measure of resources. Suppose there is an environmental disaster — perhaps an oil tanker breaks up close to a beautiful beach. This reduces the overall quality of life by degrading the landscape and preventing enjoyment of the beach. However, it does not have a negative effect on GDP; on the contrary, the money spent on clearing up the damage actually adds to GDP, so that the net effect of an environmental disaster may be to *increase* the measured level of GDP!

The Human Development Index

To deal with the criticism that GDP per capita fails to take account of other dimensions of the quality of life, in 1990 UNDP devised an alternative indicator, known as the **Human Development Index** (HDI). This was designed to provide a broader measure of the stage of development that a country had reached.

> **Key** *term*
>
> **Human Development Index:** a composite indicator of the level of a country's development, varying between 0 and 1

The basis for the HDI is that there are three key aspects of human development: resources, knowledge of how to make good use of those resources, and a reasonable life span in which to make use of those resources (see Figure 18.5). The three components are measured by, respectively, GNI per capita in PPP$, indicators of education (mean years of schooling and expected years of schooling) and life expectancy. The measurements are then combined to produce a composite index ranging between 0 and 1, with higher values reflecting higher human development.

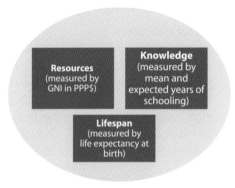

Figure 18.5 Components of the Human Development Index

GNI per capita (in PPP$) represents resources in this set-up, and is intended to reflect the extent to which people have command over resources. The education indicators pick up two rather different aspects of this important component of human development. Mean years of education can be seen as a way of reflecting educational attainment, as it measures the average number of years of schooling that were received by people aged 25 and above in their lifetime. It thus tells us something about the extent to which there has been past investment in education. Expected years of schooling, on the other hand, reveals something about the current state of education in an economy. That is, it identifies the number of years of schooling that a child of school entrance age can expect to receive given current patterns of enrolment and access to education. Life expectancy is the natural indicator of expected lifespan, and is also closely related to the general level of health of people in the country.

Values of the HDI for 2010 are charted in Figure 18.6 for the selected countries. You can see that the broad ranking of the countries is preserved, but the gap between low and high human development is less marked. Exceptions are South Africa and Brazil, which are ranked lower on the basis of the HDI than on GDP per capita: what this suggests is that these countries have achieved relatively high income levels, but other

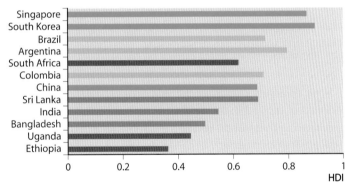

Figure 18.6 *The Human Development Index, selected countries, 2010*

Source: *Human Development Report*, 2011.

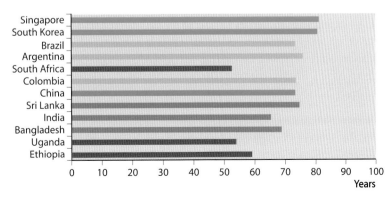

Figure 18.7 *Life expectancy at birth, selected countries*

Source: *Human Development Report*, 2011.

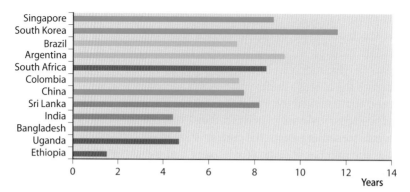

Figure 18.8 *Mean years of schooling, selected countries (% of people aged 24 and over)*

Source: *Human Development Report*, 2011.

aspects of human development have not kept pace. There are other countries in the world that share this feature. If you compare the data here with those for Figure 18.3, you will see that there are also countries that seem to perform better on HDI grounds than on GDP per capita — for example, China and Sri Lanka.

Figures 18.7 and 18.8 show the levels of two of the measures that enter into the HDI: life expectancy and mean years of schooling. It is clear that life expectancy is primarily responsible for the low ranking of South Africa in the HDI, as its level of life expectancy is not very different from that of the other sub-Saharan African countries in the sample, even though its average income level is much higher. In contrast, Bangladesh performs quite well in terms of lifespan, but relatively poorly in terms of education. By comparing these data, you can get some idea of the diversity between countries that was mentioned earlier.

In part, this diversity reflects differing priorities that governments have given to different aspects of development. Countries such as Brazil have aimed primarily at achieving economic growth, while those such as Sri Lanka have given greater priority to promoting education and healthcare.

Another way of putting a country into perspective is to construct a *development diamond*. An example is shown in Figure 18.9. This compares Ghana's performance with the average for countries in its region, i.e. sub-Saharan Africa. On each axis, the value of the variable achieved by Ghana is expressed as a proportion of the value for sub-Saharan Africa. In this instance, Ghana is seen to have lower GNI per capita but shows stronger achievement on the other indicators.

There is a view that growth should be the prime objective for development, since by expanding the resources available the benefits can begin to trickle down through the population. An opposing view claims that by providing first for basic needs, more rapid economic growth can be facilitated. The problem in some cases is that

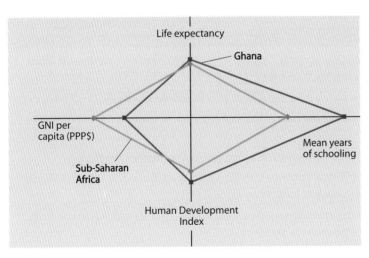

Figure 18.9 *Development diamond for Ghana compared with all countries in sub-Saharan Africa*

growth has not resulted in the trickle-down effect, and inequality remains. It may be significant that countries such as Brazil and South Africa, where the GNI per capita ranking is high relative to the HDI ranking, are countries in which there remain high levels of inequality in the distribution of income.

The HDI may be preferred to GNI per capita as a measure of development on the grounds that it reflects the key dimensions of development as opposed to growth. However, it will always be difficult to reduce a complex concept such as development to a single statistic. The diverse characteristics of LDCs demand the use of a range of alternative measures in order to identify the configuration of circumstances and problems facing a particular country.

Exercise 18.2

Table 18.1 presents some indicators for two countries, A and B.

	Country A	Country B
GDP per capita (PPP$)	10,781	11,110
Life expectancy (in years at birth)	75.6	50.8
Adult literacy rate (%)	91.6	82.4
People living with HIV/AIDS (% of adults aged 15–49)	0.3	18.8
Infant mortality rate (per 1,000 live births)	22	55

Table 18.1 *Selected standard of living indicators for two countries, 2005*

Source: *Human Development Report, 2007/08.*

a Discuss the extent to which GDP (here measured in PPP$) provides a good indication of relative living standards in the two countries.

b Discuss what other indicators might be useful in this evaluation.

Summary

➤ Less developed countries (LDCs) are largely located in four major regions: sub-Saharan Africa, Latin America, South Asia and Southeast Asia.

➤ These regions have shown contrasting patterns of growth and development.

➤ GDP is a widely used measure of the total amount of economic activity in an economy over a period of time.

➤ The trend rate of change of GDP may thus be an indicator of economic growth.

➤ However, converting from a local currency into US dollars may distort the use of GDP as a measure of the purchasing power of local incomes.

➤ There may be variation in the effectiveness of data collection agencies in different countries, and variation in the size of the informal sector.

➤ Average GDP per person also neglects the important issue of income distribution.

➤ GDP may neglect some important aspects of the quality of life.

➤ The Human Development Index (HDI) recognises that human development depends upon resources, knowledge and health, and therefore combines indicators of these key aspects.

➤ Different countries have different characteristics, and face different configurations of problems and opportunities.

Characteristics of less developed countries

Different countries are at different stages of development, as measured either by GDP per capita or by the Human Development Index (HDI). Some countries have clearly been much more successful than others in pursuing economic and human development. There are some countries in East Asia that have achieved rapid economic growth, and have been able to close the gap in living standards between them and the more developed countries. Others, especially in sub-Saharan Africa, seem to have stagnated, making little or no progress in growth since the 1960s. So what characteristics do less developed countries share? It is important to try to explain why different combinations of these characteristics may have joined with cultural, political and social influences to result in different experiences of growth and development.

The indicators that make up the HDI (namely, resources, knowledge and health) provide the first clues to the key characteristics of LDCs. LDCs have relatively low incomes, low levels of education in the population, and low levels of health. Education and health are important for many reasons. They are included in the HDI because they are seen as essential components of the quality of life, contributing directly to human development. However, they are also important because they are aspects of **human capital**. If an

 Key *term*

human capital: the stock of skills and expertise and other characteristics that contribute to a worker's productivity; can be increased through education and training, and improved nutrition and healthcare

individual undertakes education, this can be viewed as an investment, gathering skills that can be used later to generate a flow of income. Health is also a form of human capital that influences a worker's productivity.

The fact that many people in LDCs tend to have low levels of human capital has major implications for productivity in those countries, and is also a critical factor in the adoption of new technology, which typically demands high levels of skills from workers.

Demographic issues

Some other characteristics of LDCs are important in setting the scene for analysing development. It is widely believed that population growth is of special significance, and Figure 18.10 shows the past experience of population growth. The irregular pattern of this graph suggests that there is no strong correlation between income levels and population growth. However, in part this may reflect individual characteristics of some of the countries selected. For example, Singapore is a very small country with a population of only 5 million in 2010. (But imagine 5 million people living on the Isle of Wight!) Singapore has been concerned that its population is too small, and has put in place policies to encourage people to have more children. This may help to explain its relatively rapid population growth. China, on the other hand, faces the opposite problem and has imposed policies to discourage large families.

The prime concern about rapid population growth is felt by countries like Ethiopia and Uganda, where it has been suggested that the population has been growing too fast for education and healthcare services to keep up. Figure 18.11 shows one

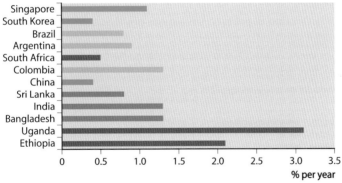

Figure 18.10 *Projected population growth, selected countries, 2010–15 (% p.a.)*

Source: *Human Development Report*, 2011.

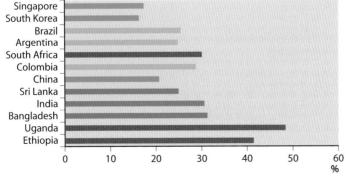

Figure 18.11 *Population below 15 years of age (%), selected countries*

Source: *Human Development Report*, 2011.

aspect of the problem: namely, the percentage of the population below 15 years of age in selected countries. In Uganda it amounts to almost half of the population, and in Ethiopia it is over 40%. These children need to be supported by the working population, and in countries where HIV/AIDS is widespread this is particularly difficult because the disease is especially prevalent among those of working age. This is one example of dependency. People who are too young or too old to be part of the working population are in a state of dependency on those in work. If the proportion of dependants increases because of shrinkage of the working population, this places added pressure on those remaining in work.

Poverty

A further characteristic of LDCs is the prevalence of poverty. One approach to measuring poverty is to define a basket of goods and services that is regarded as the minimum required to support human life: households that have incomes too low to allow them to purchase that basic bundle of goods are regarded as being in **absolute poverty**.

Research published in 2008 by the World Bank claimed that new data on incomes and prices in LDCs revealed that global poverty was more widespread than had been previously thought. It was estimated that households in which people were living on less than $1.25 per person

 term

absolute poverty: the situation describing a household if its income is insufficient to allow it to purchase the minimum bundle of goods and services needed for survival

per day (in PPP$) should be regarded as being in absolute poverty. In 2005, about 1.4 billion people in the world were said to be living below this threshold. Figure 18.12 shows a regional distribution of poverty. On a more positive note, the research showed that there had been substantial progress in the preceding years in reducing the number of people in poverty, although sub-Saharan Africa had made less progress than other regions. (More discussion of this issue may be found in 'Measuring poverty', by Peter Smith in *Economic Review*, February 2009.)

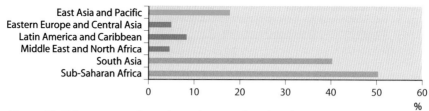

Figure 18.12 *Percentage of population living on less than $1.25 per day*
Source: International Comparison Project, 2005.

The number of people living below the poverty line is not a perfect measure. In particular, it would also be useful to know *how far* below the poverty line people are living, which would indicate the intensity of poverty. However, this is not easy to measure. In 2010, the UNDP launched a new poverty index, the Multidimensional

Poverty Index (MPI). The core idea of this index was that people may suffer deprivation in the three basic components of human development (resources, education and health). For example, households may have limited access to resources, such as clean water, sanitation, transport or assets such as a radio or refrigerator. They can also be deprived if children are unable to complete schooling, or if they are malnourished. The new index is based on data relating to ten different deprivations, assembled from a single survey of households. The severity of poverty is also related to the number of dimensions in which a household is deprived — this reflects the intensity of poverty of people in a household. The index is interpreted as depicting the share of the population that is poor across the dimensions of deprivation, but adjusted by the intensity of the deprivations. Figure 18.13 shows the index for the LDCs included in our sample. For Ethiopia, the interpretation would be that about 56% of people suffer deprivation across the dimensions of poverty reflected in the index.

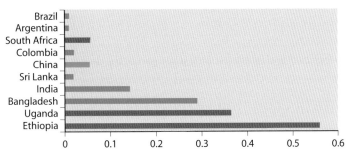

Figure 18.13 *The Multidimensional Poverty Index for selected countries, 2010*

Source: *Human Development Report*, 2011.

Poverty can also be defined in relative terms. If a household has insufficient income for its members to participate in the normal social life of the country, it is said to be in **relative poverty**. This too is defined in terms of a poverty line, this time it is 50% of the median (middle-ranked) household disposable income. Relative poverty can occur in any society.

 Key term

relative poverty: the situation applying to a household whose income falls below 50% of the median household disposable income

Absolute poverty and relative poverty reflect different things. Absolute poverty is about whether people have enough to survive, whereas relative poverty is more about inequality than about poverty. This is not to say that relative poverty should not be of concern to policy makers, but people in absolute poverty clearly require urgent action.

An important part of development is the provision of *infrastructure*. In part this is necessary to help to alleviate poverty by providing essential services. But there are other vital aspects of infrastructure that are essential for markets to operate effectively. This is particularly true of transport and communications and market facilities. Many areas of infrastructure display characteristics of public goods, so that

government intervention is essential to ensure adequate provision. (Public goods were discussed in *AS Economics, Chapter 7*.) A problem for many LDCs, however, is that the government does not have the resources to provide the necessary infrastructure.

Summary

➤ One common characteristic of LDCs is the relatively low levels of human capital in the population.

➤ Improvements in education, healthcare and nutrition are all needed in order to raise the skills and productivity of labour.

➤ Demographic factors are also important for LDCs, many of which have shown a more rapid rate of population growth than can readily be resourced.

➤ One result of the demographic situation is that many LDCs have a high proportion of the population who are aged below 15 years — in some cases, more than half of the people are young.

➤ Poverty is widespread, and its alleviation is a key part of the development process.

The structure of economic activity in LDCs

Dependence on the primary sector

In evaluating the characteristics of LDCs, it is helpful to consider the structure of economic activity. One way of viewing this is to consider the separation between primary, secondary and tertiary production activities. The *primary sector* involves the extraction of raw materials and the growing of crops. It includes agriculture, the extraction of minerals (and oil), forestry, fishing and so on. The *secondary sector* is where these raw materials or crops are processed or transformed into goods. It includes various forms of manufacturing activity, ranging from the processing of food to the manufacture of motor vehicles or computer equipment. The *tertiary sector* is concerned with the provision of services. It includes transport and communication, hairdressing, financial services and so on. A subset of tertiary activity involves intellectual services. This is sometimes known as the *quaternary sector* and includes hi-tech industry, information technology, some forms of scientific research and other 'information products'.

Figure 18.14 contrasts the structure of economic activity in two very different economies – Ethiopia and the UK. These data do not exactly correspond to the primary, secondary and tertiary divisions, as 'Industry' here includes not only manufacturing activity but also mining, construction, electricity, water and gas. Nonetheless, the contrast is striking. In the UK, the agricultural sector has dwindled almost to nothing, and services have become the dominant form of activity, although industry still accounts for more than a quarter of GDP. In Ethiopia, industry takes up only 11% of GDP – and remember this includes not only manufacturing but some other forms of

activity (notably utilities such as water and energy supply) as well. Agriculture, on the other hand, is the largest single sector.

Indeed, many LDCs have an economic structure that is strongly biased towards agriculture. Figure 18.15 shows the percentage of GDP coming from the agricultural sector (measured in terms of value added). In interpreting these data, it is important to be aware that labour productivity tends to be lower in agriculture than in other sectors. The data therefore understate the importance of agriculture in the structure of the economy, as the percentage of the labour force engaged in agriculture is higher than the agricultural share of output. This is further reinforced by the importance of unrecorded agricultural production in the subsistence sector. In other words, if farmers produce food for their own consumption, this will not be included in GDP.

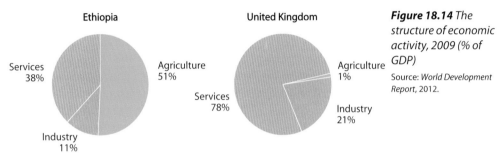

Figure 18.14 *The structure of economic activity, 2009 (% of GDP)*

Source: *World Development Report*, 2012.

Figure 18.16 underlines the situation by showing the percentage of the population living in urban areas. It would appear that, for many of the low-income countries in the group, the majority of their people are relying on rural economic activities. In many LDCs, there is a stark contrast between the urban and the rural areas. This shows up partly in terms of income differences, as you might expect from the different kinds of employment opportunities available in the urban areas. However, it shows up in other ways too – for example, in terms of access to education and healthcare, which tend to be better provided in the urban areas, partly because many teachers and doctors prefer to live there. In some countries, the inequality between different regions is tantamount to there being a *dual economy*. The economic activity in the

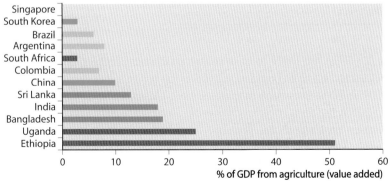

Figure 18.15 *The importance of agriculture, 2009*

Source: *World Development Report*, 2012.

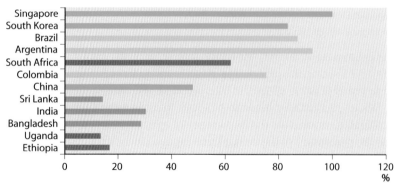

Figure 18.16
*Population living
in urban areas
(%), selected
countries*

Source: *Human
Development Report,*
2012.

country takes place in two quite different styles, and a traditional rural sector may co-exist with a burgeoning modern sector in the urban areas.

This inequality between regions in a country may have the effect of encouraging migration towards the cities. There might be many reasons for this. It may be that workers head for the cities because they are attracted by the chance of obtaining higher wages or better living conditions. Alternatively, households might decide to send some members to earn in the city while the rest remain in the rural area. This might be seen as a way of diversifying risk rather than having all household members active in the same (rural) labour market. Figure 18.17 shows something of this trend in a range of countries: it plots the percentage of the country's population living in urban areas at three points in time: 1975, 2005 and 2010.

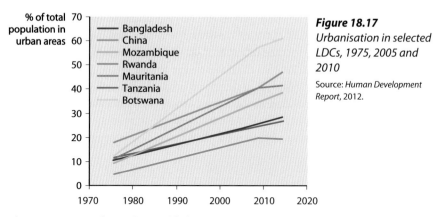

Figure 18.17
*Urbanisation in selected
LDCs, 1975, 2005 and
2010*

Source: *Human Development
Report*, 2012.

Such movements of people are likely to pose severe problems. Consider Botswana, for example. In 1975 just 11% of its population lived in the urban areas. By 2010 this had risen to more than 60%. Botswana may not have a massively large population (about 2 million in 2010), but for a government needing to provide public goods, such rapid urban expansion puts significant pressure on urban infrastructure – roads, housing, water supply, sanitation and so on. Just as important, such migration puts enormous pressure on urban labour markets, so the provision of jobs for all these additional workers becomes a major challenge. The net result is that many rural workers exchange poor living conditions in the rural areas for unemployment in an urban environment.

The informal sector

Furthermore, as employment in the newer sectors cannot expand at such a rate, the result is an expansion of the informal sector. Migrants to the city who cannot find work are forced to find other forms of employment, as most LDCs do not have well-developed social security protection. The cities of many LDCs are therefore characterised by substantial amounts of informal activity. The scale of the informal sector can be seen in Figure 18.18: for example, in Ghana nearly 80% of employment in the urban areas is made up of informal activity.

Such informal activity covers a multitude of economic activities. If you were to visit a city in an LDC, you might see many examples, such as hawkers selling food at the kerbside, roadside barbers and rickshaw drivers. However, in some cities, the informal sector has developed beyond such activities, and you might find small manufacturing concerns recycling old car tyres as shoes, or packing cases as furniture.

The growth of the urban population may have externality effects on living standards in the urban areas. If there is rapid growth of the urban population, it is unlikely that the authorities will be able to ensure adequate infrastructure to cope with the growing numbers of residents: for example, in terms of housing, water supply or sanitation. This may lead to the growth of shanty towns — informal settlements in which new arrivals congregate, often in very poor conditions. Figure 18.19 illustrates this. The assumption here is that the marginal private costs faced by an individual migrant (MPC) are lower than the marginal social costs (MSC), because of the effects of congestion. Individual migrants will continue to come to the city

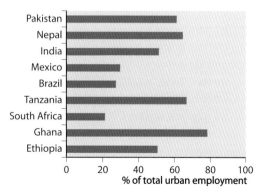

Figure 18.18 Urban informal employment as a % of total urban employment, selected countries

Note: data are for national definitions and various years

Source: International Labour Organization.

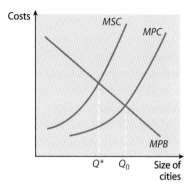

For many migrants to cities in LDCs, informal employment may be the only form of work they can find

Figure 18.19 The externality effect of migration

up to the point where their marginal private benefits are equal to their marginal private costs (at Q_0), whereas Q^* would be better for society as a whole.

In some ways the existence of the informal sector may be seen as beneficial for an LDC, as it offers a coping strategy for the poor, and may even provide some training and skills that might later help workers to find employment in the modern or formal sector. These benefits need to be weighed against the potential costs arising from the externalities mentioned earlier. Furthermore, if the informal sector acts as a cushion for migrant workers, it is possible that it will be seen as reducing the opportunity cost of unemployment, which in turn could increase the flow of migrants.

Summary

> Economic activity can be classified into primary, secondary and tertiary production activities.

> Primary activity centres around agriculture and mineral extraction; secondary activity focuses mainly on manufacturing activity; tertiary activity is concerned with the provision of services.

> Many LDCs have an economic structure that is biased towards the primary sector.

> Agriculture is often characterised by low productivity.

> The importance of agriculture is also reflected in the high proportion of the population of many LDCs that live in rural areas.

> Inequality between rural and urban areas has led to rapid internal migration in some LDCs, and to the growth of the urban informal sector.

> Migration puts pressure on urban infrastructure.

The diversity of less developed countries

Although this chapter has identified a number of characteristics that many LDCs seem to have in common, it is difficult — and dangerous — to generalise too much when trying to analyse LDCs or to devise a policy to foster development. This is because every country has its own configuration of characteristics, strengths and weaknesses. To some extent, regional groupings of countries display some common features, but even here there remains an inherent diversity.

The East Asian experience

The rapid growth achieved by the East Asian **tiger economies**, as they came to be known, was undoubtedly impressive, and held out hope that other less developed countries could begin to close the gap in living standards. Indeed, the term 'East Asian miracle' was coined to describe how quickly these **newly industrialised economies** had been able to develop. At the heart of the success were four countries: Hong Kong, Singapore, South Korea and Taiwan; others, such as Malaysia and Thailand, were not far behind.

 terms

tiger economies: a group of newly industrialised economies in the East Asian region, including Hong Kong, Singapore, South Korea and Taiwan

newly industrialised economies: economies that have experienced rapid economic growth from the 1960s to the present

How was their success achieved?

None of these countries enjoys a rich supply of natural resources. Indeed, Hong Kong and Singapore are small city-states whose only natural resources are their excellent harbours and good positions — but with small populations.

The tigers soon realised that to develop manufacturing industry it would be crucial to tap into economies of scale. This meant producing on a scale that would far outstrip the size of their domestic markets — which meant that they would have to rely on international trade. Only in this way would they be able to gain the benefits of specialisation.

By being very open to international trade and focusing on exports, the tigers were able to sell to a larger market, and thereby improve their efficiency through economies of scale. This enabled them to enjoy a period of **export-led growth**. In other words, the tiger economies expanded by selling their exports to the rest of the world, and building a reputation for high-quality merchandise. This was helped by their judicious choice of markets on which to focus: they chose to move into areas of economic activity that were being vacated by the more developed nations, which were producing new sorts of product.

> **Key term**
>
> **export-led growth:** a situation in which economic growth is achieved through the exploitation of economies of scale, made possible by focusing on exports, and so reaching a wider market than would be available within the domestic economy

The export-led growth hypothesis explains part of the success of the tiger economies, but there were other contributing factors. The tiger economies nurtured their human capital and attracted foreign investment. Their governments intervened to influence the direction of the economy, but also encouraged markets to operate effectively, fostering macroeconomic and political stability and developing good infrastructure. Moreover, these countries embarked on their growth period at a time when world trade overall was buoyant.

Sub-Saharan Africa

The experience of countries in sub-Saharan Africa is in total contrast to the success story of the tiger economies. Even accepting the limitations of the GDP per capita measure, the fact that it was lower in 2000 than it had been in 1975 (or even earlier) paints a depressing picture. Can sub-Saharan Africa learn from the experience of the tiger economies?

Part of the explanation for the failure of growth in this region lies in the fact that sub-Saharan Africa lacks many of the positive features that enabled the tiger economies to grow. Export-led growth is more difficult for countries that have specialised in the production of goods for which demand is not buoyant. Furthermore, it is not straightforward to develop new specialisations if human and physical capital levels are low, the skills for new activities are lacking and poverty is rife. On the other hand, continuing to rely on specialisation in agriculture when many of the potential export markets are characterised by strong protectionism is also fraught with difficulty.

Encouraging development when there is political instability, and when markets do not operate effectively, is a major challenge.

The experience of the 2000s was rather more encouraging, as some economies in sub-Saharan Africa began to show signs of progress in terms of economic growth and development. This is evident in Figure 18.20, which shows annual growth rates for a selection of countries in sub-Saharan Africa since 1990. For these economies at least, the 2000s offered promise of improvement. Uganda consistently outperformed growth in the world as a whole, and Tanzania did so after the late 1990s. Furthermore, these economies maintained positive growth rates when the world as a whole showed negative growth in 2009. Cameroon went through a period in the early 1990s of continuous recession, but then recovered in the 2000s. Sub-Saharan Africa as a whole experienced growth rates higher than in the world as a whole throughout the 2000s. Although this may seem encouraging, it remains to be seen whether this performance can be maintained as the global economy struggles to recover – and whether this performance can be replicated by other economies in the region. Notice that the growth rates shown here are for GDP, not for GDP per capita, so average incomes were not rising as quickly as might be inferred from the figure.

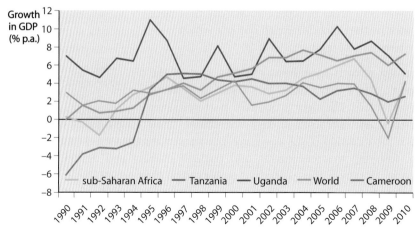

Figure 18.20 *Growth in selected countries in sub-Saharan Africa, 1990–2010*
Source: World Bank.

Latin America

Countries in Latin America followed yet another path. There was a period in which the economies of Argentina, Brazil and Mexico, among others, were able to grow rapidly, enabling them to qualify as 'newly industrialised economies'. However, such growth could not be sustained in the face of the high rates of inflation that afflicted many of the countries in this region, especially during the 1980s. Indeed, many of them experienced bouts of hyperinflation, inhibiting economic growth.

In part this reflected fiscal indiscipline, with governments undertaking high levels of expenditure which they financed by printing money. In many cases, countries in this region have tended to be relatively closed to international trade. International debt reached unsustainable levels, and continues to haunt countries such as Argentina which, in 2005, wrote off its debt by offering its creditors about 33% of the value of its outstanding debt. Around three-quarters of the creditors accepted the deal, knowing that otherwise they would probably get nothing at all. However, whether anyone will be prepared to lend to Argentina in the future remains to be seen. Latin American economies also tend to be characterised by high levels of income inequality, and poverty remains a major problem.

The BRIC countries

In the early 2000s, a group of countries were identified as experiencing rapid economic growth and closing the gap on the developed economies. These were Brazil, Russia, India and China; they became known as the BRIC economies. Although originally the group was simply a set of countries identified as having some characteristics in common, the countries began forming a political

Latin American countries, including Mexico, have run into economic difficulties after a period of rapid growth

group and having summit meetings, and in 2011 they invited South Africa to join them. At this point in time, the BRICs accounted for about 18% of world GDP and 15% of world trade, and contained about 40% of the world's population. If economic growth continues at current rates, the group will gain increasing economic and political influence relative to the G7.

Figure 18.21 shows economic growth in the original four BRIC countries since 1999, with the growth rate for the world as a whole to provide context. The consistency and rapidity of growth during the 2000s reveals why these countries were singled out for attention, although Brazil was perhaps rather less successful in terms of its growth rates. What makes this performance more startling is the size of these economies, both in population and in the size of GDP. The achievements of the economies of

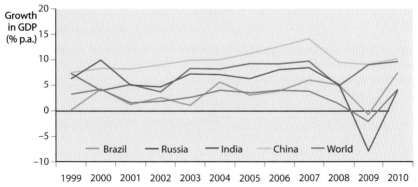

***Figure 18.21** Growth in the BRIC countries, 1999–2010*

Source: World Bank.

China and India are especially impressive, in each case starting from a relatively low base – and for these two economies, the growth seemed robust in the face of the global recession. However, the factors underlying the growth performance were different in each case, as these economies are all at very different stages in terms of average incomes and display different characteristics, both politically and economically.

Exercise 18.3

Table 18.2 provides a selection of indicators for three countries. One of these is in sub-Saharan Africa, one is in Southeast Asia and the other is in Latin America. See if you can identify which is which.

	Country A	Country B	Country C
Life expectancy at birth (years)	69.6	75.6	52.1
Adult literacy (%)	92.6	91.6	73.6
Population growth, 1975–2005 (% p.a.)	1.3	1.8	3.2
Urban population (% of total)	32.3	76.0	20.7
% of population under 15 years	21.7	30.8	42.6
% of population with access to safe water, 2004	99	97	61
% of adults aged 15–49 living with HIV/AIDS	1.4	0.3	6.1
Growth of GDP per capita, 1975–2005 (% p.a.)	4.9	1.0	0.1
Exports of primary goods (% of all merchandise exports)	22	23	79

Table 18.2 *Selected standard of living indicators for three countries*

Note: data are for 2005 unless otherwise stated.

Source: *Human Development Report*, 2007/08.

Summary

➤ A small group of countries in Southeast Asia, known as the East Asian tiger economies, underwent a period of rapid economic growth, closing the gap on the more developed countries.

➤ This success arose from a combination of circumstances, including a high degree of openness to international trade, which was seen as crucial if economies of scale were to be reaped.

➤ However, the tigers are also characterised by high levels of human capital and political and macroeconomic stability.

➤ In contrast, countries in sub-Saharan Africa have stagnated; in some cases, real per capita incomes were lower in 2000 than they had been in 1975.

➤ Countries in Latin America began well, experiencing growth for a period, but then ran into economic difficulties.

Chapter 19
Policies to promote development and sustainability

This chapter focuses on some of the obstacles that have hindered development in less developed countries, especially in sub-Saharan Africa, where very little progress seems to have been made after several decades of development efforts. This is in contrast to some countries in East Asia, which have experienced such rapid growth since the 1960s that they have successfully closed the income gap with countries that developed in earlier periods. The governments of LDCs that wish to stimulate development need to devise policies that will make the best possible use of the resources available to them domestically. However, in many cases, domestic resources are lacking, so it is important to consider the alternative possibility of mobilising resources from outside the country. This can be done by attracting foreign direct investment, accepting overseas assistance or borrowing on international capital markets.

Learning outcomes

After studying this chapter, you should:

➤ be aware of important obstacles to economic growth and development
➤ understand the causes and significance of rapid population growth
➤ understand the dangers of continued dependence on primary production, especially on low-productivity agriculture
➤ appreciate the importance of missing markets, especially financial markets
➤ be aware of the importance of social capital in promoting long-term development
➤ appreciate the significance of relationships with more developed countries
➤ be aware of the need for less developed countries to mobilise external resources for development
➤ understand the benefits and costs associated with foreign direct investment
➤ be familiar with the potential use of overseas assistance for promoting development, and the effectiveness of such flows of funds in the past

Problems facing less developed countries

Chapter 18 highlighted some of the characteristics of less developed countries (LDCs). In order to devise policies that will help to stimulate a process of development, it is first important to identify whether some of these characteristics constitute obstacles to development that will need to be overcome. These may be regarded as *internal* problems – problems that arise because of domestic issues. However, it is apparent that LDCs have also faced obstacles from outside. Such *external* problems arise in an international context because of the interactions between countries in global markets, and through political ties. Such international linkages have become more important with the spread of globalisation.

Internally, one group of issues arises in relation to the balance of factors of production available in LDCs, which tend to be characterised by a relative abundance of labour resources and a lack of capital. A second group of issues relates to the underdevelopment of markets – especially financial markets, which may be of particular importance given the stress on saving and investment in many of the models. There are also issues arising from government failure. Externally, issues arise from trade interactions and from the trend towards globalisation.

Population growth

Early writers on development were pessimists. For example, Thomas Malthus argued in the late eighteenth century that real wages would never rise above a bare subsistence level. This was based on his ideas about the relationship between population growth and real incomes.

Malthus believed that it was not possible for a society to experience sustained increases in real wages, basically because the population was capable of exponential growth, while the food supply was capable of only arithmetic growth as a result of diminishing returns.

Thomas Malthus

Although he was proved wrong (he had not anticipated the improvements in agricultural productivity that were to come), the question of whether population growth constitutes an obstacle to growth and development remains. At the heart of this is the debate about whether people should be regarded as key contributors to development, in their role as a factor of production, or as a drain on resources, consuming food, shelter, education and so on. Ultimately, the answer depends upon the quantity of resources available relative to the population size.

In global terms, world population is growing at a rapid rate: by more than 80 million people per year. In November 1999, global population went through the 6 billion mark – that is, about six times as many people as there were in 1800. But the growth is very unevenly distributed: countries such as Italy, Spain, Germany and Switzerland are projected to experience declining populations in the period 2000–15, while the

population of sub-Saharan Africa continues to grow by 2.4% per annum, and that of 'low human development' countries (according to the UNDP definition) by 2.5%. A country whose population is growing at 2.5% per annum will see a doubling in just 28 years, so the growing pressure on resources to provide education and healthcare is considerable. The proportion of the population aged below 15 is very high for much of sub-Saharan Africa, as noted in Chapter 18.

Figure 19.1 shows fertility rates for the group of countries selected in the previous chapter. The fertility rate records the average number of births per woman. Thus, in Uganda the average number of births per woman is about 6. Of course, this does not mean that the average number of *children* per family is so high, as not all the babies survive.

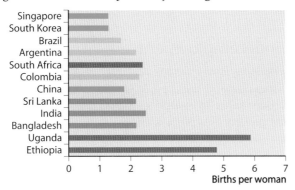

Figure 19.1 *Total fertility rates, selected countries, 2010–15*

Source: *Human Development Report,* 2012.

This pattern of high fertility has implications for the age structure of the population, leading to a high proportion of young dependants. It puts a strain on an LDC's limited resources because of the need to provide education and healthcare for so many children, and in this sense high population growth can prove an obstacle to development. This argument might be countered by pointing out that people themselves are a resource for the country. However, it is a question of the balance between population and the availability of resources.

Summary

➤ Early writers such as Malthus were pessimistic about the prospects for sustained development, believing that diminishing returns to labour would constrain economic growth.

➤ Globally, population is growing rapidly, with most of the increase taking place in less developed countries.

➤ Coupled with the age structure of the population, rapid population growth can create difficulties for LDCs because of the pressure on resources.

Exercise 19.1

Discuss the way in which the age structure of a population may influence its rate of economic growth and development.

Dependence on primary production

Another common characteristic of LDCs that was identified in Chapter 17 was the way that many LDCs, especially in sub-Saharan Africa, continue to rely heavily on the agricultural sector to provide employment and incomes. Because labour productivity in agriculture tends to be relatively low, this may keep rural incomes low. The pressures of population growth tend to reinforce this dependence.

It is worth being aware that one of the driving forces behind the Industrial Revolution in Britain was an increase in agricultural productivity, enabling more workers to shift into manufacturing activity. In an LDC context, this transition may run into a number of problems.

Unemployment and underemployment

With the rural areas experiencing low incomes and high population growth, it is perhaps natural that people should want to migrate to the urban areas in search of higher incomes and an escape from poverty — a process known as **urbanisation**.

> **Key term**
>
> **urbanisation:** process whereby an increasing proportion of the population comes to live in cities

Migration occurs in response to a number of factors. One is the attraction of the 'bright lights' of the cities — people in rural areas often perceive urban areas as offering better access to education and healthcare facilities, and better recreational opportunities. Perhaps more important are the economic gains to be made from migrating to the cities, in terms of the wage differential between urban and rural areas.

Urban wages tend to be higher for a number of reasons. Employment in the manufacturing or service sectors typically offers higher wages, in contrast to the low productivity and wages in the agricultural sector. In addition, labour in the urban areas tends to be better organised, and governments have often introduced minimum wage legislation and social protection for workers in the urban areas — especially where they rely on them for electoral support.

Such wage differentials attract a flow of migrants to the cities. However, in practice there may not be sufficient jobs available, as the new and growing sectors typically do not expand quickly enough to absorb all the migrating workers. The net result is that rural workers exchange poor living conditions in the rural areas for unemployment in the urban environment.

The impact of HIV/AIDS

The HIV/AIDS epidemic has had a major impact on LDCs, especially in sub-Saharan Africa. The relative incidence of the disease across regions is illustrated in Figure 19.2. The high prevalence in sub-Saharan Africa is clearly visible. However, this conceals large differences between countries. There are countries in sub-Saharan Africa where

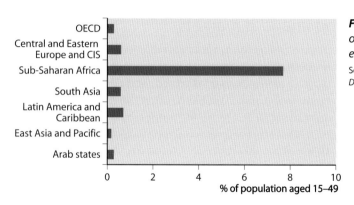

Figure 19.2 *Incidence of HIV/AIDS in the early 2000s*

Source: *Human Development Report.*

the prevalence is unimaginably high: for example, in Botswana it was estimated that in 2003 some 37.3% of the population aged 15–49 was affected; and in Swaziland the prevalence rate was 38.8%.

The repercussions of the disease are especially marked because of its impact on people of working age. This has affected the size of the labour force and left many orphans with little hope of receiving an education, which in turn has implications for the productivity of future generations.

Governments have reacted to the disease in very different ways. In countries where the government has been open about the onset of the disease and has striven to promote safe sex, the chances of keeping the disease under control are much higher. For example, in 1990 the incidence of HIV/AIDS amongst adults in Thailand and South Africa was similar, at about 1%. Thailand confronted the problem through a widespread public campaign such that, by 2001, the incidence was still about 1%. South Africa did little to stop the spread of the disease, with the president choosing to downplay the problem. In 2001 the incidence of the disease in South Africa was estimated to be about 25%. Some other governments have also kept silent, perhaps not wanting to admit that it is a problem, and in their countries the disease has run rampant. There may also be problems in measuring the incidence of HIV/AIDS accurately, as individuals may be hesitant to seek treatment or to report that they have the disease for fear of social stigma.

There is evidence that the epidemic is abating, and the number of new infections is reducing. Figure 19.3 shows this quite clearly, comparing the number of HIV infections per year in 2009 with 2001. In no region has there been an increase, and there has been a significant fall in sub-Saharan Africa. Although this is encouraging, the legacy of past infections will take some time to work through the system.

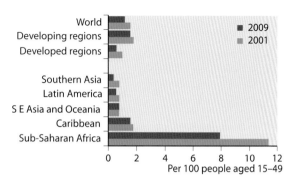

Figure 19.3 *Number of new HIV infections per year, 2001 and 2009*

Structural change and financial markets

Given the difficulties caused by overreliance on primary production and the burgeoning urban informal sector, a key question concerns structural change. A transformation of the structure of economic activity seems crucial for growth and development to take place, but how can this be initiated? A major problem is that the rate of growth that would be needed in the industrial sector to absorb the number of workers looking for employment is far in excess of what has been — or could be — achieved. This poses a substantial challenge for LDCs.

The expansion of the industrial sector requires physical capital, which most LDCs must import as they do not have the capacity to produce capital goods domestically. Furthermore, the process requires investment — which in turn requires saving. Generating a flow of savings that can be made available for investment requires a sacrifice of current consumption, which may be problematic when domestic incomes are low. Furthermore, in order for a flow of funds for investment to be mobilised, and in order for those funds to be appropriately channelled into productive investment, fully functioning financial markets are needed. The undeveloped nature of financial markets is especially problematic in the rural areas, where the lack of formal financial markets makes borrowing to invest in agricultural improvements almost impossible.

One of the problems is that the cost of establishing rural branches of financial institutions in remote areas is high; the fixed costs of making loans for relatively small-scale projects are similarly high. This is intensified by the difficulty that banks have in obtaining information about the creditworthiness of small borrowers, who typically may have no collateral to offer.

Attempts have been made to remedy this situation through *microfinance* schemes. This approach was pioneered by the Grameen Bank, which was founded in Bangladesh in 1976. The bank made small-scale loans to groups of women who otherwise would have had no access to credit, and each group was made corporately responsible for paying back the loan. The scheme has claimed great success, both in terms of the constructive use of the funds in getting small-scale projects off the ground and in terms of high payback rates.

Other schemes have involved groups of households pooling their savings in order to accumulate enough funds to launch small projects. Members of the group take it in turns to use these joint savings, paying the loan back in order for the next person to have a turn. These are known as *rotating savings and credit schemes (ROSCAs)*, and they have had some success in providing credit for small schemes. In spite of some successful enterprises, however, such schemes have been found to be less sustainable than Grameen-style arrangements, and have tended to be used to obtain consumer durable goods rather than for productive investment and innovation.

In the absence of such schemes, households may be forced to borrow from local moneylenders, often at very high rates of interest. For example, a survey by the Bank of Uganda found that households were paying rates between 0% (when borrowing from family members) and 500%. In part this may reflect a high risk of the borrower's

defaulting, but it may also reflect the ability of local moneylenders to use market power. The absence of insurance markets may also deter borrowing for productive investment, especially in rural areas.

Macroeconomic instability

In the World Bank's market-friendly view of the growth process, macroeconomic stability is highlighted as one of the key conditions that enable markets to work effectively. There are two aspects to this argument. One is that firms will be reluctant to undertake investment if they find it difficult to predict future market conditions. If inflation is high and volatile, it will not be easy for firms to form expectations about the future, so this will discourage investment. Second, it is argued that prices will fail to act as reliable signals to guide resource allocation when inflation is either high or unstable. This may then distort the pattern of resource allocation, which may be especially important for LDCs that are trying to improve the allocation of resources, and to encourage a process of structural change.

Inflation has been a feature of some – but not all – LDCs. It was a prominent feature of many Latin American economies, peaking during the 1980s at annual rates above 1,000%. However, the relationship between inflation and economic growth is a complex one. It is true that few countries that have experienced very high inflation rates have been successful in terms of economic growth. It is also the case that countries that have experienced rapid growth have maintained relatively low inflation rates. Nonetheless, there are countries that have maintained low inflation rates, but have then experienced slow (or even negative) growth rates. A tentative conclusion might be that low inflation is necessary for rapid growth to take place, but not sufficient. In other words, low inflation may be a crucial part of a growth strategy, but achieving it does not guarantee rapid growth.

Government failure

Such periods of hyperinflation partly reflected government failure. Many Latin American economies ran large fiscal deficits in this period, financing these through money creation, which led inexorably to galloping inflation. It was claimed by some (mainly Latin American) writers that inflation could be of benefit to economic growth, by redistributing income towards those in the economy with a high marginal propensity to save – namely, the government and the rich. However, there is no conclusive evidence that this does lead to higher growth, as governments cannot always be relied upon to use the funds wisely, and the rich have a tendency to indulge in luxury consumption, rather than undertaking productive investment.

Government failure has been important in many LDCs, and not only in relation to fiscal indiscipline. Governments that depend upon being re-elected may be tempted to introduce policies that are more designed to keep them in power than to foster long-term economic development. One common manifestation of this has been observed in relation to food prices. In a number of cases, governments depend primarily on the urban population to vote them back into office. Governments then may be tempted to introduce policies that are pro-urban. This might mean, for

part 4

example, imposing low prices for food in order to combat urban poverty. This has undesirable effects as it affects the incentives for farmers and may thus inhibit growth. Similarly, minimum wage legislation may have the effect of leading to higher unemployment — again, mainly in the urban areas, where such legislation is likely to bite more strongly.

Sustainability

Economic growth may have important effects on the environment, and in pursuing growth, countries must bear in mind the need for **sustainable development**, safeguarding the needs of future generations as well as the needs of the present.

Key term

sustainable development: 'development which meets the needs of the present without compromising the ability of future generations to meet their own needs' (Brundtland Commission, 1987)

These issues have been widely discussed in the context of the more developed countries. However, the issue is equally important for LDCs. Deforestation has been a problem for many LDCs that have areas of rainforest. In some cases, logging for timber has destroyed large areas of valuable land; in other cases, land has been cleared for unsuitable agricultural use. This sort of activity creates relatively little present value, and leaves a poorer environment for future generations.

Another aspect of environmental degradation concerns *biodiversity*. This refers to the way in which misuse of the environment is contributing to the loss of plant species — not to mention those of birds, insects and mammals — which are becoming extinct as their natural habitat is destroyed. Some of the lost species may not even have been discovered yet. Given the natural healing properties of many plants, this could mean the destruction of plants that might provide significant new drugs for use in medicine. But how can something be valued when its very existence is as yet unknown?

One way of viewing the environment is as a factor of production that needs to be used effectively, just like any other factor of production. In other words, each country has a stock of *environmental* capital that needs to be utilised in the best possible way.

However, if the environmental capital is to be used appropriately, it must be given an appropriate value and this can be problematic. If property rights are not firmly established — as they are not in many LDCs — it is difficult to enforce legislation to protect the environment. Furthermore, if the environment (as a factor of production) is underpriced, then 'too much' of it will be used by firms.

There are externality effects at work here too, in the sense that the loss of biodiversity is a global loss, and not just something affecting the local economy. In some cases there have been international externality effects of a more direct kind, such as when forest fires in Indonesia caused the airport in Singapore to close down because of the resulting smoke haze.

China has been one of the fastest-growing economies in the world since 1978. To have averaged almost 8% growth per annum over such a long period is extraordinary. In

OCR A2 Economics

2004 the *Asian Development Bank* reported that China's GDP had grown by 9.1% in 2003, and it predicted that in 2004 the country's growth would account for 15% of the expected expansion in the *world* economy. Exports from the rest of the world to China grew by 34.6% in 2003.

In August 2004, *The Economist* reported that 16 of the world's most polluted cities were located in China, and that around half of China's population (i.e. some 600 million people) had water supplies that were contaminated by animal and human waste. River systems were heavily polluted, and air pollution had become a serious issue, partly as a result of the country's heavy reliance on coal-fired electricity generation. Shanghai's environmental protection bureau estimated that 70% of the 1 million cars in Shanghai do not reach even the oldest European emission standard.

This illustrates the trade-off between rapid economic growth and protection of the environment. The other factor in the equation is the desire to alleviate poverty. The World Bank estimated that in 2005 some 207.7 million people in China were living in extreme poverty — defined as living on less than $1.25 per day, and that there were 645.6 million living on less than $2.50 per day. The need to bring so many people out of extreme poverty lends urgency to the drive for economic growth. However, this needs to be balanced against the need to ensure sustainable development. In other words, economic growth must be achieved in such a way that it does not destroy the environment for future generations.

There are many aspects to this issue, of which protecting the environment is just one. Sustainable development also entails taking account of the depletion rates of non-renewable resources, and ensuring that renewable resources *are* renewed in the process of economic growth. So, although economic growth is important to a society, the drive for growth must be tempered by an awareness of the possible trade-offs with other important objectives.

In 2005, some 208 million people in China were living in poverty

Measuring and monitoring sustainability is challenging, and there is no universally accepted way of going about this, other than by monitoring a whole series of different indicators. From time to time, economists have proposed alternative measures to provide a more realistic estimate of the level of economic welfare enjoyed by the inhabitants of a country. One example is the **Measure of Economic Welfare (MEW)**, which was first proposed by William Nordhaus and James Tobin in 1972. This began with GNP, and then made various adjustments so that it only included the consumption and investment items that contribute directly to economic well-being.

Key terms

Measure of Economic Welfare (MEW): indicator that amends GDP per capita so that it only reflects items that contribute directly to economic wellbeing

Index of Sustainable Economic Welfare (ISEW): indicator based on the same approach as the MEW but with a stronger focus on variables that affect sustainability

For example, they argued that the value of production in the informal sector of the economy should be included, but that deductions should be made for such things as environmental damage. In addition, they made adjustments (upward) for leisure time and (downward) for travel-to-work time. Although this measure did not really catch on, it led to considerable debate on the measurement of the standard of living in the presence of environmental and other external effects. This methodology was later used to devise an **Index of Sustainable Economic Welfare (ISEW)**. This measure begins with personal consumption spending and then introduces adjustments for income inequality, non-monetarised contributions to welfare, the costs of environmental degradation and so on. The Friends of the Earth website allows you to experiment with this measure by building up your own index. This is an instructive exercise, but it also highlights one of the problems with the index — that there is no consensus about what should be included or the weights with which the components should be combined.

Thus, one of the problems with the Nordhaus–Tobin approach is the difficulty of arriving at objective measures of the externalities that they were trying to recognise in the calculations. This led to mistrust of any precise estimates that were produced. Nonetheless, it is widely recognised that the use of GDP per capita needs to be augmented by other indicators in order to arrive at a reasonable valuation of the standard of living. In the UK, for example, the Office for National Statistics publishes a series of environmental accounts that enable the monitoring of greenhouse gas and other emissions, and energy usage.

External obstacles to growth and development

Not all of the obstacles facing LDCs in their quest for growth and development arise from domestic factors. The law of comparative advantage highlights the fact that countries can gain through specialisation. It is not necessary to have an *absolute* advantage to benefit from specialisation and trade, so long as there is some source of *comparative* advantage. In the case of most LDCs, it may be crucial to be able to import some goods that cannot be produced domestically. For example, there are few LDCs

that are capable of producing capital goods, although these are extremely important if a process of industrialisation is to be initiated.

However, although the law of comparative advantage identifies the potential gains from international trade, it does not guarantee that those gains can actually be made, and the terms under which trade takes place may put limits on the extent to which LDCs can benefit. There may thus be external obstacles that will affect LDCs. This was discussed in Chapter 16, where it was pointed out that LDCs that rely on specialising in the production and exporting of primary goods tend to suffer from volatility of export earnings in the short run and a deterioration of their terms of trade in the long run.

International debt

For some LDCs, these problems have been compounded by strategies adopted to cope with balance of payments problems. The origins of this date back to the time of the first oil price crisis in 1973/74, when oil prices were suddenly raised by a substantial percentage. For many oil-importing countries, this posed a major problem, as the demand for oil was relatively inelastic, so the increase in the price of oil led immediately to a deficit on the current account of the balance of payments. Borrowing from the International Monetary Fund (IMF) was one solution, as offering help with short-run balance of payments problems is exactly the role that the IMF was designed to fulfil. However, IMF loans come with strings attached, so many LDCs in the late 1970s looked elsewhere for funds, borrowing from commercial sources. Such loans were often on variable interest rate terms. In the 1980s, oil prices rose again. Furthermore, interest rates rose worldwide when governments in North America and western Europe adopted strict monetary policies. This created problems for many LDCs that had borrowed heavily — especially those that had not perhaps used the funds as wisely as they might have. Some countries in Latin America threatened to default on their loans, and various plans had to be devised to salvage the financial system.

The problems of debt have proved a major obstacle to development in many countries. Latin American countries were affected strongly, as they had borrowed large amounts in US dollar terms. Countries in sub-Saharan Africa had borrowed less in money terms, but accumulated debts that were substantial relative to GDP or exports. They thus found that a high share of their export revenues were being used to make payments on past debts, and were thus not available for promoting development at home. The problem reached a point at which it was clear that the debt burdens of many LDCs were unsustainable, and the World Bank launched an initiative to tackle the problem.

Diversity in development

With all these obstacles to growth and development, from both internal and external sources, it would be easy to despair of ever being able to tackle poverty in the world. However, it is important to remember that not all countries face all of the obstacles. Countries face different configurations of characteristics and problems, and such diversity needs to be matched by diversity in the design of policies to promote growth and development. Policy issues are the subject of the next chapter.

Summary

➤ The pattern of existing comparative advantage suggests that LDCs should specialise in the production of primary commodities such as agricultural goods, minerals or other raw materials.

➤ However, the prices of such goods tend to be volatile in the short run, varying from year to year as a result of instability arising from either the supply side or the demand side.

➤ Furthermore, the nature of demand for such products and the development of artificial substitutes for some raw materials may be expected to lead to a long-run deterioration in the terms of trade for primary producers.

➤ These factors will limit the extent to which LDCs benefit from international trade in primary commodities.

➤ International debt also grew to be a major obstacle to development for many countries.

Exercise 19.2

Looking back over the nature of the economic growth process and the obstacles to growth that have been outlined, discuss the extent to which countries in sub-Saharan Africa may be able to use the pattern of development that was so successful in East Asia to promote growth.

The Harrod–Domar model

Returning to the issue of economic growth, if it is seen in terms of a shift in aggregate supply, then the focus must be on investment, which enables an increase in productive capacity. This idea is supported by the **Harrod–Domar model** of economic growth, which first appeared in separate articles by Roy Harrod in the UK and Evsey Domar in the USA in 1939. This model was to become significant in influencing LDCs' attitudes towards the process of economic growth. It was developed in an attempt to determine how equilibrium could be achieved in a growing economy.

 Key *term*

Harrod–Domar model: a model of economic growth that emphasises the importance of savings and investment

The basic finding of the model was that an economy can remain in equilibrium through time only if it grows at a particular rate. This unique *stable growth path* depends on the *savings ratio* and the *productivity of capital*. Any deviation from this path will cause the economy to become unstable. This finding emphasised the importance of savings in the process of economic growth, and led to the conclusion that a country seeking economic growth must first increase its flow of savings.

Figure 19.4 illustrates the process that leads to growth in a Harrod–Domar world. Savings are crucial in enabling investment to be undertaken — always remembering that some investment will have to be used to replace existing capital that has worn out. Investment then enables capital

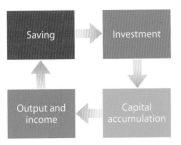

Figure 19.4 *The Harrod–Domar process of economic development*

to accumulate and technology to be improved. The accumulation of capital leads to an increase in output and incomes, which leads to a further flow of savings, and the cycle begins again. This figure highlights a number of problems that may prevent the Harrod–Domar process from being effective for LDCs.

Generating a flow of savings in an LDC may be problematic. When incomes are low, households may have to devote most of their resources to consumption, and so there may be a lack of savings. Nonetheless, some savings have proved possible. For example, in the early 1960s South Korea had an average income level that was not too different from that of countries like Sudan or Afghanistan, but it managed to build up the savings rate during that decade.

Setting aside the problem of low savings for the moment, what happens next?

Will savings lead to investment and the accumulation of capital?

If a flow of savings can be generated, the next important step is to transform the savings into investment. This is the process by which the sacrifice of current consumption leads to an increase in productive capacity in the future.

Some important preconditions must be met if savings are to be transformed into investment. First, there must be a way for potential borrowers to get access to the funds. In developed countries this takes place through the medium of financial markets. For example, it may be that households save by putting their money into a savings account at the bank; then with this money the bank can make loans to entrepreneurs, enabling them to undertake investment.

In many LDCs, however, financial markets are undeveloped, so it is much more difficult for funds to be recycled in this way. For example, a study conducted in 1997 by the Bank of Uganda found that almost 30% of households interviewed in rural Ugandan villages had undertaken savings at some time. However, almost none of these had done so through formal financial institutions, which did not reach into the rural areas. Instead, the saving that took place tended to be in the form of fixed assets, or money kept under the bed. Such savings cannot readily be transformed into productive investment.

In addition, governments in some periods have made matters worse by holding down interest rates in the hope of encouraging firms to borrow. The idea here is that a low

Singapore skyline — can saving lead to investment and economic development?

interest rate means a low cost of borrowing, which should make borrowing more attractive. However, this ignores the fact that, if interest rates are very low, there is little incentive to save because the return on saving is so low. In this case, firms may wish to invest but may not be able to obtain the funds to do so.

The other prerequisite for savings to be converted into investment is that there must be entrepreneurs with the ability to identify investment possibilities, the skill to carry them through and the willingness to bear the risk. Such entrepreneurs are in limited supply in many LDCs.

During the 1950s, Hong Kong, one of the so-called *tiger economies*, benefited from a wave of immigrant entrepreneurs, especially from Shanghai, who provided the impetus for rapid development. In Singapore the entrepreneurship came primarily from the government, and from multinational corporations which were encouraged to become established in the country. Singapore and South Korea also adopted policies that ensured a steady flow of savings, so that, for example, in Singapore gross domestic savings amounted to 52% of GDP in 1999.

Will investment lead to higher output and income?

For investment to be productive in terms of raising output and incomes in the economy, some further conditions need to be met. In particular, it is crucial for firms to have access to physical capital, which will raise production capacity. Given their limited capability of producing capital goods, many LDCs have to rely on capital imported from the more developed countries. This may be beneficial in terms of upgrading home technology, but such equipment can be imported only if the country has earned the foreign exchange to pay for it. A shortage of foreign exchange may therefore make it difficult for the country to accumulate capital.

The tiger economies were all very open to international trade, and focused on promoting exports in order to earn the foreign exchange needed to import capital goods. This strategy worked very effectively, and the economies were able to widen their access to capital and move to higher value-added activities as they developed their capabilities.

The importance of human capital

If the capital *can* be obtained, there is then a need for the skilled labour with which to operate the capital goods. Human capital, in the form of skilled, healthy and well-trained workers, is as important as physical capital if investment is to be productive.

In principle, it might be thought that today's LDCs have an advantage over the countries that developed in earlier periods. In particular, they can learn from earlier mistakes, and import technology that has already been developed, rather than having to develop it anew. This suggests that a *convergence* process should be going on, whereby LDCs are able to adopt technology that has already been produced, and thereby grow more rapidly and begin to close the gap with the more developed countries.

However, by and large this has not been happening, and a lack of human capital has been suggested as one of the key reasons for the failure. This underlines the importance of education in laying the foundations for economic growth as well as contributing directly to the quality of life.

The education systems of the tiger economies had been well established, either through the British colonial legacy (in the case of Singapore and Hong Kong) or through past Japanese occupation periods (in Taiwan and South Korea). In all of these countries, education received high priority, and cultural influences encouraged a high demand for education. The tiger economies thus benefited from having highly skilled and well-disciplined labour forces that were able to make effective use of the capital goods that had been acquired.

Harrod–Domar and external resources

Figure 19.5 extends the earlier schematic presentation of the process underlying the Harrod–Domar model of economic growth. This has been amended to underline the importance of access to technology and human capital.

The discussion above has emphasised the difficulty of mobilising domestic savings, both in generating a sufficient flow of savings and in translating such savings into productive investment.

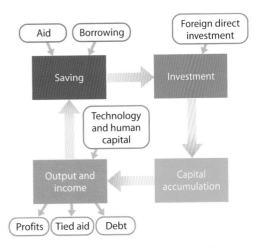

Figure 19.5 *The Harrod–Domar process of economic development augmented*

The question arises as to whether an LDC could supplement its domestic savings with a flow of funds from abroad. Figure 19.5 identifies three possible injections into the Harrod–Domar process. First, it might be possible to attract flows of overseas assistance from higher-income countries. Second, perhaps the amount of investment could be augmented directly by persuading multinational corporations to engage in foreign direct investment. Third, the LDC might be able to borrow on international capital markets to finance its domestic investment. It is worth noting that the tiger economies took full advantage of

these external sources of funds. It is worth noting that each of these ways of attracting external resources has a downside associated with it. As far as overseas assistance is concerned, in the past such flows have been seen by some donor countries as part of trade policy, and have brought less benefit to LDCs than had been hoped. In the case of the multinational corporations, there is a tendency for the profits to be repatriated out of the LDC, rather than recycled into the economy. Finally, international borrowing has to be repaid at some future date, and many LDCs have found themselves burdened by debt that they can ill afford to repay.

Summary

➤ Although development is a broader concept than economic growth, growth is a key ingredient of development.

➤ The Harrod–Domar model of economic growth highlights the importance of savings, and of transforming savings into productive investment.

➤ However, where markets are underdeveloped, this transformation may be impeded.

➤ Human capital is also a critical ingredient of economic growth.

➤ If resources cannot be generated within the domestic economy, a country may need to have recourse to external sources of funding.

Institutions and development

The design of economic policy must be considered in the context of the economic and institutional environment within which policy measures are implemented. The role of institutions in the development process has increasingly been seen as an important one in recent years. LDC governments, multilateral institutions such as the World Bank, non-governmental organisations and major trade groupings like the European Union all contribute to the policy environment. The interactions between them are also extremely important.

LDC governments

The governments of LDCs have the ultimate responsibility for designing their domestic economic and development policy, but it has often been argued that many are ill-equipped to devise and implement the sorts of policies that are required to stimulate the process of development. This is partly related to the level of development of the political and cultural systems in LDCs, and may also depend upon the existence (or absence) of a reliable and non-corrupt bureaucracy that would enable policies to be set in motion. Another major factor to remember is the constraint that LDC governments face in terms of resources. Where average incomes are low and tax collection systems are undeveloped, governments have difficulty in generating a flow of revenue domestically, which is needed in order to launch policies encouraging growth and development.

In some cases, governments have tended to rely on taxes on international trade, which are relatively easy to administer, rather than on domestic direct or indirect taxes. Naturally, this has not helped to stimulate international trade.

Some LDC governments have responded to the problem by borrowing funds from abroad. However, in many cases such funds have not been best used. They have sometimes been used for prestige projects, which impress lenders (or donors) but do little to further development. Other funds have been diverted into private use by government officials, and there are well-documented examples of politicians, officials and civil servants accumulating personal fortunes at the expense of their countries' development.

Tendencies towards corruption are likely to be more significant in countries where there is relatively little political stability, so that the government knows it will not remain in power for long. In this situation, it is not only corruption that may be problematic, as in general the incentives for such governments are weak. There is little reason to expect a government to take a long-term view of the development process, and to introduce policies that will only bring benefits in the distant future, if it only faces a short period in office, or if it perceives that it needs to bring in populist policies to ensure re-election. In other words, even in the absence of corruption, there may be little incentive for governments to take a long-term perspective.

Summary

➤ Governments in LDCs have limited resources with which to encourage a more rapid rate of economic growth and development.

➤ Corruption and poor governance have meant that some of the resources that have been available have not been used wisely in some LDCs.

Markets or state planning?

The World Bank subscribes to the notion of **market-friendly growth**. The fundamental idea of this is that countries wishing to promote development need to do so in a market-friendly way. This may entail governments doing less in those parts of the economy where markets can be relied upon, but intervening more where market failure is inevitable. The fundamental premise is that economic development should be market led.

 term

market-friendly growth: economic growth in which governments intervene less where markets can operate effectively, but more strongly where markets are seen to fail

An alternative to this approach is to rely on *central planning*. This view of the development process was attractive to many countries, with the Soviet Union being seen as a role model for many years. The breakdown of the Soviet bloc has discredited this approach to some extent, although there are still a few countries that adhere to central planning, such as Cuba and North Korea. Elsewhere, governments have come to see the benefits that derive from allowing market forces to play at least some role in resource allocation. For example, market reforms in China have contributed to that country's outstanding success in achieving rapid economic growth.

Allowing market forces to lead resource allocation has some key advantages over central planning for many LDCs. These arise from the problems mentioned above

relating to the lack of reliable bureaucracy in many LDCs and the temptations to corruption. Central planning relies very heavily on bureaucratic structures in order to manage the process of development. It also relies on reliable and detailed information about the economy. Without these, central planning cannot operate effectively. In contrast, a market system is efficient because it devolves decision making to individuals, and uses prices to provide signals and to coordinate the allocation of resources.

Problems arise where institutions do not enable the free operation of markets, and an early priority in seeking to promote development is to ensure that measures are in place that will allow markets to work. These measures would include such things as secure property rights and the provision of appropriate infrastructure. Indeed, intervention may be needed in various parts of the economy in order to counter problems arising from *market failure*.

Domestic policies for development

The objective of domestic policy is to make the best use of the resources that are available within a society. Policy must also try to balance the need to tackle short-term problems with devising a strategy that will cater for the long run.

A strategy for the long run needs to bear in mind the need for balance in the *structure* of economic activity. This means reducing the dependence on primary production, and moving towards a more diversified economy. A precondition for this is to bring about improvements in agricultural productivity. This enables food production to be secured and may then permit some release of surplus labour into new types of economic activity.

It is important to be aware of areas of potential market failure that may inhibit development, growth and structural transformation. Of particular importance may be the provision of *infrastructure*. Intervention here is justified because of the public goods

The provision of infrastructure is important to the development of LDCs

characteristics of much infrastructure, which means that there will be insufficient provision if it is left to the private sector. Improved roads and communication links, and market facilities, are examples of public goods that are essential for economic development.

Another area of potential market failure relates to aspects of *human capital*. The presence of information failures and externality effects may combine to prevent efficient provision of education and healthcare. However, these are of vital importance, not only for short-run purposes of alleviating poverty, but also because the improvement of human resources contributes to productivity improvements, and hence to economic growth. To the extent that households make inappropriate decisions on family size, there may also be a need to try to influence the rate of population growth.

LDC governments should also take steps to ensure a *stable macroeconomic environment* in order to enable the private sector to take good decisions. Only in a stable macroeconomic environment will firms be able to form reliable expectations about the future, and thus take good decisions about investment.

Given the parlous state of many LDC economies, such domestic measures are unlikely to be sufficient to stimulate self-sustained development. This partly reflects the severe scarcity of resources faced by many LDC governments. An implication of this is that LDCs must also attempt to mobilise resources from external sources.

The role of external resources in development

The shortage of resources in many LDCs has been a severe obstacle to their economic growth and development. This was emphasised by the Harrod–Domar model of economic growth which was introduced earlier in the chapter (see Figure 19.5 on page 365).

The underlying process by which growth can take place requires the generation of a flow of savings that can be transformed into investment in order to generate an increase in capital, which in turn enlarges the productive capacity of the economy. This then enables output and incomes to grow, which in turn feeds back into savings and allows the process to become self-sustaining.

However, the process will break down if savings are inadequate, or if markets do not operate sufficiently well to maintain the chain. In considering the possibility that the process could be initiated by an inflow of resources from outside the economy, there are three possible routes to be examined: foreign direct investment, overseas aid and international borrowing. As Figure 19.5 indicated, associated with each of these inflows there are likely to be some costs, and potential leakages from the system. These will be discussed in Chapter 20.

Trade policy

Another area in which policy may be important in contributing to economic development is in the area of trade policy. If a country is short of foreign exchange, there are two broad approaches that it can take in drawing up its trade policy to

deal with the problem. One is to reduce its reliance on imports in order to economise on the need for foreign currency — in other words, to produce goods at home that it previously imported. This is known as an **import substitution** policy. An alternative possibility is to try to earn more foreign exchange through **export promotion**.

Import substitution

The import substitution strategy has had some appeal for a number of countries. The idea is to boost domestic production of goods that were previously imported, thereby saving foreign exchange. A typical policy instrument used to achieve this is the imposition of a **tariff**.

 Key *terms*

import substitution: policy encouraging domestic production of goods previously imported in order to reduce the need for foreign exchange

export promotion: policy entailing encouraging domestic firms to export more goods in order to earn foreign exchange

tariff: a tax imposed on imported goods

Tariffs were discussed in Chapter 16 (pages 299–301) when it was pointed out that not all of the results of a tariff are favourable for an economy. Effectively, the government subsidises inefficient local producers, and forces domestic consumers to pay a price that is above that of the good if imported from abroad.

Some would defend this policy on the grounds that it allows the LDC to protect an *infant industry*. In other words, through such encouragement and protection, the new industry will eventually become efficient enough to compete in world markets.

There are two key problems with this argument. First, unless the domestic market is sufficiently large for the industry to reap economies of scale, local producers will never be in a position to compete globally. Second, because of such protection, domestic firms are never exposed to international competition, and so will not have an incentive to improve their efficiency to world levels. In other words, tariff protection fosters an inward-looking attitude among local producers that discourages them from trying to compete in world markets. They remain happy with the protection that allows them to reap extra profits.

Export promotion

Export promotion requires a more dynamic and outward-looking approach, as domestic producers need to be able to compete with producers already established in world markets. The choice of which products to promote is critical, as it is important that the LDC develops a new pattern of comparative advantage if it is to benefit from an export promotion strategy.

For primary producers, a tempting strategy is one that begins with existing products and tries to move along the production chain. For example, in 1997 (under encouragement from the World Bank) Mozambique launched a project whereby, instead of exporting raw cashew nuts, it would establish processing plants that would then allow it to export roasted cashew nuts. In the early 1970s Mozambique was the largest producer of cashew nuts in the world, but by the late 1990s the activity had stagnated, and the country had been overtaken by producers in Brazil and India.

This would seem to have been a good idea because it makes use of existing products and moves the industry into higher value-added activity. However, the project ran into a series of problems. On the one hand, there were internal constraints: processing the nuts requires capital equipment and skilled labour, neither of which was in plentiful supply in Mozambique. In addition, tariff rates on processed commodities are higher than on raw materials, so the producers faced more barriers to trade. They also found that they were trying to break into a market that was dominated by a few large existing producers, which were reluctant to share the market. Furthermore, the technical standards required to sell processed cashew nuts were beyond the capability of the newly established local firms. Indeed, the setting of high technical specifications for imported products is one way in which countries have tried to protect their own domestic producers — it is an example of a **non-tariff barrier**.

By the late 1990s, Brazil and India had overtaken Mozambique in cashew nut production

 Key *term*

non-tariff barrier: an obstacle to free trade other than a tariff — for example, quality standards imposed on imported products

These are just some of the difficulties that face new producers from LDCs wanting to compete in world markets. The East Asian tiger economies pursued export promotion strategies, making sure that their exchange rates supported the competitiveness of their products and that their labour was appropriately priced. However, it must be remembered that the tiger economies expanded into export-led growth at a time when world trade itself was booming, and when the developed countries were beginning to move out of labour-intensive activities, thereby creating a niche to be filled by the tigers. If many other countries had expanded their exports at the same time, it is not at all certain that they could all have been successful.

As time goes by, it becomes more difficult for other countries to follow this policy. It is particularly difficult for countries that originally chose import substitution, because the inward-looking attitudes fostered by such policies become so deeply entrenched.

It should also be remembered that there will always be dangers in trying to develop new kinds of economic activity that may entail sacrificing comparative advantage. This is not to say that LDCs should remain primary producers for ever, but it does suggest that it is important to select the new forms of activity with care in order to exploit a *potential* comparative advantage.

part **4**

Summary

➤ In designing a trade policy, an LDC may choose to go for import substitution, nurturing infant industries behind protectionist barriers in order to allow them to produce domestically goods that were formerly imported.

➤ However, such infant industries rarely seem to grow up, leaving the LDC with inefficient producers, which are unable to compete effectively with world producers.

➤ Export promotion requires a more dynamic and outward-looking approach, and a careful choice of new activities.

Exercise 19.3

Discuss the relative merits of import substitution and export promotion as trade strategies. Under what conditions might import substitution have a chance of success?

Development policy and sustainability

In a world increasingly concerned about the dangers of climate change, it is important to evaluate the impact of development policies on sustainability. In particular, it is crucial to examine whether there is a conflict between economic growth, human development and sustainability.

There are political issues in this area that cannot be ignored. The extreme differences in lifestyle between the rich nations and LDCs in which large proportions of the population live in abject poverty make it politically difficult for the former to insist that LDCs adopt sustainable growth policies, if that means that the alleviation of poverty is delayed.

It must also be recognised that for countries that lack political stability, the incentives for politicians to adopt policies with a long-term pay-off may be limited. There will always be a temptation to focus on policies that can bring short-term gains in the hope of prolonging a period in power. Such short-termism may well be incompatible with sustainability. These factors may restrict the usefulness of policies to promote sustainability.

The relationship between economic growth and environmental degradation has been discussed, and it has been argued that economic growth may bring costs in terms of the environment. However, there is no general consensus on the validity of this. Some aspects of growth may indeed have implications for the environment. For example, as real incomes rise, car ownership rises, and this is likely to lead to greater carbon dioxide emissions, thus having an impact on climate change. On the other hand, it has also been pointed out that as a society reaches a higher stage of development, it becomes able to make use of cleaner technology. This is a debate that looks set to continue for many years to come.

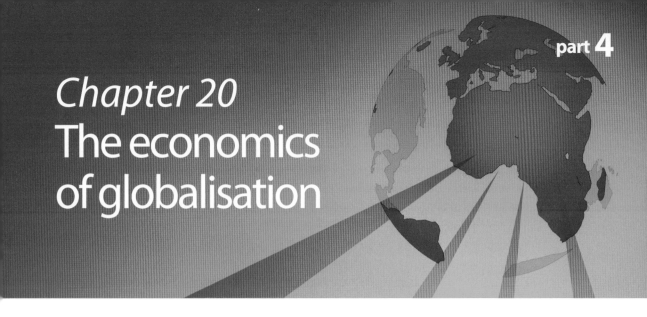

Chapter 20
The economics
of globalisation

The world is becoming increasingly more integrated in many dimensions of economic activity. International flows of factors of production and financial capital have drawn countries closer together and created new interdependencies. There have been good and bad aspects of this process. Increasing trade has opened up new opportunities for some countries, but the increased interdependence has created vulnerability, as crisis can also spread more readily between interdependent economies. Multinational firms have come to play an increasing role in global markets, and the multilateral organisations such as the World Bank, the International Monetary Fund and the World Trade Organization have faced new challenges in seeking to oversee the world's economic environment. This chapter focuses on the characteristics and consequences of globalisation.

Learning outcomes

After studying this chapter, you should:
- ➤ understand the different characteristics of globalisation
- ➤ be able to explain the factors that have contributed to the growth of globalisation
- ➤ be familiar with the different forms of international capital flows and evaluate their effects
- ➤ be able to analyse the impact of multinational corporations
- ➤ be aware of the roles of the multilateral organisations: the World Bank, International Monetary Fund and World Trade Organization
- ➤ be able to evaluate the impact of globalisation

Globalisation and comparative advantage revisited

AS Economics, Chapter 16 introduced the notion of **globalisation** — a process by which the world's economies are becoming more closely integrated. Globalisation has been characterised by a significant increase in the mobility of factors of production between countries, and increased flows of goods, services, capital, knowledge and people across international borders.

Key term

globalisation: a process by which the world's economies are becoming more closely integrated

The process of globalisation accelerated due to a number of factors. An important influence arose from the advances in the technology of transport and communication, which enabled firms to begin to fragment their production process across different locations around the world. However, also crucial to the process was the reduction of trade barriers and the deregulation of financial markets.

This whole process has led to changes in the pattern of trade between countries – for example, as the UK has become more closely integrated with the rest of Europe, there has been an increase in the share of UK trade that is with the rest of Europe, although the USA also remains a significant trading partner.

The law of comparative advantage helps to explain these changes in the pattern of trade. Indeed, globalisation may be seen as a process that enables countries to enhance the way in which their comparative advantage can be exploited. In some cases, it may enable some countries to develop new specialisations, and thus alter the pattern of their comparative advantage.

From the point of view of economic analysis, it would seem that this process of globalisation, and the increasing use of comparative advantage, would be welcomed by countries around the world. However, it seems that this is not a universal view. Countries often seem reluctant to open their economies fully to international trade, and have tended to intervene to try to protect their domestic producers from what is perceived as excessive competition from foreign firms. In evaluating the benefits and costs of globalisation, there are other issues to be taken into consideration.

External shocks

One of the issues concerning a more closely integrated global economy is the question of how robust the global economy will be to shocks. In other words, globalisation may be fine when the world economy is booming, as all nations may be able to share in the success. But if the global economy goes into recession, will all nations suffer the consequences? There are a number of situations that might cause the global economy to take a downturn.

Oil prices

Oil prices seem to provide one possible threat. In the past, sudden changes in oil prices have caused widespread disruption – for example, in 1973/74 and in 1979/80.

Figure 20.1 shows the historical time path of the price of oil from 1964 to 2004, measured in US dollars. In 1973/74 the sudden increase in

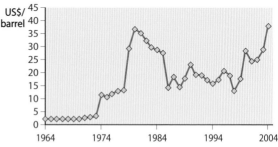

Figure 20.1 *The price of oil, 1964–2004*

Source: IMF.

the price of oil took most people by surprise. Oil prices had been steady for several years, and many economies had become dependent upon oil as an energy source, not only for running cars but for other uses such as domestic central heating. The sudden

increases in the price in 1973/74 and again in 1979/80 caused widespread problems because demand in the short run was highly inelastic, and oil-importing countries faced sudden deficits on their balance of payments current accounts. However, in time people switched away from oil for heating, firms developed more energy-efficient cars, and demand was able to adjust.

Arguably, national economies in the 2000s should have been less vulnerable to changes in the price of oil than they were in 1973. However, the movements in oil prices in the late 2000s caused some consternation. Figure 20.2 shows monthly oil prices from the beginning of 2000. The price rises in 1973/74 and 1979/80 had been primarily supply-side changes, caused by disruptions to supply following the actions of the OPEC cartel. In the 2000s, part of the upward pressure on price that is visible in the figure came from demand, with China's demand for oil being especially strong. There were also fears about the security of supplies from parts of the Middle East in the aftermath of the Iraq war, and with instability in Iran. In the event, the pressures of falling demand as the global recession began to unfold brought the price of oil tumbling. However, it was not long before oil prices began to creep up again, as some economies began to recover (and China and India continued to expand), and supplies from parts of the Middle East were disrupted – from Libya in particular.

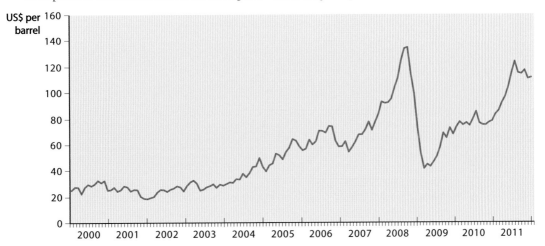

Figure 20.2 *The price of oil since 2000*

Source: IMF.

Financial crises

Given the increasing integration of financial markets, a further concern is whether globalisation increases the chances that a financial crisis will spread rapidly between countries, rather than being contained within a country or region. The 1997 Asian financial crisis provides some evidence on this issue, and the financial crisis of the late 2000s was seen to affect many economies together.

The Asian crisis began in Thailand and South Korea. Both countries had been the recipients of large flows of FDI. In the case of Thailand, a significant part of this had been investment in property, rather than in productive investment. The Thai currency (the

baht) came under speculative pressure early in 1997, and eventually the authorities had to allow a devaluation. This sparked a crisis of confidence in the region, and foreign investors began to withdraw funds, not only from Thailand but from other countries too. As far as globalisation was concerned, the key questions were how far the crisis would spread, and how long it would last.

In the event, five countries bore the main burden of the crisis: Indonesia, Malaysia, the Philippines, South Korea and Thailand. Beyond this grouping there were some knock-on effects because of the trade linkages, but arguably these were not too severe, and were probably dominated by other events taking place in the period. At the time of the crisis, Indonesia and the Philippines had been at a somewhat lower stage of development than the other countries involved, and thus suffered more deeply in terms of recession. However, with the benefit of hindsight, it seems that the region showed resilience in recovering from the crisis. Indeed, it can be argued that South Korea and Thailand in particular emerged as stronger economies after the crisis, through the weeding out of some relatively inefficient firms and institutions, and through a heightened awareness of the importance of sound financial regulation.

China and the USA

An important question in the early to mid-2000s was how the global economy would cope with two seemingly distant, but related phenomena: the rapid growth of the Chinese economy and the deficit on the US current account of the balance of payments. The US current account deficit arose partly from the heavy public expenditure programme of the Bush administration. However, the deficit grew to unprecedented levels partly through the actions of China and other East Asian economies that had chosen to peg their currencies to the US dollar. Effectively, this meant that those economies were buying US government securities as a way of maintaining their currencies against the dollar, thereby keeping US interest rates relatively low and allowing the US public to borrow to finance high consumer spending. Who gains from this situation? The USA was able to spend, and China was able to sell, fuelling its rapid rate of economic growth. For how long the situation can be sustained remains to be seen.

The credit crunch

Another example of the dangers of close interdependence began to unfold in 2007/08, when the so-called 'credit crunch' began to bite, and commercial banks in several countries found themselves in financial crisis. This followed a period in which relatively low interest rates had allowed a bubble of borrowing. When house prices began to slide, many banks in several countries found that they had over-extended themselves, and had to cut back on lending, in some cases threatening their viability. This affected a number of countries simultaneously, and the financial crisis began to affect the real economy, leading to a recession. This was a recession that affected countries all around the globe, because of the new interconnectedness of economies. It became apparent that no single country could tackle the problem alone, as measures taken to support the banks in one economy had rapid knock-on effects elsewhere. Once this

When house prices began to slide, many banks found they had overextended themselves

was realised, coordinated action was taken, and in October 2008 the central banks of several countries reduced their bank rates together. This was followed by action aiming to salvage the situation and avoid a full-blooded recession.

By early 2009, the UK economy was officially in recession, the bank rate had been driven down to an unprecedented 0.5%, and the Bank of England was introducing quantitative easing to try to stimulate the economy. One of the problems was that the commercial banks had become reluctant to lend, so firms that wanted to invest were finding it difficult to obtain funds. Attempts were made to coordinate the efforts of governments of key countries around the world — for example, at the G20 Summit held in London in April 2009. As time went by and the recession deepened, a number of countries in the Eurozone faced crises with the level of public debt. This affected Ireland, Greece and Portugal in particular, all of which needed bailouts. The danger in the early 2010s was that these problems would spread to larger countries such as Italy and Spain.

International capital flows

The changing pattern of financial flows between countries has been a feature of the globalisation era, especially (but not only) insofar as they have affected developing countries. Figure 20.3 shows the pattern of capital flows towards developing countries in 1990 and 2006.

ODA is overseas development assistance, popularly known as foreign aid. You can see that in 1990 flows of ODA were highly significant for the low human development countries, amounting to almost 10% of their GDP. In 1990 net foreign direct investment (FDI) was less important, especially for the low human development countries, but was also noticeable. Other private capital flows were relatively small. These flows include portfolio investment — in other words, where a foreign investor buys an equity stake

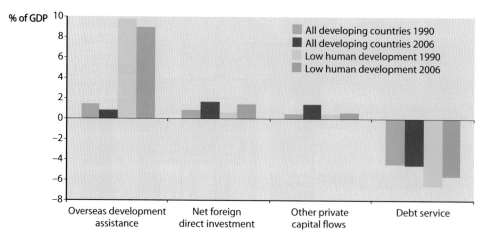

Figure 20.3 *Capital flows and developing countries, 1990 and 2006*
Source: *Human Development Report*, 2007/08.

in firms in another country; it also includes some commercial bank lending and other items. Debt service is also extremely important. This represents payments made by developing countries to their creditors, which is why it is shown as a negative flow. Notice that low human development countries were at this time devoting almost 7% of their GDP to repayment of past debts. This became a major concern later in that decade, and will be discussed later in the chapter.

The pattern had changed by 2006. ODA remained important, especially for low human development countries. FDI and other private capital flows had grown in importance for all developing countries. Debt service had decreased slightly for all developing countries, but fallen for the low human development group. For LDCs looking for capital inflows to augment domestic resources for development, these seemed to be favourable changes, but it is important to investigate more closely in order to evaluate the effectiveness of capital inflows, especially FDI and ODA.

Foreign direct investment

It is clear that **foreign direct investment (FDI)** has been attractive to many LDCs. This entails encouraging foreign **multinational corporations (MNCs)** to set up part of their production in an LDC. FDI flows between industrial nations have also been important, as can be seen in Figure 20.4, which shows the destination of FDI inflows in 2010. This shows that many FDI flows take place between the industrial nations of the world. It is also clear from this

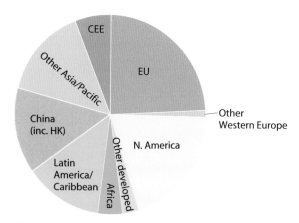

Figure 20.4 *Destination of global FDI inflows, 2010*
Source: UNCTAD, *World Investment Report 2011.*

OCR A2 Economics

figure that FDI flowing to LDCs tends to be concentrated in certain regions – notice that the flows into China and the Asia-Pacific region far outweigh the flows into Africa.

In evaluating the potential impact of MNCs operating in LDCs, it is important to consider the characteristics of such companies. Many operate on a large scale, often having an annual turnover that exceeds the less developed country's GDP. They tend to have their origins in the developed countries, although some LDCs are now beginning to develop their own MNCs.

MNCs are in business to make profits, and it can be assumed that their motivation is to maximise global after-tax profits. While they may operate in globally oligopolistic markets, they may have monopoly power within the LDCs in which they locate. They operate in a wide variety of different product markets – some are in primary production (Geest, Del Monte, BP), some are in manufacturing (General Motors, Mitsubishi) and some are in tertiary activity (WalMart, McDonald's). These characteristics are important in shaping the analysis of the likely benefits and costs of attracting FDI into an LDC.

MNCs have three basic motivations for locating in another country:
➤ market seeking
➤ resource seeking
➤ efficiency seeking

Some MNCs may engage in FDI because they want to sell their products in a particular market, and find it preferable to produce within the market rather than elsewhere: such FDI is *market seeking*. Other MNCs may undertake investment in a country in order to take advantage of some key resource – say, a natural resource such as oil or natural gas, or a labour force with certain skills, or simply cheap unskilled labour: such FDI is *resource seeking*. Still other MNCs may simply review their options globally and decide that they can produce most efficiently in a particular location, which might entail locating a part of their production chain in a certain country: such FDI is *efficiency seeking*.

To set a context for the discussion, Figure 20.5 shows the relative size of net FDI inflows for the set of countries selected previously. This reveals a very uneven pattern, with Ethiopia receiving only 0.4% of GDP as inflows of FDI and Singapore receiving 12.5%.

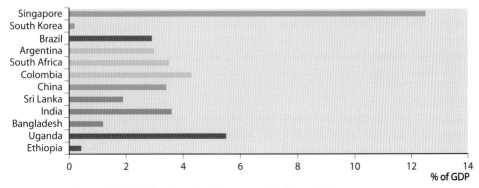

Figure 20.5 *Net foreign direct investment inflows, 2009*
Source: Human Development Report, 2011.

In some ways this chart is misleading, as it conceals the true size of FDI inflows into China. Remember that China's GDP is very large, so almost 4% of China's GDP represents a very substantial flow of investment. Some of this is market seeking, as the opening up of China's market of 1.3 billion people is a major attraction. However, it may also be partly resource seeking, with MNCs wanting to take advantage of China's resource of labour.

Potential benefits

Perhaps the prime motivation for LDCs in attracting FDI inflows is the injection they provide into the Harrod–Domar chain of development. In addition to providing *investment*, MNCs are likely to supply *capital* and *technology*, thereby helping to remedy the LDCs' limited capacity to produce capital goods. They may also assist with the development of the country's human capital, by providing training and skills development for the workers they employ, together with management expertise and entrepreneurial skills, all of which may be lacking in the LDC.

LDCs may also hope that the MNC will provide much needed modern-sector *jobs for local workers*. Given the rate of migration to urban areas, such employment could be invaluable to the LDC, where employment cannot keep up with the rapid growth of the labour force.

The LDC government may also expect to be able to collect *tax revenues*, both directly from the MNC in the form of a tax on profits, and indirectly from taxes on the workers' employment incomes. Moreover, the MNC will export its products, and thus generate a flow of foreign exchange for the LDC.

In time, there may also be *spillover effects*. As local workers learn new skills and gain management expertise and knowledge about technology, they may be able to benefit local firms if at some stage they leave the MNC and take up jobs with local companies – or use their new-found knowledge to start their own businesses. These externality effects can be significant in some cases.

BP employees in Angola — MNCs can provide training and skills development for the workers they employ

Potential costs

In evaluating the potential benefits of FDI, however, LDCs may need to temper their enthusiasm a little, as there may be costs associated with attracting MNCs to locate within their borders. This would certainly be the case if the anti-globalisation protesters are to be believed, as they have accused the MNCs of exploiting their strength and market power, the effect of which can be to damage the LDCs in various ways.

In examining such costs, it is important to be objective and to try to reach a balanced view of the matter. Some of the accusations made by the critics of globalisation may have been overstated; on the other hand, it is also important to remember that MNCs are profit-making firms and not humanitarian organisations seeking to promote justice and equality.

A first point to note is that, because most MNCs originate in more developed countries, they tend to use technology that suits the conditions with which they are familiar. In many cases, these will tend to be relatively *capital intensive*, which may not be wholly appropriate for LDC factor endowments. One upshot of this is that the employment effects may not be substantial, or may be limited to relatively low-skilled jobs.

It is dangerous to generalise here. The sort of technology that MNCs tend to use may be entirely suitable for a country like Singapore, which has progressed to the stage where it needs hi-tech capital-intensive activity to match its well-trained and disciplined workforce. However, such technology would not be appropriate in much of sub-Saharan Africa. MNCs are surely aware of such considerations when taking decisions about where to locate. A decision to set up production in China may be partly market oriented, but efficiency considerations will also affect the choice of technology.

An important consideration is whether the MNC will make use of local labour. It might hire local unskilled labour, but use expatriate skilled workers and managers. This would tend to reduce the employment and spillover effects of the MNC presence. Another possibility is that the MNC may pay wages that are higher than necessary in order to maintain a good public image, and to attract the best local workers. This is fine for the workers lucky enough to be employed at a high wage, but it can make life difficult for local firms if they cannot hold on to their best workers.

In addition, the LDC government's desire for *tax revenue* may not be fully met. In seeking to attract MNCs to locate within their borders, LDCs may find that they need to offer tax holidays or concessions as a 'carrot'. This will clearly limit the tax revenue benefits that the LDC will receive. It is also possible that MNCs can manipulate their balance sheets in order to minimise their tax liability. A high proportion of the transactions undertaken by an MNC are internal to the firm. Thus, it may be possible to set prices for internal transactions which ensure that profits are taken in the locations with the lowest tax. This process is known as *transfer pricing*. It is not strictly legal, but is difficult to monitor.

As far as the *foreign exchange earnings* are concerned, a key issue is whether the MNC will recycle its surplus within the LDC or repatriate its profits to its shareholders elsewhere in the world. If the latter is the case, this will limit the extent to which the LDC will benefit from the increase in exports. However, at least the MNC will be able to market its products internationally, and if the country becomes better known as a result then, again, there may be spillovers for local firms. Gaining credibility and the knowledge to sell in the global market is problematic for LDCs, and this is one area in which there may be definite benefits from the MNC presence.

The onset of recession in the late 2000s highlighted the potential vulnerability that may come from closer integration with the global economy. It is one thing to share in the benefits from increased trade when global demand is buoyant, and quite another to find that recession begins to spread more rapidly between countries. Naturally, it was the most open economies such as China that were among the first to suffer.

The LDC should also be aware that the MNC may use its *market power* within the country to maximise profits. Local competitors will find it difficult to compete, and the MNC may be able to restrict output and raise price. In addition, some MNCs have been accused of taking advantage of more lax environmental regulations, polluting the environment to keep their costs low. The actions of the anti-globalisation protesters in this area may have influenced MNCs to clean up their act somewhat.

Finally, MNCs tend to locate in urban areas in LDCs — unless they are purely resource seeking, in which case they may be forced to locate near the supply of whatever natural resource they are seeking. Locating in the urban areas may increase the *rural–urban inequality* discussed earlier, and encourage an even greater rate of migration.

Exercise 20.1

Draw up a list of the benefits and costs of MNC involvement in an LDC, and evaluate the benefits relative to the costs. Remember that many LDCs are enthusiastic about attracting MNCs to locate in their countries. Try to identify which are the most important benefits that they are looking for.

Given the need to evaluate the benefits and costs of FDI flows, it is important that LDC governments can negotiate good deals with the MNCs. For example, countries such as Indonesia have negotiated conditions on the share of local workers that will be employed by the MNC after a period of, say, 5 years. This helps to ensure that the benefits are not entirely dissipated. Of course, it helps if the LDC has some key resource that the MNC cannot readily acquire elsewhere. There is some recent evidence that high levels of human capital help to attract FDI flows, which may help to explain why East Asia and China have been recipients of more FDI inflows than countries in sub-Saharan Africa.

Summary

➤ Multinational corporations (MNCs) are companies whose production activities are carried out in more than one country.

➤ Foreign direct investment (FDI) by MNCs is one way in which an LDC may be able to attract external resources.

➤ MNCs may be motivated by markets, resources or cost effectiveness.

➤ LDCs hope to benefit from FDI in a wide range of ways, including capital, technology, employment, human capital, tax revenues and foreign exchange. There may also be spillover effects.

➤ However, MNCs may operate in ways that do not maximise these benefits for the LDCs.

Overseas assistance

If LDCs could enter a phase of economic growth and rising incomes, one result would be an increase in world trade. This would benefit nations around the world, and the more developed industrial countries would be likely to see an increase in the market for their products. This might be a reason for the governments of more developed countries to help LDCs with the growth and development of their economies. Of course, there may also be a humanitarian motive for providing assistance – that is, to reduce global inequality.

Indeed, there may be market failure arguments for providing aid. For example, it may be that governments have better information about the riskiness of projects in LDCs than private firms have. In relation to the provision of education and healthcare, it was argued earlier that externality effects may be involved. However, LDC governments may not have the resources needed to provide sufficient education for their citizens. Similarly, it was argued that some infrastructure may have public good characteristics that require intervention.

Official aid is known as **overseas development assistance (ODA)**, and is provided through the Development Assistance Committee of the OECD. Notice that the discussion here focuses not on short-run aid to deal with an emergency, such as a drought or tsunami, but rather on funds that are provided to foster long-term development. Figure 20.6 shows the relationship between the amount of ODA received per capita and GDP per capita of recipi-

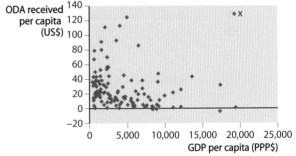

Figure 20.6 ODA and GDP per capita of recipient countries, 2000

ent LDCs in 2000. It suggests that humanitarian motives are not always paramount in determining the recipients of aid. In particular, the fact that Israel received more ODA per person than any other country in 2000, in spite of being a high-income country, suggests a political motivation. Israel (labelled 'x' in Figure 20.6) actually received more ODA as a percentage of GDP than India. There has been considerable criticism of the USA over many years for the way in which it has used aid to favour countries that have been important in US foreign policy.

A contentious issue is whether ODA should be channelled to those countries most in need of it, or focused on those countries best equipped to make good use of the funding. If humanitarian motives are uppermost, then you would expect there to be a strong relationship between flows of overseas assistance and average income levels. However, if other motives are important, this relationship might be less apparent.

In 2006, Iraq and Pakistan came high up the list of the highest recipients of ODA in dollar terms, which may reflect the importance of these countries in terms of US foreign policy in the aftermath of 9/11 and the Iraq war. It is important also to realise that some countries rely very heavily on ODA: for some this makes up almost half of their GDP.

At a meeting of the United Nations in 1974, the industrial countries agreed that they would each devote 0.7% of their GNP to ODA. This goal was reiterated at the Millennium Summit as part of the commitment to achieving the Millennium Development Goals. Progress towards this target has not been impressive, although the late 2000s saw some improvement from some countries. Figure 20.7 shows the performance of donor countries relative to this target, and you can see that only five countries had achieved the 0.7% UN target by 2010. The amount of ODA provided by the UK as a percentage of GNI increased after 1997, but the USA's share has fallen. However, it should be borne in mind that in terms of US$, the USA is by far the largest contributor.

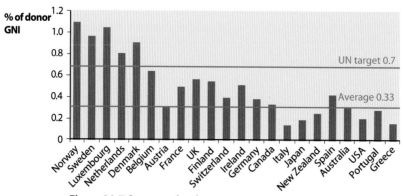

Figure 20.7 *Overseas development assistance in 2010*

Source: *Human Development Report*, 2011.

An encouraging sign is that total ODA flows increased in the late 1990s and the early years of the new millennium, as can be seen in Figure 20.8. This seemed to represent an enhanced awareness of the importance of such flows for many LDCs. Indeed, at the summit meeting of G8 at Gleneagles in July 2005 the commitment to the UN target for ODA was reiterated.

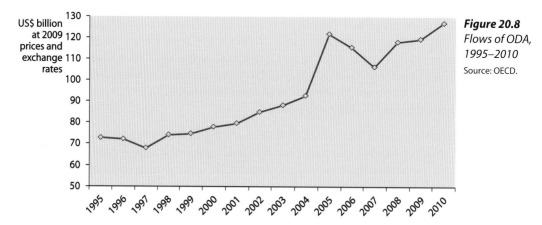

Figure 20.8
*Flows of ODA,
1995–2010*

Source: OECD.

A World Bank study of the effectiveness of aid, published in 1997, reported that 'foreign aid to developing countries since 1970 has had no net impact on either the recipients' growth rate or the quality of their economic policies'. Some evidence was found to suggest that aid was more effective in countries where 'sound economic management'

was being practised. In other words, it was argued that aid might prove effective in stimulating growth only if the country were also implementing 'good' economic policies — particularly in terms of openness to trade, low inflation and disciplined fiscal policy.

There are many possible reasons for the ineffectiveness of aid. It may simply be that providing aid to the poorest countries reduces its effectiveness, in the sense that the resources of such countries are so limited that the funding cannot be efficiently utilised. In some cases it may be related to the fact that aid flows are received by LDC governments, which can be inefficient or corrupt, so there are no guarantees that the funds are used wisely by these governments. Or it might simply be that the flows of aid have not been substantial enough to have made a difference.

There are other explanations, however. For example, some donor countries in the past have regarded aid as part of their own trade policy. By tying aid to trade deals, the net value of the aid to the recipient country is much reduced: for instance, offering aid in this way may commit the recipient country to buying goods from the donor country at inflated prices.

In other cases, aid has been tied to use in specific projects. This may help to assure the donor that the funds are being used for the purpose for which they were intended. However, it is helpful only if appropriate projects were selected in the first place. There may be a temptation for donors to select prestige projects that will be favourably regarded by others, rather than going for the LDC's top-priority development projects.

Such deals are becoming less common, as now more ODA is being channelled through multilateral organisations than bilaterally between donor and recipient directly. This may mean that aid flows will be more effective in the future. OECD reported that in 2007 only 15.2% of bilateral aid flows were tied; flows from the UK were 100% untied.

An important issue for all sorts of aid is that it should be provided in a way that does not damage incentives for local producers. For example, dumping cheap grain into LDC markets on a regular basis would be likely to damage the incentives for local farmers by depressing prices.

Summary

> Overseas development assistance (ODA) comprises grants and concessional funding provided from the OECD countries to LDCs.
> The countries most in need of ODA may not be in a position to use it effectively.
> In some cases, the direction of ODA flows is influenced by the political interests of the donor countries.
> The more developed countries have pledged to devote 0.7% of their GNPs to ODA, but few have reached this target so far.
> Some evidence suggests that aid has been ineffective except in countries that have pursued 'good' economic policies.
> The tying of aid to trade deals or to specific projects can limit the aid's benefits to recipient LDCs but the vast majority of bilateral aid is now untied.

Exercise 20.2

Discuss the view that it is only worthwhile providing long-term development aid to countries that have the infrastructure and human capital to make good use of it, even if these are not the countries in most need of assistance.

International borrowing

The final option for LDCs is to borrow the funds needed for development. This may be on concessional terms from the World Bank or the IMF, or on a commercial basis from international financial markets.

It is important to notice that, when countries borrow from the World Bank or the IMF, the loans come with strings attached. In other words, these bodies impose conditions on countries wanting to borrow, typically in relation to the sorts of economic policy that should be adopted. Such policy programmes will be considered below.

As with other forms of external finance, problems have arisen for some LDCs that have tried to borrow internationally. These problems first became apparent in the early 1980s, when Mexico announced that it could not meet its debt repayment commitments. But the stock of outstanding debt has been a major issue for many LDCs, especially in sub-Saharan Africa.

Figure 20.9 presents some data about this. It can be seen that in 1990 the debt position for many of these countries was serious indeed. In the case of Uganda, in 1990 more than 80% of the value of exports of goods and services was needed just to service the outstanding debt. For a country with limited resources, this leaves little surplus to use for promoting development. The encouraging aspect of Figure 20.9 is that for most of these countries the situation was much improved in 2010. A major problem with heavy levels of debt is that countries are forced to use precious foreign exchange in repayment of debt, rather than in tackling problems in the domestic economy.

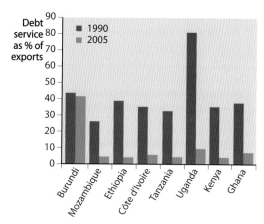

Figure 20.9 Debt servicing in sub-Saharan Africa

Source: *Human Development Report*, World Bank.

The origins of the debt crisis were discussed in Chapter 19. A number of plans (including the Baker and Brady Plans) were introduced to safeguard the international financial system, but from the LDCs' viewpoint these entailed mainly a *rescheduling* of existing debt: in other words, they were given longer to pay. A consequence was that debt levels continued to grow.

The problems were made worse because in some countries the borrowed funds were not used wisely. Development through borrowing is sustainable only if the funds are used to enable exports to grow, so that the funds can be repaid. When they do not lead to increased export earnings, repayment problems will inevitably result.

Summary

> A third way for LDCs to obtain external funds is through borrowing.

> Loans provided by the World Bank and the IMF have conditions attached that are not always palatable for LDCs.

> Many LDCs have borrowed in the past, but have then been unable to meet the repayments.

> In some cases this was because the funds were not well used.

Exercise 20.3

Discuss the extent to which good government within a developing country is a necessary condition for the successful mobilisation of internal and external resources.

Institutions and the global economy

The conduct of international trade is overseen by a number of multilateral institutions, as set out in Chapter 15. Most important are the IMF, the World Bank and the WTO. These institutions have been influential in policy design for many LDCs.

Non-governmental organisations

There are many non-governmental organisations (NGOs) that have been active in the development field. Many of these are non-profit-making charities, sometimes known as private voluntary organisations. They operate in the private sector, although they often act as channels for official development funds. NGOs have been active in providing and channelling emergency humanitarian aid to countries that have experienced some form of natural catastrophe, but have also been active in providing funds for long-term development projects.

NGOs have played an important role in areas where governments and official organisations may find difficulty. For example, they have been able to operate at the very local level, funding and overseeing small-scale projects in rural areas of many LDCs. Among the better-known NGOs are Oxfam, CAFOD and Save the Children Fund.

A further way in which NGOs have played a valuable role in promoting development is through *advocacy*. NGOs have acted as pressure groups, trying to persuade governments and the Bretton Woods institutions to adopt policies that are more favourable towards LDCs. In this, they have acted as the voice of the poor on an international stage. Perhaps the most public — and successful — example of such advocacy was the *Jubilee 2000* campaign, in which pressure was put on the World Bank and the IMF to alter their stance towards debt relief. This is discussed later in the chapter.

Trade groupings

For many LDCs, the process of development has been strongly influenced by the operations of major trade groupings and trading nations. LDCs need to engage in international trade in order to exploit comparative advantage, and to obtain goods (especially capital goods) that they are unable to produce domestically. However, the power of the USA and Japan, and of trade groupings such as the EU, is such that they are able to influence the terms under which trade takes place. This does not always work in favour of the LDCs. When the EU acts to protect its farmers, or the USA tries to protect its cotton producers, this places obstacles in the way of LDCs which are keen to be able to export their own crops. Thus it may be that, on the one hand, the World Bank encourages LDCs to focus on expanding their export activity, whilst on the other hand, the major potential importing nations set up protectionist barriers in order to protect their own markets. This naturally creates tension in international relations.

The Heavily Indebted Poor Countries (HIPC) Initiative

In the run-up to the new millennium it was clear that many countries' international debt burdens had become unsustainable. Pressure was put on the World Bank and the UN to offer *debt forgiveness* to LDCs. This pressure came in particular from non-government organisations under the banner of *Jubilee 2000.*

The World Bank was reluctant to consider this route. One of the reasons for its reluctance concerns *moral hazard.* It is argued that if a country expects to be forgiven its debt, it will have no incentive to behave responsibly – and other countries too will have less of an incentive to pay off their debts.

The response was the **HIPC Initiative**, which allows for debt forgiveness on condition that the country demonstrates a commitment to 'good' policies over a period of time. The HIPC Initiative was first launched in 1995, but the conditions were then so restrictive that few countries were able to benefit – in particular, countries were required to follow the policy package for a period of 6 years before they would qualify for any debt relief. Consequently, a number of pressure groups, including Jubilee 2000, lobbied the World Bank to allow the initiative to be more accessible.

The policies concerned overlap with a previous package of measures, which came to be known as a **Structural Adjustment Programme (SAP)**. SAPs have been on the World Bank agenda for many years, and comprise a package of policies designed to help a country initiate a process of growth and development. Under the HIPC Initiative, a new set of measures was added to encourage countries to devote funds to poverty alleviation programmes.

The HIPC policy package incorporates four main steps:

1 successful implementation of policies to enhance economic growth

2 development of a Poverty Reduction Strategy Paper (PRSP)

3 encouragement of private enterprise

4 diversification of the export base

Uganda was the first country to qualify for debt relief under HIPC, and Figure 20.9 suggests that this has had an effect, with debt service having been reduced substantially. Indeed, there is some evidence that debt levels for low-income countries are coming under control, with the ratio of total debt service to exports falling for all low-income countries from 27.1% in 1990 to 13.7% in 2005. However, the regional pattern indicates that debt levels continue to grow in Latin America and the Caribbean. It is difficult to gauge the extent to which the improvement for sub-Saharan Africa was due to the HIPC Initiative, as countries that did not qualify for HIPC relief also experienced a reduction in debt servicing over this period. For example, Bangladesh saw its debt service ratio fall from 25.8% to 5.3%.

In July 2005 government leaders from the G8 countries met at a summit meeting in Gleneagles. At this meeting the countries present pledged to cancel the debt of the world's most indebted countries — which effectively meant those countries that had qualified under the HIPC Initiative. It remains to be seen as to how this recommitment will work out in practice.

Summary

➤ The HIPC Initiative was designed to address the problems of debt in the poorest countries.

➤ Under the HIPC Initiative, debt relief is provided to countries that have shown a commitment to World Bank-approved policies and have implemented a Poverty Reduction Strategy Paper (PRSP).

Globalisation evaluated

The economic arguments in favour of allowing freer trade are strong, in the sense that there are potential gains to be made from countries specialising in the production of goods and services in which they have a comparative advantage. Globalisation facilitates and accelerates this process. And yet, there have sometimes been violent protests against globalisation, directed in particular at the WTO, whose meeting at Seattle in 1999 ended in chaos following demonstrations in the streets.

Tension has always been present during moves towards freer trade. Even if the economic arguments appear to be compelling, nations are cautious about opening up to free trade. In particular, there has been concern about jobs in the domestic economy. This is partly because there are transitional costs involved in liberalising trade, as some economic activities must contract to allow others to expand. Vested interests can then lead to lobbying and political pressure, as was apparent in the USA in the early part of the twenty-first century. There is also the question of whether globalisation will allow recession to spread more quickly between countries.

In many ways, the WTO gets caught in the middle. It has responsibility for encouraging moves towards free trade, and thus comes under pressure from nations that want to keep some degree of protection because they are unwilling to undergo the transitional

Anti-WTO protests in Seattle

costs of structural change. The WTO thus has the unpalatable job of protecting countries from themselves, enforcing short-term costs in the interests of long-term gains.

In 2000 new talks started covering agriculture and services. The fourth WTO Ministerial Conference in Doha in November 2001 incorporated these discussions into a broader work programme, the Doha Development Agenda. According to the WTO website, this agenda includes:

> ...work on non-agricultural tariffs, trade and environment, WTO rules such as anti-dumping and subsidies, investment, competition policy, trade facilitation, transparency in government procurement, intellectual property, and a range of issues raised by developing countries.

Progress on the Doha agenda has not been smooth. This is partly because agriculture is an especially contentious area, with the USA, the EU and Japan having large-scale policies in place to support their agricultural sectors. In the case of the EU's Single Market, some moves have been made towards reforming the Common Agricultural Policy, but progress has not been as rapid as developing countries would like – remembering that agriculture is especially important for many of the less developed countries. *The Economist* in 2003 drew attention to the fact that 'the rich world spends over $300 billion a year supporting its farmers, more than six times the amount it spends on foreign aid'. Reluctance on the part of the rich nations to provide concessions in these key areas, combined with determination on the part of LDCs to make genuine progress, results in a seeming deadlock.

However, the anti-globalisation protests are based on rather different arguments. One concern is that economic growth can proceed only at some cost to the environment. It has been argued that, by fragmenting the production process, the cost to the environment is high. This is partly because the need to transport goods around the world uses up valuable resources. It is also argued that nations have an incentive to lower their environmental standards in order to attract MNCs by enabling low-cost production. This is not so much an argument against globalisation as an argument that an international agency is required to monitor global environmental standards.

It has also been suggested that it is the rich countries of the world that stand to gain most from increasing global trade, as they have the market power to ensure that trading conditions work in their favour. Again, the WTO may have a role here in monitoring the conditions under which trade takes place. At the end of the day, trade allows an overall increase in global production and more choice for consumers. The challenge is to ensure that these gains are equitably distributed, and that the environment can be conserved.

Summary

➤ Globalisation is a process by which the world's economies have become more closely integrated.

➤ This has enabled greater exploitation of comparative advantage.

➤ Although closer integration may bring benefits in terms of increased global production and trade, it may also create a vulnerability by allowing adverse shocks to spread more rapidly between countries.

➤ Such shocks would include oil price changes or financial crises. However, the integrated global economy may turn out to be more resilient in reacting to adverse circumstances.

➤ Globalisation facilitates and accelerates the process by which gains from trade may be tapped.

➤ However, the transitional costs for individual economies in terms of the need for structural change have encouraged politicians to turn to protectionist measures.

➤ Critics of globalisation have pointed to the environmental costs of rapid global economic growth and the expansion of trade, and have argued that it is rich countries and multinational corporations that gain the most, rather than less developed countries.

Exercise 20.4

Evaluate the economic arguments for and against globalisation.

Glossary

abnormal, supernormal or economic profits: profits above normal profits

absolute advantage: the ability to produce a good more efficiently (e.g. with less labour)

absolute poverty: situation of a household whose income is insufficient to purchase the minimum bundle of goods and services needed for survival

accelerator: a theory by which the level of investment depends upon the change in real output

aggregate demand curve (*AD*): a curve showing the relationship between the level of aggregate demand in an economy and the overall price level; it shows planned expenditure at any given overall price level

allocative efficiency: achieved when society is producing an appropriate bundle of goods relative to consumer preferences

appreciation: a rise in the exchange rate within a floating exchange rate system

arbitrage: a process by which prices in two market segments will be equalised by a process of purchase and resale by market participants

asymmetric information: a situation in which some participants in a market have better information about market conditions than others

automatic stabilisers: process by which government expenditure and revenue vary with the economic cycle, thereby helping to stabilise the economy without any conscious intervention from government

average cost: total cost divided by the quantity produced; sometimes known as unit cost

average propensity to consume: the proportion of income that households devote to consumer expenditure

average revenue: the average revenue received by the firm per unit of output; it is total revenue divided by the quantity sold

balance of payments: a set of accounts showing the transactions conducted between residents of a country and the rest of the world

bank rate: the interest rate that is set by the Monetary Policy Committee of the Bank of England in order to influence inflation

barrier to entry: a characteristic of a market that prevents new firms from readily joining the market

broad money (M4): M0 plus sterling wholesale and retail deposits with monetary financial institutions such as banks and building societies

capital account of the balance of payments: account identifying transactions in (physical) capital between the residents of a country and the rest of the world

capital productivity: measure of output per unit of capital

capitalism: a system of production in which there is private ownership of productive resources, and individuals are free to pursue their objectives with minimal interference from government

cartel: an agreement between firms on price and output with the intention of maximising their joint profits

centrally planned economy: decisions on resource allocation are guided by the state

ceteris paribus: a Latin phrase meaning 'other things being equal'; it is used in economics when we focus on changes in one variable while holding other influences constant

claimant count of unemployment: the number of people claiming the Jobseeker's Allowance each month

common market: a set of trading arrangements in which a group of countries remove barriers to trade among them, adopt a common set of barriers against external trade, establish common tax rates and laws regulating economic activity, allow free movement of factors of production between members and have common public sector procurement policies

comparative advantage: the ability to produce a good *relatively* more efficiently (i.e. at lower opportunity cost)

comparative static analysis: examines the effect on equilibrium of a change in the external conditions affecting a market

competition policy: an area of economic policy designed to promote competition within markets to encourage efficiency and protect consumer interests

competitive market: a market in which individual firms cannot influence the price of the good or service they are selling, because of competition from other firms

complements: two goods are said to be complements if people tend to consume them jointly, so that an increase in the price of one good causes the demand for the other good to fall

constant returns to scale: found when long-run average cost remains constant with an increase in output — in other words, when output and costs rise at the same rate

consumer price index: a measure of the average level of prices in the UK; the government's inflation target is set in terms of the percentage rate of change of this index

consumer surplus: the value that consumers gain from consuming a good or service over and above the price paid

consumption externality: an externality that impacts on the consumption side of a market, which may be either positive or negative

consumption function: the relationship between consumer expenditure and disposable income; its position depends upon the other factors that affect consumer expenditure

contestable market: a market in which the existing firm makes only normal profit, as it cannot set a price higher than average cost without attracting entry, owing to the absence of barriers to entry and sunk costs

cost efficiency: the appropriate combination of inputs of factors of production, given the relative prices of those factors

cost-push inflation: inflation initiated by an increase in the costs faced by firms, arising on the supply side of the economy

cross elasticity of demand (*XED*): a measure of the sensitivity of quantity demanded of a good or service to a change in the price of some other good or service

crowding out: process by which an increase in government expenditure 'crowds out' private sector activity by raising the cost of borrowing

current account of the balance of payments: account identifying transactions in goods and services between the residents of a country and the rest of the world

customs union: a group of countries that agree to remove restrictions on trade between the member countries, and set a common set of restrictions (including tariffs) against non-member states

deadweight loss: loss of consumer surplus that arises when a monopoly restricts output and raises price

demand: the quantity of a good or service that consumers choose to buy at any possible price in a given period

demand curve: a graph showing how much of a good will be demanded by consumers at any given price

demand-deficient unemployment: unemployment that arises because of a deficiency of aggregate demand in the economy, so that the equilibrium level of output is below full employment

demand-pull inflation: inflation initiated by an increase in aggregate demand

demerit good: a good that brings less benefit to consumers than they expect, such that too much will be consumed by individuals in a free market

depreciation: the fall in value of physical capital equipment over time as it is subject to wear and tear; a fall in the exchange rate within a floating exchange rate system

derived demand: demand for a good not for its own sake, but for what it produces — for example, labour is demanded for the output that it produces

devaluation: a process whereby a country in a fixed exchange rate system reduces the price of its currency relative to an agreed rate in terms of a foreign currency

development: a process by which real per capita incomes are increased and the inhabitants of a country are able to benefit from improved living conditions: that is, lower poverty and enhanced standards of education, health, nutrition and other essentials of life

direct tax: a tax levied directly on income

discount: a process whereby the future valuation of a cost or benefit is reduced (discounted) in order to provide an estimate of its present value

discrimination: a situation in a labour market where some people receive lower wages that cannot be explained by economic factors

diseconomies of scale: occur for a firm when an increase in the scale of production leads to higher long-run average costs

disposable income: the income that households have to devote to consumption and saving, taking into account payments of direct taxes and transfer payments

division of labour: a process whereby the production procedure is broken down into a sequence of stages, and workers are assigned to particular stages

dominant strategy: a situation in game theory where a player's best strategy is independent of those chosen by others

economic and monetary union: a set of trading arrangements the same as for a common market, but in addition having fixed exchange rates between the member countries and a common monetary policy

economic cycle: a phenomenon whereby GDP fluctuates around its underlying trend, following a regular pattern

economic growth: an expansion in the productive capacity of the economy

economic rent: a payment received by a factor of production over and above what would be needed to keep it in its present use

economically active: active in the labour force, including the employed, the self-employed and the unemployed

economies of scale: occur for a firm when an increase in the scale of production leads to production at lower long-run average cost

economies of scope: economies arising when average cost falls as a firm increases output across a range of different products

effective exchange rate: the exchange rate for a country relative to a weighted average of currencies of its trading partners

elasticity: a measure of the sensitivity of one variable to changes in another variable

excess burden of a sales tax: the deadweight loss to society following the imposition of a sales tax

exchange rate: the price of one currency in terms of another

Exchange Rate Mechanism (ERM): a system which was set up by a group of European countries in 1979 with the objective of keeping member countries' currencies relatively stable against each other

export-led growth: a situation in which economic growth is achieved through the exploitation of economies of scale, made possible by focusing on exports, and so reaching a wider market than would be available within the domestic economy

export promotion: policy entailing encouraging domestic firms to export more goods in order to earn foreign exchange

external cost: a cost that is associated with an individual's (a firm or household's) production or other economic activities, which is borne by a third party

externality: a cost or a benefit that is external to a market transaction, and is thus not reflected in market prices

factors of production: resources used in the production process; *inputs* into production, including labour, capital, land and entrepreneurship

financial account of the balance of payments: account identifying transactions in financial assets between the residents of a country and the rest of the world

firm: an organisation that brings together factors of production in order to produce output

fiscal policy: decisions made by the government on its expenditure, taxation and borrowing

fixed costs: costs that do not vary with the level of output

floating exchange rate system: a system in which the exchange rate is permitted to find its own level in the market

foreign exchange reserves: stocks of foreign currency and gold owned by the central bank of a country to enable it to meet any mismatch between the demand and supply of the country's currency

franchising: under rail privatisation, a situation in which a firm is given the right to operate a particular service for a stated period

free market economy: one in which resource allocation is guided by market forces without intervention by the state

free-rider problem: when an individual cannot be excluded from consuming a good, and thus has no incentive to pay for its provision

free trade area: a group of countries that agree to remove tariffs, quotas and other restrictions on trade between the member countries, but have no agreement on a common barrier against non-members

frictional unemployment: unemployment associated with job search: that is, people who are between jobs

futures market: a market in which it is possible to buy a commodity at a fixed price for delivery at a specified future date; such a market exists for foreign exchange

game theory: a method of modelling the strategic interaction between firms in an oligopoly

GDP deflator: an implicit price index showing the relationship between real and nominal measures of GDP, providing an alternative measure of the general level of prices in the economy

General Agreement on Tariffs and Trade (GATT): the precursor of the WTO, which organised a series of 'rounds' of tariff reductions

globalisation: a process by which the world's economies are becoming more closely integrated

Golden Rule of fiscal policy: rule stating that, over the economic cycle, net government borrowing will be for investment only, and not for current spending

government budget deficit (surplus): the balance between government expenditure and revenue

government failure: a misallocation of resources arising from government intervention

gross domestic product (GDP): a measure of the economic activity carried out in an economy during a period

Harrod–Domar model: a model of economic growth that emphasises the importance of savings and investment

hot money: stocks of funds that are moved around the globe from country to country in search of the best return

human capital: the stock of skills and expertise and other characteristics that contribute to a worker's productivity; can be increased through education and training, and improved nutrition and healthcare

Human Development Index: a composite indicator of the level of a country's development, varying between 0 and 1

hypothecation: in the context of the transport sector, the principle that revenues raised from taxing transport should be used to improve the transport system

ILO unemployment rate: measure of the percentage of the workforce who are without jobs, but are available for work, willing to work and looking for work

import substitution: policy encouraging domestic production of goods previously imported in order to reduce the need for foreign exchange

incidence of a tax: the way in which the burden of paying a sales tax is divided between buyers and sellers

income elasticity of demand (*YED*): a measure of the sensitivity of quantity demanded to a change in consumer incomes

index number: a device for comparing the value of a variable in one period or location with a base observation (e.g. the retail price index measures the average level of prices relative to a base period)

Index of Sustainable Economic Welfare (ISEW): indicator based on the same approach as the MEW but with a stronger focus on variables that affect sustainability

indirect tax: a tax levied on expenditure on goods or services (as opposed to a direct tax, which is a tax charged directly to an individual based on a component of income)

industry long-run supply curve: under perfect competition, a curve that is horizontal at the price which is the minimum point of the long-run average cost curve for the typical firm in the industry

inferior good: one where the quantity demanded decreases in response to an increase in consumer incomes

inflation: the rate of change of the average price level: for example, the percentage annual rate of change of the CPI

integrated transport policy: an approach to transport policy that recognises the need to co-ordinate policy across transport modes

internalising an externality: an attempt to deal with an externality by bringing an external cost or benefit into the price system

investment: expenditure undertaken by firms to add to the capital stock

invisible hand: term used by Adam Smith to describe the way in which resources are allocated in a market economy

invisible trade: trade in services

involuntary unemployment: situation arising when an individual who would like to accept a job at the going wage rate is unable to find employment

Keynesian school: group of economists who believed that the macroeconomy could settle in an equilibrium that was below the full employment level

labour productivity: measure of output per worker, or output per hour worked

law of comparative advantage: a theory arguing that there may be gains from trade arising when countries (or individuals) specialise in the production of goods or services in which they have a comparative advantage

law of demand: a law that states that there is an inverse relationship between quantity demanded and the price of a good or service, ceteris paribus

law of diminishing returns: law stating that if a firm increases its inputs of one factor of production while holding inputs of the other factor fixed, eventually the firm will get diminishing marginal returns from the variable factor

liquidity: the extent to which an asset can be converted to cash without the holder incurring a cost

long run: the period over which the firm is able to vary the inputs of all its factors of production

long-run aggregate supply curve: a curve that shows the amount of real output that will be supplied in the economy in the long run at any given overall price level

long-run economic growth: an increase in the productive capacity of the economy

luxury good: one for which the income elasticity of demand is positive, and greater than 1, such that as income rises, consumers spend proportionally more on the good

macroeconomics: the study of the interrelationships between economic variables at an aggregate (economy-wide) level

marginal cost: the cost of producing an additional unit of output

marginal physical product of labour (MPP_L): the additional quantity of output produced by an additional unit of labour input

marginal principle: the idea that firms (and other economic agents) may take decisions by considering the effect of small changes from the existing situation

marginal propensity to consume: the proportion of additional income devoted to consumer expenditure

marginal propensity to withdraw: the sum of the marginal propensities to save, tax and import; it is the proportion of additional income that is withdrawn from the circular flow

marginal revenue: the additional revenue received by the firm if it sells an additional unit of output

marginal revenue product of labour (MRP): the additional revenue received by a firm as it increases output by using an additional unit of labour input, i.e. the marginal physical product of labour multiplied by the marginal revenue received by the firm

marginal social benefit: the additional benefit that society gains from consuming an extra unit of a good

marginal tax rate: tax on additional income, defined as the change in tax payments divided by the change in taxable income

market: a set of arrangements that allows transactions to take place

market economy: market forces are allowed to guide the allocation of resources within a society

market equilibrium: a situation that occurs in a market when the price is such that the quantity that consumers wish to buy is exactly balanced by the quantity that firms wish to supply

market failure: a situation in which the free market mechanism does not lead to an optimal allocation of resources — for example, where there is a divergence between marginal social benefit and marginal social cost

market-friendly growth: economic growth in which governments intervene less where markets can operate effectively, but more strongly where markets are seen to fail

market structure: the market environment within which firms operate

Measure of Economic Welfare (MEW): indicator that amends GDP per capita so that it only reflects items that contribute directly to economic wellbeing

merit good: a good that brings unanticipated benefits to consumers, such that society believes that it will be under-consumed in a free market

microeconomics: the study of economic decisions taken by individual economic agents, including households and firms

Millennium Development Goals (MDGs): targets set for each less developed country, reflecting a range of development objectives to be monitored each year to evaluate progress

minimum wage: legislation under which firms are not allowed to pay a wage below some threshold level set by the government

mixed economy: resources are allocated partly through price signals and partly on the basis of direction by government

model: a simplified representation of reality used to provide insight into economic decisions and events

Monetarist school: group of economists who believed that the macroeconomy always adjusts rapidly to the full employment level of output; they also argued that monetary policy should be the prime instrument for stabilising the economy

monetary policy: the decisions made by government regarding monetary variables such as the money supply or the interest rate

Monetary Policy Committee: body within the Bank of England responsible for the conduct of monetary policy

monetary transmission mechanism: the channel by which monetary policy affects aggregate demand

money stock: the quantity of money that is in circulation in the economy

monopolistic competition: a market that shares some characteristics of monopoly and some of perfect competition

monopoly: a form of market structure in which there is only one seller of a good or service

monopsony: a market in which there is a single buyer of a good, service or factor of production

multinational corporation: a company whose production activities are carried out in more than one country

multiplier: the ratio of a change in equilibrium real income to the autonomous change that brought it about; it is defined as 1 divided by the marginal propensity to withdraw

n-firm concentration ratio: a measure of the market share of the largest n firms in an industry

narrow money (M0): notes and coins in circulation and as commercial banks' deposits at the Bank of England

Nash equilibrium: situation occurring within a game when each player's chosen strategy maximises payoffs given the other player's choice, so no player has an incentive to alter behaviour

nationalisation: a process whereby an enterprise is taken into state ownership

natural monopoly: monopoly that arises in an industry in which there are such substantial economies of scale that only one firm is viable

natural rate of unemployment: equilibrium full employment level of unemployment

net investment: gross investment *minus* depreciation

net present value: the estimated value in the current time period of the discounted future net benefit of a project

newly industrialised economies: economies that have experienced rapid economic growth from the 1960s to the present

NIMBY (not in my back yard): a syndrome under which people are happy to support the construction of an unsightly or unsocial facility, so long as it is not in their back yard

nominal value: value of an economic variable based on current prices, taking no account of changing prices through time

non-pecuniary benefits: benefits offered to workers by firms that are not financial in nature

non-tariff barrier: an obstacle to free trade other than a tariff — for example, quality standards imposed on imported products

normal good: one where the quantity demanded increases in response to an increase in consumer incomes

normal profit: the return needed for a firm to stay in a market in the long run

normative statement: a statement about what *ought to be*

oligopoly: a market with a few sellers, in which each firm must take account of the behaviour and likely behaviour of rival firms in the industry

opportunity cost: in decision making, the value of the next-best alternative forgone

output gap: the difference between actual GDP and its trend value

Pareto optimum: an allocation of resources is said to be a Pareto optimum if no reallocation of resources can make an individual better off without making some other individual worse off

perfect competition: a form of market structure that produces allocative and productive efficiency in long-run equilibrium

perfect/first-degree price discrimination: situation arising in a market whereby a monopoly firm is able to charge each consumer a different price

Phillips curve: an empirical relationship suggesting that there is a trade-off between unemployment and inflation

polluter pays principle: the principle that the cost of pollution should be borne by whoever is responsible for that pollution

positive statement: a statement about what *is*, i.e. about *facts*

predatory pricing: an anti-competitive strategy in which a firm sets price below average variable cost in an attempt to force a rival or rivals out of the market and achieve market dominance

price elasticity of demand (*PED*): a measure of the sensitivity of quantity demanded to a change in the price of a good or service. It is measured as:

$$\frac{\% \text{ change in quantity demanded}}{\% \text{ change in price}}$$

price elasticity of supply (*PES*): a measure of the sensitivity of quantity supplied of a good or service to a change in the price of that good or service

price taker: a firm that must accept whatever price is set in the market as a whole

principal–agent problem: arises from conflict between the objectives of the principals and their agents, who take decisions on their behalf

prisoners' dilemma: an example of game theory with a range of applications in oligopoly theory

private cost: a cost incurred by an individual (firm or consumer) as part of its production or other economic activities

private good: a good that, once consumed by one person, cannot be consumed by somebody else; such a good has excludability and is rivalrous

privatisation: a process whereby an enterprise is transferred from public into private ownership

producer surplus: the difference between the price received by firms for a good or service and the price at which they would have been prepared to supply that good or service

product differentiation: a strategy adopted by firms that marks their product as being different from their competitors'

production externality: an externality that impacts on the production side of a market, which may be either positive or negative

production function: relationship that embodies information about technically efficient ways of combining labour and capital to produce output

production possibility curve: a curve showing the maximum combinations of goods or services that can be produced in a set period of time given available resources

productive efficiency: attained when a firm operates at minimum average total cost, choosing an appropriate combination of inputs (cost efficiency) and producing the maximum output possible from those inputs (technical efficiency)

productivity: measure of the efficiency of a factor of production

progressive tax: a tax in which the marginal tax rate rises with income, i.e. a tax bearing most heavily on the relatively well-off members of society

prohibition: an attempt to prevent the consumption of a demerit good by declaring it illegal

public good: a good that is non-exclusive and non-rivalrous — consumers cannot be excluded from consuming the good, and consumption by one person does not affect the amount of the good available for others to consume

purchasing power parity theory of exchange rates: theory stating that, in the long run, exchange rates (in a floating rate system) are determined by relative inflation rates in different countries

quantitative easing: a process by which liquidity in the economy is increased when the Bank of England purchases assets from banks

real earnings: the level of earnings adjusted for the price level; the rate of change of real earnings is thus the rate of change of earnings adjusted for inflation (the rate of change of prices)

real exchange rate: the nominal exchange rate adjusted for differences in relative inflation rates between countries

real value: value of an economic variable taking account of changing prices through time

regressive tax: a tax bearing more heavily on the relatively poorer members of society

relative poverty: situation in which household income falls below 50% of median adjusted household income

retail price index (RPI): a measure of the average level of prices in the UK

revaluation: a process whereby a country in a fixed exchange rate system raises the price of the domestic currency in terms of a foreign currency

satisficing: behaviour under which the managers of firms aim to produce satisfactory results for the firm — for example, in terms of profits — rather than trying to maximise them

scarcity: a situation that arises because people have unlimited wants in the face of limited resources

shadow price: an estimate of the monetary value of an item that does not carry a market price

short run: the period over which a firm is free to vary its input of one factor of production (e.g. labour), but faces fixed inputs of the other factors of production

short-run aggregate supply curve: a curve showing how much output firms would be prepared to supply in the short run at any given overall price level

short-run economic growth: an increase in GDP as the economy moves towards capacity output

short-run supply curve: for a firm operating under perfect competition, the curve given by its short-run marginal cost curve above the price at which $MC = SAVC$; for the industry, the short-run supply curve is the horizontal sum of the supply curves of the individual firms

social cost–benefit analysis: a process of evaluating the worth of a project by comparing its costs and benefits, including both direct and social costs and benefits — including externality effects

stagflation: a situation describing an economy in which both unemployment and inflation are high at the same time

structural unemployment: unemployment arising because of changes in the pattern of economic activity within an economy

subsidiarity: the principle that decisions should be taken as closely as possible to the citizen

subsidy: a grant given by the government to producers to encourage production of a good or service

substitutes: two goods are said to be substitutes if consumers regard them as alternatives, so that the demand for one good is likely to rise if the price of the other good rises

sunk costs: costs incurred by a firm that cannot be recovered if the firm ceases trading

supply curve: a graph showing the quantity supplied at any given price

supply-side policies: range of measures intended to have a direct impact on aggregate supply – and specifically the potential capacity output of the economy

sustainable development: 'development that meets the needs of the present without compromising the ability of future generations to meet their own needs' (Brundtland Commission, 1987)

sustainable transport development: an approach to planning the transport system which ensures that present needs can be met without compromising the ability of future generations to meet their transport needs

tacit collusion: situation occurring when firms refrain from competing on price, but without communication or formal agreement between them

tariff: a tax imposed on imported goods

technical efficiency: attaining the maximum possible output from a given set of inputs

terms of trade: the ratio of export prices to import prices

tiger economies: a group of newly industrialised economies in the East Asian region, including Hong Kong, Singapore, South Korea and Taiwan

total cost: the sum of all costs that are incurred in producing a given level of output

total factor productivity: the average productivity of all factors, measured as the total output divided by the total amount of inputs used

total physical product of labour (*TPP*): in the short run, the total amount of output produced at different levels of labour input with capital held fixed

total revenue: the revenue received by a firm from its sales of a good or service; it is the quantity sold, multiplied by the price

trade creation: the replacement of more expensive domestic production or imports with cheaper output from a partner within the trading bloc

trade diversion: the replacement of cheaper imported goods by goods from a less efficient trading partner within a bloc

trade union: an organisation of workers that negotiates with employers on behalf of its members

transfer earnings: the minimum payment required to keep a factor of production in its present use

transport: process of moving people or goods from one place to another

transport infrastructure: the permanent installations such as roads, railway track, airports and port facilities that are needed for firms to be able to provide transport services

unemployment: results when people seeking work at the going wage cannot find a job

unemployment trap: a situation in which people choose to be unemployed because the level of unemployment benefit is high relative to the wage available in low-paid occupations

unit labour cost: wages, salaries and other costs of using labour, divided by output per worker

urbanisation: process whereby an increasing proportion of the population comes to live in cities

variable costs: costs that do vary with the level of output

visible trade: trade in goods

voluntary export restraint: an agreement by a country to limit its exports to another country to a given quantity (quota)

voluntary unemployment: situation arising when an individual chooses not to accept a job at the going wage rate

World Trade Organization (WTO): a multilateral body now responsible for overseeing the conduct of international trade

X-inefficiency: occurs when a firm is not operating at minimum cost, perhaps because of organisational slack

Index

Note: Page numbers in **bold** indicate key terms. The abbreviation LDCs has been used for "less developed countries"

OCR A2 Economics